Professional Java 2 Enterprise with BEA WebLogic Server

Paco Gómez

Peter Zadrozny

Wrox Press Ltd.

Professional Java 2 Enterprise Edition
with BEA WebLogic Server

wrox

Published by Wrox Press Ltd,
Arden House, 1102 Warwick Road, Acocks Green,
Birmingham, B27 6BH, UK
Printed in Canada
ISBN 1-861002-99-8

Trademark Acknowledgements

Credits

Authors
Paco Gómez
Peter Zadrozny

Managing Editor
Paul Cooper

Technical Editors
Timothy Briggs
Daniel Robotham
Andrew Tracey

Project Manager
Chandima Nethisinghe

Production Coordinator
Tom Bartlett

Figures
Shabnam Hussain

Cover
Shelley Frazier

Production Manager
Laurent Lafon

Technical Reviewers
Lee Ackerman
Ralph Bohnet
Carl Burnham
Cosmo DiFazio
Jaeda Goodman
Scott Grant
Michael Girdley
Susan Henshaw
Andrew Hudson
Darcy Jouan
Meeraj Kunnumpurath
Alex Linde
Edward Lee
Ravi Masalthi
Tom Mitchell
Hemant More
Ron Phillips
Don Reamey
Mika Rinne

Proofing
Christopher Smith

Index
Martin Brooks

About the Authors

Peter Zadrozny started in the computer world in 1976 hacking the kernel of Unix version 6, which occupied just 22KB on a PDP-11/45. Since then he has been involved in a wide variety of assignments worldwide that used leading edge technologies in the areas of software development and IS operations. Today he is the Chief Technologist for Northern Europe at BEA Systems, and is based in London, England.

Over the past few years, Paco Gómez has specialized in Java and its related enterprise standards. He currently works for BEA Systems on architectural design and performance tuning of J2EE systems. In previous positions, Paco has worked in research and development, including providing accessible software for people with disabilities. He has a Master's degree in Robotics from Universidad Politécnica de Madrid and a B.S. degree in Computer Science from Universidad Carlos III de Madrid.

Acknowledgements

Special thanks to Angel Gutierrez for providing the base for Chapter 6 and the ASP web site. His help was invaluable in making this book happen.

To Luis Ibarz, Director of BEA Systems Iberia and all his staff in the Madrid office for putting up with us while we took over the office more times then we care to mention, to do the runs for Chapters 11 and 12.

To Skip Sauls, the pre-sales engineers, and the engineers of BEA Systems for their valuable contributions, and Eric Goirand for his help in getting us started with the WAP stuff.

To Jose Ignacio Moreno of Universidad Carlos III de Madrid for providing us with a good place to hide from everybody while working on the book.

To my wonderful mother, Manuela Marcos Sierra.

Paco

To my parents for planting the seed in fertile ground and taking very good care of it.

A la Universidad Simón Bolívar por promover y satisfacer mi necesidad de investigar y curiosear.

To Don and Brenda Lewis for giving me a break that changed my life.

To Alan Hu for trusting me on every opportunity.

A mis hijos, Johannes y la Princesa Gracie.

A mi esposa Graciela por su infinita paciencia, dedicación y permanente apoyo.

Peter

Pizza2Go

Table of Contents

Table of Contents

Table of Contents

Table of Contents

Table of Contents

Table of Contents

Introduction

Welcome to *Professional Java 2 Enterprise Edition with BEA WebLogic Server*. As the title suggests, this book uses the Java 2 Enterprise Edition (J2EE) implementation provided by BEA WebLogic Server to develop a fully functional e-commerce site.

Over the last two years, the Java platform's support for application development has expanded enormously. The Java 2 Platform, Enterprise Edition supports and provides ready-built functionality for all manner of application domains. With it you can develop web applications that:

❑   Serve dynamically generated HTML and XML

❑   Separate presentation, logic, and data into tiers

❑   Track client sessions

❑   Interface to databases, other Java applications, and directory services

❑   Make use of middleware to provide support for transactions and concurrency

❑   Support messaging

The wide availability of products to run Java applications on the server has made this a fast-moving and very competitive market, but the essential compatibility through specifications, standard APIs, and class libraries has held.

In this book we'll look at how to use J2EE in practice, mixing generic J2EE design and coding with the practicalities of configuring and deploying applications on the BEA WebLogic server. To make this more realistic, we'll use a fictitious pizza company, called Pizza2Go, as our example, developing an active e-commerce site.

This book is aimed at professional developers with some experience of programming for the web. We assume that you understand Java, and that you've a little knowledge of the J2EE APIs.

We will review key areas in server-side programming as they crop up, but this isn't a tutorial text. For more detailed introductory coverage of these topics, try *Beginning Java 2, JDK 1.3 Edition* (Ivor Horton, Wrox Press, *ISBN 1-861003-66-8*) and *Professional Java Server Programming J2EE edition* (Wrox Press, *ISBN 1-861004-65-6*) respectively.

What's Covered in this Book

The book chapters cover the following topics:

- ❑ An overview of web applications

- ❑ Setting the scene for the client-server case study we'll be developing through the book

- ❑ An introduction to servlets, JSP, JavaBeans, and how they work together to produce dynamic web content

- ❑ Further chapters covering session and entity Enterprise JavaBeans, how to design and code them, and the support WebLogic provides

- ❑ A comparison with ASP technology, and how to support a WAP interface

- ❑ The basic concepts of messaging and how these are supported in the Java Message Service (JMS) API

- ❑ Practical security issues in web applications, in relation to the basic principals of authentication and authorization, covering mechanisms such as Secure Socket Layer (SSL), ACLs, and security realms

- ❑ Tests of the robustness of the code developed in the book, and how the newly created site would manage to cope under stressfull, but ultimately realistic situations

Functionality is added to the case study incrementally, and the performance of the various application development stages tested at the end.

Appendices provide references to the HTTP protocol and JSP syntax.

What You Need to Use this Book

The code in this book was tested with the Java 2 Platform Standard Edition SDK (JDK 1.3), BEA WebLogic 5.1.0 with Service Pack 5, and Oracle 8i, on Windows NT 4.0.

We also use the following software:

- ❑ Web Browser – such as Netscape or Microsoft Internet Explorer

- ❑ A make application – we recommend GNU Make (and include a Windows version in the source code for the book)

- ❑ Sun's JNDI SDK, which is included with JDK 1.3

- ❑ A WAP phone emulator such as Nokia WAP toolkit 2.0 (from http://www.forum.nokia.com/main.html)

- ❑ IIS 4.0 and MS SQL server 7.0 (with Service Pack 1)

Most of the code in the book will work on a single machine, provided it is networked (that is, it can see http://localhost through the local browser). The final three chapters require at least three machines in order to stress test the code properly.

The complete source code from the book is available for download from http://www.wrox.com.

Conventions

To help you get the most from the text and keep track of what's happening, we use a number of conventions throughout the book.

For instance:

> **These boxes hold important, not-to-be forgotten information that is directly relevant to the surrounding text.**

While the background style is used for asides to the current discussion.

As for styles in the text:

- ❑   When we introduce them, we **highlight** important words
- ❑   We show keyboard strokes like this: *Ctrl-A*
- ❑   We show filenames and code within the text like so: `doGet()`
- ❑   Text on user interfaces and URLs are shown as: Menu

We present example code in two different ways:

```
In our code examples, the code foreground style shows new, important,
    pertinent code
while code background shows code that's less important in the present context,
    or has been seen before.
```

Pizza2Go

1

Webifying Applications

E- and M-Commerce, the Intranet, the Extranet, the Web, Business-to-Consumer and Business-to-Business – the buzzwords of the moment, grouped under the umbrella term, the Internet, are the hot stuff, a much-hyped revolution that is changing the way business is conducted and how people communicate. In this chapter, we'll take a high-level view of the Internet, including:

❑   Evolution of Internet applications

❑   What the Java 2 Enterprise Edition (J2EE) provides

❑   How BEA WebLogic Server implements J2EE

❑   An overview of the functional architecture of a web application

The Internet continues to grow in leaps and bounds (it follows an exponential curve), as more people arrive at the conclusion that they cannot escape it and that in order to keep up, they must participate. Not only is the Internet fashionable but it does promise to improve the productivity and competitiveness of the people that use it. The Internet is bigger than the sum of its parts and is definitely a force that has to be dealt with.

Over the years, more and more corporations have been using the Internet to enable what can be termed **business-to-consumer** (B2C) e-commerce. Most have followed the following route:

❑   Phase 1: Internet presence – "We are on the Internet"

❑   Phase 2: Provide information – "You can do queries"

❑   Phase 3: Receive information – "You can do updates"

These can also be characterized as the provision of static content, dynamic content, and then the use of web-enabled applications.

We're on the Internet

Usually the way that this first phase happened was that some corporate boss learned about the Internet from their children and realized that they had to be on it. More recently, the buzzwords have been omnipresent in the media and it is difficult for anyone to watch TV, listen to the radio, or read a newspaper without coming across a mention of the Internet.

The rush starts with trying to get the name of the corporation reserved in order to be able to have the precious .com trophy. This is not always a successful exercise for various reasons, but it does lead to very interesting and creative ways of representing the corporation with a .com name when the true name is not available.

The next step in this phase is to find the materials that make up the corporation brochures and either retype them or save them as an HTML file. Throw all this stuff onto a web server, add connectivity to the Internet and *voilà* you are on the Internet. Now the bosses have something to talk about at cocktail parties for the next few weeks. But just like Chinese food, they will want more after a little while. The pressure starts building again and the Chief Information Officer can no longer justify not doing more. Things conspire to take us to Phase 2...

You Can Do Queries

Even though the Management Information System departments deal with technology on a daily basis, typically they will be hesitant to quickly rush into implementing new technology. Most, being rather conservative will find a pilot project with which to experiment with these new things. The favorite application is the internal telephone directory (after all the PC at the reception has to be justified). So once again a developer is thrown on the project and after a few weeks the result is that the corporation has now really entered the Internet age with its web-based telephone directory.

> As another example, many retailers in their early web presence offered a store locator (enter your zip code and it finds the nearest store to you).

Given the spectacular success of the initial project, the next step is to seriously consider making more information available to customers over the Internet. Most of the time corporations have some sort of customer service and a toll-free telephone number. Typically the customer service representative acts as a go-between between the customer and a computer application. These are the favorite applications to web-enable. Some of the information that is available from the existing application will be given a web front end in such a way that the customers can now access this information from their web browser. This information can change over time, so dynamic generation of the HTML page for a topic when it is requested, is a big change.

At this stage most of the MIS departments struggle with security issues that range from access via a login and password combination to the use of Secure Socket Layer (SSL) to secure web communications. Query types can be as simple as retrieving a specified document all the way to getting a bank statement, but the bottom line is that at this stage the functionality is limited to queries only, that is, the information flows only from the corporation to the consumer.

As you can imagine, this phase not only has the complexity of interacting with existing applications, but also the challenge of creating a simple, consistent web front end that allows consumers to interact with these systems intuitively. More then a technical challenge, this is a sociological and human engineering challenge. Sadly though, too many of these decisions are made by programmers whose concept of ease of use is rather different from that of their target audience.

You Can Do Updates

As the developers get more familiar with the technologies and more comfortable with the kind of information they are willing to share with their customers on the Internet, the next natural step is that of allowing 'customers' to update information. Those customers can be employees on the road, trusted clients, or the general public.

This may involve changes to business processes and applications, but the Internet paves the way for bi-directional relationships, a two way street that allows the corporation to have a truly personalized relationship with its customers. By updates we understand the ability of the consumer to insert and/or modify information in the data store of the corporation.

This process is what we call 'webifying' an application. You take an existing application and you create an additional front end using web technology that allows people to interact fully with an existing application. Examples of this can be as simple a request as a change of address, to a full airline reservation system.

The intuitive web front end in this phase is (we hope) the province of Human Computer Interaction (HCI) specialists, rather than the developers. The separation of presentation from content and programming is one of the big issues in current web application development, and is a subject we'll return to later.

> There is one type of e-commerce that does not necessarily require a suitable front end – business-to-business (B2B) interaction. Generally in B2B the customer or consumer of the applications is a trained professional in the subject matter and the concentration is on efficiency and not necessarily simplicity. In some B2B applications there is no interaction between humans and applications, but instead between applications. For example, an inventory system can automatically generate purchase orders that are then sent (via the Internet) to the provider's order processing application. However this is not the focus of this book, which will be looking chiefly at business-to-consumer (B2C) web applications.

The Exception – Newborn Businesses

Not everybody has the bad luck (or good fortune, it all depends) of having to base their business on existing applications. Some are fortunate enough to be able to design their systems from scratch specifically for their use on the Internet. The new generation of .com companies is the obvious example, but any young company without legacy systems can fall into this category.

They have the opportunity to develop their applications with only one user interface in mind, the Internet, without intervening development phases. After all, without a fully interactive, working web site, what use is Internet presence and PR to a .com company? As these companies are younger and bolder they are more willing to risk it into the use of new technology and concepts, whereas their counterparts in the corporate world traditionally are more conservative. In general these newborns are the ones that have driven the evolution of the web technology, which will be reviewed now.

Evolution of Web Applications

In order to understand the way web applications have developed to date, let us quickly summarize the problems with a web application, and how these problems have been solved historically, before looking at the solution offered by Java 2 Enterprise Edition.

Web applications are different from ordinary applications in the following ways:

- ❑ Your application can have millions rather than thousands of customers, and many more simultaneous clients than in normal client-server systems. Scaling your application is a big problem, and this isn't going to go away, as the Internet expands (and extends to mobile phones).

- ❑ HTTP is a stateless protocol, which doesn't have the concept of a client session (conversational state between client and server). You have to add this in to support browsing and adding to an order, for example.

- ❑ The key to web success is provision of dynamic data on rapidly developing sites. Managing this, as a developer and a sys-admin, can be a headache.

- ❑ Transactions and security are needed for purchases online. The Internet is a public network, and that makes authorization, authentication and encryption critical.

- ❑ Impersonal as the web interface appears to be, you can and must make your customers feel welcome, perhaps personalize their view of the site information, and otherwise help them find what they want. Otherwise, the competition is just a click away.

Web application development is a hybrid of client-server development, with a thin client communicating using HTTP, web content that is dynamically generated according to the client's request, and a central data server.

Web applications can be seen as going through three generations during their evolution.

Common Gateway Interface

The first generation is based on Common Gateway Interface (CGI) technology. CGI applications are independent applications, originally implemented for Unix platforms, which are invoked by web servers – CGI providing the gateway between the Web and the existing applications. This rather clumsy and primitive way of doing things is still the heart of today's Internet. It is incredible to see how many Perl, C shell, and Bourne shell scripts control the guts of e-commerce.

The main problems with this approach are:

- ❑ Scalability is one of those things that people do not think about when they start a project but that becomes a major problem when it is successful. Granted, if we have to choose a problem, we would much rather have one derived from success; however, this one is particularly painful as there are few solid solutions out there and doing it yourself is a little like rocket science. It's difficult to retrofit scalability, as architecture is everything.

- ❑ Session handling is the application's responsibility – and CGI only provides primitive runtime information from the web server.

- ❑ The administration and maintenance of all these scripts can easily become a nightmare

Proprietary Solutions

The second generation of web applications was based on proprietary web APIs, for example, NetDynamics and Kiva (later called Netscape Application Server). Today both tools have merged into a product under the brand name iPlanet, which is a third-generation product.

These second-generation tools can be viewed as a formalization of the lessons learned with CGI. They made web applications quicker and easier to develop than CGI and in some cases included fancy development environments. The main issue with these tools was that they were based on proprietary technology, which is generally seen as an unacceptable lock-in to one vendor.

With the media blowing out of proportion every little security flaw in any Internet-related tool or system, security is a must on the checklist. This however, should not be the only reason for having a solid security support, especially now that more and more sophisticated uses of the Internet really require it. Security is not only a matter of perception for the end users, but also something that should be included from the outset, in the design of the application. Sadly though, second-generation tools did not always include support for security, and when they did it was rather basic.

Additionally, both generations often lacked built-in support for the most important functionality, something that is absolutely required in today's e-commerce environment – **transactional support**.

> A **transaction** is a series of steps or processes that are treated as a single unit of work. A transaction is successful when all the steps are completed successfully, otherwise, if any step fails, the transaction as a whole fails.
>
> For example, ordering a book over the Internet can be considered a transaction. The moment that you check out the shopping basket with that book, there are a number of steps to be executed: the application has to check if the item is available in the inventory, verify and charge the purchase on your credit card, and submit the book to shipping. If any of these steps fails, for example your credit card company denies the purchase, then the whole transaction (purchase the book) fails.

If you look at it carefully, at the end of the day absolutely everything boils down to a transaction. No matter if it is a Human Resources application used to update salary information based on the employee appraisal or if your credit card is being used at a web site to purchase some merchandise, it all ends up being a transaction. Therefore transaction support is critical for the good health of an e-commerce application.

There are a number of other issues we need to mention, which can be grouped under the operations, administration, and management umbrella. First- and second-generation web applications and tools generally did not consider anything related to theses issues as they were mainly designed to cover the needs of developers.

Some big and famous web sites have up to half of their people dedicated to the maintenance and administration of the web site. Considering that the useful life of computer applications can average 7 years (and more, as we all know about those Cobol applications that were injected with the Y2K serum to give them a new lease on life), it is clear that development is not the end of your problems. Your application should have a long life where it will have to be maintained and managed, and this ends up being the bulk of the cost of the operation.

Application Servers

The third generation of web applications forms a new market segment called application servers, or Java application servers. There is some confusion about what these application servers are, thanks to a host of marketing campaigns.

Application servers support a multi-tiered architecture rather different from a standalone, monolithic application – meaning that multiple components compose the application server. Applications that run in these servers typically have separate parts for client/UI, business logic, and database/persistence layer.

In its most basic form, an application server can be viewed as **middleware**, that is, it acts as glue that holds together web-based clients and existing applications or data stores.

❑	The clients can be the browsers, Java-based programs, or other web-enabled programming environments running on the first tier.

❑	The second tier (the glue) is the middleware, an application server. This is not absolutely required – you can always use the middle tier just as a funnel to existing applications or data stores. But normally the second tier will host a combination of presentation logic and business logic.

❑	The third tier is generally a combination of existing applications and data stores

In this context, multi-tier is used to denote the ability to break the second and third tiers into more tiers that handle with finer resolution the presentation and business logic hosted there.

As compared with the traditional two tier client-server systems, the multi-tier systems have the following benefits:

❑	Scalability and reliability – decoupling tiers 2 and 3 means that the workload can be split between machines, and multiple machines in each tier, if necessary. Clustering is an option here.

❑	Easier management – enabling division of jobs into presentation, business logic, and data management.

❑	Security – the application server is a client of the database, and so browser clients can't access all the data, only selected parts.

❑	Simpler integration – existing applications can be fitted into the architecture as just another data source, or become a web application server themselves, accessed through a URL.

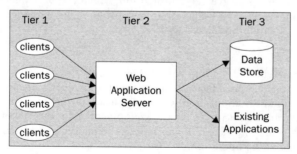

Application servers, thus defined, include Microsoft's DNA and forthcoming .NET architectures, CORBA servers, BroadVision, Vignette, and Apple WebObjects. The definition of a Java application server for this book, however, is a piece of software that implements the Java 2 Enterprise Edition APIs (J2EE) that allows you to host Java applications on a multi-tiered architecture. The J2EE specification is a standard proposed by a group of over twenty vendors that includes IBM, Sun Microsystems, BEA Systems, Hewlett Packard, Oracle, Informix, Novell, and Symantec.

> *This group learned from the experiences that the relational database vendors had about 15 years ago. When the relational database system (RDBMS) vendors started offering their products, not many people got very excited about them until they implemented a common front with Structured Query Language (SQL). SQL as a de facto, and later official, standard gave consumers relative peace of mind that they could access their data in more or less the same way independent of the actual RDBMS. Once accepted, the market for RDBMS really started growing to the point we know it today.*

Java 2 Enterprise Edition

Sun Microsystems has tried to define the function of a Java application server (http://java.sun.com/j2ee) sufficiently clearly that all implementations play on a level field. The customer of the server is thus less worried about vendor lock-in, and has a wider pool of trained developers and other resources to draw on. Because the specification isn't a standard, but industry-led, it's not slow to develop to match needs in the community.

The other advantage of using J2EE is that the issues we mentioned above that affect previous generations of web applications are part of the J2EE infrastructure and aren't tacked on as an afterthought. Specifically sessions, transactions, security, scalability, comprehensive datasource connectivity, and deployment are directly addressed by the APIs that are part of J2EE.

The common base of J2EE implementations means that, assuming that all the vendors can reach the point of conforming implementations, the race will inevitably take us to the following distinct areas:

❑ Integration with development tools

❑ Proprietary extensions to the J2EE standards

❑ Performance at different loads and for different types of web application

❑ Cost

Different servers will address different development needs, have different strengths and thus finding their niche.

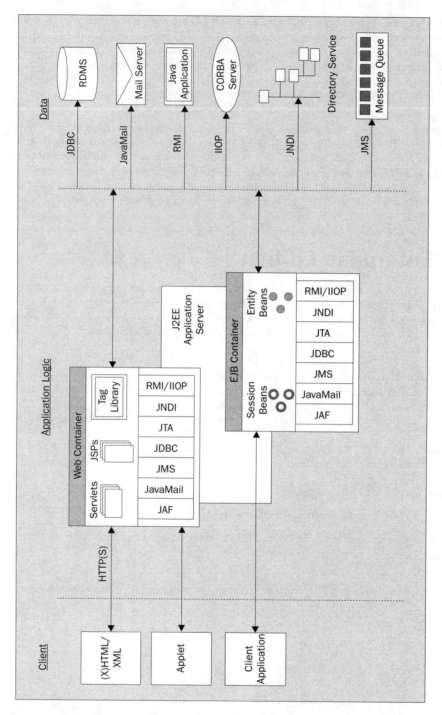

It is the intent of this book to show how the J2EE APIs work in practice. Here we'll just summarize the purpose of each API that make up the specification, and we'll provide more details as we look at each API in later chapters.

There are plenty of materials that go into more detail on the J2EE specification, starting with the documentation from Sun, http://java.sun.com/j2ee, as well as many books (for example, Professional Java Server Programming, Wrox Press, ISBN 1-861004-65-6).

Enterprise JavaBeans (EJBs)

EJB components are designed to encapsulate business logic, so that the developer does not have to worry about programming code for such mundane things as database access, transaction support, security, caching, and concurrency. These mundane problems are crucial to the success of a project, they're hard to get right, and basically they recur in every application. So, in the EJB specification they're the responsibility of the **EJB container**. With EJBs, reinventing the wheel can stop, and code that is almost too important to be left to business logic developers can be kept in the container.

Enterprise JavaBeans aren't exactly revolutionary. There's very little of the EJB specification that wasn't in the CORBA specification. Abstraction of security, transactions, data access, and naming were all in the DCE specification as well. Transaction monitors, component-container systems like MTS, and transactional databases like Oracle have been worrying about the same problems for a long time. But EJBs merge the design strengths of these earlier systems with the object-oriented programming of Java, and a specification that allows for migration between systems.

One of the really interesting advantages of EJBs is that they isolate the business logic from the actual deployment environment in such a way that when you change from, say, one database to another, you do not have to touch your EJBs, as they only contain the business logic. Moving components between different EJB containers is also possible without recompilation. The configurations for a server are specified declaratively in a file that is called the **deployment descriptor**.

EJBs components come in two flavors: session beans and entity beans.

Session beans represent the client's interaction with the web application – this is where you typically will code your business logic. Each instance of a session bean serves (that is, represents) just one client. Session beans can be one of two types, depending on the design and requirements of your application:

- ❏ Stateful – by this we mean that the bean instance can work with just that one client until it is released by that client (stateful), in which case the bean can maintain information (state) about the client between method calls, for the duration of the bean's life.

- ❏ Stateless – if the bean maintains no state between each method call, it is stateless. It can answer any client and will typically be assigned many clients by the container during its lifecycle. This request-response interaction with clients can be very fast, but places the burden of maintaining the state of the conversation elsewhere.

Both kinds of session beans are temporary – they represent the client conversation, not the outcome of the requests. The favorite example to describe the use of stateless session beans is automatic teller machine. You feed in your card, punch in your personal identification number, perform your transaction, recover your card and maybe a record of the transaction and then you leave. Our example ATM speaks with a stateless session bean assigned to the ATM for the duration of the transaction (modeled as one method call). This bean contains the logic required to perform the requested operations, very likely by acting as a dispatcher to control other beans. If the customer wants to use another service (using another method call) the EJB container assigns them another bean instance.

For stateful session beans, a good example is the ubiquitous web shopping cart. The state of the order is kept in the bean on behalf of the client; it can be changed and items added, and will be kept while the client maintains the connection with the bean. Multiple method calls affect the state of the bean, and this state is only made permanent when the order button is finally pressed. Keeping the bean's resources for just one client is more resource intensive than using stateless beans, as we'll see later in this book.

Entity beans are the persistent side of the EJB specification. They represent data that lives in some data store (we use this generic name as it can be more than just an RDBMS), in an object-oriented fashion. Entity beans are sharable, that is they can be accessed by many clients, and recoverable, meaning that their state is regularly synchronized with the data store.

The code to save and retrieve data from a data store can be developed by the programmer (bean-managed persistence, BMP) or (the easier way) by having the EJB automagically include code (container-managed persistence, CMP). For the most part, coding BMP is relatively mechanical and boring, and is much more prone to errors than CMP. As we'll see in Chapter 5, though, there are times when we need BMP. Either way, it is rather easy to access information in a data store with entity beans.

By combining session beans and entity beans you are able to create all the necessary components that make up the logic of an application. It is in the interaction between clients and the EJBs that you create the workflow that makes up the core of your web application. The EJB container allows you design the application for an individual client, as the container enables it to work for multiple clients.

Java Servlets

Remember CGI? Servlets are very similar, but they're:

- ❏ Easier to write – servlets use Java classes and streams to simplify development
- ❏ Faster to execute – servlets are compiled to Java byte code, and at runtime the servlet instance is kept in memory, and each client request spawns a new thread
- ❏ Well integrated with the web server runtime environment

HTTP is a request/response protocol, and with servlets you process every request, that is, trap the incoming data, and generate a response. Servlets make it easy to generate data to an HTTP response stream in a dynamic fashion.

The big problem (from the point of web application development) is that HTTP is a stateless protocol, that is, each request is performed as a new connection, so flow control does not come naturally between requests. **Session tracking**, or session management, maintains the state of specific clients between requests. Servlets make this very easy.

Servlets can instantiate other Java objects, and use all the other Java APIs, making their potential uses very diverse. They can access business logic that lives in EJBs or other Java objects. Neither are servlets limited to generating just HTML; they can also generate XML (including WML for WAP devices), and binary content (for example, images).

JavaServer Pages (JSP)

JavaServer Pages is an attempt to unite two very different worlds: the designer whose main concern is with the aesthetics and usefulness of an HTML page, and the developer who wants to code. JSP allows us to combine snippets of Java code in template pages (usually HTML) that will generate dynamic content on the server. The idea is that it's better for designers to add code to page templates (which they can easily edit), than for developers to add HTML to their servlets' code. As with servlets, JSPs can also handle XML and WML.

> *There's nothing new in this – there are several similar systems; ASP and ColdFusion are just two examples. But JSP is a specification, and is now supported on many web servers. Another interesting development is that you can create your own tags to support the work of the designer, hiding the details of the implementation even more.*

You can also embed JavaScript in HTML pages, to work on the client. Server-based dynamic content, however, makes more sense for the following reasons:

- ❑ Browser portability – the server can generate JSP pages for different browser types, or generic pages that will work on all browsers.

- ❑ Speed – JSP is based on servlets, that is, the JSP page is compiled to a servlet before execution.

- ❑ Control – the biggest problem with using JavaScript in the HTML page is that you are pushing business rules onto the HTML page and thus onto the client. Those rules are exposed, which is a security problem. With servlets and JSP, the rules and content remain firmly on the server, and only HTML is returned to the client.

As we'll see in Chapter 3, servlets and JSP work hand in hand.

JDBC

JDBC is a relatively portable bridge to relational databases – it's modeled on ODBC, and is thus simple and fairly well understood. It decouples the database type from the programmatic code through the use of drivers. This version of WebLogic Server provides support for advanced data types, such as Blobs, Clobs, and character streams for Oracle. Additionally there is the functionality of scrollable result sets and batch updates. Connection pooling is a new feature of the JDBC specification version 2.0, but this has been supported by WebLogic for several years.

Drivers can be one of four types.

- ❑ Type 1 is a JDBC-ODBC bridge, which comes with the JDK. It is more a proof of concept than something to be used in a serious production environment. With it, you can connect your application to any ODBC data source.

- ❑ Type 2 drivers communicate with the RDBMS using a native library, for example, in the case of Oracle, the OCI library. This means that the native library must be present on the client machine.

- ❑ Type 3 drivers are multi-tiered, that is the driver is placed between the clients and the RDMBS. It then establishes a connection with the RDBMS and acts as a funnel optimizing all the requests and responses. The client just has to load pure Java classes that communicate with the Type 3 driver.

❏ Type 4 drivers are more or less the same as Type 2 drivers, but instead of using a native library, they will communicate directly with the RDBMS using its proprietary protocol. For example, with MS/SQLServer or Sybase it would be the TDS protocol.

Both Type 2 and 4 drivers are considered two tier.

Java Message Service (JMS)

The Java Message Service is the J2EE mechanism to support the exchange of messages between Java programs. This is how Java supports **asynchronous communication**, where sender and receiver don't need to be aware of each other, and can operate essentially independently.

JMS supports two messaging models:

❏ **Point-to-point** is based on message queues. Here a **message producer** sends a message to a queue. A **message consumer** can attach itself to a queue to listen for messages. When a message arrives on the queue a consumer takes it off the queue and acts on it. Messages can be sent to just one queue, and will be used by just one consumer. Consumers can filter messages to specify the exact message types they want.

❏ In the **publish-and-subscribe** model, producers send messages to a topic and all the registered consumers for that topic retrieve those messages. In this case many consumers can receive the same message.

JMS messages can be Java streams, Java objects, maps, text, or byte streams. They can be persistent, that is, messages will be logged to a data store before being delivered to the consumer(s). This is done *once and only once*, meaning that the message cannot be lost and cannot be delivered more than once. When messages are not persistent, they can be delivered *at most once*, that is, the message can be lost but not delivered more than once.

In the particular case of publish and subscribe, there is the notion of a *durable* subscriber, that is a consumer that will receive the messages or events that occurred even while it was offline, when it restarts.

Java Transaction Support

The Java Transaction API (JTA) and Java Transaction Service (JTS) form the basis of the transactional support in J2EE and more specifically for EJB and JDBC 2.0.

> *JTS is a low-level API for transaction management that basically maps Java to OMG Object Transaction Service (OTS) for flat transactions. We've still not hit the bottom of the acronym stack, as OTS for flat transactions is based on the X/Open DTP definition of transaction function and commitment protocols. It's very unlikely you will need to use this API.*

JTA is a high level API that consists of two parts:

❏ The first is a transaction interface that allows **transaction demarcation.** Transaction demarcation enables work done by distributed components to be bound by a global transaction. It is a way of marking groups of operations to constitute a transaction.

❏ The second is an XA resource interface based on the X/Open XA interface that enables the handling of distributed transactions

You can work with JTA when you develop bean-managed persistence entity beans. Most of the time, however, you won't need to worry about programming explicit transactions with JTA, as that work is done through the JDBC and EJB APIs, handled by the container, and configured by the application deployment descriptor. This way you can focus on the design of the transaction rather than its implementation.

Java Naming and Directory Interface (JNDI)

JNDI is a common, Java-based interface to all naming and directory services. It provides support for all these interfaces by means of so-called Service Provider Interfaces, which actually communicate with the existing naming or directory services (like an LDAP based system, DNS, or Solaris NIS+).

JNDI makes a small distinction between naming services and directory services. A **naming service** associates a name with an object and basically offers binding and lookup methods. A **directory service** is a naming service that allows you to associate application attributes with a name; this way you can retrieve an object based on its attributes rather than its name.

In general JNDI is extremely easy to use. You basically have two things to do:

- ❏ A lookup for the object (usually by its name)
- ❏ A bind

We'll see JNDI in action when we work with EJBs, as JNDI is the way to acquire a bean from a container.

JavaMail

Just as JNDI provides a common interface to directory and naming services, so JavaMail provides a layer of abstraction on top of a mail provider so the client can be blissfully ignorant of the subtleties of the underlying service and whatever protocols it may employ. SMTP, POP3, IMAP, MAPI, CMC, c-client, and other mailing ideas, cease to worry you.

This way, you can add portable e-mail capabilities to Java-based applications and have JavaMail shield you from the actual mailing system.

Java Interface Definition Language (IDL)

CORBA objects use an Interface Definition Language (IDL) to specify a contract (how they are going to interact with other objects). With Java IDL you can define contracts between the Java world and the CORBA world.

To use Java IDL you will need the `idltojava` compiler, which generates portable client stubs and server skeletons that will work with any CORBA compliant Object Request Broker (ORB). Starting with Sun's JDK version 1.2 an ORB is included, which allows Java applications to invoke remote CORBA objects via the IIOP protocol.

RMI-IIOP

Just like Unix Remote Procedure Calls (RPC) but more powerful, **Remote Method Invocation** (RMI) allows a class running in one Java Virtual Machine (JVM) to execute methods on a class in another JVM. These JVMs can be in the same machine or separated by a network. RMI will handle all the details of transporting the arguments, requests, and results, including the passing of full objects as arguments. This is a Java-to-Java contract.

The **Internet Inter-ORB Protocol** (IIOP) is a protocol that, as part of the OMG CORBA spec, is implementation and language neutral, and can thus link Java components with other component systems.

RMI over IIOP can be used as a transparent bridge between Java and the CORBA world as you do not have to use any IDL or mapping between them. This way you can pass any `Serializable` Java object (object by value or by reference) between application components independently of whether they are developed in Java or any other language.

XML

Even though XML is not a standard that officially forms part of J2EE, some of the above specifications use XML. For example, EJB and JSP depend on XML to describe content.

J2EE Connector

This specification defines a standard architecture for connecting the J2EE platform to existing applications living on heterogeneous systems, in order to integrate applications with mainframes and ERPs.

BEA WebLogic Server

For this book we will be using version 5.1 of the BEA WebLogic Server. This version implements the most important APIs of J2EE, basically the specifications presented earlier, except for the J2EE Connector, Java IDL, and JavaMail. Additionally it has a bunch of extra features that go beyond the J2EE standards.

J2EE Support

WebLogic Server 5.1 includes full implementations of:

- ❑ EJB 1.1 – it also includes an implementation of EJB 2.0, even though at the time of writing this specification is still a draft.
- ❑ JavaServer Pages 1.1
- ❑ Servlets 2.2
- ❑ JNDI 1.2
- ❑ JDBC 2.0 – with WebLogic you get a choice of the Type 2 JDBC driver for Oracle or the Type 4 drivers for MS/SQLServer and Informix. You can also use third party JDBC drivers.
- ❑ JMS 1.0.1 – a native implementation based on RMI.
- ❑ JTA and JTS
- ❑ RMI 1.0 – explained in more detail in the next section

RMI Support

In the WebLogic Server, RMI has been implemented on top of three transport mechanisms: IIOP, HTTP, and T3. As explained earlier, RMI over IIOP can be used as a bridge to the CORBA world. RMI over HTTP can be used for Java-based clients when they need to communicate with WebLogic and there is a firewall in between, as it handles all the issues that are present when doing firewall tunneling.

T3, also known as rich sockets, is a BEA internal protocol that is industrial strength and very scalable. T3 is multiplexed, bi-directional, and asynchronous. It is highly optimized and uses only one socket and one thread. It is interesting to see a Java-based client instantiate as many RMI objects as it needs on the server side and still use only one socket and one thread.

Security

On the security front, WebLogic is pretty complete. It includes all the classes for:

❑   Secure Socket Layer (SSL) version 3

❑   RSA encryption

❑   Support for X.509 digital certificates, version 3

> *The encryption comes in domestic and export strength. Export strength uses 40-bit encryption and is the default version. Domestic strength uses 128-bit encryption. Strong encryption is available outside the United States in some cases. Please contact your BEA sales person for more details.*

On many of the supported platforms, WebLogic includes native SSL support to enhance the performance of the initial secure connection.

WebLogic has a very powerful Access Control List (ACL) mechanism that allows for fine-grained control of the usage of components running on the server. You can define what can be executed (or not) by which user or group of users, down to the Java method level. This way you can state things such as "all users can execute servlet ABC". This ACL mechanism covers anything that runs on WebLogic except for EJBs. These have their own access control mechanism defined in the EJB specification.

Security realms allow the administrator to import information from existing authorization or authentication systems into the ACL. You can thus import information from the NT security system, from an LDAP system (version 2), from the Unix password file, or from database proprietary system.

Another related security topic is the functionality of **firewall tunneling**. WebLogic Server provides the capability to go through firewalls and proxies via HTTP and HTTPS tunneling.

WebLogic also includes security audit and logging interfaces so that you can build your own security audit engine to generate audit trails to log security-sensitive system events.

Data Stores

In addition to RDBMS support through JDBC, WebLogic Server can use other kinds of data stores. Examples include:

❑   Object-oriented databases such as Versant and ODI

❑   Object relational mapping tools such as TOPLink from WebGain

❑   Cache accelerators like Front-Tier from TimesTen

Supported Client Types

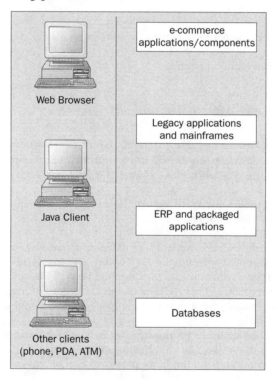

On the front end, WebLogic can handle traditional web clients and programmatic clients. By web clients we mean the HTML pages running in a browser or the deck of WML cards running in the micro-browser of a WAP device. We will also call them **thin clients**. The programmatic clients, also known as **fat clients** can be Java-based applets or standalone Java applications, which can use RMI or XML to communicate with the server.

Programmatic clients can also be based on Microsoft's Component Object Model (COM). WebLogic has a COM compiler that will take a COM object, perform introspection on it and automatically generate a Java wrapper. This allows bi-directional communication between WebLogic and the COM object. The COM object can be a client of WebLogic that can call business logic in the form of EJBs or Servlets. Because it is bi-directional, you can also call a COM object from Java. This is not much used, as most COM objects are typically clients. You can also do the same from Visual Basic programs.

Client Administration

The WebLogic Server also has the Zero Administration Client (ZAC), which provides the ability to automatically update client software. ZAC is the implementation of the W3C specification, the HTTP Distribution and Replication Protocol. The way it works is that:

❑ You create a ZAC package, which can contain pretty much anything – it could even be the WebLogic Server itself. This is done with a Publish Wizard.

❑ ZAC supplies a minimal bootstrap executable that a client can download. This bootstrap is written in native code, so that Java does not have to be present on the client.

❑ The bootstrapper can handle the initial download and the updates.

❑ The updates can be configured so that they happen when the client determines is best. It is only for this that you will need to use the ZAC API; for normal use it isn't necessary. The default is to check with the server every time the package starts execution on the client side. If there is an update, it will only copy the parts that have changed, not the whole package.

Management

WebLogic Server offers a Swing-based console to remotely monitor and update the state of applications and clusters. This console can be used to dig into the server and view detailed information on the execution of the application components, such as servlets, EJBs, and JMS queues or topics. Additionally, there is SNMP version 1 support that allows you to use any third party compliant management framework.

JVM and Platform Certification

WebLogic Server is appropriate for high Quality of Service (QoS) systems. It uses strict certification and QA procedures to ensure the robustness needed by 24x7 apps.

Because WebLogic is all written in Java, technically it runs on any Java Virtual Machine. However, not all JVMs are equal – there are good JVMs and there are those that are less good. Because of this, BEA has a JVM certification process that provides a high degree of confidence that an application written on WebLogic will behave pretty much the same on any certified JVM. This can be done because of the very stringent testing procedure the BEA folks have. The certified JVMs and the platforms on which they run on include:

❑ Linux

❑ IBM OS/390

❑ Sun Solaris – the most popular production environment

❑ NT – the favored development platform

The list of certified JVMs and platforms currently numbers over fifteen and keeps growing, so please consult the BEA web site to verify that your platform is available.

Tools Support

When developing an application, the WebLogic Server can be viewed as a library of Java classes. Because of this you can use any development tool. BEA offers tight integration with:

- ❏ IBM VisualAge for Java

- ❏ KLGroup Jprobe

- ❏ WebGain Studio – The WebGain Studio includes Visual Café Enterprise Suite, Macromedia DreamWeaver, Tendril Structure Builder, and the TOPLink object-relational mapping tool.

The same is true for developing HTML-based clients, where you can use the HTML design tool of your choice, such as DreamWeaver, Adobe Page Mill, or Microsoft Front Page.

Performance, Reliability, and Scalability

WebLogic includes a high performance HTTP web server. However, if you already have an investment in an existing web server, plug-ins are available:

- ❏ An NSAPI plug-in for the Netscape web server

- ❏ An ISAPI plug-in for Microsoft IIS

- ❏ A plug-in for Apache

Another very interesting feature is the Performance Packs. Java virtual machines are clumsy when it comes to handling sockets. The JVM listens to a socket for specific period of time. When the time-out happens it moves on to the next socket. If you have many sockets and only some of them have information you will still have to go through the time-out mechanism in turn until you reach the socket with the desired information.

The performance packs for Weblogic Server handle sockets in a native fashion (they're not available on all the supported platforms, so please consult the BEA web site). What they do is handle the sockets as interrupts so that when a socket has information it is delivered immediately to the requestor. Depending on how many sockets your application uses, you can see substantial performance gains.

Probably the most powerful performance feature of the WebLogic Server is **clustering**. With this feature, two or more WebLogic Servers run in such a way that to the user (and the programmer as well) they look like a single server. Clustering is currently limited to LANs, therefore the theoretical limit is 256 instances of WebLogic. The basic functionality offered by clustering is:

- ❏ **Load balancing** – sharing the server load between several machines. The idea here is that increased load can be met by adding another server

- ❏ **Automatic failover** – if a server fails, the other servers in the cluster step into the breach

Replication of servlets and EJBs comes as standard with clustering. Clustering is dynamic, in the sense that cluster servers can enter and leave a cluster at any moment without having to do any special operation. Because of this, failover is implicit. There are various load balancing policies available and they will be detailed in Chapter 12.

Application Support and Proprietary Extensions

The WebLogic Server provides various services and facilities to the applications it hosts. Facilities like common logs, instrumentation, configuration, and management are available to all applications that operate within the server and some of them have been described earlier.

There is another group of services that are proprietary APIs that WebLogic makes available to developers. You can choose to use them, but be aware that they are not available on other web application servers, so porting will be an issue. Having said that, you have the option of either using this functionality or coding it yourself to make your application portable.

dbKona and htmlKona

dbKona is a higher level data abstraction than JDBC. It hides the low level details and database vendor specifics from the developer.

htmlKona provides an object-oriented interface to the HTML environment that allows a developer to format an HTML document with objects.

These two APIs will be seen in detail in Chapter 3.

The WorkSpace

One of the services is the Workspace. A workspace is nothing more than a thread-safe hash table that can be assigned to programmatic clients and to the server itself. The workspace can contain any type of object and can be named, saved, and re-entered over various sessions. You can also specify that certain methods be executed before saving or destroying workspace contents.

When a programmatic client chooses to create a workspace, this is private to that particular client; no other client can gain access to it. A server workspace, in contrast, is available to all clients and threads running on the server. These workspaces are very powerful tools that can be used to minimize the amount of data that goes down the wire from the server to the client. A client can store the results of intermediary operations in the server side without having to send them over to the client side for processing. Another example is a database query that is repeatedly used by many clients. The query can be made once on the server, the result set stored in the server workspace, and the clients can look for data there instead of having to do a full query.

Scheduling

Another very useful facility is the scheduling or time API. It provides a mechanism whereby you can define actions or triggers to happen on a regular basis or at sometime in the future. These actions can be scheduled to happen on either the client's JVM or within the WebLogic server.

File IO

If your programmatic client wants to have access to the native operating system files where the WebLogic server is running, you can use the File API, which extends `java.io.InputStream` and `java.io.OutputStream` so that you can seamlessly manipulate remote files.

CGI Support

WebLogic includes the ability to execute external CGI scripts. This functionality is provided to ease the migration from a first generation application to the application server.

Connection Filtering

You can selectively block or allow connections from clients by using an API that gives you a fine-grained control where you define who can and can't access server(s).

Functional Architecture

Probably the biggest challenge for people who are new to the Web is trying to design a multi-tier application. The most common mistake is to migrate that old client-server two tier application as is to the new web world. Just take those 5,000 lines of code and cram them into a single EJB. Write an applet that calls the EJB and have that EJB communicate directly with the database via JDBC.

Of course if such a monster runs, the performance will be dreadful and then you hear that the famous application servers are not all they are advertised to be. As the vendors get blamed for faulty product they react by sending their distinguished engineers to the customer site, who start by checking the architecture of the application. When the poor design is brought up, the excuses start showing up: "We had to do it that way because we only had 30 days to go live," is quite a popular one.

The concepts presented here are very simple and common sense (the least common of all the senses), but if you knew how many projects have failed just because these principles were neglected, you would not believe it.

Think in Objects

Java is an object-oriented language. Treat it as such – it is not RPG, C, or an Oracle PL/SQL stored procedure. Go read a few books about object-oriented analysis and design (OOAD), and work your way round to design patterns for object-oriented languages. Even though EJB design is a slight departure from pure object orientation, it still is based on it.

If you don't have the necessary skills, consider hiring a mentor who can help you design the system. If hiring a mentor isn't an option, start small and be prepared to crack a few oysters before you find a pearl.

Even more important is to ensure that the system requirements are well understood – far more projects fail for management and requirements reasons than technology-related failings. This becomes increasingly critical with the scale of the system under development.

Think in Tiers

Web application servers are designed to be used in a multi-tier environment. You start with three tiers and as things get more complex and you get into some really fancy fine tuning, you add tiers.

The first tier, the client, is very simple. The whole idea is to limit the client to the very basic logic associated with capturing data and presenting results. There are some schools of thought that prefer slightly heavier clients that can also handle some business logic. This makes the most sense when the client will be disconnected from the server at times, and must maintain some state in order to continue functioning. But in principle a multi-tier architecture leans towards a thin, connected client.

The second tier, also known as the middle tier is where the majority of your business logic lives. This has a several advantages, probably the most popular one being the fact that you have all your business logic in one place, that's under your control and is thus very easy to maintain as well as to performance-tune.

The third tier is a combination of a data store and existing applications – both accessed by the middle tier. In principle clients on the first tier should not access directly the backend or third tier, but there will always be cases where this is valid. Not really kosher for the purists, but it works.

As things get more fancy, people tend to break the second tier in two, for different reasons. When JSP pages and servlets are used, they often have their own tier, with the other tier for the EJBs (session and entity). Sometimes this is more for physical, hardware reasons than anything else – the entity beans live on the same server as the data store in order to optimize data access, and the JSP/Servlets tier is on the HTTP server. Separating logical and physical architectures, through the use of tiers, means that changes can be made to the physical setup of the application, to scale it, for instance, without affecting the application.

Other fancy setups include breaking the third tier into more granular levels. Generally there is a first level that includes a transaction processing monitor and/or an object/relational mapping tool and then the data store(s) on a second level.

No matter how you do it, it is very comforting to know that all those combinations are valid and they will, in a better or worse degree, work. To summarize, this is the concept of **distributed logic**, which means you can put the logic wherever you consider best. There is also the added advantage that you can move this logic from tier to tier as your application evolves over the years of use and you understand better its behavior.

Webifying Existing Applications

The first question that comes to mind when webifying an application is which client type should be used, thin clients or Java-based clients. The general rule of thumb is that when HTML is enough to capture and display the information required by the application, then HTML is the choice. The practical reason for using HTML is when you have no control on the client side. There are three scenarios for this:

❑ The Internet, a true Wild West (or a more modern Wild East if you are in Europe); you don't really know what is out there

❑ Large corporations, when the IS department has lost control of the workstations and does not know what software or version of software is installed on the client machines; usually they will know there is a browser, but don't know which one and what version

❑ Departments with limited budgets where thin clients are a way of lowering roll-out and support costs

There are, however, many cases where HTML is just not enough, where you need a client program to perform the necessary capture and display operations. Java clients are favored, whether applets or standalone Java programs, as they can present a richer graphical user interface.

On the Internet, applets present a set of logistic problems that can diminish that sense of instant satisfaction that the users expect from computers. Because of this we suggest you limit their use to corporate intranets where there is greater network bandwidth and the browser types in use can be controlled.

When using a standalone Java client, one of the big logistic challenges is the distribution of the client application. This is where you can use the ZAC feature. It is an excellent way to handle the distribution of software. A typical ZAC package will be composed of a number of Java classes or maybe a few JAR files, and sometimes a Java Runtime Engine. By creating a package that includes a JRE you also handle updating it truly making these client side applications update free.

Sometimes neither HTML nor Java is the most obvious tool for creating a Graphical User Interface. Let's face it, Microsoft controls the desktop, so you have to be pragmatic and allow for some sort of connectivity with COM. A popular use of the WebLogic Server COM compiler is to write ActiveX components in Visual Basic that work with Excel spreadsheets that interact with a J2EE-based application.

> *Sometimes your application may not require a GUI. Automation or command-line interfaces are all valid clients of n-tier apps. The same choices apply there too.*

Multiple Clients

One of the real advantages of a multi-tier system is that you can use all the client types we've just described and have them access the same business logic. As you can see in the following figure, when the clients are HTML, the JSP/Servlet combination becomes the real client of the business logic. When the client is a Java program or a COM-based program, they can directly access the business logic as well.

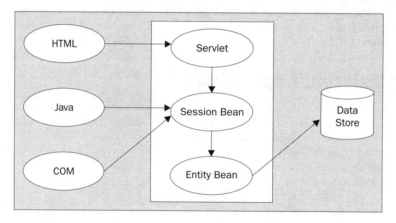

How to Use EJBs

The intended way to use EJBs is the following. The clients communicate with session beans, which can be stateful or stateless. These session beans then communicate with entity beans, which in turn communicate with the data store. Another way of looking at this is to use the session beans to represent the clients and use the entity beans to represent the data store.

When to use stateful or stateless session beans is a fairly easy and intuitive decision. Even though session beans are temporary in nature, you might have cases in which you want to remember some client data from one method call to the next in its short life – in which case you should use stateful beans. When it is a one-time shot, that is, you use that logic only once and you are done with it, then you use a stateless bean. The bottom line is that session beans form the base of the application's business logic.

The use of entity beans is a little more controversial as there is a performance penalty to be paid. In any case, the EJB model is flexible enough that you can directly use JDBC from a session bean to access your data store instead of entity beans as shown below.

These architectural choices will be the subject of tests later in the book.

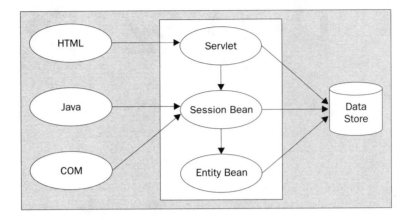

Summary

In this introductory chapter, we've raced through some overview topics, showing:

- ❑ How the Internet has evolved
- ❑ What web application servers provide developers
- ❑ How J2EE meets the needs of web applications
- ❑ Why BEA WebLogic Server is a great J2EE implementation
- ❑ First thoughts in designing a successful web application

In particular, application developers:

- ❑ Re-invent the wheel with each project
- ❑ Have difficulty scaling their apps for many clients, and keeping them robust
- ❑ Must use the same business logic to support different types of client
- ❑ Need vendor-independent solutions

This is why the multi-tier, web application architecture is so appealing.

In the next chapter, we'll outline the case study that will be developed over the rest of the book. The concepts and technologies we've skimmed over here will be covered in more detail as the case study expands.

2

Setting the Scene – Pizzas to Go

Mr Chairman of the Board is typical in having learned about the Internet from his children. In this case he did not pay too much attention, assuming it was just another fashion that would fade. But the press continues to make more and more noise about it, and seeing people use the Internet just as they would a phone, he starts to think that he wants to be part of this. With the excuse that it is for the long-term benefit of the company he embarks on an adventure that we are about to describe – the diversification of his existing bricks-and-mortar business into a new channel.

The first step is to summon his obedient right-hand man, Mr Yesman, the president of the company, and they strategize on how to become part of the Internet craze and increase the price of the stock. To become part of the Internet a strong IT group is needed, so one of their first decisions is to let go the vice-president of MIS, Mr Oldtimer. He is seen as extremely unresponsive, every project is quoted at two years and goes into production with all sorts of problems with an additional year of delay. If that where not enough, he is not as assertive and aggressive as he should be to lead an effort that will place the company in the e-commerce space.

The replacement of Mr Oldtimer is finally procured through a long and complicated process. From all the candidates, the one selected is Mr Wonderboy, and to make his position sound more important he is given the title of Chief Information Officer (CIO). Mr Wonderboy has a very outgoing personality and a great capacity for speaking his way into (as well as out of) anything. He comes from a job as a high level IT manager at some large corporation in the US, and has been wanting to be part of the Internet revolution, but internal politics kept it on hold. Even though he has no professional experience with the Internet, he figures that he can make it happen. After all, he had survived the move to the client-server technology pretty well. Additionally, since he is the boss of IT, now he gets to make all the decisions in what hopefully is a less politically charged environment.

Pizza2Go

For the purposes of this book, Mr Chairman of the Board runs a company called Pizza2Go, a chain of pizza outlets where you can place orders via telephone or just walk in. None of the outlets are restaurants, just a place to cook up your order and pick it up, if you so decide. Pizza2Go has almost 300 outlets in the US, about 25 in Canada (including French-speaking Québec) and 8 outlets in Mexico.

When ordering a pizza by telephone, the customer calls a unique toll free number for the US and Canada. (We would like to say it is 1-800-PIZZA2GO, but in real life it is already taken by another company that is totally unrelated to this book.) In Mexico the customers call another toll free number, 0800-PIZZA; but don't try it as we just made it up.

They have two operations centers that handle all the orders, one in central US that covers the US and Canada, and another smaller center in Mexico City. Each of these centers has operators to answer the phone and take the pizza order. That order is then faxed to the corresponding outlet.

One of the perceived competitive advantages of Pizza2Go is its automatic inventory system. Every time a pizza is ordered over the phone, the inventory of the outlet is updated to reflect the usage of ingredients by the order. These guys take inventory very seriously. Since orders can also be placed in the outlet (referred to as walk-ins), at the end of the day the point of sale (POS) system at the store generates a report that is faxed over to the central location to update the inventory system.

The Audit

In order to understand the situation he has gotten into, Mr Wonderboy runs an audit on the existing system. Not only does this allow him to gain important knowledge, but it also gives him the ability to blame everything that is wrong (even if just a little) on Mr Oldtimer, one of the tricks he learned in his old job.

Using the histrionic repertoire with which all management has traditionally distinguished itself, and creating enough panic that it can be bottled, the audit is set in course. The results, although emotionally very discouraging for the participants, are generally good.

What is found is a solid system that does things in a simple fashion and does them pretty well. After all, selling pizzas is relatively simple. The challenge will be to bring this system to the Internet.

Even though the core of the system, from the perspective of the folks at Pizza2Go is the inventory, it is the order entry system that will be most affected by this new focus on the Internet, so this is where the inquest will concentrate. The high level flowchart of the order process is presented opposite.

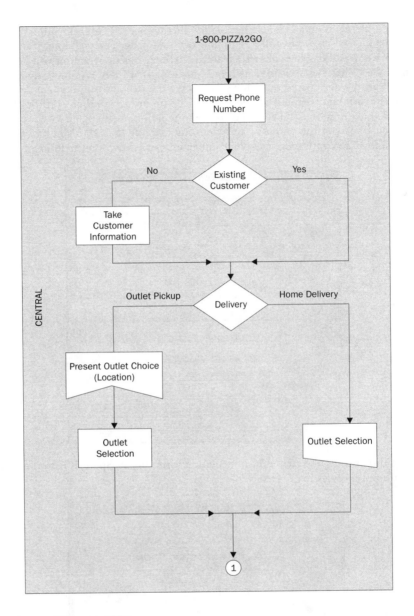

Buenos Días, Pizza2Go

When a call gets into an operations center it is routed automatically to the first operator available. The telephone system in the US operations center uses machines that route calls depending on the location of the caller. In this case, this ability is used to route calls from the French speaking areas of Canada to operators that can speak Québecois. When this happens they will use the order entry screen in French. In the Mexican operations center, the order entry system is based in Spanish.

The sophisticated phone system can also handle the infamous caller identification feature. And to prove that it is worth its high price, it has full integration with the order entry system. If the caller is not obsessed with privacy and has the caller ID feature enabled, this information will be given to the order entry system. If the caller is an existing customer, meaning that there is somebody in the database with this phone number, the designated operator will receive the call and simultaneously the customer information screen will be presented on the screen. The operator will then confirm the information with the caller, just to make sure it is the same person (phone numbers change a lot in the US). If the caller is not an existing customer, or the phone system does not provide the caller's number, then the operator is presented with a form to capture the customer information as shown in the following figure:

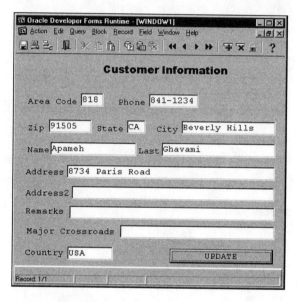

The next figure shows the same customer information form, but in Spanish with the additional field *colonia* required for addresses in Mexico:

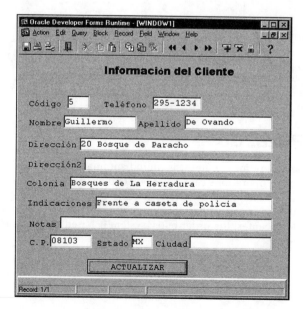

The next step for the operator is to ask if the pizza will be delivered or picked up. If it will be picked up, the customer is presented with a list of outlets (when possible) based on the postal code that was provided. The customer can then select the outlet of choice. When the pizza is ready for delivery, the system automatically selects the outlet based on the proximity to the address of delivery. This is really done by a third party product that we shall call FastAddress. This product requires a postal code, city and address. Given this information it will return either an outlet code for the closest outlet or 0 when there is no outlet available at a reasonable distance.

The customer is now presented with the Special of the Day. Mrs Marketroid, the vice president of Marketing of Pizza2Go maintains the responsibility of coming up with new special promotions on a daily basis. These typically are discounted pizzas, depending on the inventory of specific ingredients or "three for two" kind of deals. These promotions are handled as a special part of the order taking process.

When taking an order, first a unique order number is assigned and then the items are taken. Pizza2Go is a simple outfit, in the sense that the customer can only choose from a fixed menu of pizzas. It does not allow the customer to create their own pizza. The only option is the size of the pizza. The operator interacts with the following form:

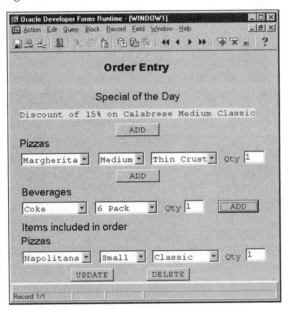

As the order is being entered the price of every item is calculated and the total price of the order is updated. This brings us to how the prices are handled. There is a price table, which depends on the size of the pizza. The price is carried in US Dollars. For Canada and Mexico, the price is calculated by taking the US price and applying a conversion factor (for example, the Canadian Dollar is 0.70 and the Mexican Peso is 0.10). Additionally, the conversion routine performs some interesting rounding logic. If the conversion is to Canadian Dollars it will round to the nearest 0.99, that is, if the result of the conversion rate is $10.62, it will round to $10.99. In the case of Mexico, the rounding is to the next full Peso, as cents are no longer handled there. So $76.89 will be rounded to $77. Incidentally, all three currencies share the same symbol, $, which makes life a little easier for the report writers.

When the order is completed, it is then faxed over to the selected outlet. Even thought the latest and greatest fax technology is being used for this, there is still no way to be sure that an outlet receives the order. This particular process is the weak link of the application and has been spotted by Mr Wonderboy as a potential big problem.

Pizza2Go has a centralized inventory system, which is updated with every order that is processed. This way the stores are stocked on time with the necessary ingredients. The inventory system also is updated with the POS information at the end of the business day to take care of the walk-in orders. Here again the POS information is faxed back to the central location. Same weak link, and even worse, they employ a legion of data entry clerks to input the data which is not always readable. Luckily, only 6% of the sales are walk-ins.

As part of their efficient inventory system and also because they have to deal with different measuring standards due to the international presence, Pizza2go has selected an empirical measure they call units. These units are used for measuring the ingredients that make up the different items in the menu. For example, a small pizza uses one unit of dough, whereas a large pizza will use three units of dough. Ingredients are packaged in multiples of units, so for example a dough package has twelve units. Another example is presented in the following table.

Pizza Quattro Stagioni	Small	Medium	Large
Tomatoes	1	2	3
Mozzarella	1	2	3
Sliced Mushrooms	0.5	1	1.5
Cooked Ham	0.5	1	1.5
Olives	1	2	3
Chopped Artichokes	1	2	3

The Stored Procedures

As with many other client-server systems, the business logic resides in the stored procedures of the database. The order entry screens store the information that makes up an order in the various tables of the application.

The system has a large number of stored procedures, mainly related to the logistics of the Just-In-Time inventory, delivery schedules, purchasing, handling the accounting books (general ledger, accounts payable, receivables, invoicing), and the maintenance of the various tables. However, we will only use the following stored procedures as the basis for the project in this book:

❑ pizzaPrice – searches for the price of a pizza in the corresponding table. If the order is from Canada or Mexico, it does the currency conversion and rounding calculations described earlier. It also handles the price of the special of the day.

❑ orderPrice – calculates the price of the order as it is at that moment.

❑ deliverOrder – prepares the order message and passes it on to the fax subsystem, and updates the inventory.

For practical purposes, we will also add a fourth stored procedure, assignOutlet, which will play the role of a rather primitive replacement of the functionality of the hypothetical FastAddress application.

The Database Schema

As we will only focus on these four stored procedures, only the tables that they manipulate need be handled. The next figure shows these tables and their relationships:

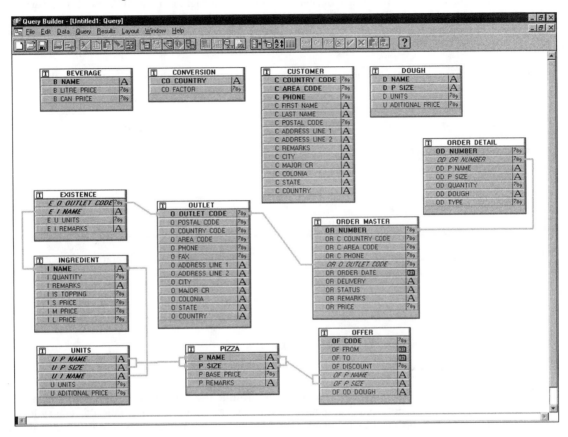

Setting up the Database

The database used for the examples of this book is Oracle 8i (version 8.1.5). You can download the Oracle Database Enterprise Edition from their web site at http://www.oracle.com. You will have to register in the Oracle Technology Network (it is free) and have a little patience for downloading the software, as it is over 250MB.

The database can be installed on the computer with the applications or on another computer in the network. In this case, the Oracle client libraries must be installed on the computer with the applications, in order to access the remote database.

We will use the BEA's type-2 JDBC driver for Oracle, WebLogic jDriver for Oracle. Other JDBC drivers can be used, like the Oracle thin driver, a type-4 driver.

On the Wrox web site (http://www.wrox.com) you can find the zip file with all the code in this book
(wlsbook_code.zip). Unzip this file under the c:\ directory and it will create the directory
c:\wlsbook, containing all the necessary files in their folders.

You will need also the BEA WebLogic Server version 5.1.0 or higher and a BEA WebLogic Server
certified JDK, like the SUN JDK version 1.3.0. You can download them from http://www.bea.com and
http://java.sun.com respectively. BEA also provides service packs for WebLogic Server that resolves
issues of the product. The examples in the book were run with version 5.1.0 and service pack 5.

For the rest of the book, we will assume that the products and applications are installed in the default
directories, as shown in the following table:

Software	Version	Installation directory
BEA WebLogic Server	5.1.0 sp 5	c:\weblogic
SUN JDK	1.3.0-C	c:\jdk1.3
Oracle database	8.1.5.0.0	c:\oracle\ora81
Application	1.0	c:\wlsbook

Usually, these directories are configurable. If you select another installation directory, keep it in mind
when reading the instructions and programs.

After all the products are installed, you will have to set up the database following these simple
instructions:

❑ Set up the scripts setEnv.cmd and setDB.cmd

❑ Run the scripts

The c:\wlsbook\setEnv.cmd script sets up the environment variables for a command line session.
At the beginning of this script there is a section where you can set up the installation directory for the
products. These directories must be changed if the installation was not made with the default values.

```
rem file: setEnv.cmd
rem =======================================
rem TO DO: change the defaults as necessary

rem Project settings (P)
SET P_H=c:\wlsbook

rem BEA WebLogic Server settings (W)
SET W_H=c:\weblogic

rem Java settings (J)
SET J_H=c:\jdk1.3

REM Oracle
SET PATH=c:\oracle\ora81\bin;%PATH%

rem end TO DO
rem =======================================
```

In order to set up the database, first you must know the server name, a user name, and its password. In the examples the database name is 'zeppelin', the user is 'scott', and the password is 'tiger'.

The environment setup and database connection can be checked by just following these steps:

❑   Start a command-line session

❑   Change to directory `c:\wlsbook`

❑   Execute the environment setup script `setEnv.cmd`, specifying the chapter number (2):

```
setenv 2
```

❑   Check the database connection by using the `dbping` utility, included in the WebLogic distribution:

```
java utils.dbping oracle scott tiger zeppelin
```

The steps are shown in the following screenshot:

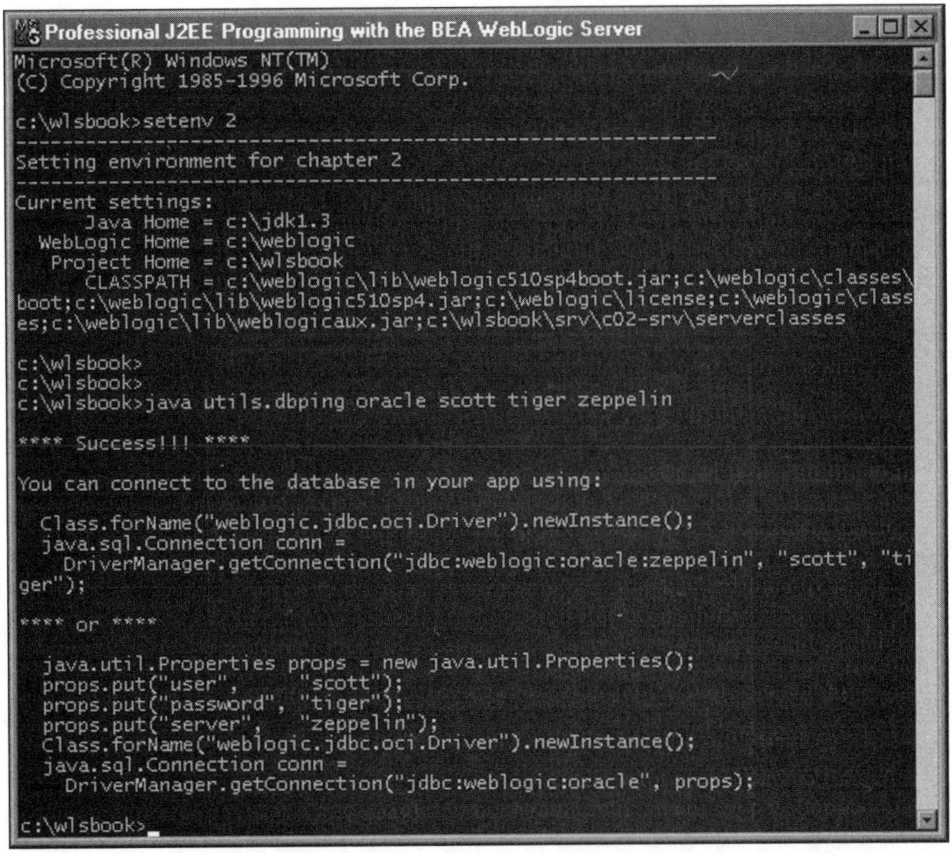

The script `c:\wlsbook\setDB.cmd` creates in the database the tables, data, and stored procedures required to follow the applications of the book. Before executing the script, check and edit the script header to set the right values for access to the database.

```
rem file: setDB.cmd
rem ======================================
rem TO DO: change the defaults as necessary

SET DBUSER=scott
SET DBPASS=tiger
SET DBSERVER=zeppelin

rem end TO DO
rem ======================================
```

The script will create the tables and stored procedures on the schema of the selected user (by default 'scott'). The names of the tables and stored procedures are shown in the following table. If there are tables or stored procedures with the same name in that schema, then use another database user (schema), as the existing objects will be replaced by the new ones after running the script.

The tables created by the script are:

Table Name	Table Name
base_price	manager
beverage	match
conversion	match_seq
custom_pizza	offer
customer	order_detail
dough	order_detail_seq
existence	order_master
ingredient	order_master_seq
JMSConsumer	outlet
JMSDestination	pizza
JMSMessage	ticket
JMSMessageQueue	ticket_seq
JMSTableId	units

The stored procedures created by the script are:

Stored Procedure Name
assignOutlet
deliverOrder
orderPrice
pizzaPrice

After modifying the file `setDB.cmd`, it can be executed from the command line as shown in the following screenshot.

```
Professional J2EE Programming with the BEA WebLogic Server

c:\wlsbook>setDB
----------------------------------------------------------------
Initializing the database...
----------------------------------------------------------------
utils.Schema will use these parameters:
        url: jdbc:weblogic:oracle
     driver: weblogic.jdbc.oci.Driver
   dbserver: zeppelin
       user: scott
   password: tiger
   SQL file: c:\wlsbook\src\sql\oracle\dbCreation.ddl
+++ WebLogic Native Layer for OCI 8.x (BETA-2)
DROP TABLE existence
DROP TABLE conversion
DROP TABLE dough
DROP TABLE beverage
DROP TABLE custom_pizza
DROP SEQUENCE order_detail_seq
DROP TABLE order_detail
DROP SEQUENCE order_master_seq
DROP TABLE order_master
DROP TABLE offer
DROP TABLE units
DROP TABLE ingredient
DROP TABLE base_price
DROP TABLE pizza
DROP TABLE outlet
DROP TABLE customer
DROP TABLE manager
DROP SEQUENCE ticket_seq
DROP TABLE ticket
DROP SEQUENCE match_seq
DROP TABLE match
COMMIT
CREATE TABLE manager( mgr_email              VARCHAR(30),  CONSTRAINT mgr_pk PRI
MARY KEY (mgr_email) )
INSERT INTO manager VALUES('paco.gomez@terra.com')
COMMIT
CREATE TABLE customer ( c_country_code    NUMBER(3) NOT NULL,  c_area_code
   NUMBER(3) NOT NULL, c_phone          NUMBER(10) NOT NULL, c_first_name
   VARCHAR(20), c_last_name       VARCHAR(20), c_postal_code      NUMBER(10),
   c_address_line_1 VARCHAR(30), c_address_line_2 VARCHAR(30), c_remarks
     VARCHAR(30), c_city           VARCHAR(20), c_major_cr         VARCHAR(30),
   c_colonia        VARCHAR(30), c_state          VARCHAR(10), c_country
       VARCHAR(10), c_uname          VARCHAR(20), c_password         VARCHAR(20
), c_company        VARCHAR(20), c_phone_ext      VARCHAR(10), c_apt
       VARCHAR(10), c_user_level     NUMBER(3), c_email            VARCHAR(30)
, CONSTRAINT c_pk PRIMARY KEY (c_country_code, c_area_code, c_phone) )
INSERT INTO customer VALUES (1, 305, 9758841, 'Juancho', 'Otaola', 33180, '24
 Doral Blvd.', '', '', 'Miami', '', '', 'FL', 'USA', 'juancho', 'juancho', 'A
cme', '', '', 1, '')
INSERT INTO customer VALUES (1, 303, 6589745, 'Tim', 'Mather', 80110, '563 Bo
ulder Way', '', '', 'Englewood', '', '', 'CO', 'USA', 'tim', 'tim', '', '',  '
', 1, '')
```

The environment and the database are now ready to run the applications.

The Plan

Given the circumstances and the fact that Mr Wonderboy is very astute, caution is the name of his game.

The first step is to get a good understanding of his staff and their capabilities. This is very important because no matter what technology you use, the understanding of a specific domain area provides a competitive advantage over the knowledge of a particular technology. At the end of the day, you can train people into new technologies, whereas it is harder to teach them industry know-how. In this particular case, offering the current staff a professional growth plan into e-commerce and all the fantastic leading edge Java technology is a mayor incentive to retain the current staff, particularly the talented ones.

Within his new staff Mr Wonderboy finds two powerful players, Mrs Chief Architect and Mr Senior Developer. Both of them have been long enough in Pizza2Go to have a complete knowledge of the processes. They both lead teams of developers who may not have experience of the Internet, but are motivated to learn.

The second part of the plan is the choice of technology. Java comes to mind immediately when thinking of the Internet. Java has passed the point of hype and has come of age. The idea of using it for this project was not just mere résumé building – there are a number of good reasons to choose it:

❑ Probably most attractive to the people on the operational side of the IT groups is its platform independence. This means that you can create Java code on one platform and execute it without a change on another one.

❑ Java is modular and efficient. It allows the architect easily to create multiple tiers.

❑ Java is object oriented, which promotes code reusability and increases developer productivity.

❑ The most important thing for Mr Wonderboy is the fact that Java is not only a language, but also a full set of Application Programming Interfaces (APIs) that address most (if not all) the needs of an enterprise. The J2EE standards have been described earlier in this book.

Once this first decision was made, the next one was choosing a product that implemented the J2EE specifications. This was relatively easy. For all practical purposes there are only two serious products in the market that implement J2EE:

❑ WebLogic Server from BEA Systems

❑ WebSphere from IBM

When Mrs Chief Architect and Mr Senior Developer started researching these products it quickly became obvious that WebLogic was a more mature product then WebSphere. Not only does WebLogic implement more J2EE APIs but those implementations are more complete then those of the competitors. Additionally, the fact that it has more functionality, such as the clustering, which allows for scalability, load balancing and fail over are not only interesting features, but a guarantee that you can grow with the product. Another nice feature of WebLogic is that a developer can use basically any development tool. All the way from vi to Visual Café, even IBM Visual Age for Java. The pricing is roughly the same for both products.

The clincher for BEA was the relative number of live sites on the Internet based on each server. The number of WebSphere sites did not even reach 1% of the web sites that are using WebLogic. All in all Mr Wonderboy and his team felt much more comfortable with the WebLogic Server.

The next step in this project is the implementation of the new system. Here Mr Wonderboy is in violent agreement with Mrs Chief Architect and Mr Senior Developer. They all furiously oppose a Big Bang approach, where a new system will completely replace the old one once the new one is ready. The plan they agree to is that everything will be done as a very smooth transition of the current system to the new one, incorporating and integrating new parts that replace the old ones on a phased approach. The smooth transition will be done in three phases:

❑ Replace the front end used by the call center with a combination of JavaServer Pages and servlets. The original front end was developed using Oracle Developer version 6. There are no tools or magic formulas for doing this, so the conversion will be done manually, replacing the current screens one-by-one. This will be the subject of Chapter 3.

❑ Replace the business logic programmed in stored procedures with Enterprise JavaBeans, specifically session beans. The transition will be made first to stateless session beans, and then one of them will be converted to a stateful bean. This will the subject of Chapter 4.

❑ Replace the code that directly accesses the database with entity beans. This will be the subject of Chapter 5.

Now that we know all this, we are ready for the adventure into the new brave world of the Java 2 Enterprise Edition Standards and the BEA WebLogic Server.

Creating a Web Front End

Following orders from Mr Wonderboy, Mrs Chief Architect and Mr Senior Developer will use this first stage, the development of a web interface to the application, more as an experiment to get familiar with the new technology then anything else. The idea is for the developers to experiment with different programming techniques for JavaServer Pages (JSP) and servlets, to test out all the ways that make sense for handling the front end. This code will form the basis on which the following chapters will build.

In this chapter, we'll:

- ❏ Introduce servlets, JavaServer Pages, and JavaBeans and show how they work together to provide a dynamic web interface to our application

- ❏ Introduce Model 1 and Model 2 architectures

- ❏ Show the Pizza2Go site design and get the code running

- ❏ Look at how WebLogic Server supports JDBC connection pools

- ❏ Examine the detail of searching for a customer, ordering a pizza, customers' order history, and inventory listing

- ❏ Highlight the benefits of dbKona and htmlKona for WebLogic-only application development

- ❏ Re-examine Model 1, Model 2, and hybrid architectures in the light of the implementations in the chapter

- ❏ Summarize the different ways of communicating data in a web application – via application or session attributes, or through HTTP GET and POST requests

Introducing Servlets

A **servlet** is a Java class that executes on the server side to generate dynamic output in response to a client request. A servlet's lifecycle is managed by a container, which also provides basic network services, such as decoding requests and formatting responses.

Servlets can be viewed as web components that interact with web clients, usually through the Hypertext Transfer Protocol (HTTP). The Servlet API links the request/response web model to Java's object-oriented programming model. A typical interaction with a servlet is as follows:

❑   A web browser accesses a web server with an HTTP request.

❑   The request is passed on to the servlet container.

❑   The container decodes the request and converts that information into a request object (of the class `HttpServletRequest`).

❑   The container determines which servlet is to be executed and calls it. (If an instance of the servlet exists, it is called. If not, the container will create and initialize a servlet instance.)

❑   The servlet uses the request object to acquire information such as the values of HTML form parameters, who the remote user is, and what they requested.

❑   The servlet executes its programmed logic and the resulting output stream, if any, is placed in a response object (of the type `HttpServletResponse`). This output doesn't have to be HTML; it can be any MIME type, including binary data.

❑   The servlet container passes control back to the web server, which sends the HTTP response to the client.

> **For more information on the HTTP protocol, see Appendix A.**

The Servlet API is currently in version 2.2, which is the version supported by WebLogic Server 5.1.0, and the one we'll use in this book.

The servlet has the following lifecycle, as defined in the `javax.servlet.Servlet` interface, and implemented in `GenericServlet` and its subclass `HttpServlet`:

❑   Initialization – the container creates an instance of the servlet and calls `init()` to initialize the servlet. After this method the servlet should be ready to service requests from multiple clients.

❑   Servicing requests – the servlet usually runs in a multithreaded container, and each client request spawns a new thread (or takes a thread from a pool) to handle the `service()` method of that servlet. You must handle any concurrency issues with resources shared between clients in your code.

❑   Destruction – the container calls `destroy()` prior to garbage collecting and finalizing the servlet instance.

One additional feature that the `HttpServlet` class provides is a series of convenience methods to handle different HTTP requests – `doGet()`, `doPost()`, `doPut()`, and `doDelete()`. The `service()` method dispatches the request to the appropriate method. In developing your own servlet, you typically subclass `HttpServlet` and override the methods you need.

The servlets framework also provides support for application-level and session-level data, through the `ServletContext` and `HttpSession` objects respectively.

A Servlet Example

Here's a very simple example of a servlet, in which the servlet retrieves the username from a request parameter and creates an HTML page with a welcome message for that user. The servlet can be invoked by typing the following URL into your browser:

http://localhost:7001/MyFirstServlet?username=Manu

Alternatively, an HTML form can be used to set the `username` parameter.

You'll find the code in `c:\wlsbook\src\MyFirst\MyFirstServlet.java`. First all the necessary packages are imported:

```
import javax.servlet.*;
import javax.servlet.http.*;
import java.io.*;
```

Then the servlet itself is defined. It extends `javax.servlet.http.HttpServlet`, which provides methods to query the container, and the lifecycle methods we saw above.

Here, we override the `service()` method (the one that handles the requests and produces the responses):

```
public class MyFirstServlet extends HttpServlet {

  public void service(HttpServletRequest request,
                      HttpServletResponse response)
      throws IOException {

    PrintWriter out;
    String title = "My First Servlet Output";

    String username = request.getParameter("username");

    response.setContentType("text/html");

    out = response.getWriter();

    out.println("<HTML><HEAD><TITLE>");
    out.println(title);
    out.println("</TITLE></HEAD><BODY>");
    out.println("<H1>" + title + "</H1>");
    out.println("<P>Hello ");
    if ((username != null) && (!username.equals(""))) {
      out.println("<B>" + username + "</B>");
    }
    out.println("!!!");
    out.println("</BODY></HTML>");
  }
}
```

We'll take a look at how to start the WebLogic server later in this chapter. In the meantime, this servlet generates the following screenshot:

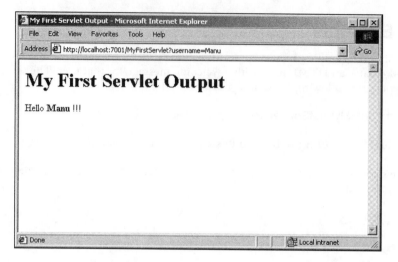

In the service() method, we are provided with the request object, and we query this for the username parameter. The response object is also available; we use it to set the MIME content type for the response, and get a writer object into which we stream the output.

We'll see more of servlets as we code the examples in this chapter.

Introducing JavaServer Pages

JavaServer Pages are an extension to servlets. Basically they are a mirror image of servlets, allowing you to embed Java in HTML pages, whereas servlets embed HTML output in Java code. JSP pages provide the ability to combine snippets of Java code with a page template, and have that template filled with data in response to a client request. The JSP page is automatically compiled to a servlet class before its first use, converting the HTML information into out.println("") statements like those used in the servlet above.

This intermixing of Java code and HTML allows a clearer separation between the design of the page and mechanisms of dynamic content generation. This separation can make development and maintenance easier. For example, the look of a page can be changed without affecting the code that generates the dynamic content.

In the WebLogic server, the way a JSP page works is the following:

❑   A web client requests a page with the .jsp extension.

❑   The container has a mapping for .jsp to a special servlet, called JSPServlet (in wlsbook\srv\c03-srv\weblogic.properties). This servlet finds the requested JSP file. If necessary it will translate the JSP page to a servlet and compile it, before creating an instance of the page to answer the request. This only happens the first time it is used or when there has been a change in the JSP. This is why the first use of a JSP page is slower than subsequent requests.

❑   The request is forwarded to the generated servlet.

JavaServer Pages uses tags to mark sections of Java code. There are a variety of tags (a full reference to the tags in version 1.1 is provided in Appendix B, or the syntax card from http://java.sun.com/products/jsp), and they fall into the following categories:

❑   Directives – these provide global information to the container that is independent of any particular request, and can be incorporated at translation time. Directives do not produce any output to the current out stream.

❑   Actions – these are request-specific actions that the JSP page must handle dynamically.

Tag	Shortened Syntax	Description
Page directive	`<%@ page ... %>`	Configuration information for the page, including: Script language; Java packages and classes to import; Whether session support is enable; (on by default); Which page to go to in the event of an error; What MIME type the output will be (text/html by default); Whether the page is thread-safe (true by default).
Include directive	`<%@ include file="relativeURL" %>`	Include the referenced page at translation time.
Taglib directive	`<%@ taglib uri="relativeURL" prefix="tagPrefix" %>`	Reference to any tag libraries that will be used in the page, with the prefix that will identify them. JSP 1.1 supports a mechanism to add custom tags to JSP pages that call Java classes for their functionality, thus reducing the scripting code on a JSP page. This is used for the BEA Commerce Server portlet framework.
Declaration	`<%! declaration[;...] %>`	Declares variables or methods.
Expression	`<%= expression %>`	Evaluates the expression and places the result, cast to a String, in the out stream.
Scriptlet	`<% scriptlet %>`	Contains a Java code fragment, over as many lines as necessary.
Forward action	`<jsp:forward page="relativeURL" />`	Forwards the request to another URL.
Include action	`<jsp:include page="relativeURL" />`	Includes a page at run time, so can include a static file, or request a file dynamically.

We'll meet a few more tags that help handle JavaBeans in the next section.

> *The tags have XML-compatible equivalents, so that a JSP page can be created and validated by XML tools. We'll see these tags later in this chapter.*

There are also several implicit objects that JSP makes available to developers within the page:

Implicit Object	Description
request	The client request
response	The response object
pageContext	Provides access to the session, output stream, and page object
session	Provides session-level storage of data
application	Provides access to global variables that are made available to all JSPs and servlets within a servlet context
out	The output stream for the page
page	The instance of the page's class; equivalent to this in a Java class

A JSP Example

Here is another simple that illustrates a JSP page. Basically the JSP page does the same as the previous example but the welcome message will be repeated as many times as stated in the request parameter repeat. The page could be invoked with the following URL:

http://localhost:7001/MyFirstJsp.jsp?username=Manu&repeat=5

First in this JSP page, we declare some variables and initialize them:

```
<%
    String title = "My First JSP Output";
    String username = request.getParameter("username");
    int repeat = 1;
    try {
      repeat = Integer.parseInt(request.getParameter("repeat"));
    } catch(Exception e) {
      System.err.println(e);
    }
%>
```

Then the HTML code is written, including some expressions:

```
<HTML>
<HEAD>
<TITLE><%=title%></TITLE>
<META HTTP-EQUIV="Content-Type" CONTENT="text/html; CHARSET=iso-8859-1">
</HEAD>
<BODY>
  <H1><%=title%></H1>
```

Finally, the HTML code can be enclosed between Java scriptlets. This allows control of the execution flow and the resulting HTML page.

```
<% for (int i = 1; i <= repeat; i++) { %>
  <P>Hello
<%
    if ((username != null) && (!username.equals(""))) {
      %><B><%= username %></B><%
    }
%>
!!!
<%}%>
</BODY>
</HTML>
```

The resultant JSP page will look like this:

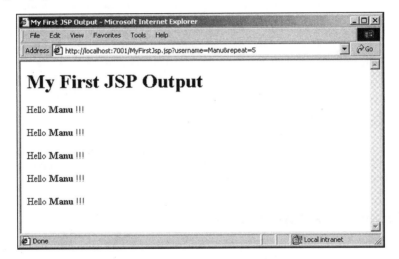

Introducing JavaBeans

Another important element in a Java-based web application is the JavaBean. A JavaBean is simply a Java class that conforms to certain patterns – has a public, no-args constructor, provides get/set methods to work with its properties and is serializable. For web applications, a JavaBean is a *component* that will typically encapsulate state. Sometimes a JavaBean will also encapsulate behavior, but this is not common, as it is better to place business logic in components that provide more built-in support for business processes, such as servlets or EJBs (more on this in the next section).

> **Don't confuse JavaBeans with an Enterprise JavaBean as they are different, as we'll see in the next chapter.**

JSP provides three action tags specifically to work with JavaBeans:

Tag	Syntax	Description
UseBean	`<jsp:useBean id="nameForPage" scope="scope" class="fullyQualifiedName" />`	Finds the bean of the specified name and scope, instantiates it if necessary, and makes it available to the following tags. Scope is `page` by default, but can be set to `session`, `request`, or `application`. Note that the `jsp:useBean` tag can be non-empty, containing tags that initialize the bean.
Get	`<jsp:getProperty name="bean" property="name"/>`	Returns the value of the specified property for the named bean.
Set	`<jsp:setProperty name="bean" property="name" value="newValue"/>`	Sets the property with the value specified. The special case `property="*"` sets all properties whose names match the request parameters.

JSP Architectures

When working with JSP, there are two approaches to building an application – called the JSP Model 1 and Model 2 architectures. They are concerned with the division of labor involved in processing the request, acting on it, and presenting the results.

The JSP Model 1 Architecture

The Model 1 architecture, shown in the figure below, takes the view that it is the JSP page that communicates with the client, handling all the requests and responses. Data access is performed by directly calling the data source, sometimes with the assistance of JavaBeans. In this context, JavaBeans are used to exchange information between JSP pages or between servlets and JSP pages.

So, in the diagram, the sequence for answering the request is something like:

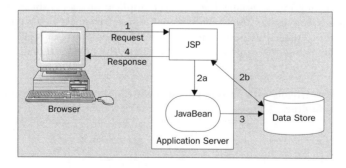

❑   1 – A request is received, which the JSP page processes

❑   2a – The JSP page uses a JavaBean to access shared state (for the application or the session, for example)

❑   2b – Alternatively, the JSP page can go direct to the data source, or use another enterprise Java API

❑   3 – The JavaBean accesses the data source, for example, to update the data it stores or add an order to the system

❑   4 – The JSP page formats and outputs a response to the browser

Even though there is some level of separation of the presentation logic from the actual data, the business logic is embedded within the JSP page.

The JSP Model 2 Architecture

The Model 2 architecture, shown in the next figure, is generally deemed a better approach, in the sense that it allows for the separation of presentation logic (placed in the JSP pages), from business logic (placed in servlets).

The following figure shows how the architecture prepares a response:

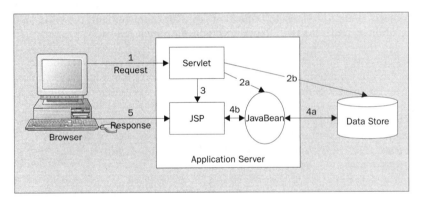

❑   1 – You can consider the servlet as a **controller** that is responsible for processing the request from the client

❑   2a – Depending on the type of the request, the servlet may instantiate a JavaBean and initialize it with the information that results from processing the request

❑   2b – Or the servlet can use some other methods to access the data requested by the client, for example, the direct access to the data source shown here, or a layer of business objects

❑   3 – Then it will forward the request to the appropriate JSP page, which will eventually send the response to the client

❑   4a and 4b – The JSP page only has to take care of *retrieving* data from any JavaBeans or other data access mechanisms that the servlet might have created; that data is then inserted into the appropriate places in the HTML templates

❑   5 – The JSP page is returned to the client as a response stream

In this model the servlet does not generate an HTML response, it only generates the interim data (often stored in the session in the form of JavaBeans), which the JSP page formats into a view.

> *A point has to be made regarding the size of these objects if they are attached to a session. The larger they are the bigger the impact on the scalability of the system. When using the clustering option in WebLogic server, these objects must be replicated between servers to facilitate fail-over. Keep the size of these objects to an absolute minimum.*

The most obvious benefits of this architecture are in the development process:

- ❑ Although JSP pages are compiled into servlets, the developer has no access to the servlet as a class, which can be hard for those used to being able to see the whole control structure of a class. Currently the IDEs for JSP pages do not give the same level of sophistication as Java IDEs, which means that when you are writing the Java code for a JSP page you have less ability to check your code. And if it doesn't work, you won't see the error until you deploy your JSP page, by which time it is very hard to track it down.

- ❑ An important benefit of this architecture is the fact that, by removing the business logic from JSP pages, you no longer need an experienced Java developer to create JSP pages. Put another way, the JSP pages can and should be developed by an HTML specialist who knows how to create great pages, with the required knowledge of Java kept to a minimum (syntax and control statements) to enable design of dynamic pages.

- ❑ The actual business logic that requires Java developers is now contained in servlets and other Java objects. This addresses an important issue for management, providing a clear split in responsibilities that suits the talents of the development teams.

The model uses either the `RequestDispatcher` interface's `forward()` method or `HttpServletResponse` interface's `sendRedirect()` method. Both methods eliminate the possibility of the servlet generating part of the response, as that causes an exception to be thrown at execution time.

> *Note that they differ quite a lot. The `forward()` method retains the existing request and response objects (and URL in the browser), while the `sendRedirect()` method causes a new request/response object to be created when the request comes back. A redirect is also much slower as there are two extra network steps involved.*

The Architecture of Pizza2Go

As stated in the last chapter, the main objective of this series of experiments is to reproduce the functionality of the front end currently being used in the Oracle-based system by creating a new one based on JSP and servlets. The new front end will continue to call the stored procedures that exist on the current system and the database structure remains the same. From the business standpoint, the intent is that this new front end will only be used by the operators of Pizza2Go.

As all this technology is quite new for Mrs Chief Architect and Mr Senior Developer, they are not quite sure which architecture to adopt. The Model 1 architecture seems to be simpler and more efficient, however, having the Java code intermixed with HTML promises maintenance problems, and doesn't play to the team's strengths. The Model 2 architecture solves the maintenance problems by separating the HTML and the Java code, but it tends to consume more memory. Armed with this information, they decide to use both architectures – Model 1 when addressing simple pages and Model 2 when the processing is more complex. They will also combine both models when it makes sense and turns out to be easier for the developers.

We'll return to these front-end architecture models at the end of the chapter, once we have some code to illustrate the workings with. For now, here's a summary flow diagram of the organization of the Pizza2Go Intranet web site:

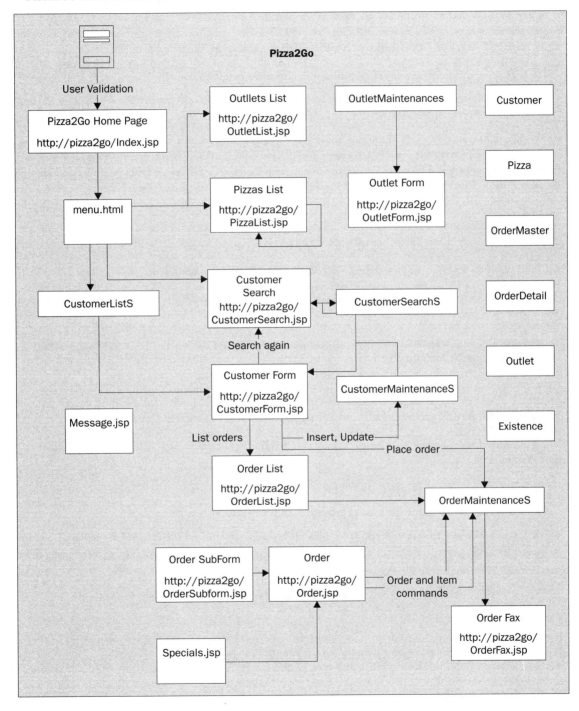

Getting Started

The code used in this book is available from the Wrox web site (http://www.wrox.com). After installation (see Chapter 2) the source code is located in the directory c:\wlsbook\src and is organized by chapters. The executables and related files for execution are deployed in the directory c:\wlsbook\srv, also organized by chapters. This organization allows two things:

❑   Having different and independent applications by chapters

❑   The separation between the source code and its compiled code (under the directory src) from the complete application (under the directory srv)

For example, the code for this chapter is under c:\wlsbook\src\c03. The two types of source code, Java classes and JSP/HTML, are kept in the directories java and jsp respectively. The Java binary files are kept under the directories serverclasses and servletclasses. It is necessary to 'deploy' the application, that is, copy the application from the src to the srv directory.

To make the compilation and deployment processes easier, a makefile (GNUmakefile) is included with the following targets: all, common, servlets, deploy, deployJSP, redeploy, javadoc, and clean. The syntax of this file is compatible with the GNU make utility.

All the Java code has the package name jsw, which stands for *Java Solutions with WebLogic*, and a further sub-package name corresponding with the chapter to which it belongs. The Java code for Chapter 3 is in the package jsw.c03. There is also the javadoc documentation for all the Java code under the directory c:\wlsbook\doc.

To run the application for Chapter 3 we will assume the required software is installed in the default locations, as described in Chapter 2.

First, we need to compile and deploy the files for this chapter's application. Bring up a command prompt, call setenv 3, change directory to src\c03, and type make all, followed by make deploy. The application for this chapter is now under the c:\wlsbook\srv\c03-srv directory.

In addition to the configuration files described in Chapter 2 (setEnv.cmd), a list of other important files is as follows:

❑   c:\wlsbook\startWls.cmd. This command starts the server.

❑   c:\wlsbook\stopWls.cmd. This command stops the server.

❑   c:\wlsbook\weblogic.policy. This file configures the server for Java 2 security.

❑   c:\wlsbook\weblogic.properties. This file has the configuration properties of the server, common to all chapters.

❑   c:\wlsbook\srv\c03-srv\weblogic.properties. This file has the configuration properties of the server specific to Chapter 3.

If everything is installed in the default locations, the one final thing to set up is the properties of the JDBC connection pool (more on this later) in the file c:\wlsbook\srv\c03-srv\ weblogic.properties. Edit the file and modify the props line, at the end of the pool definition. Set the username, password, and database name to those configured in your installation. The default configuration is as follows:

```
#                      THE WEBLOGIC PROPERTIES FILE
# # # # # # # # # # # # # # # # # # # # # # # # # # # # # # # # # # # # #
#

#
# <Pizza2Go chapter 03>
#

#
# database dependant properties
#

weblogic.jdbc.connectionPool.p2gPool=\
        url=jdbc:weblogic:oracle,\
        driver=weblogic.jdbc.oci.Driver,\
        loginDelaySecs=1,\
        initialCapacity=1,\
        maxCapacity=10,\
        capacityIncrement=2,\
        allowShrinking=true,\
        shrinkPeriodMins=15,\
        refreshTestMinutes=10,\
        testTable=dual,\
        props=user=scott;password=tiger;server=zeppelin
```

After modifying these properties, the server can be started following these steps:

❑   Start a command line session

❑   Change to directory `c:\wlsbook`

❑   Execute the environment setup script `setEnv.cmd` specifying the chapter number (3):

```
C:\> cd \wlsbook
C:\wlsbook> setenv 3
-------------------------------------------------------------
Setting environment for chapter 3
-------------------------------------------------------------
Current settings:
        Java Home = c:\jdk1.3
  WebLogic Home = c:\weblogic
   Project Home = c:\wlsbook
        CLASSPATH =
c:\weblogic\lib\weblogic510sp4boot.jar;c:\weblogic\classes\boot;c:\weblogic\lib\we
blogic510sp4.jar;c:\weblogic\license;c:\weblogic\classes;c:\weblogic\lib\weblogica
ux.jar;c:\wlsbook\srv\c03-srv\serverclasses
```

❑   Execute the `startWls.cmd` command:

```
C:\wlsbook> startwls
```

The WebLogic Server will output a large number of messages. To know that it has started correctly look first at the last line of the output. If it is "WebLogic Server started", that's hopeful. Then go backwards through the messages making sure that there are no exceptions. A typical output is shown here:

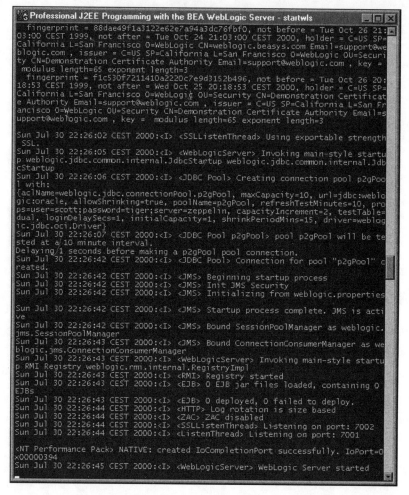

The output from starting the server is also written to `weblogic.log` in the `srv\c03-srv` directory.

To get the application running, you have to start a browser and point it to the following URL: http://localhost:7001/index.jsp.

To stop the server, just follow these steps:

❑ Start a command line session

❑ Change to directory `c:\wlsbook`

❑ Execute the environment setup script `setEnv.cmd` specifying the chapter number (3):

```
C:\> cd \wlsbook
C:\wlsbook> setenv 3
------------------------------------------------------------
Setting environment for chapter 3
------------------------------------------------------------
Current settings:
        Java Home = c:\jdk1.3
    WebLogic Home = c:\weblogic
     Project Home = c:\wlsbook
        CLASSPATH =
c:\weblogic\lib\weblogic510sp4boot.jar;c:\weblogic\classes\boot;c:\weblogic\lib\we
blogic510sp4.jar;c:\weblogic\license;c:\weblogic\classes;c:\weblogic\lib\weblogica
ux.jar;c:\wlsbook\srv\c03-srv\serverclasses
```

❑   Execute the stopWls.cmd command:

```
C:\wlsbook> stopwls
Shutdown initiated
Shutdown sequence initiated
```

The WebLogic server reads its configuration information from a file called
`weblogic.properties`. *There may be more than one properties file: a globally shared
properties file, a per-cluster properties file, and per-server properties file for each WebLogic server
that you run. Every chapter contains an appropriate set of properties files, and the* `setenv.cmd`
file selects the right ones.

Naming Conventions

The examples in this book use the following naming convention. The names of the classes can be one or
more words. The first character of every word is in upper case. The names are suffixed according to the
class type:

Class Type	Suffix	Example
Servlet	S	CustomerListS
Stateless session bean	SL	OrderServicesSL
Stateful session bean	SF	OrderSF
Entity bean	EB	OrderMasterEB

In the case of JSP pages, as they are just a filename, they are identified by the .jsp extension.

*Registered names in JNDI (Java Naming and Directory Interface) or the servlet engine, which are
used to look up the Java classes at runtime, are the same as the corresponding class names.*

The Main Menu

This is the first item the Pizza2go operator sees when they start using the system. The main JSP page is called `index.jsp`, so that it becomes the default page when providing the URL of the application with no specific file to be executed. The first thing that is done in this JSP page is to start a session. In this particular case the session will be maintained until the browser is closed or a timeout occurs. The value of the timeout can be defined in the properties file:

```
weblogic.httpd.session.timeoutSecs=integer
```

The default is 3600 seconds, that is, 1 hour, and this is what we'll use here.

The session is started with the following directive on the first line of the JSP page:

```
<%@ page session="true" import="java.util.*,java.sql.*" %>
<html>
<head>
<title>Pizza2Go Home Page</title>
<meta http-equiv="Content-Type" content="text/html; charset=iso-8859-1">
</head>

<body bgcolor="#FFFFFF">
<h1><center>
Pizza2Go Main Menu
</center>
</h1>
<hr>
```

The `page` directive is used to define attributes for this page. This directive not only starts the session but also imports the Java classes that will be used in the code that follows. Note that `session` is set to `true` in the page directive by default.

```
<%@ include file="menu.html" %>
```

This next directive in the JSP page includes a static HTML page using the `<%@ include file=...%>` directive.

We could also have used the `<jsp:include page=.../>` action instead of the `<%@ include` directive. The difference between the two is that the content pointed to by the `<%@ include` directive is parsed by the JSP processor when the JSP is translated to a servlet (it becomes part of the servlet source), while the content pointed to by the `<jsp:include` action is not parsed, just included in place at runtime.

The file `menu.html` contains the menu that will be used pretty much all through the system. The actual file is the following:

```
<table width="100%" border="1">
  <tr>
    <td bordercolor="#FFFFFF"><h4>Main menu:</h4></td>
    <td><a href="/CustomerSearch.jsp">Customer Search</a> </td>
    <td><a href="/CustomerListS">Customers</a> </td>
    <td><a href="/CustomerForm.jsp">Current Customer</a> </td>
    <td><a href="/OutletList.jsp">Outlets</a> </td>
    <td><a href="/PizzaList.jsp">Pizzas</a> </td>
  </tr>
</table>
```

This is a very simple HTML page that just calls other JSP pages. Note that `CustomerListS` is not a JSP page, but the registered name of a servlet. In the chapter's `weblogic.properties` file it appears as follows:

```
weblogic.httpd.register.CustomerListS =jsw.c03.CustomerListS
```

The actual output of this HTML page is the following:

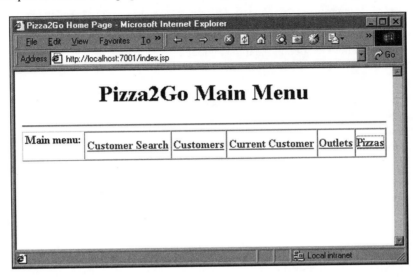

This JSP page continues with a scriptlet, a bunch of Java code enclosed in <% ... %> tags.

```
try {
  Class.forName("weblogic.jdbc.pool.Driver");
} catch(Exception e) {
  out.println(e);
}
```

The first part of this scriptlet checks to see if a JDBC connection pool has already been loaded, in which case nothing happens. Otherwise the call to `Class.forName()` loads the driver class, which instantiates and registers itself with the `DriverManager`.

The second part of the scriptlet stores all the pizza names in a vector. The names are stored as an attribute of the implicit `application` object, a global object that can be used by all the servlets. This avoids having to access the database every time this information is needed.

The decision to keep the pizza names in memory while the Pizza2Go application is running makes sense because the pizza names change very rarely. However, for items that might go out of stock during the run-time life of the application, it may be necessary to regularly query the database for an updated list.

59

Here you can also see how a connection is requested from a pool configured with the name p2gPool:

```
Vector pizzaNames = (Vector)application.getAttribute("pizzaNames");
if (pizzaNames == null) {
  try {
    pizzaNames = new Vector();

    Connection conn =
      DriverManager.getConnection("jdbc:weblogic:pool:p2gPool");

    String select = "select distinct p_name from pizza";
    Statement stmt = conn.createStatement();
    ResultSet resultSet = stmt.executeQuery(select);

    while(resultSet.next()) {
      pizzaNames.addElement(resultSet.getString("p_name"));
    }
    resultSet.close();
    stmt.close();
    conn.close();

    application.setAttribute("pizzaNames", pizzaNames);
  } catch(Exception e) {
    System.err.println(e);
  }
}
```

This particular JSP page illustrates the use of the implicit object called `application` to give global access to some variables. The Servlet 2.2 specification defines a **web application** as a combination of all the server-side resources, such as servlets and JSPs, together with an XML-based **deployment descriptor**. The deployment descriptor describes how the application is deployed on the web server, and if used properly ensures that the resources used by the application do not have to be hard-coded. The application can be deployed on different web servers without any changes to the code (all changes are made to the deployment descriptor).

The web application operates within the **servlet context** and is thus isolated from other web applications that might be running on the same server. Note that the servlet context is not shared between different VMs, even if the web application is distributed, so application and servlet context aren't identical.

By setting the pizza names as an application attribute, they will be available throughout the application; that is to all the servlets, and for all the sessions. This technique differs from storing information in a session value, which we'll see later on.

JDBC Connection Pools

Establishing a connection to a database is a pretty expensive operation in the sense that it can take up to a second. Because of this, the traditional way of handling database connections from a client is to establish a connection between the client and database when the client application starts (for example at the beginning of the work day) and then maintain the connection until the client ends. This architecture is also costly because you need as many connections as active clients, and worse still, the connection is not being used efficiently, as the interaction with the database is intermittent. and the connection is almost always idle.

A more efficient alternative is the use of **connection pools**. The idea is that a predefined number of database connections are established initially and then made available to the clients when needed. As the connection has already been established, when the client requests one it is available immediately. When the client is done with the connection, it is not dropped but returned to the pool so and made available to other clients.

> When using connection pools the correct way for the client to interact with the database is to obtain a connection from the pool every time a query or set of queries will be done and then return the connection to the pool when the set of queries is completed.

WebLogic provides connection pool functionality that works with any JDBC drivers, that is, drivers provided by BEA or third party drivers that comply with the JDBC specification. A connection pool is defined in the properties file as follows:

```
weblogic.jdbc.connectionPool.p2gPool=\
        url=jdbc:weblogic:oracle,\
        driver=weblogic.jdbc.oci.Driver,\
        loginDelaySecs=1,\
        initialCapacity=4,\
        maxCapacity=10,\
        capacityIncrement=2,\
        allowShrinking=true,\
        shrinkPeriodMins=15,\
        refreshTestMinutes=10,\
        testTable=dual,\
        props=user=scott;password=tiger;server=zeppelin
```

❑   In this example the p2gpool is defined as using the WebLogic jDriver for Oracle that conforms to the JDBC specification 1.2. If you want to use the WebLogic jDriver that conforms with the JDBC specification 2.0, just change the url to jdbc20:weblogic:oracle and the driver to weblogic.jdbc20.oci.Driver. This new driver adds support for Blobs, Clobs, and batch updates.

❑   The loginDelaySecs property is optional and allows you to define the number of seconds to wait between each attempt to open a connection to the database. This is needed because some databases cannot handle multiple requests for connections in a rapid succession.

❑   The initialCapacity property defines the number of connections that have to be established when the WebLogic server is starting.

❑   maxCapacity defines the maximum number of connections a pool can have.

❑   When all the connections are in use and an additional one is requested, WebLogic will automatically increment the number of connections. This implies that the requestor will have to wait until the new connections are established. This dynamic growth is controlled by the capacityIncrement property, which is used to define how many new connections have to be established and placed in the pool every time the current capacity is reached and more connections are requested.

❑   WebLogic also allows shrinking the size of the connection pool after it has been increased to meet the demand. With the allowShrinking property this feature is enabled and it can be used in combination with the shrinkPeriodMins to specify how many minutes it has to wait before shrinking the size of the pool.

❑ The `refreshTestMinutes` property is used to verify that the connections with the database are still active. What happens is that each unused connection in the pool is tested using a simple SQL query. If the test fails, the connection resources are dropped and a new connection is established. This property is used in conjunction with `testTable`, which defines the name of the table to be used for the test. In this particular case, Oracle offers a table called `dual` that can be used for this purpose. This is very useful in the case that the database has been rebooted and the connections become stale.

❑ Finally, the `props` property is used to define the properties necessary to connect to the database. In this case the user, password, and database name are defined.

These are the basic properties used to define a connection pool. There are many other properties available. Please consult the WebLogic documentation to learn more about them.

Searching for Customers

Starting with the design premise that each customer has an entry, and if an entry does not exist one is created, the developers created a JSP page, `CustomerSearch.jsp`, which provides search information to a servlet, `CustomerSearchS`. The servlet searches for the customer and if the data entry is incomplete or incorrect, control is transferred back to the JSP page to refill the necessary fields.

The first part of the `CustomerSearch.jsp` file is the following:

```
<html>
<head>
<title>Customer Search</title>
<meta http-equiv="Content-Type" content="text/html; charset=iso-8859-1">
</head>

<body bgcolor="#FFFFFF">
<a href="index.jsp">Main Menu</a>
```

The last statement is a way back to the main menu, and is provided with the `href` tag. This is one of the cardinal rules of web site etiquette; every page should have a way back to a central location. Next, as this JSP page can be called by the `CustomerSearchS` servlet, we present any error in filling the fields detected by the servlet with:

```
<%= request.getParameter("message") %>
```

Notice here that the `<%=` tag is used to evaluate the expression and place the resulting string in the `out` stream. The code continues with:

```
<% String sDefaultCountryCode = request.getParameter("c_country_code");
   if ((sDefaultCountryCode == null) || (sDefaultCountryCode.equals(""))){
     String location = System.getProperty("jsw.location", "US");
     if (location.equals("MX"))
       sDefaultCountryCode = "52";
     else
       sDefaultCountryCode = "1";
   }
%>
```

One of the main objectives of the new system is to make it easily localizable. One way to do this is to have a system-wide property that specifies the country where the server is located. This information should be available throughout the system to enable all the necessary changes in functionality. In this application, it is decided that the telephone country code is going to be part of the customer key and that it should default to the country specified by the system-wide property. In this case, the property will have two possible values, and the country codes will be 1 for the United States and 52 for Mexico.

To define a system-wide property we take advantage of the `weblogic.properties` file and include the following:

```
java.system.property.jsw.location=MX
```

This defines a system-wide property called `jsw.location` and assigns it the value `MX` for Mexico. Here the developers agree to use the two letter ISO country codes to define the country.

Another way of handling localization is by using the Java Internationalization and Localization Tool Kit (http://java.sun.com/products/jilkit/). However, this would only handle the differences in output, not the calculations that are being done with the prices. Modifying the code to include the usage of this tool kit is left as an exercise for the reader.

After the scriptlet, the JSP page has the necessary HTML code for the data entry form:

```
<table align="center" border="0">
<tr>
 <td>
<form method="post" action="CustomerSearchS">
  <p>Telephone: (Country code: <%= sDefaultCountryCode %>)</p>
    <input type="hidden" name="c_country_code"
           value="<%= sDefaultCountryCode %>">
  <p>Area code:
    <input type="text" name="c_area_code"
           value="<%= request.getParameter("c_area_code") %>">
  </p>
  <p>Phone:
    <input type="text" name="c_phone"
           value="<%= request.getParameter("c_phone") %>">
  </p>
  <p>
    <input type="submit" name="Submit" value="Search">
    <input type="reset" name="reset" value="Clear">
  </p>
</form>
 </td>
</tr>
</table>

</body>
</html>
```

The form data is posted to the `CustomerSearchS` servlet. The code of this servlet starts with:

```
package jsw.c03;

import java.util.*;
import java.io.*;
import java.net.*;
import javax.servlet.*;
import javax.servlet.http.*;
import java.sql.*;

/**
 * This class is a servlet that searches for a customer.
 *
 */
public class CustomerSearchS extends HttpServlet {

  /**
   * This is the static initializer,
   * executed the first time this class is referred to.
   * It makes sure the JDBC pool driver is loaded.
   */
  static {
    try {
      Class.forName("weblogic.jdbc.pool.Driver");
    } catch(Exception e) {
      System.err.println(e);
    }
  }

  /**
   * This method examines an HTTP request and searches for the
   * specified customer in the database. It then redirects
   * the response to the <tt>CustomerForm.jsp</tt> JSP page.
   */
  public void service(HttpServletRequest req, HttpServletResponse res)
      throws IOException
  {
    HttpSession session = req.getSession(true);

    if (! checkParams(req, res))
      return;
```

The servlet `service()` checks that the parameters captured by the form are complete and correct by calling `checkParams()`. Server-side validation of form data is an alternative to the more popular method of using some JavaScript on the client side, something we don't recommend because:

❑ JavaScript is not compatible between the various browsers

❑ You also have to provide some level of functionality for the users that turn off JavaScript support in their browsers through security concerns

The code for the `checkParams()` method is the following:

```
/**
 * This method examines an HTTP request and performs a
 * server-side validation of the received parameters.
 */
public boolean checkParams(HttpServletRequest req,
                           HttpServletResponse res) {

  String c_country_code    = req.getParameter("c_country_code");
  String c_area_code       = req.getParameter("c_area_code");
  String c_phone           = req.getParameter("c_phone");

  String message = null;

  if (c_country_code.equals("") || c_country_code.equals(null) ||
      c_area_code.equals("") || c_area_code.equals(null) ||
      c_phone.equals("") || c_phone.equals(null)) {
    message = "Please, fill in all fields";
  } else {
    try {
      Integer.parseInt(c_country_code);
      Integer.parseInt(c_area_code);
      Long.parseLong(c_phone);
    } catch(NumberFormatException e) {
      message = "Please, enter numbers in the boxes";
    }
  }

  if (message != null) {
    String sParams = "?";
    sParams += URLEncoder.encode("c_country_code") + "=" +
          URLEncoder.encode(c_country_code);
    sParams += "&" +
            URLEncoder.encode("c_area_code") + "=" +
          URLEncoder.encode(c_area_code);
    sParams += "&" +
            URLEncoder.encode("c_phone") + "=" +
          URLEncoder.encode(c_phone);
    sParams += "&" +
            URLEncoder.encode("message") + "=" +
            URLEncoder.encode(message);

    String sURL res.encodeRedirectURL("/CustomerSearch.jsp"
                                      + sParams);

    try {
      res.sendRedirect(sURL);
      return false;
    } catch(Exception e) {
      System.err.println("Exception: CustomerSearchS.checkParams: " + e);
    }
  }
  return true;
}
```

If there is an error in the form, a suitable message is created, and assigned as a parameter. The customer details and message parameters are all encoded using URLEncoder.encode() and execution is redirected to the CustomerSearch JSP page as a GET method, that is, sending the parameters as part of the URL.

Let us continue with the code from the service() method of the CustomerSearchS servlet:

```java
String c_country_code   = req.getParameter("c_country_code");
String c_area_code      = req.getParameter("c_area_code");
String c_phone          = req.getParameter("c_phone");

Connection conn = null;

try {

  conn = DriverManager.getConnection("jdbc:weblogic:pool:p2gPool");

  Statement stmt = conn.createStatement();
  String select = "select * from customer where " +
                  "(c_country_code = " + c_country_code +
                  " AND c_area_code = " + c_area_code +
                  " AND c_phone = " + c_phone +
                  ")";

  stmt.execute(select);

  ResultSet resultSet = stmt.getResultSet();

  Customer customer       = new Customer();
  customer.c_country_code = Integer.parseInt(c_country_code);
  customer.c_area_code    = Integer.parseInt(c_area_code);
  customer.c_phone        = Long.parseLong(c_phone);

  if (resultSet.next()) {
    customer.c_first_name    = resultSet.getString("c_first_name");
    customer.c_last_name     = resultSet.getString("c_last_name");
    customer.c_postal_code   = resultSet.getLong("c_postal_code");
    customer.c_address_line_1 = resultSet.getString("c_address_line_1");
    customer.c_address_line_2 = resultSet.getString("c_address_line_2");
    customer.c_remarks       = resultSet.getString("c_remarks");
    customer.c_city          = resultSet.getString("c_city");
    customer.c_major_cr      = resultSet.getString("c_major_cr");
    customer.c_colonia       = resultSet.getString("c_colonia");
    customer.c_state         = resultSet.getString("c_state");
    customer.c_country       = resultSet.getString("c_country");
    session.setAttribute("isNewCustomer", new Boolean(false));
  } else {
    session.setAttribute("isNewCustomer", new Boolean(true));
    System.out.println(
        "<DEBUG> <CustomerSearchS-service> Customer not found: "
        + customer);
  }

  session.setAttribute("customer", customer);
```

```
      stmt.close();
      conn.close();

      String sURL = res.encodeRedirectURL("/CustomerForm.jsp");
      String location = System.getProperty("jsw.location", "US");
      if (location.equals("MX"))
        sURL = res.encodeRedirectURL("/CustomerFormSpanish.jsp");
      try {
        res.sendRedirect(sURL);
      } catch(Exception e) {
        System.err.println("Exception: CustomerSearchS.service: " + e);
      }
    } catch (Exception e) {
      System.err.println("Exception: CustomerSearchS.service: " + e);
    }
  }
```

If there was no problem with the parameters, this code will establish a JDBC connection and search for the desired customer. If the customer exists, the associated data for that customer is stored in a `Customer` object and a Boolean variable is set to indicate whether the customer record existed previously. Then the `service()` method returns the JDBC connection to the pool.

The HTTP session is used here to store conversational state about the `Customer` on the server. The session ID is stored in a cookie that goes from the server to the browser and vice versa. The servlets and JSPs can transparently retrieve the session from the session ID, whether it comes from a cookie or from the URL, using `request.getSession()`.

When a user simultaneously opens two browser windows, usually both browsers have the same cookie so both refer to the same HTTP session on the server. This is like maintaining two lines of conversation with the same person at the same time. The Servlet specification is not designed to support this 'unnatural' behavior, even if the browser allows it. There are synchronization issues here, for example: if two JSPs simultaneously store and retrieve values on the session, which is the valid value that is stored/retrieved?

In summary, there is nothing in the Servlet specification to prevent simultaneous access to the same session object or to handle access in a 'transactional' mode. This problem is addressed by other stateful containers that are transactional: for example, the stateful session beans we'll see in the next chapter.

Another important issue is that when the session is used to store conversational state, as for example in a multiple form 'web transaction', the result of each step is stored in the session for the next step. In this case, the application in the server must be flexible enough to allow loose coupling between the browser and the server, but without compromising consistency. Usually the user tends to navigate back and forth through links and through the browser page cache. One solution here is to include a 'state machine' in the application on the server to keep track of the current state in the server, the input of the browser, and the corresponding transitions and output.

Here the support for multiple locations with the system-wide country property continues by checking if the location is Mexico, in which case it will call the `CustomerFormSpanish` JSP page. Otherwise the call to `encodeRedirectURL()` and then `sendRedirect()` will call the English version of the `CustomerForm` JSP page.

The Customers

The CustomerSearchS servlet will transfer execution to the appropriate customer form (English or Spanish) when the parameters are correctly set. Providing the customer exists, the page will present all the information associated with this customer as in the figure below. The page offers options to add a new order or list the orders this customer has made in the past.

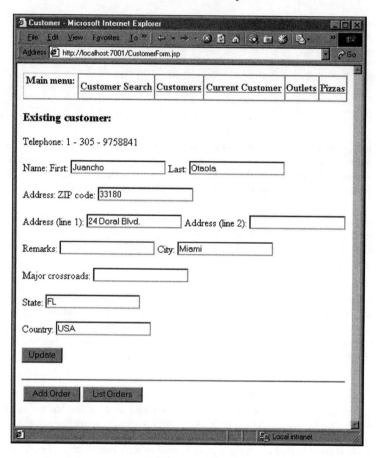

The code for CustomerForm.jsp starts with some JavaScript:

```
<html>
<head>
<title>Customer</title>
<meta http-equiv="Content-Type" content="text/html; charset=iso-8859-1">

<script language="JavaScript">
function goBack() {
  if (parent.history.length > 0) {
    parent.history.back()
  }
}
```

```
function goForward() {
  if (parent.history.length > 0) {
    parent.history.forward()
  }
}
</script>
</head>

<body bgcolor="#FFFFFF">
<%@ include file="menu.html" %>
```

This script will be used in the next block of the JSP page. We have just said that you should avoid using JavaScript in your pages, but Mr Senior Developer was curious to try out some helpful client-side code. The code continues with the following scriptlet:

```
<h3>
<%
  Customer customer = (Customer)session.getAttribute("customer");
  if (customer == null) {
    String destinationPage = "/CustomerSearch.jsp";
    %> <jsp:forward page='<%= destinationPage %>' />
    <%
  }
  if (session.getAttribute("message") != null) {
    out.println(session.getAttribute("message") + "<p>");
    session.removeAttribute("message");
  }
  if (((Boolean)session.getAttribute("isNewCustomer")).booleanValue()) {
    out.println("Customer not found.<p>");
    out.println(
        "You can <a href=\"javascript:goBack()\">search again</a>,");
    out.println("or insert a new customer:");
  }
  else
    out.println("Existing customer:<p>");
%>
</h3>
```

If the customer does not exist, this Java code gives the user the opportunity to search again or to insert a new customer. You can see how a link is provided to the JavaScript code so the client can go back to the previous search page in the browser. The browser only executes this JavaScript if the user clicks on the link. If for any reason the user arrived at this page without a current customer, a forward is done to the customer search JSP page using the `jsp:forward` action.

The code continues with the presentation of the form:

```
<form method="post" action="CustomerMaintenanceS">
  <p>Telephone:
    <%= customer.c_country_code %> - <%= customer.c_area_code %> -
    <%= customer.c_phone %>
  <input type="hidden" name="c_country_code" size="3"
         value="<%= customer.c_country_code %>">
  <input type="hidden" name="c_area_code" size="3"
```

```
                       value="<%= customer.c_area_code %>">
        <input type="hidden" name="c_phone" size="10"
                       value="<%= customer.c_phone %>">
    </p>
    <p>Name: First:
        <input type="text" name="c_first_name"
                       value="<%= customer.c_first_name %>">
      Last:
        <input type="text" name="c_last_name"
                       value="<%= customer.c_last_name %>">
    </p>
    <p>Address: ZIP code:
        <input type="text" name="c_postal_code"
                       value="<%= customer.c_postal_code %>">
    </p>
    <p>Address (line 1):
        <input type="text" name="c_address_line_1"
                       value="<%= customer.c_address_line_1 %>">
      Address (line 2):
        <input type="text" name="c_address_line_2"
                       value="<%= customer.c_address_line_2 %>">
    </p>
    <p>Remarks:
        <input type="text" name="c_remarks" value="<%= customer.c_remarks %>">
      City:
        <input type="text" name="c_city" value="<%= customer.c_city %>">
    </p>
    <p>Major crossroads:
        <input type="text" name="c_major_cr"
                       value="<%= customer.c_major_cr %>">
<%
      String location = System.getProperty("jsw.location", "US");
      if (location.equals("MX")) {
%>
      Colonia:
        <input type="text" name="c_colonia" value="<%= customer.c_colonia %>">
<%
      } else {
%>
        <input type="hidden" name="c_colonia" value="">
<%
      }
%>
    </p>
    <p>State:
        <input type="text" name="c_state"
                       value="<%= customer.c_state %>">
    </p>
    <p>Country:
        <input type="text" name="c_country" value="<%= customer.c_country %>">
    </p>
    <p>
<% String sAction = "Update";
    if (((Boolean)session.getAttribute("isNewCustomer")).booleanValue())
      sAction = "Insert";
```

```
%>
    <input type="submit" name="command" value="<%=sAction%>">
  </p>
  </form>
  <hr>

<% if (!((Boolean)session.getAttribute("isNewCustomer")).booleanValue()) { %>
<table>
 <tr>
  <td>
   <form method="post" action="OrderMaintenanceS">
    <input type="submit" name="command" value="Add Order">
   </form>
  </td>
  <td>
   <form method="post" action="OrderList.jsp">
    <input type="submit" name="command" value="List Orders">
   </form>
  </td>
 </tr>
</table>
<%}%>

</body>
</html>
```

The following points are worth noting in the code above:

❑ The code to include the Colonia field if the system-wide property, jsw.location, is MX

❑ The action for the form can be either Update or Insert depending on the value of the session isNewCustomer attribute

❑ If the form is for a new customer, the user cannot go to the orders pages until they have an entry

Ordering Pizza

Now we have the customer, we need to order the pizza. We'll use the Model 2 architecture in this part of the application, with the servlet OrderMaintenanceS processing client requests and forwarding that data to the JSP page OrderForm.jsp for presentation. The communication of the data between the two is performed using a JavaBean.

The JSP specification provides an alternative XML syntax. Even though this syntax is designed for use by XML tools, Mr Senior Developer decides to experiment using it. The actual page presented to the user consists of five parts, which:

❑ Include the main site menu and a message box with the date and any messages relating to this customer

❑ View basic order status information

❑ Display the special offers

❑ Enable the user to select a pizza to add to the order

❑ Show the current pizzas ordered

The first part of the `OrderForm.jsp` JSP page looks like:

```
<html>
<head>
<title>Order</title>
<meta http-equiv="Content-Type" content="text/html; charset=iso-8859-1">
</head>
<body bgcolor="#FFFFFF">

<jsp:include page="menu.html" flush="true" />
<jsp:include page="Message.jsp" flush="true" />

<jsp:scriptlet>
   Customer customer = (Customer)session.getAttribute("customer");
</jsp:scriptlet>
```

Using the `jsp:include` action, this portion of the page presents the main menu and a message that we'll discuss later.

The second part of the page is an information and action section. It allows the user to view basic information on the order and act upon it by updating, deleting, or delivering it.

```
<h3>Place an order for customer
<jsp:expression>customer.c_first_name</jsp:expression>
<jsp:expression>customer.c_last_name</jsp:expression>
<jsp:useBean id="order" class="jsw.c03.OrderMaster" scope="session">
</jsp:useBean>
 (Order #: <jsp:getProperty name="order" property="or_number"/>):
</h3>

<form method="post" action="OrderMaintenanceS" name="form1">
  <input type="hidden" name="od_number"
         value="<jsp:getProperty name="order" property="or_number"/>">
  <p>
  <table width="100%" border="1" cellspacing="0" cellpadding="0">
    <tr>
      <td>Date: <jsp:getProperty name="order" property="or_order_date"/>
      </td>
      <td>Status: <jsp:getProperty name="order" property="or_status"/>
      </td>
      <td>
        <input type="submit" name="command" value="Delete Order">
      </td>
    </tr>
    <tr>
      <td>Delivery:
            Address: <input type="radio" name="Delivery" value="Address"
              <jsp:scriptlet>
              if (order.getOr_delivery().equals("Address"))
                out.print( "checked");
              </jsp:scriptlet>
              >
            Outlet: <input type="radio" name="Delivery" value="Outlet"
              <jsp:scriptlet>
```

```
                    if (order.getOr_delivery().equals("Outlet"))
                       out.print( "checked");
                  </jsp:scriptlet>
                  >
      </td>
      <td>Remarks:
         <textarea name="Remarks" rows="2">
         <jsp:getProperty name="order" property="or_remarks"/>
         </textarea>
      </td>
      <td>
        <input type="submit" name="command" value="Update Order">
      </td>
    </tr>
    <tr>
      <td>Outlet: <input type="text" name="or_o_outlet_code" size="5"
                      value="<jsp:getProperty name="order"
                            property="or_o_outlet_code"/>"
              >
      </td>
      <td>Price: $<jsp:getProperty name="order" property="or_price"/></td>
      <td><input type="submit" name="command" value="Deliver">
         <input type="submit" name="command" value="View Fax"></td>
    </tr>
  </table>
</form>
```

This section uses the `jsp:useBean` tag to obtain the attributes of the order from the `OrderMaster` bean. It then is uses the `jsp:getProperty` action to access the attributes.

The result of these two first sections can be seen on the following screenshot:

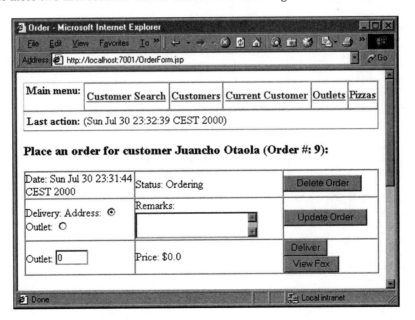

The JSP page continues by presenting the special offer of the day.

```
<h3>Specials:</h3>
<jsp:include page="Specials.jsp" flush="true" />
```

The code for Specials.jsp is the following:

```
<%@ page import="java.util.*,java.sql.*"%>

<%
  int discount = 15;
  String pizzaName = "";
  String pizzaSize = "";
  String pizzaDough = "";
  boolean found = false;
%>

<%
  try {
    Class.forName("weblogic.jdbc.pool.Driver");
  } catch(Exception e) {
    out.println(e);
  }

  try {
    Connection conn =
      DriverManager.getConnection("jdbc:weblogic:pool:p2gPool");

    String select =
      "select * from offer where of_from <= ? and of_to >= ?";
    PreparedStatement pstmt = conn.prepareStatement(select);

    java.sql.Timestamp now =
      new java.sql.Timestamp(System.currentTimeMillis());

    pstmt.setTimestamp(1, now);
    pstmt.setTimestamp(2, now);

    ResultSet resultSet = pstmt.executeQuery();

    if (resultSet.next()) {
      found = true;
      discount = resultSet.getInt("of_discount");
      pizzaName = resultSet.getString("of_p_name");
      pizzaSize = resultSet.getString("of_p_size");
      pizzaDough = resultSet.getString("of_od_dough");
    } else
      found = false;

    resultSet.close();
    pstmt.close();
    conn.close();
  } catch(Exception e) {
    System.err.println(e);
  }
```

```
%>
<% if (found) {%>
<form method="post" action="OrderMaintenanceS" name="">
  <table width="100%" align="center">
    <tr align="center">
      <td>
        <b>Special of the day:</b> Discount of <%=discount%>% on
            <%=pizzaName%> <%=pizzaSize%> <%=pizzaDough%>!!!
        <input type="hidden" name="Pizza" value="<%=pizzaName%>">
        <input type="hidden" name="Size" value="<%=pizzaSize%>">
        <input type="hidden" name="Dough" value="<%=pizzaDough%>">
        <input type="hidden" name="Quantity" value="1">
        <input type="submit" name="command" value="Add">
      </td>
    </tr>
  </table>
</form>
<% } else {%> <center>No Specials Today</center> <%}%>
```

This JSP page will establish a connection to the database and query for the special offer that corresponds to the current day. It then closes the connection and displays the information, giving the user the opportunity to add it to the order.

Returning to `OrderForm.jsp`, the fourth section builds an input line from which a selection can be made and added to the order. This is done with the following code:

```
<form method="post" action="OrderMaintenanceS" name="form2">
<input type="hidden" name="od_number"
       value="<jsp:getProperty name="order" property="or_number"/>">
  <h3>Pizzas:</h3>
  <p> <b>Pizza</b>:
    <select name="Pizza">
<jsp:scriptlet>
  String pizzaName;
  int n = 0;
  Vector pizzaNames = (Vector)application.getAttribute("pizzaNames");
  for (Enumeration pizzas = pizzaNames.elements() ;
        pizzas.hasMoreElements() ;) {
    pizzaName = (String)pizzas.nextElement();
    out.print("<option value=\"" + pizzaName + "\"");
    if (n == 0) out.print(" selected ");n++;
    out.print(">" + pizzaName + "</option>");
  }
</jsp:scriptlet>
    </select>
    Size:
    <select name="Size">
      <option value="Small">Small</option>
      <option value="Medium" selected>Medium</option>
      <option value="Large">Large</option>
    </select>
    Dough:
    <select name="Dough">
```

```
              <option value="Thin Crust" selected>Thin Crust</option>
              <option value="Classic">Classic</option>
          </select>
          Quantity:
          <input type="text" name="Quantity" value="1" size="5">
          <input type="submit" name="command" value="Add">
      </p>
      </form>
  <hr>
```

The result of the last two sections can be seen in the following screenshot:

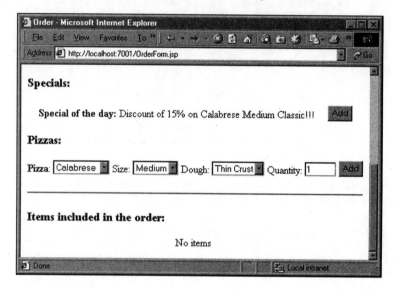

The fifth and last section presents the items included in the current order. This is done by calling OrderSubform.jsp:

```
<jsp:include page="OrderSubForm.jsp" flush="true" />
</body>
</html>
```

The code of the OrderSubForm.jsp JSP page is the following:

```
<%@ page import="java.util.*,java.sql.*"%>

<h3>Items included in the order:</h3>

<%
  try {
    Class.forName("weblogic.jdbc.pool.Driver");
  } catch(Exception e) {
    out.println(e);
  }
  OrderMaster order = (OrderMaster)session.getAttribute("order");
  if (order == null) {
```

```
      out.println("non existing object");
  } else {
    try {
      Connection conn =
        DriverManager.getConnection("jdbc:weblogic:pool:p2gPool");

      String select = "select * from order_detail " +
        "where od_or_number = ? order by od_number";
      PreparedStatement pstmt = conn.prepareStatement(select);

      pstmt.setLong(1, order.getOr_number());

      ResultSet resultSet = pstmt.executeQuery();

      Vector pizzaNames;
      String sValue;
      int nRows = 0;
      while(resultSet.next()) {
        nRows++;
%>
<form method="post" action="OrderMaintenanceS">
  <p> <b>Pizza</b>:
    <input type="hidden" name="od_number"
           value="<%= resultSet.getString("od_number") %>">
    <select name="Pizza">
<%
  sValue = resultSet.getString("od_p_name");
  pizzaNames = (Vector)application.getAttribute("pizzaNames");
  for (Enumeration pizzas = pizzaNames.elements() ;
        pizzas.hasMoreElements() ;) {
    String pizzaName = (String)pizzas.nextElement();
    out.print("<option value=\"" + pizzaName + "\"");
    if(pizzaName.equals(sValue)) out.print(" selected ");
    out.print(">" + pizzaName + "</option>");
  }
%>
    </select>
    Size:
    <select name="Size">
      <% sValue = resultSet.getString("od_p_size"); %>
      <option value="Small"
        <%= (sValue.equals("Small") ? "selected" : "") %>>Small
      </option>
      <option value="Medium"
        <%= (sValue.equals("Medium") ? "selected" : "") %>>Medium
      </option>
      <option value="Large"
        <%= (sValue.equals("Large") ? "selected" : "") %>>Large
      </option>
    </select>
    Dough:
    <select name="Dough">
      <% sValue = resultSet.getString("od_dough"); %>
      <option value="Thin Crust"
```

```
            <%= (sValue.equals("Thin Crust") ? "selected" : "") %>>Thin Crust
        </option>
        <option value="Classic"
            <%= (sValue.equals("Classic") ? "selected" : "") %>>Classic
        </option>
      </select>
      Quantity:
      <input type="text" name="Quantity"
            value="<%= resultSet.getInt("od_quantity")%>" size="5">
      <input type="submit" name="command" value="Update">
      <input type="submit" name="command" value="Delete">

    </p>
  </form>

<%
      }

      if (nRows == 0) {
        %> <center> No items </center> <%
      }

      resultSet.close();
      pstmt.close();
      conn.close();
    } catch(Exception e) {
      System.err.println(e);
    }
  }
%>
```

The page uses the order information stored in the session to retrieve the items included in the order from the database.

The page presents every item that makes up the order, and gives the user the option to delete or update the item. To update any item of the order the user just has to reselect the component from the pull-down menu and click on **Update**. The request goes to the `OrderMaintenanceS` servlet, where it's handled by the `updatePizza()` method. A similar method, `deletePizza()` is used to delete an item from the order.

Each item is presented on its own line so that the user can modify or delete it. To make it easier for users, the form of each item presents the types of pizza available. The JSP page uses the pizza information stored as an attribute of the `application` object, which acts as a cache for the database, in order to build up the selection options. The default value of the item is the one ordered. This is a very convenient way for the user to see and update the information.

An example of the output generated by this JSP page can be seen here:

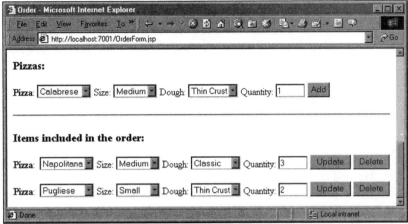

The `Message.jsp` page mentioned earlier is a very interesting way of sending messages of the 'successful update' kind from a servlet to a JSP page. It is simple, yet powerful. All it does is present the message object that is stored in the session and clear it up when it is done. Here is the code for `Message.jsp`:

```
<table width="100%" border="1">
  <tr>
    <td bordercolor="#FFFFFF"><b>Last action:</b>
      (<jsp:expression>new Date()</jsp:expression>)
      <jsp:scriptlet>if (session.getAttribute("message") != null)
{</jsp:scriptlet>
        <jsp:expression>session.getAttribute("message")</jsp:expression>
      <jsp:scriptlet>}
                   session.removeAttribute("message");
      </jsp:scriptlet>
    </td>
  </tr>
</table>
```

The message object is updated in `CustomerForm.jsp` and the `checkParams()` method of the `CustomerSearchS` servlet. `Message.jsp` is important in giving feedback on an order – the message attribute is set with each action, whether successful or not, as you can see in the `OrderMaintenanceS` class.

When the message data is only for the consumption of the destination page, the servlet can also forward the data as part of the request object sent to the JSP.

When a user requests a history of the orders placed by a specific customer, `OrderList.jsp` is called. The developers who wrote this JSP page used a mish-mash of <% directives and the JSP XML syntax, but it works just as well. The code starts with:

```
<%@ page import="java.util.*,java.sql.*"%>

<html>
<head>
<title>Order List</title>
<meta http-equiv="Content-Type" content="text/html; charset=iso-8859-1">
</head>
<body bgcolor="#FFFFFF">

<jsp:directive.include file="menu.html" />
<jsp:include page="Message.jsp" flush="true" />
```

As we saw earlier, the include directive parses the static page, menu.html, at translation time, whereas the include action for the JSP page, Message.jsp, is processed at runtime (so that it can show the current message). The code continues with:

```
<jsp:scriptlet>
    Customer c = (Customer)session.getAttribute("customer");
</jsp:scriptlet>

<h3>List orders for customer
<jsp:expression>c.c_first_name</jsp:expression>
<jsp:expression>c.c_last_name</jsp:expression>:
</h3>

<%
  try {
    Class.forName("weblogic.jdbc.pool.Driver");

    try {
      Connection conn =
        DriverManager.getConnection("jdbc:weblogic:pool:p2gPool");

      String select =
        "select * from order_master where " +
        "or_c_country_code = ? and or_c_area_code = ? and or_c_phone = ?"+
        " order by or_order_date";
      PreparedStatement pstmt = conn.prepareStatement(select);

      pstmt.setInt(1, c.c_country_code);
      pstmt.setInt(2, c.c_area_code);
      pstmt.setLong(3, c.c_phone);

      ResultSet resultSet = pstmt.executeQuery();
%>
```

This part of the scriptlet sends a prepared statement as a query to the database via a connection obtained from the pool. Next, the result of that query is prepared as a table:

```
      int nRows = 0;
      while(resultSet.next()) {
        nRows++;
        if (nRows == 1) {
%>
```

```
                     <table width="100%" border="1" cellspacing="0" cellpadding="0">
                     <tr><th>Order#</th>
                         <th>Date</th>
                         <th>Price</th>
                         <th>Delivery</th>
                         <th>Outlet</th>
                         <th>Status</th>
                         <th>Remarks</th>
                         <th>Action</th>
                     </tr>
<%
            }
%>
```

If the record is the first of the resultset, it first presents the headers of the table:

```
        <tr>
        <form method="post" action="OrderMaintenanceS" name="">
        <input type="hidden" name="or_number"
               value="<%= resultSet.getLong("or_number") %>">
        <td><%= resultSet.getLong("or_number")%></td>
        <td><%= new java.util.Date(resultSet.getTimeStamp("or_order_date")
                                       .getTime())%></td>
        <td><%= resultSet.getFloat("or_price")%></td>
        <td><%= resultSet.getString("or_delivery")%></td>
        <td><%= resultSet.getLong("or_o_outlet_code")%></td>
        <td><%= resultSet.getString("or_status")%></td>
        <td><%= resultSet.getString("or_remarks")%></td>
        <td><input type="submit" name="command" value="View"></td>
        </form>
        <tr>
<%
        }
        if (nRows == 0) {
          %> <center> No orders </center> <%
        } else {
          %> </table> <%
        }
        resultSet.close();
        pstmt.close();
        conn.close();
    } catch(Exception e) {
        out.println(e);
    }

  } catch(Exception e) {
    out.println(e);
  }

%>

</body>
</html>
```

Otherwise, it presents each of the records in the result set by placing every element in a cell of the table. The output of this JSP page can be seen on the following screenshot:

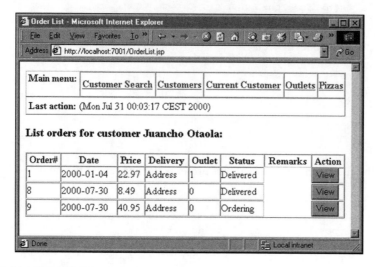

To list the available pizzas, a JSP page using the Model 1 architecture was produced. `PizzaList.jsp` is mostly Java code. It starts by preparing the table that it will use to present the list of pizzas:

```
<%@ page import="
          java.util.*,
          java.sql.*,
          java.net.*,
          java.text.*
          "
%>

<html>
<head>
<title>Pizzas List</title>
<meta http-equiv="Content-Type" content="text/html; charset=iso-8859-1">
</head>

<body bgcolor="#FFFFFF">
<a href="index.jsp">Main Menu</a>
<h2 align="center">Pizzas List</h2>

<table width="100%" border="1" cellspacing="0" cellpadding="0">
  <tr>
    <th bordercolor="#FFFFFF"></th>
    <th bordercolor="#FFFFFF"></th>
    <th colspan="3">Prices</th>
  </tr>
  <tr>
    <th>Name</th>
    <th>Ingredients</th>
    <th>Small</th>
    <th>Medium</th>
    <th>Large</th>
  </tr>
```

The code continues with the customary request to the JDBC connection pool:

```
<%
    Connection conn = null;
    String sPName = "";
    String s = "";
    DecimalFormat frmt = new DecimalFormat("0.00");


    try {
      Class.forName("weblogic.jdbc.pool.Driver");
      conn = DriverManager.getConnection("jdbc:weblogic:pool:p2gPool");

      Statement stmt = null;
      PreparedStatement pstmt = null;
      String select = "";
      ResultSet resultSet = null;
      ResultSet resultSetPrice = null;
      float conversionFactor = 1.0f;
      String sParams = null;

      stmt = conn.createStatement();
      select = "select co_factor from conversion where co_country = '" +
               System.getProperty("jsw.location", "US") + "'";
      resultSet = stmt.executeQuery(select);
      if (resultSet.next())
        conversionFactor = resultSet.getFloat("co_factor");
      resultSet.close();
      stmt.close();
```

This particular connection to the database is used for many queries. The first one, presented above, searches the `conversion` table for the right currency conversion for the country specified in the `jsw.location` system property.

```
      stmt = conn.createStatement();
      select = "select distinct u_p_name, u_i_name from units";
      stmt.execute(select);
      resultSet = stmt.getResultSet();

      while(resultSet.next()) {
        if (!(sPName.equals(resultSet.getString("u_p_name")))) {
          if (!(sPName.equals(""))) {
            out.println("</td>");
```

The `units` table contains one record per pizza ingredient and uses the pizza name as the primary key. The idea for this page is to build one table row with the name of the pizza, the ingredients, and the prices for the different sizes. The query presented above obtains the pizza name (`u_p_name`) and the ingredients (`u_i_name`).

The negated `if` statements are used to include the prices after the pizza name and ingredients. They kick in when the `resultSet` is on the next row, but `sPName` is still set to the previous pizza (and thus isn't equal to the current `u_p_name`), and this is used to retrieve the prices in the following query. The second `if` statement is needed for the first run through of the `while` loop, when `sPName` equals `null`.

83

```
        select = "select p_base_price from pizza " +
          "where p_name = ? order by p_size desc";
        pstmt = conn.prepareStatement(select);
        pstmt.setString(1, sPName);
        resultSetPrice = pstmt.executeQuery();

        resultSetPrice.next();
        out.println("<td>" + "$" +
          (conversionFactor * resultSetPrice.getFloat("p_base_price"))
            + "</td>");
        resultSetPrice.next();
        out.println("<td>" + "$" +
          (conversionFactor * resultSetPrice.getFloat("p_base_price"))
            + "</td>");
        resultSetPrice.next();
        out.println("<td>" + "$" +
          (conversionFactor * resultSetPrice.getFloat("p_base_price"))
            + "</td>");
        out.println("</tr>");
        resultSetPrice.close();
        pstmt.close();

        out.println("</tr>");
      } // End if (!(sPName.equals("")))
```

This code will present the localized prices for the three sizes of the pizza. Even though this part of the code comes first, because of the negated `if` statements, it will be executed last. Before that, the name and the description of the pizza ingredients are presented:

```
        out.println("<tr>");
        sPName = resultSet.getString("u_p_name");
        sParams = "?";
        sParams += URLEncoder.encode("u_p_name") + "=" +
                   URLEncoder.encode(sPName);

        out.print  ("<td> <a href=\"PizzaList.jsp" + sParams + "\">");
        out.println(sPName + "</a></td>");
        out.print  ("<td>");
      } // End if (!sPName.equals(resultSet.getString("u_p_name")))
      out.print(resultSet.getString("u_i_name")+ ", ");
    } // End while loop
  out.println("</td>");
```

What is really interesting in this part of the code is that this JSP page has the ability to call itself when more detailed information about a specific pizza is requested. This is done is by building a hyperlink to `PizzaList.jsp` with a parameter specifying the pizza name. In the next HTML table column the ingredients are included as a comma-delimited list.

The code continues by handling the special case of the last record and closing the table:

```
            select = "select p_base_price from pizza " +
              "where p_name = ? order by p_size desc";
            pstmt = conn.prepareStatement(select);
            pstmt.setString(1, sPName);
            resultSetPrice = pstmt.executeQuery();

            resultSetPrice.next();
            out.println("<td>" + "$" +
              (conversionFactor * resultSetPrice.getFloat("p_base_price"))
               + "</td>");
            resultSetPrice.next();
            out.println("<td>" + "$" +
              (conversionFactor * resultSetPrice.getFloat("p_base_price"))
               + "</td>");
            resultSetPrice.next();
            out.println("<td>" + "$" +
              (conversionFactor * resultSetPrice.getFloat("p_base_price"))
               + "</td>");
            out.println("</tr>");
            resultSetPrice.close();
            pstmt.close();

            conn.close();
        } catch (Exception e) {
          System.err.print(e);
        }
    %>

    </table>
    <p> </p>
```

When this JSP page is executed with no parameter, that is, only a listing of the available pizzas is desired, the output is the following:

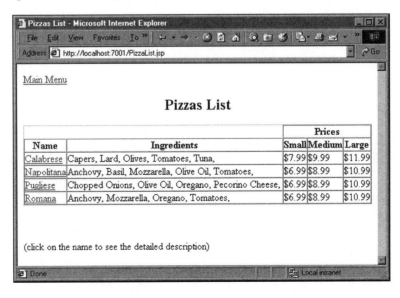

The code of `PizzaList.jsp` continues with the code used to display the detailed information for a specific pizza:

```
<%
   sPName = request.getParameter("u_p_name");
   if (sPName != null) {
%>
```

This scriptlet checks to see if there is a parameter called u_p_name, and if there is, it executes the following code:

```
<h2><center><%= sPName%></center></h2>
<table width="75%" border="1" align="center" cellpadding="0" cellspacing="0">
<tr>
  <th colspan="2" bordercolor="#FFFFFF"></th>
  <th colspan="3">Units</th>
</tr>
<tr>
  <th colspan="2">Ingredient</th>
  <th>Small</th>
  <th>Medium</th>
  <th>Large</th>
</tr>

<%
   try {

      conn = DriverManager.getConnection("jdbc:weblogic:pool:p2gPool");

      String select = "select u_i_name, u_p_size, u_units from units " +
               "where u_p_name = ? order by u_i_name asc, u_p_size desc";

      PreparedStatement pstmt = conn.prepareStatement(select);

      pstmt.setString(1, sPName);

      ResultSet resultSet = pstmt.executeQuery();

      String sParams = null;
      while(resultSet.next()) {
        %>
        <tr>
          <td colspan="2"><%= resultSet.getString("u_i_name")%></td>
          <% for(int i = 0; i < 3; i++) {%>
            <td><%= frmt.parse(resultSet.getString("u_units"))%></td>
          <% if(i < 2) resultSet.next(); }%>
        </tr>
        <%
      }
      resultSet.close();
      pstmt.close();
```

The Java code queries for every ingredient that is used in the pizza specified in the u_p_name parameter and then presents each ingredient as a table row along with the number of units each pizza size requires. The code of this JSP page finishes as follows:

```
            select = "select d_name, d_units from dough " +
                     "where d_p_size <> 'Calzone' " +
                     "order by d_name desc, d_p_size desc";

            pstmt = conn.prepareStatement(select);
            resultSet = pstmt.executeQuery();

            boolean b = true;
            while(resultSet.next()) {
              %>
              <tr>
                <%if(b) {out.println("<td rowspan=\"2\">Dough</td>");b=false;}%>
                <td><%= resultSet.getString("d_name")%></td>
                <% for(int i = 0; i < 3; i++) {%>
                  <td><%= frmt.parse(resultSet.getString("d_units"))%></td>
                <% if(i < 2) resultSet.next();}%>
              </tr>
              <%
            }
            resultSet.close();
            pstmt.close();
            conn.close();
        } catch (Exception e) {
            System.err.print(e);
        }
    %>

    </table>

    <%
      } else {
    %>
      (click on the name to see the detailed description)
    <%
      }
    %>
    </body>
    </html>
```

Since the units of dough required are different depending on the size of the pizza, the previous code handles the presentation accordingly.

The output of this part of the JSP page is shown below. Note the pizza name as a parameter in the location area of the browser.

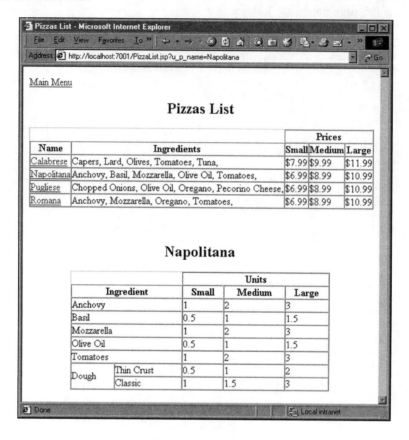

Using dbKona and htmlKona

Time for a breather from servlets, JSP pages, and beans. One advantage of the WebLogic Server, in our opinion, is the ease of programming provided by the pure Java dbKona and htmlKona APIs. They are proprietary to this server and not part of J2EE, so you do sacrifice portability. But we do want to show you how much easier they make web development.

dbKona

dbKona hides the low-level details and database vendor specifics of the database connection from the developer by providing high level abstract objects. The general container object is a `DataSet`, which contain objects of type `Record`, which in turn contain objects of type `Value`, thus offering a very simple way to interact with the database.

Another useful feature of dbKona is that it has methods and objects to automatically generate SQL and which will work with any JDBC driver.

htmlKona

htmlKona provides an object-oriented interface to the HTML environment that allows a developer to create an HTML document using objects that define a series of elements on a page. The web page is considered a canvas that will be rendered when one of the output methods is called.

When dbKona and htmlKona are used together their power and simplicity is unbeatable. To show you how dramatically different programming them can be compared to using JDBC and HTML directly, let us have a look at the `CustomerListS` servlet. This servlet uses the traditional JDBC and HTML statements to present a list of all the customers in the database:

```java
package jsw.c03;

import javax.servlet.*;
import javax.servlet.http.*;
import java.sql.*;
import java.io.*;
import java.net.URLEncoder;

/**
 * This class is a servlet that lists the registered customers
 * and their personal data.
 *
 */
public class CustomerListS extends HttpServlet {

  /**
   * This is the static initializer,
   * executed the first time this class is referred to.
   * It makes sure the JDBC pool driver is loaded.
   */
  static{
    try{
      Class.forName("weblogic.jdbc.pool.Driver");
    }
    catch(Exception e){
      System.err.println(e);
    }
  }

  /**
   * This method opens a JDBC connection to the database and retrieves
   * all the existing customers, creating an HTML page with their data.
   */
  public void service(HttpServletRequest req, HttpServletResponse res)
      throws IOException
  {
    res.setContentType("text/html");
    PrintWriter out = res.getWriter();

    out.println("<html><head><title>Customers List</title></head>");
    out.println("<body>");
```

```
out.println("<a href=\"index.jsp\">Main Menu</a>");

out.println("<h1><center>Customers List</center></h1>");

out.println("<table width=\"100%\" border=\"1\"");
out.println(" cellspacing=\"0\" cellpadding=\"0\">");
out.println("<tr><th>First Name</th><th>Last Name</th><th>ZIP</th>");
out.println("<th>City</th><th>State</th><th>Country</th>" +
            "<th>Phone</th></tr>");

Connection conn = null;
```

At the start of the service() method, the HTML table is prepared with the columns headers. The code continues with the JDBC connection to the database and the corresponding query:

```
try {

    conn = DriverManager.getConnection("jdbc:weblogic:pool:p2gPool");

    Statement stmt =
    conn.createStatement();
    String select = "select * from customer";

    stmt.execute(select);

    ResultSet resultSet = stmt.getResultSet();
```

Then it continues by manually presenting every customer one line at a time:

```
String sParams = null;
while (resultSet.next()) {
  out.println("<tr>");
  out.println("<td>" + resultSet.getString("c_first_name") +
              "</td>");
  out.println("<td>" + resultSet.getString("c_last_name")  +
              "</td>");
  out.println("<td>" + resultSet.getLong("c_postal_code")  +
              "</td>");
  out.println("<td>" + resultSet.getString("c_city")       +
              "</td>");
  out.println("<td>" + resultSet.getString("c_state")      +
              "</td>");
  out.println("<td>" + resultSet.getString("c_country")    +
              "</td>");

  sParams = "?";
  sParams += URLEncoder.encode("c_country_code") + "=" +
          URLEncoder.encode("" +
          resultSet.getInt("c_country_code"));
  sParams += "&" +
          URLEncoder.encode("c_area_code") + "=" +
          URLEncoder.encode("" +
          resultSet.getInt("c_area_code"));
  sParams += "&" +
```

```
                        URLEncoder.encode("c_phone") + "=" +
                        URLEncoder.encode("" +
                        resultSet.getLong("c_phone"));
              out.println("<td>" + "<a href=\"CustomerSearchS" +
                                   sParams + "\">"
                        + "+" + resultSet.getInt("c_country_code")
                        + "-" + resultSet.getInt("c_area_code")
                        + "-" + resultSet.getLong("c_phone")
                        + "</a></td>");
              out.println("</tr>");
            }
```

And finishes cleanly with:

```
        resultSet.close();
        stmt.close();
        conn.close();
      } catch (Exception e) {
        System.err.println("Exception: CustomerListS.service: " + e);
      }
      out.println("</table>");

      out.println("</body></html>");
      out.close();
    }
}
```

Now, let us see some code that uses dbKona and htmlKona instead. An example of this is `OutletList.jsp`, which is used to list all the outlets of Pizza2Go:

```
<%@ page import="
        java.util.*,
        java.sql.*,
        weblogic.db.jdbc.*,
        weblogic.html.*
        "
%>

<html>
<head>
<title>Outlets List</title>
<meta http-equiv="Content-Type" content="text/html; charset=iso-8859-1">
</head>

<body bgcolor="#FFFFFF">
<a href="index.jsp">Main Menu</a>
<h2 align="center">Outlets List</h2>

<%
    Connection conn;

    try {
      Class.forName("weblogic.jdbc.pool.Driver").newInstance();
      conn = DriverManager.getConnection("jdbc:weblogic:pool:p2gPool");
```

As usual, the JDBC driver is loaded and a connection is obtained from the pool.

```
DataSet dSet = new TableDataSet(conn, "outlet").fetchRecords();
```

With this single line a `DataSet` is made available that contains all the records of the `outlet` table.

```
TableElement tE = new TableElement(dSet);
```

This statement plus `out.print(tE);` would be enough to present the whole table – that is how simple it is. The developers, however, wanted to offer the user the ability to click on a specific outlet to obtain more detailed information about it. This is done with the following code:

```
tE.setBorder(1);

TableDataElement cell = null;
AnchorElement aE = null;
StringElement sE = null;

for (int i = 1; i < tE.getNumRows(); i++) {
  cell = tE.getCellAt(i, 0);
  String objstr = cell.getElement().toString();
  int index = objstr.indexOf('.');
  objstr = objstr.substring(0, index);
  cell.setElement(
      new LinkElement("OutletMaintenanceS?o_outlet_code=" + objstr,
      objstr));
}
out.print(tE);

dSet.close();
conn.close();
} catch (Exception e) {
  e.printStackTrace(System.err);
  out.print(e);
}
%>
</body>
</html>
```

Within the `for` loop, the outlet number is extracted and used to create a link in the first column. The `linkElement()` method defines a link with the `OutletMaintenanceS` servlet with the appropriate parameter, which is the outlet number. A sample output of this JSP page is shown in the following screenshot:

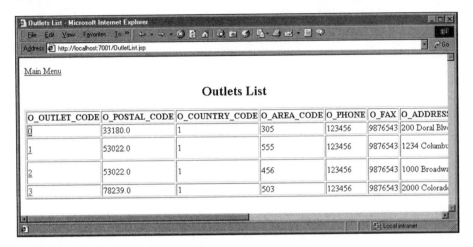

We do not hesitate in recommending the use of dbKona and htmlKona, because of the gains in productivity they provide, if you're working exclusively with WebLogic. More information and examples on these APIs can be found in the WebLogic documentation.

Architecture Overview

During the course of this chapter we have seen how Mrs Chief Architect, Mr Senior Developer, and their team familiarized themselves with the servlet and JSP APIs and experimented with different architectures for their web interface.

It's useful to review these models, this time using specific code developed in the chapter.

Model 1 Architecture

The order list is a good example of Model 1 Architecture. The content and the presentation of the list are implemented in `OrderList.jsp`, which is responsible both for searching the database for orders belonging to a given customer, and for presenting the results.

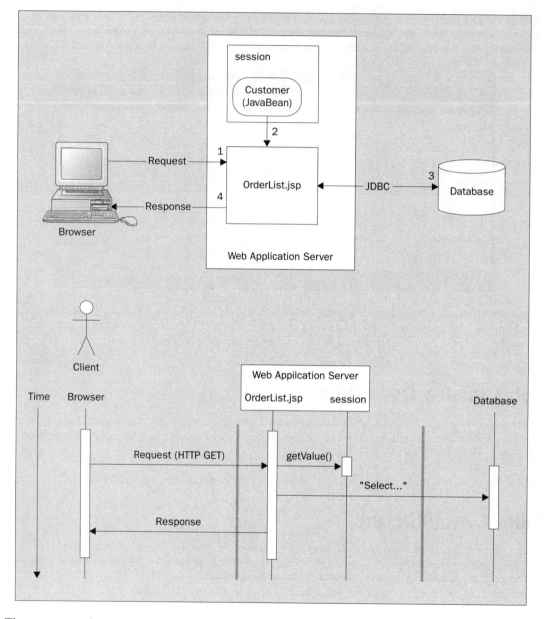

The sequence of events presented in the figure above is:

1. The JSP page receives a request issued by the browser with the HTTP GET command

2. The JSP page accesses its session to get the current customer info and store it in a JavaBean

3. Then it searches for orders in the database using JDBC

4. Finally it constructs an HTML table, which it sends back to the browser

Model 2 Architecture

The customer search and maintenance part of the application is a clear example of the Model 2 architecture. Here CustomerForm.jsp is responsible for the customer data presentation. It expects all the necessary customer data in a JavaBean in the session. It is the responsibility of the servlets (CustomerSearchS and CustomerMaintenanceS) to store the relevant information in the Customer JavaBean before calling the JSP page.

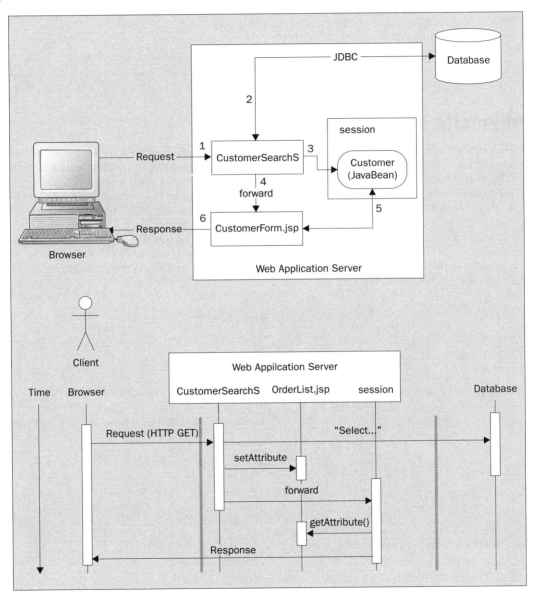

The sequence of events presented above relates to the `CustomerSearchS` servlet:

1. The servlet receives the request

2. The servlet searches for the data in the database

3. It stores the data in the `Customer` JavaBean in the session

4. The servlet forwards the request to the JSP page

5. The JSP page retrieves the customer data from the JavaBean in the session

6. The JSP page presents the customer information to the browser in HTML form

A Pragmatic Variation

Mrs Chief Architect is not exactly known for being a purist. She feels very strongly that when deadlines are around the corner a sensible combination of gut feeling and experience leads to useful variations of theoretical perfection. Such is the case with the way `OrderMaintenanceS` servlet and `OrderForm.jsp` interact between themselves and with other JSP pages. It is neither a perfect Model 2 nor a Model 1 architecture, but a combination of both, which is shown in the following figure.

Mrs Chief Architect's main reason for designing the hybrid system was that it provided the easiest way for the developers to break down the page's functionality. In a large-scale system, however, the short-term benefits of this approach might be outweighed by the need to use a common architecture over the whole site to improve maintainability.

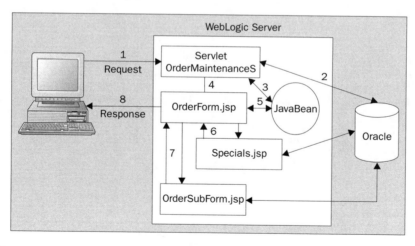

The flow of events in this figure is the following:

1. The servlet receives and processes the request

2. The servlet accesses the database

3. The servlet stores results in the JavaBean in the servlet session

4. The servlet transfers control to `OrderForm.jsp`

5. The JSP page recovers data from the JavaBean

6. The JSP page calls `Specials.jsp`, which has direct access to the database

7. The JSP page also calls `OrderSubform.jsp`, which also accesses the database

8. All this generates the response back to the browser

Communication Techniques for JSP, Servlets, and Browsers

The development team of Pizza2Go has also experimented with many techniques to pass data between JSP pages, servlets, and Browsers. Here's a summary.

Session Values

The session object is used extensively within the Pizza2Go site to store and retrieve data, as a way to share information between all the modules (JSP and servlets). Examples of this technique are presented in the descriptions of both Model 1 and 2 architectures.

The basis of this technique is that when a module wants to share data with another module that will be executed later, but within the same user session, it stores data in the session using the `setAttribute()` method. The receiving module will gain access to this data by using `getAttribute()` method. The example presented for the Model 1 architecture depicts this clearly.

Application Attributes

You can also store attributes in the servlet context. `Index.jsp` stores all the names of the pizzas as application attributes, which are later retrieved by other modules, for example `OrderForm.jsp`. The application is an implicit object that is shared by all the servlet instances and JSP pages independently of the session of which they are a part.

HTTP GET

Some modules communicate with others using the `GET` command from the HTTP protocol. The information that will be transmitted is encoded in the URL and is recovered using the `getParameter()` function of the request object. One example of this technique can be found in the code for a customer search, when the entry data is validated on the server side.

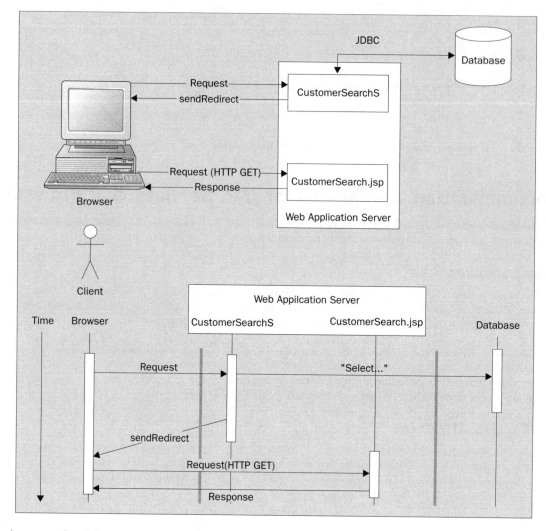

An example of this technique is presented above:

1. The CustomerSearchS servlet receives the request and checks the data in the checkParams() method

2. If it is incorrect, it sends the customer information back to CustomerSearch.jsp encoded as parameters in the URL

3. The JSP page retrieves the data from the GET request

4. The JSP page presents the search form with these values

In this case, instead of using the RequestDispatcher object's forward() method, the HttpServletResponse object's sendRedirect() method is used, instructing the browser to look up a new CustomerSearch.jsp.

HTTP POST

The POST command included in the HTTP protocol allows the values of form fields to be passed to the web server, and from there to a servlet or a JSP page. These are recovered with the getParameter() function of the request object.

In some cases, the module that builds the form sends information to the module that processes the form by means of hidden fields. This is quite a popular technique used to enhance the data that the user supplies.

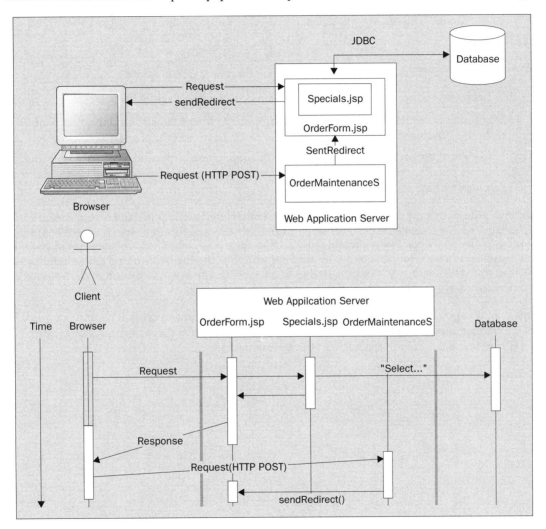

One example of this technique can be found in the processing of special offers, as illustrated above.

1. Specials.jsp is requested by the browser, as part of OrderForm.jsp

2. It searches for the offer of the day in the database

3. It then displays the offer of the day including an option to order it. The button is part of a form that has hidden fields that include the details of the special of the day, which the user doesn't need to see, but which allow the servlet to process the special like any other pizza.

4. The form sends the details to the `OrderMaintenanceS` servlet via the `POST` method, which retrieves the values of the hidden fields via the `getParameter()` method in the `addPizza()` method.

Summary

In this chapter we have:

- ❑ Recapped the basic features of the servlet and JavaServer Pages APIs from J2EE

- ❑ Seen the potential of the dbKona and htmlKona APIs and the JDBC connection pools from the WebLogic server

- ❑ Reviewed the architectural models used in conjunction with these APIs as well as the communication techniques that can be used to transfer data between JSP pages, servlets, and browsers

Through a series of experiments in using the different architectural models and web communication techniques, we have created a new front end for the Pizza2Go application described in Chapter 2. Because of the many possible techniques and architectures, the code for this chapter should be viewed as a set of experiments to gain familiarity with the technology rather than trying to find out the most efficient way of doing things. We'll return to the question of efficiency at the end of the book. We'll also improve the user interface in Chapter 6.

The code developed in this chapter still communicates with the stored procedures and data structures in the Oracle database. The objective of the next chapter is to replace the stored procedures with Enterprise JavaBeans (EJBs), specifically with session beans.

Stored Procedures Mutate to Session Beans

Enterprise JavaBeans (EJBs), as we saw in Chapter 1, are a subject everybody is talking about – the programming paradigm for the new web world. Mr Wonderboy and his troops are very excited with the success of their first experiment with servlets and JSP pages. Now they really want to get into this EJB thing.

In this chapter, we'll:

- ❑ Provide an overview of the EJB component specification
- ❑ Look at EJB container services for lifecycle management and transactions
- ❑ Recap roles in EJB work – developer, assembler, and deployer
- ❑ Discuss different design models for EJBs, and how the container supports each model
- ❑ See how to replace the Pizza2Go Oracle stored procedures with stateless session beans
- ❑ Examine the lifecycle of stateless session beans in the WebLogic server
- ❑ Make alterations to last chapter's front-end code
- ❑ Use the deployment descriptor to configure EJBs
- ❑ See how to hot deploy EJBs
- ❑ Develop a stateful session bean
- ❑ Contrast the lifecycle of stateless and stateful session beans in WebLogic server

Introducing Enterprise JavaBeans

Enterprise JavaBeans are the basis of a server-side component architecture, allowing developers to quickly create distributed object-oriented applications.

Component architectures seem like a great idea – split the functionality of an application into coarse-grained units, thus decoupling their interaction with each other and making the system more robust and flexible, able to work between several machines, and able to scale to many users. Better still, with a variety of components, it should be possible to assemble an application by tying the components together, and swap in new versions of components independently.

But the difficulties of creating robust components are legion. And much of this difficulty is in the lack of support from the container, in insufficient standardization of the container's duties or 7the repetitive coding of essential support functionality.

The Enterprise JavaBeans specification is grounded in the desire to free the application developer from dealing with low-level issues such as multi-threading, caching, concurrency control, and resource management. Handling multiple users, transactions, and allowing the application to scale are parts of a business framework that are much more generic than the business processes themselves, and coding them yourself is like reinventing the wheel, as well as being rather difficult. With EJB, this becomes the container's responsibility.

Writing to the EJB specification, the vendors' implementations are better tested, in competition, and focused not just on getting the job done, but on meeting diverse customer requirements. The specification was developed by Sun with wide industry backing. Politics aside, the result has been a specification that is sufficiently complete to allow applications to be deployed between different EJB servers substantially unchanged.

The basic idea of EJB components is that the developer encapsulates business logic in them, without having to worry about what kind of client calls them or about infrastructure issues.

An interesting part of the EJB specification, which we'll come back to in a few sections' time, is that it makes explicit support for the different component types. **Session beans** represent a process or workflow that the bean performs on behalf of a client, while **entity beans** represent a data view (something which we'll consider in more detail in the next chapter). One further distinction for session beans is whether they maintain state between method requests.

One other point to which we'll return is that the EJB specification makes plain and supports the different roles for people working with the application.

The EJB Architecture

A high level view of the architecture of the EJB model is presented in the following figure:

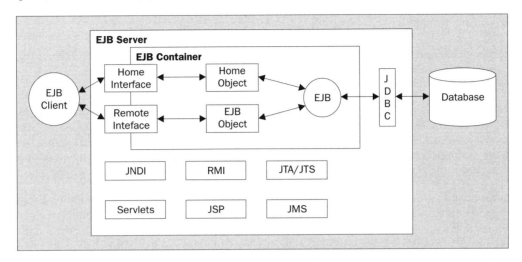

Here you can see that the EJB component lives in what is called an **EJB container**, which in turn is hosted by an **EJB server**.

The container provides the following services:

❑ Transaction support

❑ Lifecycle management

❑ Security management

❑ Persistency

❑ Resource management

❑ Concurrency

The server provides the container with the lower-level infrastructure and services such as connectivity to other J2EE APIs and applications. As the diagram shows, connectivity to databases, naming services, mail, and other servers is provided by the server.

A client of the EJB communicates with the EJB by means of two interfaces, namely the **home interface** and the **remote interface**. It cannot get a direct reference to an EJB component instance.

This interface programming is very important for scalability, as the container decouples the client and server component interaction. What are the benefits of this? Well if a client is long-lived and has a handle to an EJB component, but uses it intermittently, dedicating that component instance and the resources it uses to the client is very wasteful. But give the client a handle to a component, which the container has to match with an actual bean instance whenever a method is called, and you break the client-server mapping. Then, the container can control the lifecycle of the component to best suit the server's load and resource availability. Thus, when there are many simultaneous clients, the container can pool components to best service clients.

The home interface for a component is shared by all the clients and is tasked with the lifecycle duties such as the creation and removal of the EJBs. The home interface extends `javax.ejb.EJBHome`, which itself extends `java.rmi.Remote`. The bean's home interface must define all the methods for creating a new bean, as they cannot be created in the usual way, that is, by using their constructors. The **home object** is the actual implementation of the home interface. The developer only has to define the interface as the object is automatically generated by a vendor-supplied tool.

> The `Remote` interface is a placeholder interface, that is, it has no methods, but signals to the compiler that the class may be called from a non-local virtual machine, and that `RemoteException` must be supported by all the methods in the class.

The remote interface lists the signatures of the methods that will implement the particular business logic of the EJB. The remote interface extends `javax.ejb.EJBObject`, which itself extends `java.rmi.Remote`. The remote interface defines all the business methods of the bean, that is, those that a client wants to call. The **EJB object** is the automatically generated implementation of the remote interface and is the client's view of the actual bean.

The bean class does not actually implement the home and remote interfaces, although it must provide corresponding methods, as if it does implement them. We'll see more on this in a moment.

The EJB itself is isolated by the container, and only the container can access the EJB. This way the container can handle all the low-level and infrastructure issues without any interference from the clients. The reason why the home object and the EJB object are generated automatically is so that the container can act as a mediator between the client and the EJB – and this is the mechanism by which the container manages security and transactions. This is the real magic of EJBs.

> An alternative way of looking at this is that there is no one class that corresponds to the 'real EJB': instead it is a combination of the bean class provided by the developer, the home and remote interfaces provided by the developer, and the classes generated by the container.

One important feature is that the use of these services can be defined independently from the actual business logic. For the most part, the developer will concentrate on business logic, allowing the container to handle the transaction logic. It is possible to influence the way in which transactions are handled, in a declarative way through the **deployment descriptor**. A deployment descriptor is defined as a properties file for the bean that is used by the container to handle transactions and other run-time behaviors. In the EJB 1.0 specification these were serialized files, but in the later specs, they are XML files. We'll come back to these in a later section when we have some beans to deploy.

EJB Design Models

The EJB specification offers three component types for use in EJB applications. Typically, you'll see all three in use:

❑ **No State** – represented by the **stateless session beans**. They do not keep state on behalf of the client between calls of their methods, and so can be shared between many clients. They are relatively short-lived and can be viewed as providing a single-use service. An example is a bean with a method that calculates the Value Added Tax of an item; the method just returns its calculation and is ready for the next request, no matter which client that comes from.

❑ **Session Oriented** – represented by stateful session beans, which maintain state across methods calls and transactions. Their life is determined by the life of their client. A typical example is a shopping cart at a web site because the output depends very much on its caller.

❑ **Persistent** – known as entity beans, they are a representation or view of data from a data store (a relational database, an object-oriented database, a file, etc.). Because of this they are transactional. As examples, entity beans can represent the information associated with a driver's license, an order, or a resultset from a query. We'll leave detailed explanations of entity beans until the next chapter.

In this chapter we'll cover session beans. Firstly we'll be interested in replacing the functionality of the Oracle PL/SQL stored procedures by stateless session beans. Then we'll look at stateful session beans.

Transaction Support in EJBs

Transactions are everywhere and often need to be mapped to software – they can be defined as any workflow that is 'all or nothing', that is, it must all succeed or be returned to its original state (or 'rolled back').

There are four very important properties that must be guaranteed by systems that support transactions: atomicity, consistency, isolation, and durability. These four properties are generally known better by the 'ACID' acronym:

❑ **Atomicity** – all the actions that make up a transaction form a logical unit. As such they must all complete successfully or the transaction is undone and no actions complete.

❑ **Consistency** – the data store used by for the transaction must always be in a consistent state. That is, if a transaction fails half way through, the data store must not retain partially modified data. Uncommitted changes to the data store must be capable of being rolled back.

❑ **Isolation** – the state of the transaction is not available outside itself until it has been successfully completed, so it can execute without interference.

❑ **Durability** – once the transaction has been completed successfully, the state is stored permanently.

The EJB specification has declarative support for various modes of transactional management. As we mentioned in the previous section, the deployment descriptor tells the container how to manage transactions when methods on a bean are invoked. The modes are illustrated in the following table:

Transaction Support	Description
Mandatory	The caller must start the transaction before it uses the bean. An error occurs if no transaction is available.
Required	The bean requires a transaction; the container will start one if the caller hasn't already done so.
NotSupported	The container suspends the caller's transaction before calling the bean.
RequiresNew	The container starts a new transaction for every call, even if there is already a transaction in progress, in which case it will suspend it.
Supports	The container just passes the caller's transaction along. If there is no transaction in progress, no new one is created.
Never	The bean does not participate within a transaction context.

We'll see these in action later in the chapter, when we deploy our beans. In the next chapter, we'll look at further transaction support in deployment descriptors.

As you can see, the transactional support offered by the EJB specification makes it pretty easy to develop transactional components without having to get into the low-level stuff.

Other Services

The EJB container also provides the lifecycle management for components. It takes care of the component from the time it is instantiated, when it is initialized, to the time it is removed from the container.

The EJBs do not exist in the container until the clients start calling them. At this moment the container will create a new bean instance, initialize it with context information, and place it in the container.

Context information is provided to the EJB from the container by passing an object implementing `javax.ejb.SessionContext` (or `javax.ejb.EntityContext` for an entity bean). The container calls the EJB's `setSessionContext()` method with an object implementing the `SessionContext` interface as the argument. This object is usually stored as an EJB field, allowing the bean instance to obtain run-time information from the container. The `setSessionContext()` method is called by the container just before the `ejbCreate()` method.

> *There's also an option for stateless session beans to pre-create a pool of bean instances at server startup.*

As the container starts to reach capacity limits, it can **passivate** some beans, that is, it can swap some beans out of the container to the hard disk. Passivation involves detaching the bean instance from the EJB object, and saving its state by serializing its attributes. The clients are unaware of this process because they don't ever have access to the actual bean instances.

> *Fields of the bean that are declared `transient` aren't serialized and so won't survive passivation, and so won't be present when the bean is activated. Conversely, all non-transient fields must support the `java.io.Serializable` interface, so they can be serialized.*

Since this implies that the bean has state worth saving, that a client may call for again, this applies only to stateful session beans, and we will come back to the details of passivation at the end of the chapter, when we create a stateful bean.

Beans can also be removed from the container. This happens to inactive beans when the container decides that it is not worth passivating them, as the resource consumption will likely be more expensive than initializing them again.

EJB's security management is very powerful as it gives the developer the ability to create the components without having to hard code security issues. The developer uses an abstraction called a **security role**. A security role is a grouping of user permissions that enable the execution of the various components that make up an application. The security roles are assigned at deployment time according to the corresponding security policies of the operational environment.

Persistence is a service that will be specifically discussed in Chapter 5.

EJB Architecture Roles

The EJB specification has broken down beans into various independent portions that clearly require different skill sets. Because of this, the specification defines certain development roles. The job specs are the following:

❑ **Enterprise Bean Provider** – creates the components that contain the business logic. Has J2EE programming experience. Typically these persons are knowledgeable in their vertical business domain, although not usually as knowledgeable as the Application Assembler.

❑ **Application Assembler** – creates the actual application by putting all the pieces together. The person uses the EJBs created by the Enterprise Bean Providers and combines them with a front end, using servlets and JSPs perhaps, to produce the final application.

❑ **Deployer** – knows the actual operational environment where the application will run. This person defines the security roles of the application, the database that will be used, and all the external dependencies related to the application that are not defined by the provider and the assembler. Basically this person deals with the deployment descriptor.

❑ **EJB server Provider** – the software company that provides the EJB server. In this case it is BEA Systems.

❑ **EJB Container Provider** – the software company that provides the container. Typically it is the same provider as for the server. In this book we are dealing with the WebLogic server from BEA Systems.

❑ **System Administrator** – responsible for the configuration and administration of the computing and networking infrastructure where the application will run. They are also responsible for day-to-day operation of the application.

Naming Convention

In addition to the naming convention proposed in Chapter 3, here's a naming convention for EJBs to minimize the confusion. The idea is that the remote interface has a name that identifies the functionality of the EJB. This name is reused for the home interface and the EJB class with the word Home or Bean appended to it. The SL suffix stands for stateless, while SF stands for stateful.

The following table shows some examples:

Remote Interface	Home Interface	EJB Class
BeanName	*BeanName***Home**	*BeanName***Bean**
PizzaServicesSL	PizzaServicesSLHome	PizzaServicesSLBean
OrderSF	OrderSFHome	OrderSFBean
OrderMasterEB	OrderMasterEBHome	OrderMasterEBBean

Stateless Session Pizzas

As you may remember from Chapter 2, the original Oracle application had four PL/SQL stored procedures, assignOutlet, deliverOrder, orderPrice, and pizzaPrice. In Chapter 3, the Wonder Troops created a new web front end, which uses these stored procedures. The way the stored procedures are used fits the stateless session bean model perfectly well. The servlets and JSP pages call the stored procedures to persist the order as it is built.

The Troops can replace the stored procedures with stateless session beans that provide the same functionality. The stateless session EJBs perform the same function as the stored procedures (for example, calculating the price of a pizza) but in Java instead of the database-specific language used by the stored prodedures (Oracle PL-SQL, in this case). These EJBs are providing data source independence, while the code in Chapter 3 is data source dependent.

Mrs Chief Architect organizes these new beans into functional services. The result is the following three beans:

❑   PizzaServicesSL, which replaces the pizzaPrice stored procedure.

❑   OrderServicesSL, which provides all related functionality for pizza orders and replaces the orderPrice and deliverOrder stored procedures.

❑   OutletServicesSL, which replaces the assignOutlet stored procedure.

As you can see, by organizing the beans this way, as new functionality is required, it can be easily placed in the appropriate bean.

Because of these changes, the Intranet web site of Pizza2Go has to be reorganized. The new flowchart is presented in the figure opposite.

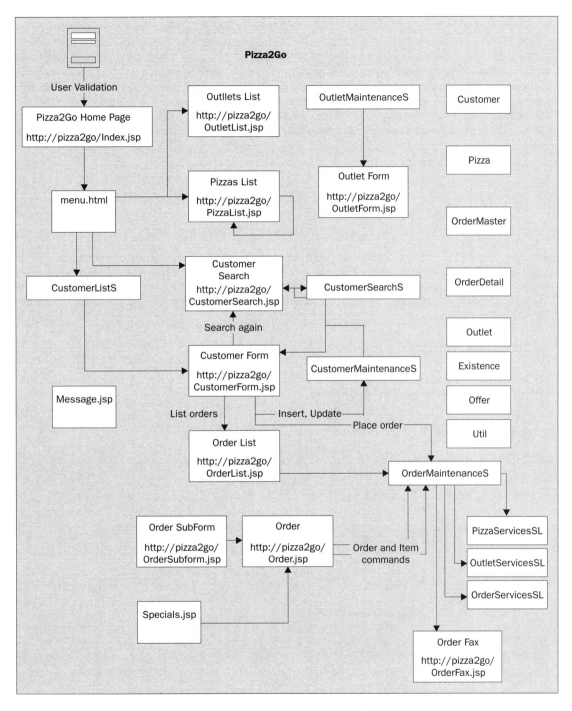

One thing that Mr Senior Developer notices is that the stored procedures handle the transactional integrity of the system. As they are replaced, this has to be moved to the EJBs. The way to solve this issue is by using the WebLogic JTS drivers instead of the connection pools and JDBC drivers we saw in the last chapter.

Java Transaction Service (JTS) is the Java implementation of the OMG Object Transaction Service (OTS).

Continued use of JDBC connection pools is a common mistake for developers of J2EE applications, and you can get away with it, but the application will not be transactionally safe. Even if you do not need transaction integrity because your application does not seem to require it, you should, for code robustness in the future development of your application, use the JTS drivers. The change is not painful either – in every instance where you call the connection pool, you replace the word `pool` with `jts`:

```
Class.forName("weblogic.jdbc.pool.Driver");
```

becomes:

```
Class.forName("weblogic.jdbc.jts.Driver");
```

Another thing to be careful about is the JavaBeans handling the representation of the database tables. They must implement the `java.io.Serializable` interface, so that they can freely travel on the network, as it is not known where these beans will execute. The existing JavaBeans already implement the `Serializable` interface, as this is the recommendation of the Servlet v2.2 specification for a distributed environment.

```
public class Customer implements java.io.Serializable {
```

We will now look at the home and remote interfaces, and the actual bean implementations that the Wonder Team has developed for these beans.

Pizza Services

The Home interface for the `PizzaServicesSL` bean is pretty simple:

```
package jsw.c04a;

import javax.ejb.*;
import java.rmi.RemoteException;

/**
 * This is the Home Interface for the Stateless Session EJB
 * <tt>PizzaServicesSL</tt>.
 *
 * @see      jsw.c04a.PizzaServicesSL
 * @see      jsw.c04a.PizzaServicesSLBean
 */
public interface PizzaServicesSLHome extends EJBHome {

  /**
    * Creates a Stateless Session EJB to access to pizza services.
    */
  public PizzaServicesSL create()
    throws CreateException, RemoteException;
}
```

Only one function of the lifecycle is necessary, the creation of the bean. This maps to the corresponding `ejbCreate()` method in `PizzaServicesSLBean`, which we'll see in a moment. The `EJBHome` interface defines methods for removing the EJB from the container, and for acquiring meta data about the EJB component.

The remote interface is also very simple:

```
package jsw.c04a;

import javax.ejb.*;
import java.rmi.RemoteException;
import java.util.Date;

/**
 * This is the Remote Interface for the Stateless Session EJB
 * <tt>PizzaServicesSL</tt>.
 *
 * @see     jsw.c04a.PizzaServicesSLHome
 * @see     jsw.c04a.PizzaServicesSLBean
 */
public interface PizzaServicesSL extends EJBObject {

  /**
   * Returns the base price of a pizza.
   * The price is localized based on the system
   * property <tt>jsw.location</tt>.
   * It does not consider the special offer of the day.
   */
  public float getPrice(Pizza pizza)
    throws RemoteException, P2GException;

  /**
   * Returns the base price of a pizza.
   * The price is localized based on the <tt>location</tt> parameter.
   * It does not consider the special offer of the day.
   */
  public float getPrice(Pizza pizza, String location)
    throws RemoteException, P2GException;

  /**
   * Returns the price of a pizza.
   * The price is localized based on the <tt>location</tt> parameter.
   * It does consider the special offer of the day, passed in the
   * <tt>date</tt> parameter.
   */
  public float getPrice(Pizza pizza, String location,
                        java.util.Date date, String dough)
    throws RemoteException, P2GException;

  /**
   * Returns the special offer of the day.
   * The day is passed in the <tt>date</tt> parameter.
   */
  public Offer getSpecial(java.util.Date date)
    throws RemoteException, P2GException;

}
```

The remote interface defines two methods, `getSpecial()` and `getPrice()`, which has three signatures that are explained next.

The actual bean implementation is the following:

```
package jsw.c04a;

import javax.ejb.*;
import javax.naming.*;
import java.util.*;
import java.rmi.RemoteException;
import java.sql.*;
import java.text.ParseException;

/**
 * This class is the Bean Implementation for the Stateless Session EJB
 * <tt>PizzaServicesSL</tt>.
 * The methods in this class return the price of a pizza and the special
 * offer of the day.
 *
 * @see      jsw.c04a.PizzaServicesSLHome
 * @see      jsw.c04a.PizzaServicesSL
 */
public class PizzaServicesSLBean implements SessionBean
{
  private SessionContext ctx;

  /**
   * This is the static initializer,
   * executed the first time this class is referred to.
   * It makes sure the JDBC JTS driver is loaded.
   */
  static {
    try {
      Class.forName("weblogic.jdbc.jts.Driver");
    } catch(Exception e) {
      System.err.println(e);
    }
  }

  /**
   * Returns the base price of a pizza.
   * The price is localized based on the system
   * property <tt>jsw.location</tt>.
   * It does not consider the special offer of the day.
   */
  public float getPrice(Pizza pizza)
    throws P2GException {
    String location = System.getProperty("jsw.location", "US");
    return getPrice(pizza, location);
  }
```

It implements the `javax.ejb.SessionBean` interface. The first signature of the `getPrice()` method will get the country where the application is running and then call the actual method to do the database search for the price.

> *Alternatives to explicitly loading drivers statically in every session bean are to load them once in a system-wide class, or alternatively to specify them in the `jdbc.drivers` system property.*

The second signature of the `getPrice()` method will calculate the price considering the special of the day. Again, it calls the actual method that does the database search for the price.

```
/**
 * Returns the price of a pizza.
 * Both pizza and dough types needed to calculate this.
 * The price is localized based on the <tt>location</tt> parameter.
 * It does consider the special offer of the day, passed in the
 * <tt>date</tt> parameter.
 */
public float getPrice(Pizza pizza, String location,
                      java.util.Date date, String dough)
    throws P2GException {
    float price = 0.0f;
    Offer offer = null;

    price = getPrice(pizza, location);
    offer = getSpecial(date);

    if (offer != null) {
        Pizza specialPizza = offer.getOf_pizza();

        if ( (specialPizza.getP_name().equals(pizza.getP_name())) &&
             (specialPizza.getP_size().equals(pizza.getP_size())) &&
             (dough.equals(offer.getOf_od_dough())) ) {
            price *= (1.0f - (offer.getOf_discount()/100.0f));
            try {
                price = Util.format(price);
            } catch(ParseException pe) {
                throw new P2GException(Util.getStackTraceAsString(pe));
            }
        }
    }

    return price;
}
```

The third signature is the one that actually searches the database for the price of the pizza. Notice that this method does not verify that the JTS driver is loaded as this has been done in the static intializer.

```
/**
 * Returns the base price of a pizza.
 * The price is localized based on the <tt>location</tt> parameter.
 * It does not consider the special offer of the day.
 */
public float getPrice(Pizza pizza, String location)
    throws P2GException {
    float conversionFactor = 1.0f;
    float price = 0.0f;
    Connection conn = null;

    try {
        String select = "";
        PreparedStatement pstmt = null;
        ResultSet resultSet = null;
```

```
       conn = DriverManager.getConnection("jdbc:weblogic:jts:p2gPool");

       select = "select p_base_price from pizza " +
                " where p_name = ? and p_size = ?";
       pstmt = conn.prepareStatement(select);
       pstmt.setString(1, pizza.getP_name());
       pstmt.setString(2, pizza.getP_size());
       resultSet = pstmt.executeQuery();
       if (resultSet.next()) {
         price = resultSet.getFloat("p_base_price");
       } else {
         throw new P2GException("Pizza not found: " + pizza.getP_name());
       }
       resultSet.close();
       pstmt.close();
```

Once the pizza price has been found, the method proceeds to calculate the real price according to the country the application is running in. It does this by checking the currency conversion table in the database.

```
       select = "select co_factor from conversion where co_country = ?";
       pstmt = conn.prepareStatement(select);
       pstmt.setString(1, location);
       resultSet = pstmt.executeQuery();
       if (resultSet.next()) {
         conversionFactor = resultSet.getFloat("co_factor");
       } else {
         throw new P2GException("Conversion factor not found for location"
                                 + location);
       }
       resultSet.close();
       pstmt.close();

       conn.close();
    } catch (Exception e) {
       System.err.println(e);
       try {
         conn.close();
       } catch(SQLException se) {
         throw new P2GException(se.toString());
       }
    }

    try {
       price = Util.format(price * conversionFactor);
    } catch(ParseException pe) {
       throw new P2GException(Util.getStackTraceAsString(pe));
    }

    return price;
  }
```

The `getSpecial()` method obtains the special of the day from the database. It includes a change in the way the front end interacts with these beans. As you may remember, in Chapter 3 the special of the day was obtained in `OrderForm.jsp`. In order to minimize the amount of Java code in the JSP page, Mr Senior Developer decides to move this functionality to this bean. This is good programming practice as business and presentation logic should be kept separate whenever possible, something that the Model 2 architecture advocates. This method pretty much does the same thing as the page: opens a connection to the database and queries for the special given a date, and then updates the `Offer` object.

```java
/**
 * Returns the special offer of the day.
 * The day is passed in the <tt>date</tt> parameter.
 */
public Offer getSpecial(java.util.Date date)
  throws P2GException {

  Offer offer = null;
  Connection conn = null;

  try {
    conn = DriverManager.getConnection("jdbc:weblogic:jts:p2gPool");

    String sSelect =
          "select * from offer where of_from <= ? and of_to >= ?";

    PreparedStatement pstmt = conn.prepareStatement(sSelect);

    java.sql.Timestamp d = new java.sql.Timestamp(date.getTime());

    pstmt.setTimestamp(1, d);
    pstmt.setTimestamp(2, d);

    ResultSet resultSet = pstmt.executeQuery();
    if (resultSet.next()) {
      offer = new Offer();
      offer.setOf_code(resultSet.getLong("of_code"));
      offer.setOf_discount(resultSet.getInt("of_discount"));
      offer.setOf_from(resultSet.getTimestamp("of_from"));
      offer.setOf_to(resultSet.getTimestamp("of_to"));
      offer.setOf_od_dough(resultSet.getString("of_od_dough"));

      Pizza pizza = new Pizza();
      pizza.setP_name(resultSet.getString("of_p_name"));
      pizza.setP_size(resultSet.getString("of_p_size"));
      offer.setOf_pizza(pizza);
    }

    resultSet.close();
    pstmt.close();
    conn.close();
  } catch(Exception e) {
    try {
      conn.close();
    } catch(SQLException se) {
      throw new P2GException(se.toString());
    }
    throw(new P2GException(e.toString()));
  }
  return offer;
}
```

Finally, the code for the bean is completed with the following required methods:

```
public void ejbCreate() { }

public void setSessionContext(SessionContext ctx)
  throws RemoteException {
  this.ctx = ctx;
}

public void ejbActivate()
  throws RemoteException {
}

public void ejbPassivate()
  throws RemoteException {
}

public void ejbRemove()
  throws RemoteException {
}
```

These methods form part of the contract between the EJB and the container. The container will call these methods during the lifecycle of the EJB:

❑ Creation

❑ Context setting

❑ Passivation

❑ Activation

❑ Removal

The first method, `ejbCreate()`, matches the parameters we defined for the `create()` method of the home interface, `PizzaServicesSLHome`. The other four methods are defined in the `SessionBean` interface.

In this particular EJB, no special implementation is needed for most of the lifecycle methods, as no initialization/finalization is needed, and passivation/activation won't be needed for the stateless bean. The `setSessionContext()` method is called by the container to associate the EJB with the context maintained by the container. The EJB can use this context to retrieve run-time information from the container.

Order Services

The home interface of the `OrderServicesSL` bean is similar to that of `PizzaServicesSL`, as it only declares the `create()` method:

```
package jsw.c04a;

import javax.ejb.*;
import java.rmi.RemoteException;
```

```
/**
 * This is the Home Interface for the Stateless Session EJB
 * <tt>OrderServicesSL</tt>.
 *
 * @see       jsw.c04a.OrderServicesSL
 * @see       jsw.c04a.OrderServicesSLBean
 */
public interface OrderServicesSLHome extends EJBHome {

  /**
   * Creates a Stateless Session EJB to access to order services.
   */
  public OrderServicesSL create()
    throws CreateException, RemoteException;

}
```

The remote interface follows:

```
package jsw.c04a;

import javax.ejb.*;
import java.rmi.RemoteException;

/**
 * This is the Remote Interface for the Stateless Session EJB
 * <tt>OrderServicesSL</tt>.
 *
 * @see       jsw.c04a.OrderServicesSLHome
 * @see       jsw.c04a.OrderServicesSLBean
 */
public interface OrderServicesSL extends EJBObject{

  /**
   * This method updates in the database the total price of an order.
   * The order is specified by its order number (primary key).
   */
  public float updatePrice(long orderNum)
    throws RemoteException, P2GException;

  /**
   * This method delivers an order.
   * The order is specified by its order number (primary key).
   * The method updates the existences in the assigned outlet.
   */
  public String deliverOrder(long orderNum)
    throws RemoteException, P2GException;

}
```

Notice that these two methods can throw a P2GException in addition to a RemoteException. A P2GException is an example of an application-defined exception that can be thrown in an EJB business method, and used to convey application-specific information. In this case, no special information is added to it. The code for this exception is the following:

119

```
package jsw.c04a;

/**
 * An exception that can provide information specific to the Pizza2Go
 * application.
 *
 */
public class P2GException
  extends java.lang.Exception {

  public P2GException() {}

  public P2GException(String message) { super(message); }

}
```

The actual implementation of the bean is:

```
package jsw.c04a;

import javax.ejb.*;
import javax.naming.*;
import java.util.*;
import java.sql.*;
import java.rmi.RemoteException;
import java.text.ParseException;

/**
 * This class is the Bean Implementation for the Stateless Session EJB
 * <tt>OrderServicesSL</tt>.
 * The methods in this class perform operations related to orders.
 *
 * @see      jsw.c04a.OrderServicesSLHome
 * @see      jsw.c04a.OrderServicesSL
 */
public class OrderServicesSLBean implements SessionBean {
  private SessionContext ctx;

  /**
   * This is the static initializer,
   * executed the first time this class is referred to.
   * It makes sure the JDBC JTS driver is loaded.
   */
  static {
    try {
      Class.forName("weblogic.jdbc.jts.Driver");
    } catch(Exception e) {
      System.err.println(e);
    }
  }
```

At the core of this bean are the methods that replace the two stored procedures. The first one is `updatePrice()`. This method is interesting in the sense that it calls another bean:

```
/**
 * This method updates in the database the total price of an order.
 * The order is specified by its order number (primary key).
 */
public float updatePrice(long orderNum)
  throws P2GException {

  float price = 0.0f;
  Connection conn = null;
  PizzaServicesSL pizzaServices = null;

  try {
    Context context = new InitialContext();
    PizzaServicesSLHome pizzaServicesHome =
      (PizzaServicesSLHome) context.lookup("jsw.c04a.PizzaServicesSL");
    pizzaServices = pizzaServicesHome.create();
```

These statements are the standard way to call the `PizzaServicesSL` bean. We will go through them in more detail when the lifecycle of a stateless session bean is presented later in this section.

What is important to notice now is that `OrderServicesSL` bean does not use the instance of the EJB that is in the session of the servlet. Instead it creates another one, uses it, and destroys it. This is more convenient as the EJB has no direct access to the servlet session – the context is taken from its own environment.

Note that for code robustness, the bean will also be destroyed when catching exceptions.

The code continues by getting the order from the database and calculating the price of it:

```
PreparedStatement pstmt = null;
String select = "";
ResultSet resultSet = null;
conn = DriverManager.getConnection("jdbc:weblogic:jts:p2gPool");
select = "select od_p_name, od_p_size, od_dough, od_quantity " +
         " from order_detail where od_or_number = ?";
pstmt = conn.prepareStatement(select);
pstmt.setLong(1, orderNum);
resultSet = pstmt.executeQuery();
Pizza pizza = new Pizza();
java.util.Date date = new java.util.Date();
while (resultSet.next()) {
  pizza.setP_name(resultSet.getString("od_p_name"));
  pizza.setP_size(resultSet.getString("od_p_size"));
  price += resultSet.getInt("od_quantity") *
           pizzaServices.getPrice(pizza,
                     System.getProperty("jsw.location", "US"),
                     date, resultSet.getString("od_dough"));
}
resultSet.close();
pstmt.close();
```

Then the order record is updated with the price of the order, the update is verified, and the bean that was created is removed:

```
String insert = "update order_master set or_price = ? " +
        " where (or_number = ?)";

pstmt = conn.prepareStatement(insert);

pstmt.setFloat(1, Util.format(price));
pstmt.setLong(2, orderNum);

pstmt.execute();

int n = pstmt.getUpdateCount();
if (n != 1) {
   throw new Exception("<E> OrderServicesSLBean:updatePrice: "+
                       "the price order could not be updated");
}
pstmt.close();

conn.close();
pizzaServices.remove();
}
```

The code of this method finishes with a careful handling of possible errors:

```
catch (Exception e) {
  System.err.println(e);
  try {
    if (pizzaServices != null) pizzaServices.remove();
  } catch(Exception ex) {
    throw new P2GException(ex.toString());
  }
  try {
    conn.close();
  } catch(SQLException se) {
    throw new P2GException(se.toString());
  }
}

try {
  price = Util.format(price);
} catch(ParseException pe) {
  throw new P2GException(Util.getStackTraceAsString(pe));
}

return price;
}
```

The `deliverOrder()` method is used to assemble the final order and update the inventory:

```
/**
 * This method delivers an order.
 * The order is specified by its order number (primary key).
 * The method updates the inventory in the assigned outlet.
 */
public String deliverOrder(long orderNum)
   throws P2GException {

   String res = "The order could not be delivered";
   Connection conn = null;

   try {
      PreparedStatement pstmt = null;
      PreparedStatement pstmt2 = null;
      PreparedStatement pstmt3 = null;
      String select = "";
      String select2 = "";
      String select3 = "";
      ResultSet resultSet = null;
      ResultSet resultSet2 = null;
      long outletNum = 0;

      conn = DriverManager.getConnection("jdbc:weblogic:jts:p2gPool");
```

It starts by finding the outlet for the order in the database:

```
      select = "select or_o_outlet_code from order_master " +
               " where or_number = ?";
      pstmt = conn.prepareStatement(select);
      pstmt.setLong(1, orderNum);
      resultSet = pstmt.executeQuery();
      if (resultSet.next()) {
         outletNum = resultSet.getLong("or_o_outlet_code");
      } else {
         throw new Exception("<E> OrderServicesSLBean:deliverOrder: "+
                             "the order could not be found");
      }
      resultSet.close();
      pstmt.close();
```

It then sets the necessary prepared statements to handle the inventory:

```
      select = "select od_p_name, od_p_size, od_quantity, od_dough " +
               "from order_detail where od_or_number = ?";
      select2 = "select u_i_name, u_units " +
                "from units where u_p_name = ? and u_p_size = ?";
      select3 = "update existence set e_u_units = e_u_units - ? " +
                "where ((e_o_outlet_code = ?) and (e_i_name = ?))";

      pstmt = conn.prepareStatement(select);
      pstmt.setLong(1, orderNum);
      resultSet = pstmt.executeQuery();
```

Now, for every item in the order it updates the inventory for the specific outlet, based on the ingredient units that are defined in the corresponding table:

```
while (resultSet.next()) {
  pstmt2 = conn.prepareStatement(select2);
  pstmt2.setString(1, resultSet.getString("od_p_name"));
  pstmt2.setString(2, resultSet.getString("od_p_size"));
  resultSet2 = pstmt2.executeQuery();
  float q = 0.0f;
  while (resultSet2.next()) {
    q = resultSet.getInt("od_quantity") *
        resultSet2.getFloat("u_units");
    pstmt3 = conn.prepareStatement(select3);
    pstmt3.setFloat(1, q);
    pstmt3.setLong(2, outletNum);
    pstmt3.setString(3, resultSet2.getString("u_i_name"));
    pstmt3.execute();
    int n = pstmt3.getUpdateCount();
    if (n != 1) {
      throw new Exception("<E> OrderServicesSLBean:deliverOrder: "+
                "the ingredients inventory could not be updated");
    }
    pstmt3.close();
  }
  resultSet2.close();
  pstmt2.close();

  // Update dough quantities
  pstmt2 = conn.prepareStatement("select d_units from dough " +
          "where d_name = ? and d_p_size = ?");
  pstmt2.setString(1, resultSet.getString("od_dough"));
  pstmt2.setString(2, resultSet.getString("od_p_size"));
  resultSet2 = pstmt2.executeQuery();
  if (resultSet2.next()) {
    q = resultSet.getInt("od_quantity") *
        resultSet2.getFloat("d_units");
    pstmt3 = conn.prepareStatement(select3);
    pstmt3.setFloat(1, q);
    pstmt3.setLong(2, outletNum);
    pstmt3.setString(3, "Dough");
    pstmt3.execute();
    int n = pstmt3.getUpdateCount();
    if (n != 1) {
      throw new Exception("<E> OrderServicesSLBean:deliverOrder: " +
                "the dough inventory could not be updated");
    }
    pstmt3.close();
  } else {
    throw new Exception("<E> OrderServicesSLBean:deliverOrder: " +
                "the units could not be found");
  }
  resultSet2.close();
  pstmt2.close();
}
resultSet.close();
pstmt.close();
```

It then marks the order as delivered even though this has not happened yet. For all practical purposes, it has been delivered, as the inventory has been updated to reflect the fact that the ingredients necessary to make the pizza have been used.

```
        select = "update order_master set or_status = 'Delivered' " +
                 " where or_number = ?";
        pstmt = conn.prepareStatement(select);
        pstmt.setLong(1, orderNum);
        int n = pstmt.executeUpdate();
        if (n != 1) {
           throw new Exception("<E> OrderServicesSLBean:deliverOrder: " +
                               "the status order could not be updated");
        }
        pstmt.close();
        conn.close();

        res = "ok";
    } catch (Exception e) {
        System.err.println(e);
        try {
           conn.close();
        } catch(SQLException se) {
           throw new P2GException(se.toString());
        }
    }

    return res;
}
```

The bean finishes by defining container contract methods just as the `PizzaServicesSL` EJB does.

Outlet Services

By now you should be pretty familiar with the drill. The home interface of the `OutletServicesSL` bean is very similar to the previous ones:

```
package jsw.c04a;

import javax.ejb.*;
import java.rmi.RemoteException;

/**
 * This is the Home Interface for the Stateless Session EJB
 * <tt>OutletServicesSL</tt>.
 *
 * @see     jsw.c04a.OutletServicesSL
 * @see     jsw.c04a.OutletServicesSLBean
 */
public interface OutletServicesSLHome extends EJBHome {

   /**
    * Creates a Stateless Session EJB to access to outlet services.
    */
   public OutletServicesSL create()
      throws CreateException, RemoteException;

}
```

The same goes for the remote interface, which only includes one method:

```
package jsw.c04a;

import javax.ejb.*;
import java.rmi.RemoteException;

/**
 * This is the Remote Interface for the Stateless Session EJB
 * <tt>OutletServicesSL</tt>.
 *
 * @see       jsw.c04a.OutletServicesSLHome
 * @see       jsw.c04a.OutletServicesSLBean
 */
public interface OutletServicesSL extends EJBObject {

  /**
   * This method assigns an outlet to an order.
   * The assignment is based on the postal code and city.
   * @param orderNum the order identifier
   * @returns the outlet identifier assigned to the order
   */
  public long assignOutlet(long orderNum)
    throws RemoteException, P2GException;

}
```

The actual implementation of the bean is responsible for assigning an outlet to an order. The EJB method replaces the stored procedure `assignOutlet`. It is interesting to note the fact that this bean does not update the database. This continues to be the responsibility of the `OrderMaintenanceS` servlet, which updates the database with the values provided by this bean.

In a fully developed system, however, servlets would not usually update the database. This would be the responsibility of the entity bean, which will be covered more fully in Chapter 5.

A Stateless Session Bean's Lifecycle

Before we look at the way that these beans are called by a client, let us examine the lifecycle of a stateless session bean in the WebLogic container.

The WebLogic server has a pool of free stateless session beans. The beans in the free pool are not bound to any client instance. When a client calls a method on a stateless session bean, the container obtains an instance from the free pool and executes the method. When the method is completed, the bean is unbound and placed back in the free pool. This design ensures a high performance for the execution of these beans. This lifecycle is presented above opposite.

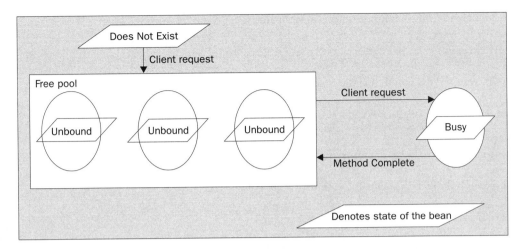

You can prime the free pool by specifying that the container populate the pool at startup, using the `initial-beans-in-free-pool` element in the deployment descriptor. By default, the maximum size of the pool is limited by the available memory. You can specify the maximum size, in terms of bean instances, by setting the `max-beans-in-free-pool` tag.

If all the beans available are busy and `max-beans-in-free-pool` has been reached, new requests will be blocked until a bean is available. If a blocked request is involved in a transaction and it times out, a remote exception is thrown by the container and communicated back to the client. The same exception will be thrown after five minutes of waiting if the blocked request is not part of a transaction.

Client to a Session Bean

To recap, for a client to use an EJB, the following steps must be performed:

❑   Locate the home interface

❑   Gain access to the bean (by calling `create()` on the home interface, and storing the handle returned)

❑   Call the bean methods

❑   Discard the bean handle (by calling the bean's `remove()` method)

To locate the home interface in WebLogic, JNDI is used as follows. First you get the JNDI naming context:

```
Context context = new InitialContext();
```

If the initial context is created without parameters, it will use the current environment properties. This usually means that the JNDI context resides in the server in which the code is running.

Then you use the context to look up the EJB home interface for the bean:

```
PizzaServicesSLHome pizzaServicesHome =
        (PizzaServicesSLHome)context.lookup("jsw.c04a.PizzaServices");
```

Next, you create (bind to) an instance of the bean:

```
pizzaServices = pizzaServicesHome.create();
```

Now that you have a handle for the bean, you can use it as required, for example:

```
price += resultSet.getInt("od_quantity") *
        pizzaServices.getPrice(pizza,
                              System.getProperty("jsw.location", "US"),
        date, resultSet.getString("od_dough"));
```

Once you are done with the bean, you just remove it:

```
pizzaServices.remove();
```

This code is taken from the `OrderServicesSL` bean's `updatePrice()` method, which uses the `PizzaServicesSL` bean.

The Stateless Front End

The front end created in Chapter 3 was designed to use the Oracle stored procedures, so it will have to be changed to accommodate the use of the stateless session beans. In principle this is relatively simple, as all that has to be done is replace the calls to the stored procedures with calls to the EJBs. The reality, though, is that the lifecycle of the bean has to be considered, specifically the question of when to create the bean. This is the subject of some debate between Mrs Chief Architect and Mr Senior Developer.

Mrs Chief Architect is of the opinion that the beans that will be used at various times in a session should be created at the start of that session, the handles stored as session variables, and these used to bind bean instances for method calls.

Mr Senior Developer, who has been looking at the inner workings of WebLogic, thinks that if he primes the free pool and acquires a bean instance for each method, it will be faster. His argument is based on the way WebLogic handles the stateless session beans, using the free pool. Using a smart twist on his argument, Mrs Chief Architect counters that if the internals of WebLogic are so efficient, it can only increase the application's efficiency to create the beans once at the beginning, and keep the handle.

The other point of contention is the removal of beans. Mr Senior Developer believes that, since the beans are not really being removed by the container, just recycled into the free pool, it is not necessary to code explicit `remove()` statements.

The argument is finally won by Mrs Chief Architect. Rather than program to the specific characteristics of an EJB container, which could change in future versions, she advocated the idea of doing things cleanly. The beans that will be used quite often will be created once at the beginning, whereas the beans used only occasionally will be created as required. These latter beans will also be removed after each use or when an error occurs. For this application, `PizzaServicesSL` and `OrderServicesSL` are the beans that will be created once at the beginning. The `OutletServicesSL` bean will be created just before it is used, which only happens once per order.

The only issue with this approach is when to 'remove' the beans that were created at the beginning. Remember that calling `remove()` just invalidates the handle, but won't destroy the stateless session bean instance – the free pool size is controlled by the container.

The logical answer is to remove them at the end, but there is really no end defined in this existing application. The solution here is to create a logout function, where the EJBs can be removed and other housekeeping duties performed. Mr Senior Developer decides to create a JSP page that will perform this function. The `Logout.jsp` page can be called from the main menu. The code looks like the following:

```
<%@ page import="java.util.*,java.sql.*,javax.naming.*"%>

<html>
<head>
<title>Pizza2Go logout</title>
<meta http-equiv="Content-Type" content="text/html; charset=iso-8859-1">
</head>

<body bgcolor="#FFFFFF">
<h1><center>Pizza2Go</center></h1>
<hr>

<%
  PizzaServicesSL pizzaServices =
                 (PizzaServicesSL) session.getAttribute("pizzaServices");
  if (pizzaServices != null) {
    try {
      pizzaServices.remove();
      session.removeAttribute("pizzaServices");
    } catch(Exception e) {
      out.println(Util.getStackTraceAsString(e));
      System.err.println(e);
    }
  }
  OrderServicesSL orderServices =
                 (OrderServicesSL) session.getAttribute("orderServices");
  if (orderServices != null) {
    try {
      orderServices.remove();
      session.removeAttribute("orderServices");
    } catch(Exception e) {
      out.println(Util.getStackTraceAsString(e));
      System.err.println(e);
    }
  }
  session.invalidate();
%>

<center>Session successfully ended</center>

<p>
<table align="center" border="1" cellspacing="0" cellpadding="1">
<tr><th><a href="index.jsp">Login</a></th></tr>
</table>
</p>

</body>
</html>
```

Here the handles to the `PizzaServiceSL` and `OrderServicesSL` beans are retrieved, and if they're not null, the `remove()` method is called on them. Notice also the use of the `session.invalidate()` method to invalidate the HTTP session and unbind all the objects bound to it.

Now, let us have a look in more detail at how the Wonder Troops coded the changes to the front end to handle the new stateless session beans.

Before moving on, let's summarize the outcome of the discussion:

❏ Pre-initialization of the free pool for stateless session beans is a WebLogic server feature, whereas creating beans for each client session is a more generic version. The Wonder Troops chose the latter option.

❏ When you call `create()` on a stateless session bean, the container looks for a matching and free bean instance in the free pool, and binds it if it can. If not, and the number of bean instances is within the maximum allowed, it'll create one.

❏ Searching for a bean and storing the handle for as long as you need is more efficient than searching and acquiring a handle just when you need it. Unlike JDBC pools, where the connection is direct, the indirect connection with the session bean means that you can hold onto the handle.

The limits on the time for which you can hold the handle are set by the timeouts for the EJB instance in the container, and for the session variable.

All object references and handles to the bean instances become invalid on the container timeout and if a client attempts to invoke a method on the bean, the container will throw the `java.rmi.NoSuchObjectException` to the client. You can serialize the handle to a session bean to some store, but you must make sure that the session object can last that long as well.

The timeout of the session variable won't cause a call to `remove()` on the bean instance, it'll just remove the handle. Currently there's no callback code for a session being invalidated, but it's part of the Servlet 2.3 specification.

❏ The container unbinds the stateless session bean between each method call, so that it can make the best use of the bean instances.

Changes to the JavaServer Pages

The biggest change is to `index.jsp`, the main page of the application. The first change is to the initial import declaration, which now includes the additional Java libraries.

```
<%@ page session="true"
    import="java.util.*,java.sql.*,javax.naming.*" %>
```

The rest of the code remains the same, except that the code to create the beans is added at the end. First `PizzaServicesSL` is created and the handle stored as a session value. This is done so that the bean can be used all through the session:

```
    PizzaServicesSL pizzaServices =
                (PizzaServicesSL) session.getAttribute("pizzaServices");
    if (pizzaServices == null) {
      try {
        Context ctx = Util.getInitialContext();
        PizzaServicesSLHome pizzaServicesHome =
              (PizzaServicesSLHome) ctx.lookup("jsw.c04a.PizzaServicesSL");
        pizzaServices = pizzaServicesHome.create();
        session.setAttribute("pizzaServices", pizzaServices);
      } catch(Exception e) {
        System.err.println(e);
      }
    }
```

Then the `OrderServicesSL` bean is created and the handle is also placed in the session:

```
    OrderServicesSL orderServices =
                (OrderServicesSL) session.getAttribute("orderServices");
    if (orderServices == null) {
      try {
        Context ctx = Util.getInitialContext();
        OrderServicesSLHome orderServicesHome =
              (OrderServicesSLHome) ctx.lookup("jsw.c04a.OrderServicesSL");
        orderServices = orderServicesHome.create();
        session.setAttribute("orderServices", orderServices);
      } catch(Exception e) {
        System.err.println(e);
      }
    }
    //c04a<--
```

The next JSP page that is changed is `Specials.jsp`. This page is now very simple as the actual process of obtaining the special of the day is a method in the `PizzaServicesSL` bean. All the JDBC access code has been replaced by the following code:

```
<jsp:useBean id="offer" class="jsw.c04a.Offer" scope="session"/>

<% if (offer.getOf_code() > 0) {
  String pizzaName = offer.getOf_pizza().getP_name();
  String pizzaSize = offer.getOf_pizza().getP_size();
%>
<form method="post" action="OrderMaintenanceS" name="">
  <table width="100%" align="center">
    <tr align="center">
      <td>
        <b>Special of the day:</b> Discount of
          <jsp:getProperty name="offer" property="of_discount"/>%
        on <%= pizzaName %> <%= pizzaSize %>
          <jsp:getProperty name="offer" property="of_od_dough"/>!!!
        <input type="hidden" name="Pizza" value="<%= pizzaName %>">
        <input type="hidden" name="Size" value="<%= pizzaSize %>">
        <input type="hidden" name="Dough" value="
          <jsp:getProperty name="offer" property="of_od_dough"/>">
        <input type="hidden" name="Quantity" value="1">
        <input type="submit" name="command" value="Add">
      </td>
    </tr>
  </table>
</form>
<%} else {%> <center>No Specials Today</center> <%}%>
```

131

The `offer` bean is part of the session, and has been initialized in the `service()` method of the `OrderMaintenanceS` servlet. We'll see the code for this in the next section.

Note that the way of referencing the information changes from:

```
<input type="hidden" name="Dough" value="<%= pizzaDough %>">
```

to using the `offer` JavaBean which contains all the corresponding information of the special:

```
<input type="hidden" name="Dough" value="
    <jsp:getProperty name="offer" property="of_od_dough"/>">
```

The other JSP page that is modified is `PizzaList.jsp`. Here all the database access to obtain the prices of the pizzas is replaced by calls to the `PizzaServicesSL` bean and therefore the way that the actual data is referred to changes. The following code fragment illustrates the original way things were done in Chapter 3:

```
select = "select p_base_price from pizza " +
    "where p_name = ? order by p_size desc";
pstmt = conn.prepareStatement(select);
pstmt.setString(1, sPName);
resultSetPrice = pstmt.executeQuery();

resultSetPrice.next();
out.println("<td>" + "$" +
    (conversionFactor * resultSetPrice.getFloat("p_base_price"))+
    "</td>");
resultSetPrice.next();
out.println("<td>" + "$" +
    (conversionFactor * resultSetPrice.getFloat("p_base_price"))+
    "</td>");
resultSetPrice.next();
out.println("<td>" + "$" +
    (conversionFactor * resultSetPrice.getFloat("p_base_price"))+
    "</td>");
out.println("</tr>");
resultSetPrice.close();
pstmt.close();
conn.close();
```

In contrast, here's how the session bean is used:

```
PizzaServicesSL pizzaServices =
            (PizzaServicesSL)session.getAttribute("pizzaServices");
...
pizza.setP_name(sPName);

pizza.setP_size("Small");
%><td align="right">$<%= pizzaServices.getPrice(pizza) %></td><%
pizza.setP_size("Medium");
%><td align="right">$<%= pizzaServices.getPrice(pizza) %></td><%
pizza.setP_size("Large");
%><td align="right">$<%= pizzaServices.getPrice(pizza) %></td><%
```

Things ends up being a lot simpler in the front end as all the data access and calculations are done in the `PizzaServicesSL` bean.

Changes to Servlets

The only servlet that has changed is OrderMaintenanceS.java. As we saw earlier, the developers decided to move the functionality of the special of the day to the PizzaServicesSL bean, therefore the EJB has to be accessed to obtain the information, which is then placed in the servlet session. The following fragment of code is from the end of the service() method:

```
try {
  if (sURL.equals("/OrderForm.jsp")) {
    HttpSession session = req.getSession(true);
    Offer offer = (Offer)session.getAttribute("offer");
    if (offer == null) {
      PizzaServicesSL pizzaServices =
                (PizzaServicesSL)session.getAttribute("pizzaServices");
      if (pizzaServices == null) {
        try {
          Context ctx = Util.getInitialContext();
          PizzaServicesSLHome pizzaServicesHome =
          (PizzaServicesSLHome)ctx.lookup("jsw.c04a.PizzaServicesSL");
          pizzaServices = pizzaServicesHome.create();
          session.setAttribute("pizzaServices", pizzaServices);
        } catch(Exception e) {
          System.err.println(e);
        }
      }
      offer = pizzaServices.getSpecial(new java.util.Date());
      if (offer != null)
        session.setAttribute("offer", offer);
    }
  }
  res.sendRedirect(sURL);
} catch(Exception e) {
  System.err.println("Exception: OrderMaintenanceS.service: " + e);
}
```

The other change that was made is to the updateOrder() method. Whereas before it called the Oracle PL/SQL stored procedure to obtain the outlet where the order was going to be fulfilled, it now calls the OutletServicesSL bean. As discussed earlier, this bean is created, used, and then removed as and when it is needed, as can be seen in this fragment of code:

```
if (order.getOr_delivery().equals("Address")) {
  long outletNum = 0;
  OutletServicesSL outletServices = null;
  try {
    Context ctx = Util.getInitialContext();
    OutletServicesSLHome outletServicesHome =
      (OutletServicesSLHome) ctx.lookup("jsw.c04a.OutletServicesSL");
    outletServices = outletServicesHome.create();
    outletNum = outletServices.assignOutlet(order.getOr_number());
    outletServices.remove();
    order.setOr_o_outlet_code(outletNum);
    session.setAttribute("order", order);
  } catch(Exception e) {
    System.err.println(e);
  }
}
```

The other methods modified are deliverOrder() and updatePrice(), where the JDBC call for execution of a stored procedure is replaced by calls to the OrderServicesSL bean.

Additions

To make life a little easier while developing, a few classes have been added. These classes are Util, P2GException, and Offer. They include a number of methods such as getInitialContext(), which will get a specific initial context with or without a parameter.

Putting It All Together

Let us go over the checklist of what the Wonder Troops have done so far:

- ❏ Define the new architecture of the application
- ❏ Define the home interfaces of the beans
- ❏ Define the remote interfaces
- ❏ Implement the beans
- ❏ Modify the front end

The next steps needed to put this application together are:

- ❏ Compile the EJB classes
- ❏ Create the deployment descriptors for the beans
- ❏ Create the EJB JAR files
- ❏ Deploy the JAR files
- ❏ Run the application

It's time to go through these steps in more detail.

Compiling the EJB Classes

As in the previous chapter, a GNU make compliant makefile is created to compile and deploy all the application code.

After modifying these properties, the server can be started following these steps:

1. Start a command-line session

2. Change to directory c:\wlsbook

3. Execute the environment setup script setEnv.cmd specifying the chapter number (4a)

```
C:\> cd \wlsbook
C:\wlsbook> setenv 4a
------------------------------------------------------------
Setting environment for chapter 4a
------------------------------------------------------------
Current settings:
      Java Home = c:\jdk1.3
   WebLogic Home = c:\weblogic
    Project Home = c:\wlsbook
```

```
     CLASSPATH =
c:\weblogic\lib\weblogic510sp5boot.jar;c:\weblogic\classes\boot;c:\weblogic\lib\we
blogic510sp5.jar;c:\weblogic\license;c:\weblogic\classes;c:\weblogic\lib\weblogica
ux.jar;c:\wlsbook\srv\c04a-srv\serverclasses
```

4. Change to directory c:\wlsbook\src\c04a. Execute the make command with the clean parameter:

```
C:\wlsbook> cd src\c04a
C:\wlsbook\src\c04a> make clean
if exist c:\wlsbook\src\c04a\serverclasses\jsw rd /S /Q
c:\wlsbook\src\c04a\serverclasses\jsw
if exist c:\wlsbook\src\c04a\servletclasses\jsw rd /S /Q
c:\wlsbook\src\c04a\servletclasses\jsw
...
```

5. This will remove previously generated code and temporary files. Execute the make command without parameters to build all of the application:

```
C:\wlsbook\src\c04a> make
building common...
c:\jdk1.3\bin\javac.exe -classpath c:\weblogic\lib\weblogic510sp5boot.jar;c:\
weblogic\classes\boot;c:\weblogic\lib\weblogic510sp5.jar;c:\weblogic\license;c:\we
blogic\classes;c:\weblogic\lib\weblogicaux.jar -d serverclasses
c:\wlsbook\src\c04a\java\jsw\c04a\Customer.java
c:\wlsbook\src\c04a\java\jsw\c04a\Outlet.java
c:\wlsbook\src\c04a\java\jsw\c04a\Pizza.java c:\wlsbook\src\c04a\jav
a\jsw\c04a\Offer.java c:\wlsbook\src\c04a\java\jsw\c04a\Existence.java
c:\wlsbook\src\c04a\java\jsw\c04a\OrderMaster.java
c:\wlsbook\src\c04a\java\jsw\c04a\OrderDetail.java
c:\wlsbook\src\c04a\java\jsw\c04a\Util.java
c:\wlsbook\src\c04a\java\jsw\c04a\P2GException.java
building PizzaServicesSL...
...
```

6. Finally, copy the application from the src directory to the srv directory by again executing make with the deploy target:

```
C:\wlsbook\src\c04a> make deploy
deploying JSPs...
xcopy /E c:\wlsbook\src\c04a\jsp\\*.jsp c:\wlsbook\srv\c04a-srv\public_html
C:\wlsbook\src\c04a\jsp\CustomerForm.jsp
...
14 File(s) copied
xcopy /E c:\wlsbook\src\c04a\jsp\\*.html
c:\wlsbook\srv\c04a-srv\public_html
C:\wlsbook\src\c04a\jsp\menu.html
1 File(s) copied
deploying...
xcopy /E c:\wlsbook\src\c04a\serverclasses\\*.class
c:\wlsbook\srv\c04a-srv\serverclasses
C:\wlsbook\src\c04a\serverclasses\jsw\c04a\Customer.class
...
```

```
9 File(s) copied
xcopy /E c:\wlsbook\src\c04a\servletclasses\\*.class
c:\wlsbook\srv\c04a-srv\servletclasses
C:\wlsbook\src\c04a\servletclasses\jsw\c04a\CustomerListS.class
...
5 File(s) copied
cold deploy of ejbs
copy c:\wlsbook\src\c04a\ejb\PizzaServicesSL\PizzaServicesSLBean.jar
c:\wlsbook\srv\c04a-srv\ejb
        1 file(s) copied.
copy c:\wlsbook\src\c04a\ejb\OrderServicesSL\OrderServicesSLBean.jar
c:\wlsbook\srv\c04a-srv\ejb
        1 file(s) copied.
copy c:\wlsbook\src\c04a\ejb\OutletServicesSL\OutletServicesSLBean.jar
c:\wlsbook\srv\c04a-srv\ejb
        1 file(s) copied.
```

The Deployment Descriptor

The **deployment descriptor** allows the person responsible for the deployer role of the application to define parameters that control the execution of the EJBs without having to touch the beans at all – no delving in the Java files and recompilation. Two XML files compose the deployment descriptor for each EJB in Chapter 4; they are `ejb-jar.xml` and `weblogic-ejb-jar.xml`. Here's a quick list of the kinds of parameters:

❑   Transaction attributes, where the level of transaction support and isolation can be defined

❑   Security, which can be used to define the access control and identification attributes

❑   Developer-defined properties

❑   Interface details and class names

WebLogic provides a tool to create and maintain deployment descriptors. It is called the EJB Deployer Tool. We will use this tool to create the deployment descriptor for this chapter's beans. The EJB Deployer Tool can be started from the WebLogic program group in the Windows start menu or by typing the following command:

```
C:\wlsbook\src\c04a> java weblogic.EJBDeployerTool
```

The Deployer Tool is shown in the following screenshot:

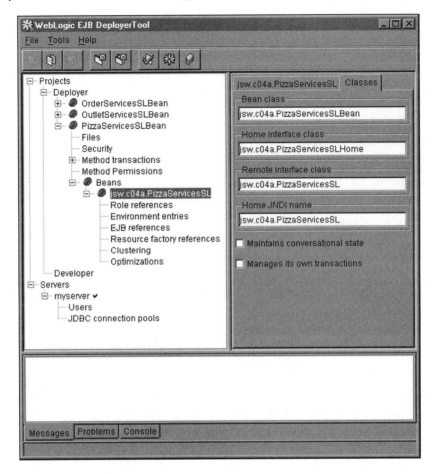

The deployment process can also be done by hand editing the XML deployment descriptors and running the command line program `weblogic.ejbc`. The makefile target for deploying the PizzaServicesSL EJB shows this program in action:

```
###
### PizzaServicesSL EJB
###
PIZZASRV_J = \
     $(P_SRC)\java\$(P_PKG)\PizzaServicesSL.java \
     $(P_SRC)\java\$(P_PKG)\PizzaServicesSLHome.java \
     $(P_SRC)\java\$(P_PKG)\PizzaServicesSLBean.java

PIZZASRV_C = \
     $(P_SRC)\ejb\PizzaServicesSL\$(P_PKG)\PizzaServicesSL.class \
     $(P_SRC)\ejb\PizzaServicesSL\$(P_PKG)\PizzaServicesSLHome.class \
     $(P_SRC)\ejb\PizzaServicesSL\$(P_PKG)\PizzaServicesSLBean.class \
     $(PIZZASRV_R)

PIZZASRV_R = $(P_SRC)\ejb\PizzaServicesSL\PizzaServicesSLBean.jar
```

```
PizzaServicesSL: common $(PIZZASRV_C)

$(PIZZASRV_C): $(PIZZASRV_J)
    @echo building PizzaServicesSL...
    -if exist ejb\PizzaServicesSL rmdir /S /Q ejb\PizzaServicesSL
    mkdir ejb\PizzaServicesSL
    $(J_JC) -deprecation -classpath $(CLASSPATH);serverclasses \
           -d ejb\PizzaServicesSL $(PIZZASRV_J)
    -if exist jartemp rmdir /S /Q jartemp
    mkdir jartemp
    mkdir jartemp\META-INF
    mkdir jartemp\$(P_PKG)
    copy DD\PizzaServicesSL\*.xml jartemp\META-INF
    copy ejb\PizzaServicesSL\$(P_PKG)\*.class jartemp\$(P_PKG)
    cd jartemp && $(J_B)\jar cvf PizzaServicesSLBean.jar META-INF \
      $(P_PKG) $(J_J) \
      -classpath $(CLASSPATH);ejb\PizzaServicesSL;serverclasses \
      weblogic.ejbc \
      -keepgenerated jartemp\PizzaServicesSLBean.jar \
     ejb\PizzaServicesSL\PizzaServicesSLBean.jar
```

The deployment descriptors are under the directory `c:\wlsbook\src\c04a\DD` organized by EJB name. For every bean there are two XML deployment descriptors, the `ejb-jar.xml` file and the `weblogic-ejb-jar.xml`.

Let us have a look at both descriptors for the `PizzaServicesSL` bean, starting with the `ejb-jar.xml`:

```xml
<?xml version="1.0"?>

<!DOCTYPE ejb-jar PUBLIC '-//Sun Microsystems, Inc.//DTD Enterprise JavaBeans
1.1//EN' 'http://java.sun.com/j2ee/dtds/ejb-jar_1_1.dtd'>

<ejb-jar>
  <enterprise-beans>
    <session>
      <ejb-name>jsw.c04a.PizzaServicesSL</ejb-name>
      <home>jsw.c04a.PizzaServicesSLHome</home>
      <remote>jsw.c04a.PizzaServicesSL</remote>
      <ejb-class>jsw.c04a.PizzaServicesSLBean</ejb-class>
      <session-type>Stateless</session-type>
      <transaction-type>Container</transaction-type>
    </session>
  </enterprise-beans>
  <assembly-descriptor>
    <container-transaction>
      <method>
        <ejb-name>jsw.c04a.PizzaServicesSL</ejb-name>
        <method-intf>Remote</method-intf>
        <method-name>*</method-name>
      </method>
      <trans-attribute>Required</trans-attribute>
    </container-transaction>
  </assembly-descriptor>
</ejb-jar>
```

And now let us have a look at the `weblogic-ejb-jar.xml`, which looks after WebLogic-specific configuration:

```xml
<?xml version="1.0"?>

<!DOCTYPE weblogic-ejb-jar PUBLIC '-//BEA Systems, Inc.//DTD WebLogic 5.1.0
EJB//EN' 'http://www.bea.com/servers/wls510/dtd/weblogic-ejb-jar.dtd'>

<weblogic-ejb-jar>
  <weblogic-enterprise-bean>
    <ejb-name>jsw.c04a.PizzaServicesSL</ejb-name>
    <caching-descriptor>
      <max-beans-in-free-pool>100</max-beans-in-free-pool>
    </caching-descriptor>
    <jndi-name>jsw.c04a.PizzaServicesSL</jndi-name>
  </weblogic-enterprise-bean>
</weblogic-ejb-jar>
```

If the EJB provider does not specify a transaction attribute in the `ejb-jar.xml` file, WebLogic Server uses `Supports` by default. We use `Required` here because we are accessing the database and we want that to be transactional. Not specifying a transaction can increase your server's performance, but make sure that you fully understand what you are doing when you specify different transactional attributes.

Hot Deployment

The WebLogic server has a feature known as 'hot deployment', which is its ability to dynamically deploy and remove EJBs from the server, without restarting that server, using the EJB Deployer Tool or a command line program.

You have to specify in the `weblogic.properties` file for c04a which beans can be redeployed as follows:

```
weblogic.ejb.deploy=\
    c:/wlsbook/srv/c04a-srv/ejb/PizzaServicesSLBean.jar,\
    c:/wlsbook/srv/c04a-srv/ejb/OrderServicesSLBean.jar,\
    c:/wlsbook/srv/c04a-srv/ejb/OutletServicesSLBean.jar
```

The command line Java program for hot deploy, `weblogic.deploy`, is very convenient while the EJB is being developed, as it can be tested without restarting the server. This is the approach taken in the `redeploy` target of the makefile:

```
redeploy: deploy
        @echo redeploying...
        $(J_J) -classpath $(CLASSPATH) weblogic.deploy -host localhost \
            -port 7001 -debug update weblogic \
                c:/wlsbook/srv/$(P_VER)-srv/ejb/PizzaServicesSLBean.jar
        $(J_J) -classpath $(CLASSPATH) weblogic.deploy -host localhost \
            -port 7001 -debug update weblogic \
                c:/wlsbook/srv/$(P_VER)-srv/ejb/OrderServicesSLBean.jar
        $(J_J) -classpath $(CLASSPATH) weblogic.deploy -host localhost \
            -port 7001 -debug update weblogic \
                c:/wlsbook/srv/$(P_VER)-srv/ejb/OutletServicesSLBean.jar
```

139

Running the Application

Now that we have completed all the steps to assemble the application, the execution is very simple. Start the server as you did in Chapter 3, but now setting the environment to 4a. Start your browser and point it to http://localhost:7001. It should produce as screen similar to the following screenshot, with the new Logout option the only clue to the changes we've made:

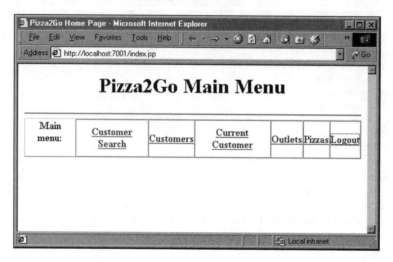

Stateful Session Pizzas

The experiment with the stateless beans was successful enough for the Wonder Troops to want to try the next stage. So far the original Oracle application, the change to the front end in Chapter 3, and the experiment with stateless beans have had a common architecture. The pizza order was built by keeping every item (the order detail) in the database. This means that every time an item was added or some change made to the order, a JDBC call was made to keep the 'state' of the order in the database.

The idea in this section is to use a stateful session bean to keep the items of the order in memory, instead of keeping them in the database. In comparison to the application that just uses stateless beans, Mr Senior Developer has high expectations that keeping the order detail as the state of the bean will improve performance by minimizing the number of database accesses. In Chapter 11, when the Wonder Troops stress test the application, they will be able to compare the performance of this version with the previous one.

For this next stage, a big part of the functionality that lives in the `OrderMaintenanceS` servlet is moved into this new stateful bean. The stateless session beans that were created in the previous section are still used, as their services are still required.

The order will be stored in the database only when the **deliver** or the **store** button has been selected. At this moment the database will also update the inventory and send the fax to the corresponding outlet. A new option will also be added to the main menu, **current order**, which will take the user to the order being created at the moment. The operation is easy, as the order is just the state of the session bean. Otherwise, if there is no current order it will take the user to **current customer** where a new order can be started by selecting **add order**. If there is no current customer the option will send the user to **search customer**. A **store** option has also been added so that an order contained in the bean can be committed to the database.

The changes in the Intranet web site created by adding this stateful session bean are reflected in the following figure:

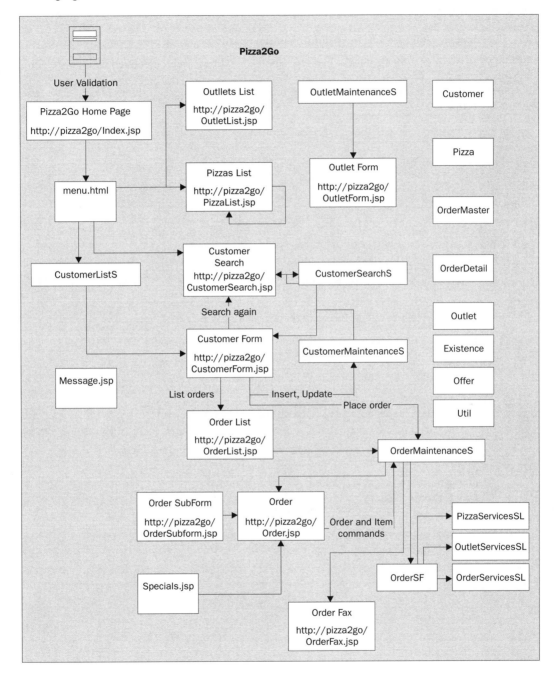

The Stateful Order

Let us start by writing the home interface of the OrderSF bean. This interface has two create() methods:

❑ The first signature creates the bean to handle a brand new order for a customer

❑ The second signature creates the bean to handle an existing order, identified by an order number

This is pretty smart, as it allows the usage of the bean at different stages of the application for essentially the same operations.

```java
package jsw.c04b;

import javax.ejb.*;
import java.rmi.RemoteException;

/**
 * This is the Home Interface for the Stateful Session EJB
 * <tt>OrderSF</tt>.
 *
 * @see        jsw.c04b.OrderSF
 * @see        jsw.c04b.OrderSFBean
 */
public interface OrderSFHome extends EJBHome {

    /**
     * Creates a Stateful Session EJB to manage a new order.
     *
     * @param      customer the customer this order belongs to.
     * @return     the created order.
     * @exception P2GException
     *                 if the customer doesn't exist.
     */
    OrderSF create(Customer customer)
      throws CreateException, RemoteException, P2GException;

    /**
     * Creates a Stateful Session EJB to manage an existing order.
     *
     * @param      orderNum the primary key of the existing order.
     * @return     the created order.
     * @exception P2GException
     *                 if the order doesn't exist.
     */
    OrderSF create(long orderNum)
      throws CreateException, RemoteException, P2GException;

}
```

The remote interface defines a large number of methods that are available in the implementation of the bean:

```
package jsw.c04b;

import javax.ejb.*;
import java.rmi.RemoteException;
import java.util.Vector;

/**
 * This is the remote interface for the Stateful Session EJB
 * <tt>OrderSF</tt>.
 * Remote Interface for the Stateful Session EJB "Order".
 *
 * @see      jsw.c04b.OrderSFHome
 * @see      jsw.c04b.OrderSFBean
 */
public interface OrderSF extends EJBObject {

  /**
   * Returns this order's customer.
   *
   * @return    the customer.
   */
  public Customer getCustomer()
    throws RemoteException;

  /**
   * Returns this order's OrderMaster information.
   *
   * @return    the OrderMaster.
   */
  public OrderMaster getOrderMaster()
    throws RemoteException;

  /**
   * Returns all the order details included in the order.
   *
   * @return    a Vector with all the order details.
   */
  public Vector getOrderDetail()
    throws RemoteException;

  /**
   * This method sets the outlet code the customer will
   * get the order from. It automatically sets the delivery mode
   * to "Outlet".
   *
   * @exception P2GException
   *                if the status order is already delivered.
   */
  public void setOutlet(long outletNum)
    throws RemoteException, P2GException;
```

```
/**
 * This method sets the delivery mode to the value
 * "Outlet" or "Address", specified in its parameter.
 * If the delivery mode is "Outlet", the method
 * <tt>setOutlet</tt> must be called to set the
 * desired outlet.
 *
 * @param       deliveryMode: "Outlet" or "Address".
 * @exception P2GException
 *                 if the status order is already delivered.
 */
public void setDelivery(String deliveryMode)
  throws RemoteException, P2GException;

/**
 * Updates the order remarks.
 *
 * @param       remaks the new remarks.
 * @exception P2GException
 *                 if the status order is already delivered.
 */
public void setRemarks(String remarks)
  throws RemoteException, P2GException;

/**
 * Stores the order in the database.
 * It stores the order master and all the order details.
 * It the order is already in the database, then it is
 * replaced by this one.
 *
 * @exception P2GException
 *                 if the status order is already delivered.
 */
public void storeOrder()
  throws RemoteException, P2GException;

/**
 * Remove the order in the database.
 * It removes the order and its details from the database.
 * The state of this EJB became undetermined after calling this method
 * and it should no longer be used.
 * A new EJB must be created to work with a new order.
 */
public void removeOrder()
  throws RemoteException, P2GException;

/**
 * Delivers the order. It stores the order in the database.
 * It stores the order master and all the order details.
 * Overwrites the details if they already exist
 *
 * @exception P2GException
 *                 if the status order is already delivered.
 */
```

```
   public void deliverOrder()
     throws RemoteException, P2GException;

  /**
   * Adds an order detail to the order.
   *
   * @exception P2GException
   *                 if the status order is already delivered.
   */
   public int addOrderDetail(OrderDetail orderDetail)
     throws RemoteException, P2GException;

  /**
   * Updates an order detail.
   *
   * @exception P2GException
   *                 if the status order is already delivered or
   *                 if the order detail doesn't exist in the order.
   */
   public int setOrderDetail(OrderDetail orderDetail)
     throws RemoteException, P2GException;

  /**
   * Deletes an order detail.
   *
   * @exception P2GException
   *                 if the status order is already delivered,
   *                 if the order detail doesn't exist in the order.
   */
   public int delOrderDetail(OrderDetail orderDetail)
     throws RemoteException, P2GException;

}
```

Let us have a look at the bean implementation, starting with the declarations:

```
package jsw.c04b;

import java.io.Serializable;
import java.util.*;
import java.sql.*;
import java.text.*;
import javax.ejb.*;
import javax.naming.*;

/**
 * This class is the bean implementation for the Stateful Session EJB
 * <tt>OrderSF</tt>.
 * The methods in this class perform operations related to an order.
 *
 * @see     jsw.c04b.OrderSFHome
 * @see     jsw.c04b.OrderSF
 */
public class OrderSFBean implements SessionBean {
```

```
private SessionContext ctx;

/**
 * This order's customer.
 */
public Customer customer;

/**
 * This order's OrderMaster.
 */
public OrderMaster orderMaster;

/**
 * This order's details.
 */
public Vector orderDetailVector;

/**
    * If the order is a new one or loaded from the database.
    *
    * @see #ejbCreate(Customer customer)
    * @see #ejbCreate(long orderNum)
    * @see #storeOrder()
    * @see #deliverOrder()
    */
private boolean isNew;

/**
    * A key used to identify the order details in this order.
    *
    * @see #addOrderDetail(OrderDetail orderDetail)
    * @see #setOrderDetail(OrderDetail orderDetail)
    * @see #delOrderDetail(OrderDetail orderDetail)
    */
public long orderDetailNumber;

private transient PizzaServicesSL  pizzaServices;
private transient OrderServicesSL  orderServices;
private transient OutletServicesSL outletServices;

/**
 * This is the static initializer,
 * executed the first time this class is referred to.
 * It makes sure the JDBC JTS driver is loaded.
 */
static {
  try {
    Class.forName("weblogic.jdbc.jts.Driver");
  } catch(Exception e) {
    System.err.println(e);
  }
}
```

Let us start by reviewing the implementation of the ejbCreate() methods.

Just as in the previous section, the question of when to create the session beans arises. Once again Mr Senior Developer has a different point of view from Mrs Chief Architect. This time, he proposes that the structure of the previous section should be left the same, that is, create all the stateless session beans at the beginning and the stateful session bean every time a new order is started. Mrs Chief Architect agrees with him regarding the stateful bean, however her opinion is that the structure of an order is more important and proposes that the stateless beans be created and removed from within the stateful bean. Her feeling is that using this strategy she has full control of when and where they are created and destroyed, instead of having a bunch of 'stray' beans. The Troops consider her proposal as the cleaner of the two, and decide to implement it.

The result is that when a new order is created, the stateful bean executes the following code:

```
/**
 * Creates a Stateful Session EJB to manage a new order.
 *
 * @param     customer the customer this order belongs to.
 * @return    the created order.
 * @exception P2GException
 *                  if the customer doesn't exist.
 */
public void ejbCreate(Customer customer)
  throws P2GException {

  createServices();
  this.customer = customer;
  orderMaster = new OrderMaster();
  orderMaster.setOr_number(0);
  orderMaster.setOr_c_country_code(customer.c_country_code);
  orderMaster.setOr_c_area_code(customer.c_area_code);
  orderMaster.setOr_c_phone(customer.c_phone);
  orderMaster.setOr_o_outlet_code(0);
  orderMaster.setOr_order_date(new java.util.Date());
  orderMaster.setOr_delivery("Address");
  orderMaster.setOr_status("Ordering");
  orderMaster.setOr_remarks("");
  orderMaster.setOr_price(0.0f);
  orderDetailVector = new Vector();
  orderDetailNumber = 0;
  isNew = true;
  if (orderMaster.getOr_delivery().equals("Address")) {
    try {
      orderMaster = outletServices.assignOutlet(orderMaster);
    } catch(Exception e) {
      throw new P2GException(e.toString());
    }
  }
}
```

This method first creates the stateless session beans by calling the `createServices()` method, and then initializes the corresponding fields. If the pizza is for delivery, the method goes ahead and assigns it to an outlet. The developers don't worry about assigning an outlet if the pizza is for pickup, as the user will select the desired outlet.

Here's the `createServices()` method:

```
private void createServices() {
  try {
    Context context = new InitialContext();
    PizzaServicesSLHome pizzaServicesHome =
        (PizzaServicesSLHome) context.lookup("jsw.c04b.PizzaServicesSL");
    pizzaServices = pizzaServicesHome.create();
    OrderServicesSLHome orderServicesHome =
        (OrderServicesSLHome) context.lookup("jsw.c04b.OrderServicesSL");
    orderServices = orderServicesHome.create();
    OutletServicesSLHome outletServicesHome =
      (OutletServicesSLHome) context.lookup("jsw.c04b.OutletServicesSL");
    outletServices = outletServicesHome.create();
  } catch(Exception e) {
    System.err.println(e);
  }
}
```

The second signature of the `ejbCreate()` method, shown below, is called from an existing order. In this case, the method executes these steps:

❑ Creates the stateless session beans that correspond to the available services.

❑ Issues, via JDBC, a prepared statement that searches the database for the required order.

❑ Traverses the order detail table in the database searching for the items that make up the order.

❑ If the order has not been delivered, it gets its price by calling the `updatePrice()` method.

The code for this method follows:

```
/**
 * Creates a Stateful Session EJB to manage an existing order.
 *
 * @param      orderNum the primary key of the existing order.
 * @return     the created order.
 * @exception P2GException
 *                if the order doesn't exist.
 */
public void ejbCreate(long orderNum)
    throws P2GException {
  try {
    createServices();
    orderMaster = null;
    Connection conn =
      DriverManager.getConnection("jdbc:weblogic:jts:p2gPool");
    String select = "select * from order_master where or_number = ?";
    PreparedStatement pstmt = conn.prepareStatement(select);
    pstmt.setLong(1, orderNum);
    ResultSet resultSet = pstmt.executeQuery();
    if (resultSet.next()) {
      orderMaster = new OrderMaster();
      orderMaster.setOr_number(resultSet.getLong("or_number"));
      orderMaster.setOr_c_country_code(
              resultSet.getInt("or_c_country_code"));
      orderMaster.setOr_c_area_code(resultSet.getInt("or_c_area_code"));
      orderMaster.setOr_c_phone(resultSet.getLong("or_c_phone"));
```

```
            orderMaster.setOr_o_outlet_code(
                    resultSet.getInt("or_o_outlet_code"));
            orderMaster.setOr_order_date(
                    resultSet.getTimestamp("or_order_date"));
            orderMaster.setOr_delivery(resultSet.getString("or_delivery"));
            orderMaster.setOr_status(resultSet.getString("or_status"));
            orderMaster.setOr_remarks(resultSet.getString("or_remarks"));
            orderMaster.setOr_price(resultSet.getFloat("or_price"));
        }
        resultSet.close();
        pstmt.close();

        customer = findCustomer(orderMaster);
        orderDetailVector = new Vector();
        orderDetailNumber = 0;

        select = "select * from order_detail " +
                " where od_or_number = ? order by od_number";
        pstmt = conn.prepareStatement(select);
        pstmt.setLong(1, orderNum);
        resultSet = pstmt.executeQuery();
        while(resultSet.next()) {
          OrderDetail orderDetail = new OrderDetail();
          orderDetail.setOd_number(orderDetailNumber);
          orderDetail.setOd_or_number(orderNum);
          Pizza pizza = new Pizza();
          pizza.setP_name(resultSet.getString("od_p_name"));
          pizza.setP_size(resultSet.getString("od_p_size"));
          orderDetail.setOd_pizza(pizza);
          orderDetail.setOd_quantity(resultSet.getInt("od_quantity"));
          orderDetail.setOd_dough(resultSet.getString("od_dough"));
          if(orderMaster.getOr_status().equals("Delivered")) {
            orderDetail.setOd_price(-1.0f);
          } else {
            //this is the "enable-call-by-reference=true" optimized version:
            //pizzaServices.updatePrice(orderDetail, new java.util.Date());

            //this is the "enable-call-by-reference=false" standard version:
            orderDetail = pizzaServices.getUpdatedPrice(orderDetail,
                                            new java.util.Date());
          }
          orderDetailVector.addElement(orderDetail);
          orderDetailNumber++;
        }
        resultSet.close();
        pstmt.close();
        conn.close();
        updatePrice();
        isNew = false;
    } catch(Exception e) {
      System.err.println(e);
      throw new P2GException("Order not found");
    }
    if (orderMaster == null)
      throw new P2GException("Order not found");
}
```

The assumption is that the caller of this method already has the knowledge of the order number. Therefore the exception thrown when the order does not exist is there only for code robustness.

Calling Beans by Reference

The second `ejbCreate()` method has two ways to calculate the order price by calling one of two new methods in `PizzaServicesSL`:

❑ The code above calls `getUpdatedPrice()`. This corresponds to the standard way of calling EJB methods, that is, by value. The result is returned and the `orderDetail` variable is updated.

❑ The second method uses a feature of the WebLogic Server that allows calling *by reference*. Nothing needs to be returned as both caller and called reference the same object. This can only be used when the caller and called are in the same Virtual Machine.

In Java, arguments in a method call are always passed by reference, except when the argument is a Java primitive. In contrast, the EJB specification states that arguments are passed to an EJB business method by value. The method argument must be one of the legal types specified by RMI/IIOP, that is, that can be serialized and sent between virtual machines.

WebLogic takes advantage of the default argument passing mechanism in Java when the EJB method caller and EJB instance are in the same virtual machine.

In this second case, the deployment descriptor of the `PizzaServicesSL` EJB has to have the following entry (in its `weblogic-ejb-jar.xml`):

```
<enable-call-by-reference>true</enable-call-by-reference>
```

This is the default value and usually results in a big performance improvement, as `PizzaServicesSL` can update the shared price inside the method without needing a return value.

```
//this is the "enable-call-by-reference=true" optimized version:
pizzaServices.updatePrice(orderDetail, new java.util.Date());
```

The two versions of the method are:

```
/**
 * Calculates the price of an order detail.
 * The price is localized based on the system
 * property <tt>jsw.location</tt>.
 * It does consider the special offer of the day.
 * This is a <tt>call-by-reference</tt> version as the result
 * is updated in the parameter <tt>orderDetail</tt>.
 */
public void updatePrice(OrderDetail orderDetail, java.util.Date date)
    throws P2GException {
  String location = System.getProperty("jsw.location", "US");
  float price = getPrice(orderDetail.getOd_pizza(), location,
                    date, orderDetail.getOd_dough());
  price *= orderDetail.getOd_quantity();
  try {
    price = Util.format(price);
  } catch(ParseException pe) {
    throw new P2GException(Util.getStackTraceAsString(pe));
  }
```

```
    orderDetail.setOd_price(price);
}

/**
 * Calculates the price of an order detail.
 * The price is localized based on the system
 * property <tt>jsw.location</tt>.
 * It does consider the special offer of the day.
 * This is NOT a <tt>call-by-reference</tt> version as the result
 * is returned by the function.
 */
public OrderDetail getUpdatedPrice(OrderDetail orderDetail,
                                   java.util.Date date)
    throws P2GException {

  updatePrice(orderDetail, date);

  return orderDetail;
}
```

Other Supporting Methods

Let us continue with the other methods of the `OrderSFBean` bean:

- ❑ The `getCustomer()`, `getOrderMaster()`, and `getOrderDetail()` methods just return the corresponding values.

- ❑ `setOutlet()` verifies that the order has not been delivered yet, and then it assigns the outlet to the order.

- ❑ The `setDelivery()` method will, after verifying that the order has not been delivered, assign the delivery mode. Note that if the pizza is to be picked up at the outlet, the caller of this method will also have to call the `setOutlet()` method to specify which outlet will be used.

- ❑ The `setRemarks()` method just does that.

- ❑ The `storeOrder()` takes the order as it is in the bean and stores it in the database. First it verifies if it is a new order, in which case it inserts a new record in the database, otherwise it just updates it. Then it does the same with the order detail table and the items that make up the order.

`removeOrder()` deletes the order and its items from the database, if they are present. It is important to note that because of the way in which this particular bean has been implemented, the EJB remains in limbo after this; therefore this instance cannot be used again. The caller of this method has the responsibility to remove the bean.

This is not always the case for session beans, but reflects the fact that `OrderSFBean` assumes an order with which it works.

```
/**
 * Remove the order in the database.
 * It removes the order and its details from the database.
 * The state of this EJB became undetermined after calling this method
```

```
  * and it should no longer be used.
  * A new EJB must be created to work with a new order.
  */
  public void removeOrder()
        throws P2GException {
    if (!isNew) {
      Connection conn = null;
      String select;
      PreparedStatement pstmt;
      try {
        conn = DriverManager.getConnection("jdbc:weblogic:jts:p2gPool");
        select = "delete from order_detail where od_or_number = ?";
        pstmt = conn.prepareStatement(select);
        pstmt.setLong(1, orderMaster.getOr_number());
        pstmt.execute();
        pstmt.close();
        select = "delete from order_master where or_number = ?";
        pstmt = conn.prepareStatement(select);
        pstmt.setLong(1, orderMaster.getOr_number());
        pstmt.execute();
        pstmt.close();
      } catch(Exception e) {
        throw new P2GException("<E> OrderBeanSF:removeOrder: "+
                           "the order could not be removed. reason:"+e);
      } finally {
        try {
          conn.close();
        } catch(SQLException se) {
          System.err.println(se.toString());
        }
      }
    }
  }
```

The `deliverOrder()` method calls the `storeOrder()` method and then calls the `deliverOrder()` method of the `OrderServicesSL` bean to update the inventory and send the fax to the outlet:

```
/**
 * Delivers the order. It stores the order in the database.
 * It stores the order master and all the order details.
 * Overwrites the details if they already exist
 *
 * @exception P2GException
 *            if the status order is already delivered.
 */
public void deliverOrder()
  throws P2GException {
  storeOrder();
  try {
    String res = orderServices.deliverOrder(orderMaster.getOr_number());
    if (!res.equalsIgnoreCase("ok")) {
      throw new P2GException(res);
    }
    orderMaster.setOr_status("Delivered");
  } catch(Exception e) {
    throw new P2GException("<E> OrderBeanSF:deliverOrder: "+
                       "the order could not be delivered. reason:" + e);
  }
}
```

The implementation of the bean continues with `addOrderDetail()`, `setOrderDetail()`, and `delOrderDetail()` methods, which do what their names indicate.

Additionally the implementation of the bean includes a few private methods. Worth mentioning is `findCustomer()`, which has two signatures. The first one will return a customer given an order number:

```
/**
 * This is a helper function that searches for the order's customer.
 *
 */
private Customer findCustomer(OrderMaster orderMaster)
  throws P2GException {
  Customer customer = new Customer();
  customer.c_country_code   = orderMaster.getOr_c_country_code();
  customer.c_area_code      = orderMaster.getOr_c_area_code();
  customer.c_phone          = orderMaster.getOr_c_phone();
  customer = findCustomer(customer);
  if (customer == null)
    throw new P2GException("No customer found for this order");
  return customer;
}
```

The second one takes a `Customer` object and fills out the details:

```
/**
 * This is a helper function that searches for a customer.
 *
 */
private Customer findCustomer(Customer customer) {

  Customer aCustomer = null;
  Connection conn = null;
  PreparedStatement pstmt = null;
  ResultSet resultSet = null;
  try {
    conn = DriverManager.getConnection("jdbc:weblogic:jts:p2gPool");
    String select = "select * from customer where c_country_code = ? " +
                    " and c_area_code = ? and c_phone = ?";
    pstmt = conn.prepareStatement(select);
    pstmt.setInt(1, customer.c_country_code);
    pstmt.setInt(2, customer.c_area_code);
    pstmt.setLong(3, customer.c_phone);
    resultSet = pstmt.executeQuery();
    if (resultSet.next()) {
      aCustomer = new Customer();
      aCustomer.c_country_code  = customer.c_country_code;
      aCustomer.c_area_code     = customer.c_area_code;
      aCustomer.c_phone         = customer.c_phone;
      aCustomer.c_first_name    = resultSet.getString("c_first_name");
      aCustomer.c_last_name     = resultSet.getString("c_last_name");
      aCustomer.c_postal_code   = resultSet.getLong("c_postal_code");
      aCustomer.c_address_line_1 =
                          resultSet.getString("c_address_line_1");
      aCustomer.c_address_line_2 =
```

```
                                      resultSet.getString("c_address_line_2");
        aCustomer.c_remarks    = resultSet.getString("c_remarks");
        aCustomer.c_city       = resultSet.getString("c_city");
        aCustomer.c_major_cr   = resultSet.getString("c_major_cr");
        aCustomer.c_colonia    = resultSet.getString("c_colonia");
        aCustomer.c_state      = resultSet.getString("c_state");
        aCustomer.c_country    = resultSet.getString("c_country");
      }
    } catch(Exception e) {
      System.err.println(e);
    } finally {
      try {
        resultSet.close();
        pstmt.close();
        conn.close();
      } catch(SQLException se) {
          System.err.println(se.toString());
      }
    }
    return aCustomer;
  }
```

The ejbActivate() method calls the createServices() method:

```
public void ejbActivate() {
   createServices();
}
```

In a similar fashion, ejbPassivate() and ejbRemove() are used to call the removeServices() method:

```
public void ejbPassivate() {
   removeServices();
}

public void ejbRemove() {
   removeServices();
}
```

The container will passivate and activate the stateful session bean OrderSF. The OrderSF bean holds handles to the following stateless session beans:

```
private transient PizzaServicesSL  pizzaServices;
private transient OrderServicesSL  orderServices;
private transient OutletServicesSL outletServices;
```

What happens to those handles when the bean is passivated? There are two approaches here:

❑ Keep the handles as transient fields and remove and create the stateless beans when passivating and activating the stateful bean respectively. This is the approach we chose here.

❑ Create the stateless session beans at the OrderSF creation and keep the handles as non-transient fields by storing the Serializable version of the handles, so the container can automatically store and load them when passivation and activation occur.

We took the first approach because in the second one, when trying to call a business method with a handle to an EJB that has been created a long time ago, there is a possibility that the associated EJB won't be valid (because it has timed out). When the stateless beans are created with the caller bean (OrderSF) and re-created every time it is activated, we can guarantee the stateless beans handles are valid when they're needed.

The Stateful Client's View

Let us have a look at the lifecycle of a stateful session bean. In order to improve performance, the WebLogic Server uses a cache of stateful beans. Unlike the stateless bean free pool, the stateful beans in the cache are bound to a specific client and they are the active instances of stateful beans. This is so they are immediately available for client requests. In the cache there will also be instances that were recently used. The lifecycle is depicted below.

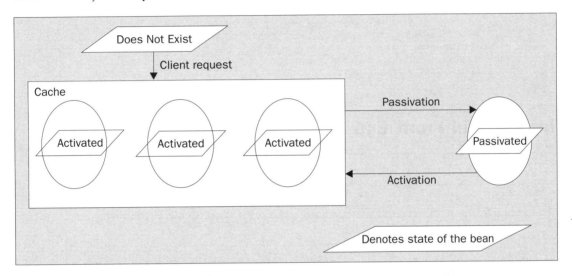

At startup time there are no stateful bean instances in the cache of the WebLogic server. They are placed in the cache as the clients start calling them. When the beans are no longer in use, they become eligible for passivation. As we saw earlier, passivation is when a bean is swapped out of the cache and its state serialized to disk. When a bean is eligible for passivation, it does not mean that passivation will occur immediately; it will only happen when there is the need for the resources or during regular cache maintenance.

There are two deployment elements that can be used to gain some level of control over the passivation and removal of stateful beans: max-beans-in-cache and idle-timeout-seconds.

If max-beans-in-cache is reached and all the beans are active, WebLogic will throw a CacheFullException. In consequence, if there are beans that are not being used, some of these will be passivated, even if the beans have not reached their idle-timeout-seconds limit.

When the idle-timeout-seconds limit has been reached for a bean instance, WebLogic may remove that bean from the cache even if the max-beans-in-cache has not been reached. Note that the action may be removal and not passivation. In a similar fashion, when the max-beans-in-cache value is approached, the server will remove the beans that have reached the idle-timeout-seconds limit. The removal is done to ensure that no resources of the server are being wasted.

If a bean is passivated, the client must use the instance before `idle-timeout-seconds` is reached, otherwise the bean will be removed.

We can see these two tags in the `weblogic-ejb-jar.xml` deployment descriptor for the OrderSFBean:

```xml
<?xml version="1.0"?>

<!DOCTYPE weblogic-ejb-jar PUBLIC '-//BEA Systems, Inc.//DTD WebLogic 5.1.0
EJB//EN' 'http://www.bea.com/servers/wls510/dtd/weblogic-ejb-jar.dtd'>

<weblogic-ejb-jar>
  <weblogic-enterprise-bean>
    <ejb-name>jsw.c04b.OrderSF</ejb-name>
    <caching-descriptor>
      <max-beans-in-cache>500</max-beans-in-cache>
      <idle-timeout-seconds>60</idle-timeout-seconds>
    </caching-descriptor>
    <jndi-name>jsw.c04b.OrderSF</jndi-name>
  </weblogic-enterprise-bean>
</weblogic-ejb-jar>
```

The Stateful Front End

As mentioned earlier, the `OrderMaintenanceS` servlet is changed extensively to reflect the usage of this stateful bean. Basically, wherever there is an access to the database regarding the order, it is replaced by the functionality now offered by `OrderSF`.

For example, the `viewOrder()` method used in the previous section is as follows:

```java
/**
 * This method retrieves an existing order from the database.
 * The order retrieved is stored in the HTTP session.
 */
private void viewOrder(HttpServletRequest req)
    throws IOException {

  Connection conn = null;
  PreparedStatement pstmt = null;
  ResultSet resultSet = null;
  try {
    OrderMaster order = new OrderMaster();
    order.setOr_number(Long.parseLong(req.getParameter("or_number")));

    conn = DriverManager.getConnection("jdbc:weblogic:pool:p2gPool");

    String select = "select * from order_master where or_number = ?";
    pstmt = conn.prepareStatement(select);

    pstmt.setLong(1, order.getOr_number());

    resultSet = pstmt.executeQuery();
```

```
          if (resultSet.next()) {
            order.setOr_c_country_code(resultSet.getInt("or_c_country_code"));
            order.setOr_c_area_code(resultSet.getInt("or_c_area_code"));
            order.setOr_c_phone(resultSet.getLong("or_c_phone"));
            order.setOr_o_outlet_code(resultSet.getInt("or_o_outlet_code"));
            order.setOr_order_date(resultSet.getTimestamp("or_order_date"));
            order.setOr_delivery(resultSet.getString("or_delivery"));
            order.setOr_status(resultSet.getString("or_status"));
            order.setOr_remarks(resultSet.getString("or_remarks"));
            order.setOr_price(resultSet.getFloat("or_price"));
          } else {
            throw new Exception("the order could not be found");
          }
          HttpSession session = req.getSession(true);
          session.setAttribute("order", order);
        } catch(Exception e) {
          System.err.println("Exception: OrderMaintenanceS.viewOrder: " + e);
        } finally {
          try {
            if (resultSet != null) resultSet.close();
            if (pstmt != null)     pstmt.close();
            if (conn != null)      conn.close();
          } catch(Exception w) {
            System.err.println("Warning: OrderMaintenanceS.viewOrder: " + w);
          }
        }
    }
```

This code is simplified by using the stateful bean:

```
/**
 * This method retrieves an existing order from the database.
 * The order retrieved is stored in the HTTP session.
 */
private void viewOrder(HttpServletRequest req)
    throws IOException {

  HttpSession session = req.getSession(true);
  OrderSF currentOrder = (OrderSF) session.getAttribute("currentOrder");
  session.setAttribute("message", "The order could not be loaded");
  try {
    if (currentOrder != null)
      currentOrder.remove();
    Context ctx = Util.getInitialContext();
    OrderSFHome orderHome = (OrderSFHome)
                        ctx.lookup("jsw.c04b.OrderSF");
    currentOrder = orderHome.create(
                    Long.parseLong(req.getParameter("or_number")));
    session.setAttribute("currentOrder", currentOrder);
    session.setAttribute("order", currentOrder.getOrderMaster());
    session.setAttribute("message", "Order succesfully loaded!");
  } catch(Exception e) {
    System.err.println("Exception: OrderMaintenanceS.viewOrder: " + e);
  }
}
```

OrderForm.jsp is modified to add the *store* option and OrderSubform.jsp is changed to use the information from the OrderSF bean. The main menu, index.jsp, was enhanced by adding the option to present the current order.

For easier handling from the programming standpoint, the OrderDetail JavaBean now includes the price of an item from an order, even though it is not a field in the order detail table. A new method that updates the price of an item in an order has been added to the PizzaServicesSL bean.

Finally, another signature has been added to the assignOutlet() method in the OutletServicesSL bean. It will return an outlet based on the OrderMaster object. It first searches for the postal code and city for that specific customer. Then it assigns the first outlet that matches the postal code, otherwise it will assign the first outlet in that city. This is a rather poor algorithm, but the Wonder Troops just needed something to use for testing the application.

Setting It Up

The process for handling a stateful EJB is similar to the one described for stateless EJBs in the previous section. The identifier for this section is 4b. The steps are the same as for the stateless beans.

Summary

In this chapter we have seen the Troops convert the functionality provided by the Oracle stored procedures into stateless session beans. Then, as an additional step, a stateful session bean was added to handle the state of the pizza order. So we have seen how to handle both cases of session beans.

More specifically, we've seen:

❑ The basics of the EJB model, including the interface-based programming, the jobs the container does for you, support for transactions, and the developer roles

❑ How session beans represent the user's view of an application, and so model process

❑ How stateless session beans can replace database stored procedures, and thus generalize the data handling to include other data sources

❑ How stateful session beans can, by representing the state of a process that's under way in memory, cut down on network traffic

❑ How to deploy beans, and what features WebLogic provides to configure how the container manages beans

❑ The changes needed to the application's front end to use beans

In the next chapter we will be converting direct JTS/JDBC calls to database tables to calls via entity beans.

5

Easy Data Access with Entity Beans

In Chapter 4 we covered some of the EJB architecture and worked with both stateless and stateful session beans. In this chapter we will concentrate on entity beans, which present an object view of persistent data. These beans are a dream for the programmers, as very little coding need be done to access data.

Continuing with their experiments, the Wonder Troops are set the task of testing the entity beans, to see how much less code they have to write. They will use the code that was developed in the second section of the previous chapter, the code for the stateful session bean, as a base. The intent is to replace some of the direct calls to the database via JDBC with entity beans.

Specifically, in this chapter we'll cover:

❑ What entity beans are for

❑ How entity beans are put together

❑ Container-managed persistence

❑ Bean-managed persistence

❑ Some initial pointers as to when to use entity beans

Entity Beans

Entity beans provides EJB object representations of data that lives or persists in a data store. An entity bean is best thought of as representing a logical unit of data, whether that be a row of a table in a relational database, a single column in a row, related information stored across several tables, or the result of a query.

The key point to grasp with entity beans is that many clients can use them at the same time. Here is the main difference between them and session beans: the client and the session bean have, at least for the time it takes to run a method, a one-to-one relationship. An entity bean, in contrast, has a one-to-many relationship with its clients. When many clients are accessing the same entity bean, they will do so in a serial fashion. That is, when the first client is accessing the bean, the others are blocked while waiting for the first one to finish. This does place a limit on the complexity of the methods called on the bean.

> *That all the coding in an EJB is singly threaded from the point of view of the application developer simplifies the code in the bean, and keeps threading issues firmly in the container. If you need a faster response, get more beans.*

Another important concept is that the beans, even when they are called by other beans, are only accessible through their remote interface. This is important when thinking about how session beans call entity beans. Many clients can appear to call the same pizza bean, for example, to get its price as part of their order. But the container manages the number of instances of that bean to keep the server scalable and reliable.

There are overheads associated with an entity bean, but these should be counteracted by the usefulness of the grouped information to a large number of clients. You'll see what entity beans need to add over a JavaBean data structure or a database result set, as we work through the chapter.

Entity beans represent data, so they must be able to 'find' data on behalf of clients, and, more importantly, persist it to the data store. The EJB specification offers the developer a lot of flexibility in how they support persistence of the state of an entity bean. The developer can delegate the data access to the container, or write their own database access. The first model is **container-managed persistence** (CMP), the latter is **bean-managed persistence** (BMP). We'll look at examples of each in this chapter.

Entity beans can also have business methods – these are typically used to transform the data into a more suitable representation for the application.

The data store can be a relational database, an object-oriented database, a view on data through an application, such as TOPLink, or a flat file.

> *The way that WebLogic implements entity beans is by using the JTA driver, which itself uses a JDBC driver (in the case of relational databases). Therefore, you can persist data to any database that has a compliant JDBC driver. In the case of object-oriented databases, WebLogic provides direct connections with Versant and ODI.*

More on Transactions

An entity bean can be part of a transaction, just as a session bean can. As with session beans, much of the transaction work can be left to the container and specified declaratively.

There's an additional level of declarative control that we didn't cover in the last chapter. **Translation isolation** allows you to define how transactions interact between themselves, by controlling the level of access a bean has to shared data.

The disadvantage of sharing data is the increased prevalence of dirty, non-repeatable, and phantom reads:

- ❑ A **dirty read** can happen when a transaction *modifies* a row in a database table but has not yet committed it. If another transaction reads it, and then the first transaction does a rollback (because of some error), the changes to the row are eliminated. The second transaction has data that is inconsistent.

- ❑ A **non-repeatable read** can happen when a transaction reads a row, then a second transaction modifies that row. If the first transaction reads that row again it gets different values.

- ❑ Suppose that a transaction selects a set of rows that match a query, then a second transaction inserts new rows that also match the query of the first transaction. When the first transaction executes the same query again it will get those additional rows. This is called a **phantom read**.

To minimize these consequences, isolation levels can be set for the methods of the bean. Even though these can be defined in the deployment descriptor of a bean, the functionality is really provided by the database. The isolation levels defined are:

Transaction Isolation Level	Description
TRANSACTION_READ_UNCOMMITTED	Transactions can read uncommitted changes to data.
	Dirty reads, non-repeatable reads, and phantom reads can occur.
TRANSACTION_READ_COMMITTED	Transactions can read committed changes to data, but not uncommitted data.
	Dirty reads are prevented; non-repeatable and phantom reads are possible.
TRANSACTION_REPEATABLE_READ	Transactions can't change data that is being read by other transactions.
	Dirty and non-repeatable reads are prevented; phantom reads are possible.
TRANSACTION_SERIALIZABLE	Transactions operate serially on data.
	The strictest isolation level; all of the above problems are avoided.

In the majority of cases, your beans will use TRANSACTION_SERIALIZABLE as the isolation level. Once the application has been in production for a while and there is the need for serious fine-tuning in the performance, this in one of the parameters that should be considered.

Of course, your application determines how far you can go in setting isolation levels. Read-only transactions that publish information can be interleaved, while transactions that update data need more thought.

Keep in mind that not all the databases support all the isolation levels, even though they might appear to be accepted by the JDBC driver of choice.

To understand how entity beans work, we'll look at the following topics before delving into the changes to the example:

- ❑ Support for a primary key
- ❑ The programming interfaces
- ❑ The bean's lifecycle in the container.
- ❑ Configuring the container for entity beans

The Primary Key of an Entity Bean

The basic difference between entity and session beans is that, instead of the bean being bound to a client, an entity bean is bound to a **primary key** – some unique way of describing the data the bean holds. The primary key is defined as a `Serializable` Java class. As an example from later in this chapter:

```
package jsw.c05;

/**
 * This is the Primary Key for the Entity EJB <tt>OrderMasterEB</tt>.
 *
 * @see       jsw.c05.OrderMaster
 * @see       jsw.c05.OrderMasterEB
 * @see       jsw.c05.OrderMasterEBHome
 * @see       jsw.c05.OrderMasterEBBean
 */
public class OrderMasterEBPK implements java.io.Serializable {

    /**
     * This is the primary key.
     * It is the order number, which is the primary key
     * in table <tt>order_master</tt>.
     */
    public long or_number;

    /**
     * This is the equals method.
     * @param obj java.lang.Object
     * @return boolean
     */
    public boolean equals(Object obj) {
      if (obj instanceof OrderMasterEBPK) {
        OrderMasterEBPK otherKey = (OrderMasterEBPK) obj;
        return ((this.or_number == otherKey.or_number));
      } else
        return false;
    }
```

```
    /**
     * This is the hashCode method.
     * @return int
     */
    public int hashCode() {
      return (int)this.or_number;
    }
}
```

This class defines the order number, `or_number`, as the primary key of the `OrderMasterEB` entity bean.

Notice the naming conventions we've used. Classes to define entity beans follow the naming convention described in the last chapter, but end in EB, while the primary key class appends the letters PK at the end of the name of the class.

The Home Interface

The home interface of an entity bean extends `javax.ejb.EJBHome`, just as session beans do. In your interface you define the `create()` methods that clients will call to acquire an instance of the bean (entity beans cannot be instantiated using constructors), again as before. But entity beans also add **finder methods** to the mix, which correspond to SQL queries, to return entity beans that match the search criteria.

A very basic home interface will look something like:

```
import javax.ejb.*;
import java.rmi.RemoteException;

public interface SimpleEBHome extends EJBHome {

  public SimpleEB create() throws CreateException, RemoteException;

  public SimpleEB findByPrimaryKey(SimpleEBPK primaryKey)
    throws FinderException, RemoteException;

}
```

Every entity bean home interface will always define a `findByPrimaryKey()` method, which returns an entity bean instance with the first match for the primary key. If the method can't find a match, it will throw a `FinderException`.

You can define additional finder methods with other search parameters. You can also define different return types, so you can return one instance or a collection (or enumeration) of instances that match the request.

With WebLogic container-managed persistence, additional finder methods can be specified using the Deployer Tool. The method search terms are defined using a Lisp-like syntax that works by generating the SQL for the finder methods behind the scenes. For bean-managed persistence, the developer must write their own finder method implementations. For access to a relational database, normal JDBC and SQL will be used in those methods.

Entity Bean Lifecycle

The entity bean implementation implements the `EntityBean` interface, which defines the following methods:

- ❑ `ejbRemove()`
- ❑ `ejbActivate()`
- ❑ `ejbPassivate()`
- ❑ `setEntityContext()`
- ❑ `unsetEntityContext()`
- ❑ `ejbLoad()`
- ❑ `ejbStore()`

The lifecycle is as shown in the following diagram:

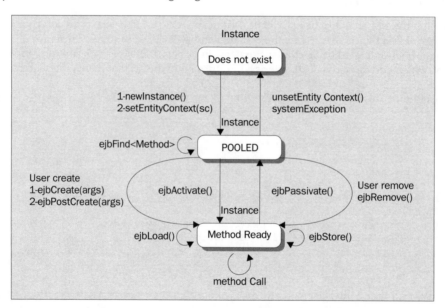

As you can see, you must specify both `ejbCreate()` and `ejbPostCreate()` methods in the entity bean. Both have the same signature, so EJB container can match the call to the `ejbCreate()` method with a subsequent one to the `ejbPostCreate()` method. The `ejbPostCreate()` method is called once the bean identity is available to the bean instance, so the bean can use it for initialization, for example, with its primary key.

The core of an entity bean's behavior is in the two methods, `ejbLoad()` and `ejbStore()`. These synchronize data between the bean and the data source.

- ❑ The `ejbLoad()` method is called by WebLogic to read the most recent version of the data from the data store

- ❑ The `ejbStore()` method is called to persist the data back into the data store when a transaction commits

When a developer chooses to use CMP, these control methods are provided by the WebLogic container. When BMP is chosen, the developer overrides these control methods.

The default behavior of an entity bean, where the `ejbLoad()` method is called every time a read of the data store is necessary, and `ejbStore()` is called at every commit, might not be desirable under certain circumstances. In these cases, the default behavior can be changed by manipulating some deployment descriptor elements of the bean, as we'll see next.

Declarative Control of an Entity Bean

The behavior of the entity bean can be configured with the following tags:

- ❑ `db-is-shared`
- ❑ `is-modified-method-name`
- ❑ `delay-updates-until-end-of-tx`
- ❑ `passivation-strategy`
- ❑ `read-write`
- ❑ `read-only`

You can change the behavior of `ejbLoad()` in a CMP entity bean by using the `db-is-shared` element in the deployment descriptor. If you are sure that there is only one instance of the WebLogic server accessing a particular entity bean and there are no external applications modifying the underlying data, then calling `ejbLoad()` every time is unnecessary. For this particular case you can set the value of `db-is-shared` to `false` (the default is `true`) in the deployment descriptor. The effect is that `ejbLoad()` will only be called when this is the first reference from a client for the bean in question or when a transaction rolls back, with the result being a better performance. Due to caching limitations, this will not work when WebLogic is configured to work in a cluster.

To change the behavior of the `ejbStore()` method, you can use two elements in the deployment descriptor. The first one is `is-modified-method-name`. The default behavior is that `ejbStore()` is called every time a commit occurs, independently of whether the data to be persisted has changed or not. The trick here is for the developer to write a method that will return `true` if the data has changed or `false` if it has not. This method is then used as the parameter for the `is-modified-method-name` tag, which will be called before `ejbStore()` to determine if it is necessary to persist the data. This will work on both CMP and BMP, but make sure that you have fully tested the logic for using this method, as this is one of the places where developers typically get into trouble.

The data store does not get updated until a commit is done, so no intermediate results are available. However, if you want other clients to be able to view intermediate results for transactions that are in progress, and your database can support a transaction isolation level of read uncommitted, you can make it happen by setting the value of the `delay-updates-until-end-of-tx` element to `false`. What will happen is that `ejbStore()` will be called at the end of each method and the information sent over to the database, instead of waiting until the commit. Note that the data sent at the end of each method is not committed to the database, just stored, until the transaction concludes.

There are also mechanisms to control the lifecycle of an entity bean. For example, entity beans follow the normal lifecycle of passivation described in the previous chapter for stateful beans. However, by setting the value of the `passivation-strategy` element in the deployment descriptor of the bean to `transaction`, it will passivate the instance of the bean at the completion of each transaction.

The default caching strategy of the container is called `read-write`. This is basically where the data is brought into the cache at the beginning of each transaction with `ejbLoad()`, and sent to the data store using `ejbStore()` at the end of each transaction. This behavior can be modified as described earlier. WebLogic has another cache strategy available, which is called `read-only`. This strategy will not execute the `ejbStore()` method, and will execute the `ejbLoad()` method at the beginning and at regular intervals thereafter. The intervals are defined by the `read-timeout-seconds` element. Note that the transaction attribute for a bean using a read-only caching strategy has to be set to `NotSupported`.

WebLogic does not implement `read-mostly` caching; this is defined as `read-only` exported to most machines. However, the same effect can be achieved manually with a combination of `read-write` and `read-only` EJBs. You start with a `read-only` bean that reads the data at the specified intervals. Then you define a separate `read-write` bean that models the same data as the `read-only` bean, which gets updated as required.

Enough theory, let's try out entity bean development.

Container-Managed Persistence

The marketing brochures claim that no programming has to be done to access the database and the Wonder Troops want to check out this claim. Mrs Chief Architect thinks that the ideal test would be to use the entity bean at the core of the application, the `order_master` and `order_detail` tables. One entity bean for each table will be defined. Using as a base the code of the previous chapter, modifications will be made so that direct calls to these database tables via JDBC will be replaced by calls to entity beans.

Order Master

`OrderMasterEB` is the entity bean that corresponds to the `order_master` table in the database. To minimize the changes to the existing code, Mrs Chief Architect decides to use the `OrderMaster` JavaBean to pass information to its clients. That way, no changes have to be made in the JSP page and servlets, which already expect to receive the attributes as part of this JavaBean.

Mr Senior Developer doesn't agree with this decision. He is always trying to optimize any process as much as possible, and for him, sending the whole JavaBean down the wire is inefficient. His position is based on the fact that most of the time only one or two attributes of the bean are needed. He thinks the application should be written in such a way that only the required attributes are the ones transmitted.

In principle Mrs Chief Architect agrees, but thinks writing specialized code to send specific attributes of the JavaBean over the network is a distraction from the current focus on entity bean development. Mr WonderBoy chimes in his agreement, for reasons of cost, and so it is slated for inclusion in version 2.0.

The Home Interface

Let us have a look at the home interface of this bean:

```
package jsw.c05;

import javax.ejb.*;
import java.rmi.RemoteException;
import java.util.Enumeration;
```

```
/**
 * This is the Home Interface for the Entity EJB <tt>OrderMasterEB</tt>.
 *
 * @see      jsw.c05.OrderMaster
 * @see      jsw.c05.OrderMasterEB
 * @see      jsw.c05.OrderMasterEBPK
 * @see      jsw.c05.OrderMasterEBBean
 */
public interface OrderMasterEBHome extends EJBHome {

  /**
   * Creates a new OrderMaster Entity EJB.
   */
  public OrderMasterEB create(OrderMaster orderMaster)
    throws CreateException, RemoteException;

  /**
   * Searches for an OrderMaster Entity EJB, by its primary key.
   */
  public OrderMasterEB findByPrimaryKey(OrderMasterEBPK primaryKey)
    throws FinderException, RemoteException;

  /**
   * Searches for one or more OrderMaster Entity EJB, by customer.
   * The method returns the orders of a given customer.
   */
  public Enumeration findByCustomer(int country, int area, long phone)
    throws FinderException, RemoteException;

}
```

The interface defines the compulsory `create()` and `findByPrimaryKey()` methods. The `findByPrimaryKey()` method uses the primary key class we showed earlier.

There's an additional finder method called `findByCustomer()`, which provides the user of the bean with the ability to locate a bean based on country, telephone area code, and telephone number. This finder method is defined in the `weblogic-cmp-rdbms-jar.xml` deployment descriptor as:

```
<finder-list>
  <finder>
    <method-name>findByCustomer</method-name>
    <method-params>
      <method-param>int</method-param>
      <method-param>int</method-param>
      <method-param>long</method-param>
    </method-params>
    <finder-query>
      <![CDATA[(orderBy 'or_number'
                      (& (= or_c_country_code $0)
                         (= or_c_area_code $1)
                         (= or_c_phone $2)
                      )
                )
      ]]>
    </finder-query>
  </finder>
</finder-list>
```

169

The finder expression in the deployment descriptor uses a Lisp-like syntax that is based on expressions of the form:

```
Operator operand1 operand2
```

So, in the finder query defined above, the three parameters to the method, $0, $1, and $2, are set equal to their column names. orderBy *is a WebLogic Query Language (WLQL) keyword.*

Note that the WebLogic 5.1.0 documentation states that WLQL is no longer supported. This isn't true, as this code will still work. It will not work in web applications using EJB 2.0, which is in Beta at the time of writing. In the EJB 2.0 specification, finder methods in CMP are standardized between containers, and coded in a more SQL-like fashion. See http://www.weblogic.com/ docs51/classdocs/API_ejb20/cmp.html for more details.

The finder method can also be set up with the EJB Deployer Tool. The following screenshot shows the finder methods:

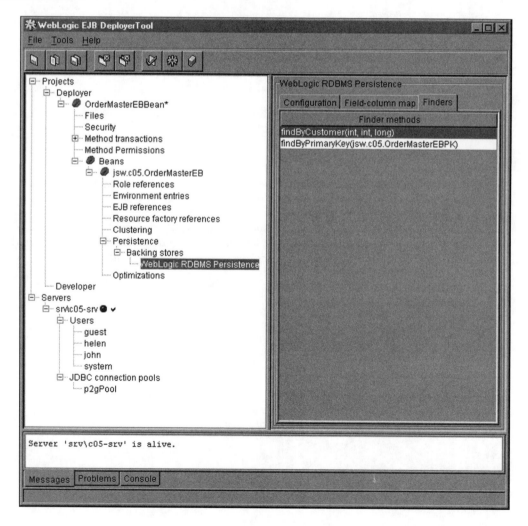

Double-clicking the finder method brings up the following dialog and the finder expression can be edited:

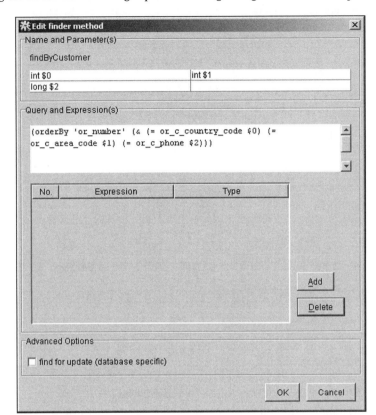

Mr Senior Developer decides that this finder method will return an enumeration with references to all the records that match the criteria, instead of a collection. Using the Collections API defined in JDK 1.2 is probably more efficient, but it is not available in JDK 1.1. As the Wonder Team wants to experiment with both versions of the JDK, enumeration will provide backwards compatibility.

What's interesting is that the developers do not have to program the finder methods. They just define the condition in the deployment descriptor and the signature in the home interface. During the deployment process the classes will be generated automatically.

The Remote Interface

The remote interface is very simple:

```
package jsw.c05;

import java.rmi.RemoteException;
import javax.ejb.*;
```

```
/**
 * This is the Remote Interface for the Entity EJB <tt>OrderMasterEB</tt>.
 *
 * @see        jsw.c05.OrderMaster
 * @see        jsw.c05.OrderMasterEBHome
 * @see        jsw.c05.OrderMasterEBPK
 * @see        jsw.c05.OrderMasterEBBean
 */
public interface OrderMasterEB extends EJBObject {

    /**
     * Returns the OrderMaster information of this Entity EJB.
     */
    public OrderMaster getOrderMaster()
      throws RemoteException;

    /**
     * Sets the OrderMaster information of this Entity EJB.
     * @exception P2GException
     *               If the given OrderMaster <tt>or_number</tt> field
     *               does not match the primary key that is in the Entity EJB.
     */
    public void setOrderMaster(OrderMaster orderMaster)
      throws RemoteException, P2GException;

}
```

Here only two methods are defined:

❑   One to obtain the data related to a specific order_master record

❑   Another to commit new data to a specific order_master record

In general, these kinds of methods in an entity bean are called **accessor methods**.

The bean implementation starts with the following declarations, including those for its primary key:

```
package jsw.c05;

import javax.ejb.*;
import java.util.Date;
import java.sql.*;

/**
 * This class is the Bean Implementation for the Entity EJB
 * <tt>OrderMasterEB</tt>.
 *
 * @see        jsw.c05.OrderMaster
 * @see        jsw.c05.OrderMasterEB
 * @see        jsw.c05.OrderMasterEBPK
 * @see        jsw.c05.OrderMasterEBHome
 */
public class OrderMasterEBBean implements EntityBean {
```

```
    private EntityContext ctx;
/**
  * This is the static initializer,
  * executed the first time this class is referred to.
  * It makes sure the JDBC JTS driver is loaded.
  */
static {
  try {
    Class.forName("weblogic.jdbc.jts.Driver");
  } catch(Exception e) {
    System.err.println(e);
  }
}

/**
  * This is the primary key.
  * It is the order number, which is the primary key
  * in table <tt>order_master</tt>.
  */
public long or_number            = 0;

public int or_c_country_code    = 0;
public int or_c_area_code       = 0;
public long or_c_phone          = 0;
public long or_o_outlet_code    = 0;
public java.sql.Timestamp or_order_date = null;
public String or_delivery       = "";
public String or_status         = "";
public String or_remarks        = "";
public float or_price           = 0.0f;
```

The `getOrderMaster()` accessor method is used by the EJB client to get the data stored in the entity bean as an `OrderMaster` JavaBean:

```
/**
  * Returns the OrderMaster information of this Entity EJB.
  */
public OrderMaster getOrderMaster() {
  OrderMaster orderMaster = new OrderMaster();

  orderMaster.setOr_number(or_number);
  orderMaster.setOr_c_country_code(or_c_country_code);
  orderMaster.setOr_c_area_code(or_c_area_code);
  orderMaster.setOr_c_phone(or_c_phone);
  orderMaster.setOr_o_outlet_code(or_o_outlet_code);
  orderMaster.setOr_order_date(or_order_date);
  orderMaster.setOr_delivery(or_delivery);
  orderMaster.setOr_status(or_status);
  orderMaster.setOr_remarks(or_remarks);
  orderMaster.setOr_price(or_price);

  return orderMaster;
}
```

To make the bean's use of network bandwidth more efficient, we would need to define accessor methods for each field, as well as the full bean.

The `setOrderMaster()` method reverses the process:

```
/**
 * Sets the OrderMaster information of this Entity EJB.
 * @exception P2GException
 *                  If the given OrderMaster <tt>or_number</tt> field
 *                  does not match the primary key that is in the E-EJB.
 */
public void setOrderMaster(OrderMaster orderMaster)
  throws P2GException {

  // The primary key is never modified!!
  if (or_number != orderMaster.getOr_number())
    throw new P2GException("Cannot modify a different order");

  or_c_country_code = orderMaster.getOr_c_country_code();
  or_c_area_code = orderMaster.getOr_c_area_code();
  or_c_phone = orderMaster.getOr_c_phone();
  or_o_outlet_code = orderMaster.getOr_o_outlet_code();
  or_order_date =
    new Timestamp(orderMaster.getOr_order_date().getTime());
  or_delivery = orderMaster.getOr_delivery();
  or_status = orderMaster.getOr_status();
  or_remarks = orderMaster.getOr_remarks();
  or_price = orderMaster.getOr_price();
}
```

The `setOrderMaster()` method will throw a `P2GException` if there is no primary key available in the entity bean. The primary key is the order number. It will also throw an exception if the primary key of the JavaBean, which comes as a property of the `OrderMaster` class, does not match the primary key in the entity bean.

The `ejbCreate()` method is used to create a new order master record, which will be assigned the data contained in the `OrderMaster` Java Bean:

```
/**
 * This function initializes the OrderMaster
 * information of this Entity EJB.
 * It assigns a new primary key to the order.
 * @see #getNewOrderNum()
 */
public OrderMasterEBPK ejbCreate(OrderMaster orderMaster)
  throws CreateException {
  try {
    or_number = getNewOrderNum().longValue();
  } catch (Exception e) {
    throw new CreateException (e.getMessage());
  }
  or_c_country_code = orderMaster.getOr_c_country_code();
  or_c_area_code = orderMaster.getOr_c_area_code();
  or_c_phone = orderMaster.getOr_c_phone();
  or_o_outlet_code = orderMaster.getOr_o_outlet_code();
  or_order_date =
    new Timestamp(orderMaster.getOr_order_date().getTime());
  or_delivery = orderMaster.getOr_delivery();
  or_status = orderMaster.getOr_status();
  or_remarks = orderMaster.getOr_remarks();
  or_price = orderMaster.getOr_price();

  return null;
}
```

The `ejbCreate()` method returns `null`, despite having a return type of the primary key, to follow the EJB 1.1 specification (section 9.4.2):

"The `ejbCreate()` methods must be defined to return the primary key class type. The implementation of the `ejbCreate()` methods should be coded to return a `null`. The returned value is ignored by the Container."

The key method in this bean is `getNewOrderNum()` called from the `ejbCreate()` method. As the name suggests it returns a new, unique order number. To do this, a JDBC request is sent to the database to obtain the next sequence value of the order master table:

```
/**
 * This function finds a new primary key for this EJB.
 * It uses a sequence value from the database
 * (<tt>order_master_seq</tt>).
 * @see #ejbCreate(OrderMaster orderMaster)
 */
private Long getNewOrderNum() throws Exception {

  Connection conn       = null;
  Statement  stmt       = null;
  ResultSet  resultSet= null;
  long       orderNum = 0;

  try {
    conn = DriverManager.getConnection("jdbc:weblogic:jts:p2gPool");
    stmt = conn.createStatement();
    stmt.executeQuery("select order_master_seq.NEXTVAL from DUAL");
    resultSet = stmt.getResultSet();
    if ((resultSet != null) && (resultSet.next())) {
      orderNum  = resultSet.getLong(1);
    } else {
      throw new CreateException (
              "ejbCreate: sequence failed to return a value");
    }
  } catch (SQLException sqe) {
    throw new CreateException (sqe.getMessage());
  } finally {
    try {
      if (resultSet != null) resultSet.close();
      if (stmt != null)      stmt.close();
      if (conn != null)      conn.close();
    } catch(Exception w) {
      System.err.println("Warning: OrderMasterEBBean.getNewOrderNum: " +
                          w);
    }
  }
  return new Long(orderNum);
}
```

*The code above uses an Oracle sequence, `order_master_seq`, to get the primary key for the entity bean. This would need to be rewritten if the database changed. One way around this is to use a **data access object** to hide database-specific code. The data access object can be configured at deployment time, for example by setting a `System` property indicating the target database. This is left as an exercise for the gentle reader.*

The code of the bean continues with the declaration of the obligatory methods related to the EJB lifecycle:

```
public void ejbPostCreate(OrderMaster orderMaster) {
}

public void ejbActivate() {
}

public void ejbPassivate() {
}

public void setEntityContext(EntityContext ctx) {
  this.ctx = ctx;
}

public void unsetEntityContext() {
  this.ctx = null;
}

public void ejbLoad() {
}

public void ejbStore() {
}

public void ejbRemove()
  throws RemoveException {
}
}
```

Note that the compulsory `ejbPostCreate()` method matches the parameters of its corresponding `ejbCreate()`.

Order Detail

`OrderDetailEB` is the entity bean that has been defined to access all the information from the `order_detail` table. The home interface is defined pretty much the same way as that for the `order_master` table:

```
package jsw.c05;

import javax.ejb.*;
import java.rmi.RemoteException;
import java.util.Enumeration;
/**
 * This is the Home Interface for the Entity EJB <tt>OrderDetailEB</tt>.
 *
 * @see     jsw.c05.OrderDetail
 * @see     jsw.c05.OrderDetailEB
 * @see     jsw.c05.OrderDetailEBPK
 * @see     jsw.c05.OrderDetailEBBean
 */
public interface OrderDetailEBHome extends EJBHome {

  /**
   * Creates a new OrderDetail Entity EJB.
   */
  public OrderDetailEB create(OrderDetail orderDetail)
    throws CreateException, RemoteException;
```

```
  /**
   * Searches for an OrderDetail Entity EJB, by its primary key.
   */
  public OrderDetailEB findByPrimaryKey(OrderDetailEBPK primaryKey)
    throws FinderException, RemoteException;

  /**
   * Searches for one or more OrderDetail Entity EJB, by order number.
   * The method returns the order details of a given order master.
   */
  public Enumeration findByOrderMaster(long orderNum)
    throws FinderException, RemoteException;

}
```

It is interesting to notice that the default finder method and the `findByOrderMaster()` method seem to be the same, since the primary key class of this bean is defined as:

```
package jsw.c05;

/**
 * This is the Primary Key for the Entity EJB <tt>OrderDetailEB</tt>.
 *
 * @see       jsw.c05.OrderDetail
 * @see       jsw.c05.OrderDetailEB
 * @see       jsw.c05.OrderDetailEBHome
 * @see       jsw.c05.OrderDetailEBBean
 */
public class OrderDetailEBPK implements java.io.Serializable {

  /**
   * This is the primary key.
   * It is the order detail number, which is the primary key
   * in table <tt>order_detail</tt>.
   */
  public long od_number;

  /**
   * This is the equals method.
   * @param obj java.lang.Object
   * @return boolean
   */
  public boolean equals(Object obj) {
    if (obj instanceof OrderDetailEBPK) {
      OrderDetailEBPK otherKey = (OrderDetailEBPK) obj;
      return ((this.od_number == otherKey.od_number));
    } else
      return false;
  }

  /**
   * This is the hashCode method.
   * @return int
   */
  public int hashCode() {
    return (int)this.od_number;
  }
}
```

However, the additional finder method has been defined as:

```
<finder-list>
  <finder>
    <method-name>findByOrderMaster</method-name>
    <method-params>
      <method-param>long</method-param>
    </method-params>
    <finder-query>
      <![CDATA[(orderBy 'od_number' (= od_or_number $0))]]>
    </finder-query>
  </finder>
</finder-list>
```

This means that the enumeration returned will be in numeric order.

The remote interface and the rest of the methods in this bean are pretty much the same as those for `OrderMasterEB`. It has a `getNewOrderDetailNum()`, which is used by `ejbCreate()`, and similar accessor methods as `getOrderDetail()` and `setOrderDetail()`, to get a new order detail number.

What is really interesting in this bean is the way that the methods `ejbLoad()` and `ejbStore()` are used to transform the data type. In the application, the pizza name and pizza size are used through the field `od_pizza`, which is of type `Pizza`; however in the database they are of type `String`, and the container will load and store them by using the fields `od_p_name` and `od_p_size`. So when the contents of this entity bean are being loaded, they must be converted from type `String` to type `Pizza`:

```
private transient Pizza od_pizza = null;

/**
 * This function transforms the data loaded from the database.
 * It creates a Pizza object initialized with the loaded
 * data, and stores it in the <tt>od_pizza</tt> field for later use.
 */
public void ejbLoad() {

  od_pizza = new Pizza();
  od_pizza.setP_name(od_p_name);
  od_pizza.setP_size(od_p_size);

  setModified(false); //"isModified" version: to avoid writing
}
```

In a similar fashion, when the contents of this entity bean are ready to be stored, they are converted from type `Pizza` to type `String`:

```
/**
 * This function transforms the data to be stored in the database.
 * It updates the data in fields <tt>od_p_name</tt> and
 * <tt>od_p_size</tt> from the data in field <tt>od_pizza</tt>.
 */
public void ejbStore() {

  od_p_name = od_pizza.getP_name();
  od_p_size = od_pizza.getP_size();

  setModified(false); //"isModified" version: to avoid writing
}
```

The `ejbStore()` and `ejbLoad()` methods are the ideal place to handle any data conversion that your application might need. For example, if the data is encrypted in the database, or if the data contains measurement units, this is the place you can convert them to the desired working units.

The `setModified()` method marks an `isDirty` Boolean flag as `true` when called:

```
/**
 * This field is for the "isModified" version.
 */
private transient boolean isDirty;

/**
 * Returns whether the bean has been modified or not.
 * This is for the "isModified" version.
 *
 * @return                      boolean isDirty
 */
public boolean isModified() {
  return isDirty;
}

/**
 * Sets the bean's modified flag.
 * This is for the "isModified" version.
 *
 * @param flag                Modified Flag
 */
public void setModified(boolean flag) {
  isDirty = flag;
}
```

The `isModified()` method is tagged in the `weblogic-ejb-jar.xml` deployment descriptor as the method to call from the `is-modified-method-name` tag:

```
<weblogic-ejb-jar>
  <weblogic-enterprise-bean>
    <ejb-name>jsw.c05.OrderDetailEB</ejb-name>
    ...
    <persistence-descriptor>
      <is-modified-method-name>isModified</is-modified-method-name>
      ...
    </persistence-descriptor>
    ...
  </weblogic-enterprise-bean>
</weblogic-ejb-jar>
```

The `isDirty` flag is reset in `ejbLoad()` and `ejbStore()` and set `true` in the `setOrderDetail()` method. The `isModified()` method is called by the container before committing the data, to find out whether the `ejbStore()` method needs to be called to store changes.

The Client's View

The changes to the client code are relatively simple. For example, originally `OrderList.jsp` contained the following JDBC garble:

```
<%
  try {
    Class.forName("weblogic.jdbc.pool.Driver");

    try {
      Connection conn =
        DriverManager.getConnection("jdbc:weblogic:pool:p2gPool");

      String select =
        "select * from order_master where " +
        " or_c_country_code = ? and or_c_area_code = ? and " +
        " or_c_phone = ? order by or_order_date";
      PreparedStatement pstmt = conn.prepareStatement(select);

      pstmt.setInt(1, customer.c_country_code);
      pstmt.setInt(2, customer.c_area_code);
      pstmt.setLong(3, customer.c_phone);

      ResultSet resultSet = pstmt.executeQuery();

      int nRows = 0;
      while(resultSet.next()) {
        nRows++;
        if (nRows == 1) {
%>
```

This has now been replaced with the following code:

```
<%
  try {
    Context ctx = Util.getInitialContext();
    OrderMasterEBHome orderMasterHome = (OrderMasterEBHome)
      ctx.lookup("jsw.c05.OrderMasterEB");
    Enumeration orderMasterList =
      orderMasterHome.findByCustomer(customer.c_country_code,
                                     customer.c_area_code,
                                     customer.c_phone);
    int nRows = 0;
    while(orderMasterList.hasMoreElements()) {
      if (nRows == 0) {
%>
```

The Wonder Troops are amazed that all the JDBC code has been replaced by a JNDI lookup and a call to a finder method, simplifying the JSP page of all its JDBC calls and embedded SQL.

Changes to the OrderServicesSL Bean

In the `OrderServicesSL` stateless session bean, things also get a lot easier. The `updatePrice()` and the `deliverOrder()` methods perform the search by primary key using the default finder method:

```
/**
 * This method updates in the database the total price of an order.
 * The order is specified by its order number (primary key).
 */
public float updatePrice(long orderNum)
  throws P2GException {

  float price = 0.0f;
  PizzaServicesSL pizzaServices = null;
  try {
    // Acquire handle to PizzaServiceSL session bean
    Context context = new InitialContext();

    PizzaServicesSLHome pizzaServicesHome =
      (PizzaServicesSLHome) context.lookup("jsw.c05.PizzaServicesSL");
    pizzaServices = pizzaServicesHome.create();

    // Acquire handle to OrderDetailEB entity bean
    // and get the enumeration of OrderDetail objects for this
    // order number
    OrderDetailEBHome orderDetailHome = (OrderDetailEBHome)
      context.lookup("jsw.c05.OrderDetailEB");
    Enumeration orderDetails =
      orderDetailHome.findByOrderMaster(orderNum);

    java.util.Date date = new java.util.Date();

    // Work through enumeration
    while(orderDetails.hasMoreElements()) {

      // Get detail
      OrderDetailEB orderDetailEB =
        (OrderDetailEB)orderDetails.nextElement();
      OrderDetail orderDetail = orderDetailEB.getOrderDetail();

      // Get price for that part of the pizza, from PizzaServiceSL
      price += orderDetail.getOd_quantity() *
             pizzaServices.getPrice(orderDetail.getOd_pizza(),
                          System.getProperty("jsw.location", "US"),
                          date, orderDetail.getOd_dough());
    }

    // Get OrderMasterEB for this order number,
    // and set new price
    OrderMasterEBHome orderMasterHome =
      (OrderMasterEBHome) context.lookup("jsw.c05.OrderMasterEB");
    OrderMasterEBPK primaryKey = new OrderMasterEBPK();
    primaryKey.or_number = orderNum;
    OrderMasterEB orderMasterEB =
      orderMasterHome.findByPrimaryKey(primaryKey);
```

```
            OrderMaster orderMaster = orderMasterEB.getOrderMaster();
            orderMaster.setOr_price(Util.format(price));
            orderMasterEB.setOrderMaster(orderMaster);

        pizzaServices.remove();
      } catch (Exception e) {
        System.err.println(e);
      }

      try {
        price = Util.format(price);
      } catch(ParseException pe) {
        throw new P2GException(Util.getStackTraceAsString(pe));
      }

      return price;
    }
```

In the `OrderMaintenanceSL` stateless session bean, the `viewOrder()` and `updateOrder()` methods use this entity bean in pretty much the same way as described above.

Changes to the OrderSF Bean

The first change to the `OrderSF` bean is the addition of transient references to the two entity beans we've just created:

```
      private transient OrderMasterEBHome orderMasterHome;
      private transient OrderDetailEBHome orderDetailHome;
```

In the `removeOrder()` method of the stateful bean `OrderSF`, you can see two different ways of deleting records:

❑   The first uses the remote object, of type `OrderDetailEB` to remove the order detail records

❑   The second uses the home object, of type `OrderMasterEBHome`, and the primary key, to delete the actual order master record using its ID

Here's the code:

```
    /**
     * Remove the order in the database.
     * It removes the order and its details from the database.
     * The state of this EJB became undetermined after calling this method
     * and it should no longer be used.
     * A new EJB must be created to work with a new order.
     */
    public void removeOrder()
        throws P2GException {

      if (!isNew) {
        try {
          Enumeration orderDetails =
            orderDetailHome.findByOrderMaster(orderMaster.getOr_number());
```

```
        while(orderDetails.hasMoreElements()) {
          OrderDetailEB orderDetailEB =
            (OrderDetailEB)orderDetails.nextElement();
          orderDetailEB.remove();
        }

        OrderMasterEBPK primaryKey = new OrderMasterEBPK();
        primaryKey.or_number = orderMaster.getOr_number();

        orderMasterHome.remove(primaryKey);
      } catch(Exception e) {
      System.err.println(e);
      throw new P2GException("<E> OrderBeanSF:removeOrder: "+
                             "the order could not be removed. reason:" +
                             e);
      }
    }
  }
}
```

The stateful bean `OrderSF` uses this entity bean to create a new order in the `storeOrder()` method as follows:

```
/**
 * Stores the order in the database.
 * It stores the order master and all the order details.
 * If the order is already in the database, then it is
 * replaced by this one.
 *
 * @exception P2GException
 *                  if the status order is already delivered.
 */
public void storeOrder()
    throws P2GException {

  try {
    if (!isNew) {
        // If the order has been loaded from a database,
        // remove the existing components of that order
        Enumeration orderDetails =
          orderDetailHome.findByOrderMaster(orderMaster.getOr_number());

        while(orderDetails.hasMoreElements()) {
          OrderDetailEB orderDetailEB =
            (OrderDetailEB)orderDetails.nextElement();
          orderDetailEB.remove();
        }

        // Get order number from OrderMaster instance
        // and use it to set the new OrderMasterEB object
        OrderMasterEBPK primaryKey = new OrderMasterEBPK();
        primaryKey.or_number = orderMaster.getOr_number();
        OrderMasterEB orderMasterEB =
          orderMasterHome.findByPrimaryKey(primaryKey);
```

```
                    orderMasterEB.setOrderMaster(orderMaster);
                } else {
                    // New order, and new OrderMasterEB instance
                    OrderMasterEB orderMasterEB = orderMasterHome.create(orderMaster);
                    orderMaster = orderMasterEB.getOrderMaster();
                    isNew = false;
                }

                // Iterate the orderDetailVector,
                // which holds the elements of the order
                for (Enumeration en = orderDetailVector.elements() ;
                     en.hasMoreElements(); ) {

                    // Retrieve the OrderDetail object and create a new OrderDetailEB
                    OrderDetail orderDetail = (OrderDetail)en.nextElement();
                    orderDetail.setOd_or_number(orderMaster.getOr_number());
                    orderDetailHome.create(orderDetail);
                }
            } catch(Exception e) {
            System.err.println(e);
            throw new P2GException("<E> OrderBeanSF:storeOrder: "+
                                    "the order could not be stored. reason:" +
                                    e);
        }
    }
```

Hybrid Data Access with the OutletServicesSL Bean

You can still combine the use of an entity bean with a straight JDBC query. Since the WonderTroops have only converted access to the `order_master` and `order_detail` tables to entity beans, the rest of the tables still have to be accessed using JDBC. An example of this hybrid access can be seen in the following code fragment from the `assignOutlet()` method of the `OutletServicesSL`, stateless bean:

```
/**
 * This method assigns an outlet to an order.
 * The assignment is based on the postal code and city.
 * @param orderNum the order identifier
 * @returns the outlet identifier assigned to the order
 */
public long assignOutlet(long orderNum)
  throws P2GException {

  long outletNum = 0;
  Connection conn = null;
  String select = "";

  try {
      // Get the order master for this order number
      Context context = new InitialContext();
      OrderMasterEBPK primaryKey = new OrderMasterEBPK();
      primaryKey.or_number = orderNum;
      OrderMasterEBHome orderMasterHome =
        (OrderMasterEBHome) context.lookup("jsw.c05.OrderMasterEB");
      OrderMasterEB orderMasterEB =
        orderMasterHome.findByPrimaryKey(primaryKey);
      OrderMaster orderMaster = orderMasterEB.getOrderMaster();
```

```
                  // Extract information from the customer table
                  // in order to assign the outlet
                  conn = DriverManager.getConnection("jdbc:weblogic:jts:p2gPool");
                  select = "select customer.c_postal_code, customer.c_city from " +
                          " customer " +
                          " where customer.c_country_code = ? and " +
                          " customer.c_area_code = ? and " +
                          " customer.c_phone = ? ";
                  PreparedStatement pstmt = conn.prepareStatement(select);
                  pstmt.setInt(1, orderMaster.getOr_c_country_code());
                  pstmt.setInt(2, orderMaster.getOr_c_area_code());
                  pstmt.setLong(3, orderMaster.getOr_c_phone());
                  ResultSet resultSet = pstmt.executeQuery();
                  long zipCode = 0;
                  String city = "";
                  if (resultSet.next()) {
                    zipCode = resultSet.getLong("c_postal_code");
                    city = resultSet.getString("c_city");
                  } else {
                    throw new Exception("<E> OutletServicesSLBean:assignOutlet: "+
                                   "the order could not be assigned to any outlet");
                  }
                  resultSet.close();
                  pstmt.close();
                  ....
```

Here, the `order_master` table is accessed via the entity bean, but the `customer` table is accessed using JDBC.

Deploying Entity Beans

The deployment descriptor attributes of the entity beans are kept in three files:

❑   `ejb-jar.xml`

❑   `weblogic-ejb-jar.xml`

❑   `weblogic-cmp-rdbms-jar.xml`

In a real-life application, with potentially hundreds of entity beans, related beans are likely to be packaged up within the same `.jar` file and can share these XML files. Our example has relatively few entity beans and, for simplicity, we will keep the files separate.

In the file `ejb-jar.xml` for the `OrderMasterEB` bean, the container managed fields are defined in the following fragment:

```
<ejb-jar>
  <enterprise-beans>
    <entity>
      <ejb-name>jsw.c05.OrderMasterEB</ejb-name>
      <home>jsw.c05.OrderMasterEBHome</home>
      <remote>jsw.c05.OrderMasterEB</remote>
      <ejb-class>jsw.c05.OrderMasterEBBean</ejb-class>
      <persistence-type>Container</persistence-type>
      <prim-key-class>jsw.c05.OrderMasterEBPK</prim-key-class>
      <reentrant>False</reentrant>
      <cmp-field>
```

185

```
            <field-name>or_order_date</field-name>
        </cmp-field>
        <cmp-field>
            <field-name>or_number</field-name>
        </cmp-field>
        ...
    </entity>
  </enterprise-beans>
  <assembly-descriptor>
    <container-transaction>
      <method>
        <ejb-name>jsw.c05.OrderMasterEB</ejb-name>
        <method-intf>Remote</method-intf>
        <method-name>*</method-name>
      </method>
      <trans-attribute>Required</trans-attribute>
    </container-transaction>
  </assembly-descriptor>
</ejb-jar>
```

In the descriptor, we can see:

❑ How the entity bean's persistence mechanism is defined as `Container`

❑ That the primary key class for the bean is defined in the `prim-key-class` tag

❑ That the `reentrant` tag is declared `False` to prevent loopbacks between beans. This is discouraged in the EJB specification because it can lead to deadlocks between beans.

The file `weblogic-ejb-jar.xml` (used for WebLogic-specific configuration) includes the persistence descriptor entry, which defines the type of persistence as follows:

```
<persistence-descriptor>
    <delay-updates-until-end-of-tx>false</delay-updates-until-end-of-tx>
    <persistence-type>
        <type-identifier>WebLogic_CMP_RDBMS</type-identifier>
        <type-version>5.1.0</type-version>
        <type-storage>META-INF/weblogic-cmp-rdbms-jar.xml</type-storage>
    </persistence-type>
    <db-is-shared>true</db-is-shared>
    <persistence-use>
        <type-identifier>WebLogic_CMP_RDBMS</type-identifier>
        <type-version>5.1.0</type-version>
    </persistence-use>
</persistence-descriptor>
```

Finally, the file `weblogic-cmp-rdbms-jar.xml` includes the information needed to actually perform container-managed persistence. This comprises:

❑ The JDBC pool name

❑ The table name

❑ The field-column mapping

❑ The finder descriptors

❑ The transaction isolation level

The following fragment of the `weblogic-cmp-rdbms-jar.xml` file shows this information (some field-column mappings are omitted):

```xml
<weblogic-rdbms-bean>
  <pool-name>p2gPool</pool-name>
  <table-name>order_master</table-name>
  <attribute-map>
    <object-link>
      <bean-field>or_order_date</bean-field>
      <dbms-column>or_order_date</dbms-column>
    </object-link>
    <object-link>
      <bean-field>or_number</bean-field>
      <dbms-column>or_number</dbms-column>
    </object-link>
    ...
    <object-link>
      <bean-field>or_delivery</bean-field>
      <dbms-column>or_delivery</dbms-column>
    </object-link>
  </attribute-map>
  <finder-list>
    <finder>
      <method-name>findByCustomer</method-name>
      <method-params>
        <method-param>int</method-param>
        <method-param>int</method-param>
        <method-param>long</method-param>
      </method-params>
      <finder-query>
        <![CDATA[(orderBy 'or_number'
                    (& (= or_c_country_code $0)
                       (= or_c_area_code $1)
                       (= or_c_phone $2)
                    )
                 )
        ]]>
      </finder-query>
    </finder>
  </finder-list>
  <options>
    <use-quoted-names>false</use-quoted-names>
    <transaction-isolation>TRANSACTION_SERIALIZABLE
                                </transaction-isolation>
  </options>
</weblogic-rdbms-bean>
```

Bean-Managed Persistence

This form of persistence is used to bypass the standard access and updates to the database performed by the EJB container. It is typically used by people who need to handle aggregations of data from various tables or have to persist to a data store that is not available via container managed persistence (CMP), for example a flat file. It is also useful when there is the need for some sophisticated finder methods that cannot be defined with CMP, or when there is the need to do some really weird stuff with the database.

> *TOPlink, an object relational mapping tool which is part of the WebGain studio, allows developers to write beans which use CMP, but which can still incorporate developer-written SQL and complex database relations.*

WebLogic has one limitation on using entity beans with container managed persistence – a single entity bean cannot span various tables. That is something TOPlink tackles, but we are often asked how to handle these cases with WebLogic alone. There are basically two ways.

The first uses a session bean to handle a set of entity beans, just as is done with the stateful session bean `OrderSF` as presented earlier in this chapter and illustrated below.

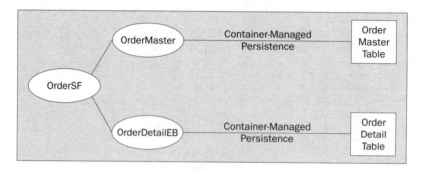

The second way is to manage the persistence yourself with BMP. It is this way that we'll look at in further detail here.

The Wonder Troops got together to decide how to use BMP with their application. As you might remember from Chapter 3, the relationship between a pizza and its ingredients is not straightforward. It is an n-to-n relationship with attributes, which happen to be the units of an ingredient in a pizza. This relation defines the amounts or units of each ingredient that makes up a pizza. Additionally, the data lives in three different tables. Mrs Chief Architect proposes that this case is used to explore the use of BMP in this application and the troops agree.

Mr Senior Developer sets out to design an entity bean, `PizzaUnitsEB`, that will present a view of the data contained in the three tables, as depicted opposite above.

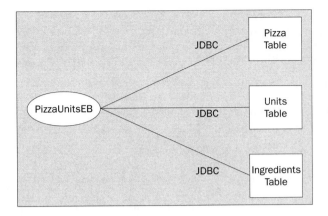

The following is a list of the fields handled by `PizzaUnitsEB`:

❏ `p_name`, `p_size`, `i_name`, and `u_units` in the `units` table. The first three fields make the primary key of the relation.

❏ `p_base_price` and `p_remarks` from the `pizza` table

❏ `i_remarks` from the `ingredient` table

The fields `p_name` and `p_size` are the foreign keys for the `Pizza` table, and `i_name` is the foreign key to the `Ingredient` table, as the following figure illustrates (taken from the database diagram in Chapter 2):

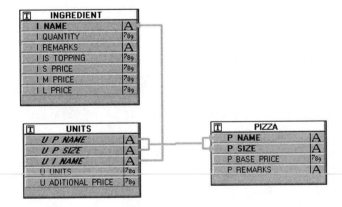

`PizzaUnitsEB` provides functionality to create, modify, update, and delete units of pizza ingredients. It also permits the changing of the fields of the tables that have a corresponding representation in this entity bean.

The home interface of this bean is the following:

```
package jsw.c05;

import javax.ejb.*;
import java.rmi.RemoteException;
import java.util.*;
```

```
/**
 * This is the home interface for the Entity EJB <tt>PizzaUnitsEB</tt>.
 *
 * @see      jsw.c05.PizzaUnitsEB
 * @see      jsw.c05.PizzaUnitsEBPK
 * @see      jsw.c05.PizzaUnitsEBBean
 */
public interface PizzaUnitsEBHome extends EJBHome {

  /**
   * Creates a new PizzaUnitsEB Entity EJB.
   */
  public PizzaUnitsEB create(Pizza pizza, String ingredientName,
                             float units)
    throws CreateException, RemoteException;

  /**
   * Searches for a PizzaUnitsEB Entity EJB, by its primary key.
   */
  public PizzaUnitsEB findByPrimaryKey(PizzaUnitsEBPK primaryKey)
    throws FinderException, RemoteException;

  /**
   * Searches for one or more ingredients and units of a given Pizza.
   * It returns all the primary keys of the Entity EJB found.
   * The enumeration is ordered by ingredient name.
   *
   * @param pizza the Pizza
   * @return                      Enumeration EJB Primary Keys
   * @exception                   javax.ejb.FinderException
   * @exception                   java.rmi.RemoteException
   */
  public Enumeration findByPizza(Pizza pizza)
    throws FinderException, RemoteException;

  /**
   * Searches for one or more ingredients and units of a given Pizza,
   * regardless of its size.
   * It returns all the primary keys of the Entity EJB found.
   * The enumeration is ordered by ingredient name and
   * pizza size (Small, Medium & Large).
   *
   * @param pizza the Pizza pizza, only the pizza name counts
   * @return                      Enumeration EJB Primary Keys
   * @exception                   javax.ejb.FinderException
   * @exception                   java.rmi.RemoteException
   */
  public Enumeration findByPizzaName(Pizza pizza)
    throws FinderException, RemoteException;

  /**
   * Searches for all ingredients and units.
   * It returns all the primary keys of the Entity EJB found.
   * The enumeration is alphabetically ordered by pizza name,
   * pizza size (Small, Medium & Large) and ingredient name.
   *
```

```
   * @return               Enumeration EJB Primary Keys
   * @exception            javax.ejb.FinderException
   * @exception            java.rmi.RemoteException
   */
  public Enumeration findAll()
    throws FinderException, RemoteException;


}
```

The primary key class is the following:

```
package jsw.c05;

/**
 * This is the Primary Key for the Entity EJB <tt>PizzaUnitsEB</tt>.
 *
 * @see      jsw.c05.PizzaUnitsEB
 * @see      jsw.c05.PizzaUnitsEBHome
 * @see      jsw.c05.PizzaUnitsEBBean
 */
public class PizzaUnitsEBPK implements java.io.Serializable {

  /**
   * This field is part of the primary key.
   * It is the pizza name, which is part of the primary key
   * in table <tt>units</tt>.
   */
  public String p_name;

  /**
   * This field is part of the primary key.
   * It is the pizza size, which is part of the primary key
   * in table <tt>units</tt>.
   */
  public String p_size;

  /**
   * This field is part of the primary key.
   * It is the ingredient name, which is part of the primary key
   * in table <tt>units</tt>.
   */
  public String i_name;

  /**
   * This is the equals method.
   * @param obj java.lang.Object
   * @return boolean
   */
  public boolean equals(Object obj) {
    if (obj instanceof PizzaUnitsEBPK) {
      PizzaUnitsEBPK otherKey = (PizzaUnitsEBPK) obj;
        return (this.p_name.equals(otherKey.p_name) &&
                this.p_size.equals(otherKey.p_size) &&
                this.i_name.equals(otherKey.i_name)
               );
```

```
      } else
        return false;
    }

    /**
     * This is the hashCode method.
     * @return int
     */
    public int hashCode() {
      String fullName = p_name + p_size + i_name;
        return fullName.hashCode();
    }
  }
```

As you can see, this bean has four finder methods:

- ❑   findByPrimaryKey()
- ❑   findByPizza()
- ❑   findByPizzaName()
- ❑   findAll()

Since the Troops are now using BMP, all the finder methods have to be hand-coded, so let us have a look at each of them, starting with the basic findByPrimaryKey().

Implementing Finder Methods in Bean-Managed Persistence

The finder method in the home interface is related to the corresponding finder method implementation in the EJB object by a convention established in the EJB specification. Both methods have the same parameters and return type, but the method name also includes the prefix ejb. For example, the findFoo() in the home interface is implemented by the EJB object method ejbFindFoo(). This follows the convention for the create() and ejbCreate() methods.

The ejbFindByPrimaryKey() method implementation in the PizzaUnitsEB bean is as follows:

```
    /**
     * Searches for a PizzaUnitsEB Entity EJB, by its primary key.
     */
    public PizzaUnitsEBPK ejbFindByPrimaryKey(PizzaUnitsEBPK primaryKey)
      throws FinderException {

      if ((primaryKey == null) || (primaryKey.p_name == null) ||
          (primaryKey.p_size == null) || (primaryKey.i_name == null))
        throw new FinderException ("primary key cannot be null");

      refresh(primaryKey);

      return primaryKey;
    }
```

The implementation includes a helper method, refresh(), used internally to load the information from the database into the bean. It does this by accessing all three tables and getting all the defined fields. All the database access is done using JDBC. Basically, this method does all the hard work of retrieving the data. It can be considered the equivalent of the ejbLoad() method in the CMP case.

```
/**
 * This method does the actual load of data from the database.
 * The loaded fields are from the tables: <tt>units</tt>,
 * <tt>pizza</tt> and <tt>ingredient</tt>
 *
 * @param primaryKey PizzaUnitsEBPK Primary Key
 * @exception javax.ejb.EJBException
 */
private void refresh(PizzaUnitsEBPK primaryKey)
    throws EJBException {

  if (primaryKey == null) {
    throw new EJBException ("primary key cannot be null");
  }

  Connection conn = null;
  PreparedStatement pstmt = null;
  ResultSet resultSet = null;
  try {
    // Given pizza name and size, and ingredient name, get units
    // This information is kept in the PizzaUnitsEBPK class
    conn = DriverManager.getConnection("jdbc:weblogic:jts:p2gPool");
    String select = "select u_units from units " +
      " where units.u_p_name = ? and units.u_p_size = ? and " +
      " units.u_i_name = ? ";
    pstmt = conn.prepareStatement(select);
    pstmt.setString(1, primaryKey.p_name);
    pstmt.setString(2, primaryKey.p_size);
    pstmt.setString(3, primaryKey.i_name);
    pstmt.executeQuery();

    resultSet = pstmt.getResultSet();
    if (resultSet.next()) {
      p_name  = primaryKey.p_name;
      p_size  = primaryKey.p_size;
      i_name  = primaryKey.i_name;
      u_units = resultSet.getFloat("u_units");
    } else {
      throw new EJBException ("Refresh: PizzaUnitsEB ("
          + primaryKey.p_name + "," + primaryKey.p_size + ","
          + primaryKey.i_name + ") not found");
    }
    resultSet.close();
    pstmt.close();

    // Get the price for the pizza, depends on its name and size
    select = "select p_base_price from pizza " +
          " where pizza.p_name = ? and pizza.p_size = ? ";
    pstmt = conn.prepareStatement(select);
    pstmt.setString(1, primaryKey.p_name);
    pstmt.setString(2, primaryKey.p_size);
    pstmt.executeQuery();
```

```
      resultSet = pstmt.getResultSet();
      if (resultSet.next()) {
        p_base_price = resultSet.getFloat("p_base_price");
      } else {
        throw new EJBException ("Refresh: PizzaUnitsEB ("
              + primaryKey.p_name + "," + primaryKey.p_size + ","
              + primaryKey.i_name + ") not found");
      }
      resultSet.close();
      pstmt.close();

      // Get the ingredient details
      select = "select i_remarks from ingredient " +
              " where ingredient.i_name = ? ";
      pstmt = conn.prepareStatement(select);
      pstmt.setString(1, primaryKey.i_name);
      pstmt.executeQuery();
      resultSet = pstmt.getResultSet();

      if (resultSet.next()) {
        i_remarks = resultSet.getString("i_remarks");
      } else {
        throw new EJBException ("Refresh: PizzaUnitsEB ("
              + primaryKey.p_name + "," + primaryKey.p_size + ","
              + primaryKey.i_name + ") not found");
      }
    } catch (SQLException sqe) {
      throw new EJBException (sqe.getMessage());
    } finally {
      try {
        if (resultSet    != null) resultSet.close();
        if (pstmt != null) pstmt.close();
        if (conn   != null) conn.close();
      } catch (Exception e) {
        throw new EJBException (e.getMessage());
      }
    }
  }
}
```

The `ejbFindByPizza()` method searches for all the beans that are ingredients of a specified pizza. It returns an enumeration of the primary keys of the beans that match the condition. The enumeration is ordered alphabetically by ingredient name. The sort is requested in the prepared statement used to call the database.

```
/**
 * Searches for one or more ingredients and units of a given Pizza.
 * It returns all the primary keys of the E-EJB found.
 * The enumeration is ordered by ingredient name.
 *
 * @param pizza the Pizza
 * @return                    Enumeration EJB Primary Keys
 * @exception                 javax.ejb.FinderException
 */
public Enumeration ejbFindByPizza(Pizza pizza)
    throws FinderException {
```

```
      Connection conn = null;
      PreparedStatement pstmt = null;
      ResultSet resultSet = null;
      try {
        conn = DriverManager.getConnection("jdbc:weblogic:jts:p2gPool");
        String select = "select u_i_name from units " +
          " where units.u_p_name = ? and units.u_p_size = ? " +
          " order by u_i_name";
        pstmt = conn.prepareStatement(select);
        pstmt.setString(1, pizza.getP_name());
        pstmt.setString(2, pizza.getP_size());
        pstmt.executeQuery();

        resultSet = pstmt.getResultSet();
        Vector v = new Vector();
        PizzaUnitsEBPK primaryKey;

        while (resultSet.next()) {
          primaryKey = new PizzaUnitsEBPK();
          primaryKey.p_name = pizza.getP_name();
          primaryKey.p_size = pizza.getP_size();
          primaryKey.i_name = resultSet.getString("u_i_name");
          v.addElement(primaryKey);
        }

        resultSet.close();
        pstmt.close();
        conn.close();

        return v.elements();
      } catch (SQLException sqe) {
        throw new FinderException(sqe.getMessage());
      }
    }
```

The `ejbFindByPizzaName()` finder method searches for all the ingredients of a specified pizza, no matter what its size. It converts the query results to an enumeration of the primary keys of the beans which it returns. The enumeration is ordered alphabetically by ingredient and size (in descending order; small, medium, and large).

```
/**
 * Searches for one or more ingredients and units of a given Pizza,
 * regardless of its size.
 * It returns all the primary keys of the E-EJB found.
 * The enumeration is ordered by ingredient name and
 * pizza size (Small, Medium & Large).
 *
 * @param pizza the Pizza pizza, only the pizza name counts
 * @return                  Enumeration EJB Primary Keys
 * @exception               javax.ejb.FinderException
 */
public Enumeration ejbFindByPizzaName(Pizza pizza)
    throws FinderException {
```

```
      Connection conn = null;
      PreparedStatement pstmt = null;
      ResultSet resultSet = null;

      try {
        conn = DriverManager.getConnection("jdbc:weblogic:jts:p2gPool");
        String select = "select u_p_size, u_i_name from units " +
          " where units.u_p_name = ? order by u_i_name asc, u_p_size desc";
        pstmt = conn.prepareStatement(select);
        pstmt.setString(1, pizza.getP_name());
        pstmt.executeQuery();

        resultSet = pstmt.getResultSet();
        Vector v = new Vector();
        PizzaUnitsEBPK primaryKey;

        while (resultSet.next()) {
          primaryKey = new PizzaUnitsEBPK();
          primaryKey.p_name = pizza.getP_name();
          primaryKey.p_size = resultSet.getString("u_p_size");
          primaryKey.i_name = resultSet.getString("u_i_name");
          v.addElement(primaryKey);
        }

        resultSet.close();
        pstmt.close();
        conn.close();

        return v.elements();
      } catch (SQLException sqe) {
        throw new FinderException(sqe.getMessage());
      }
    }
```

Lastly, the `findAll()` method returns an enumeration of all the primary keys of the EJBs found. The enumeration is sorted alphabetically by ascending pizza name, descending pizza size (small, medium, and large), and ascending ingredient.

```
/**
 * Searches for all ingredients and units.
 * It returns all the primary keys of the Entity EJB found.
 * The enumeration is alphabetically ordered by pizza name,
 * pizza size (Small, Medium & Large) and ingredient name.
 *
 * @return              Enumeration EJB Primary Keys
 * @exception           javax.ejb.FinderException
 */
public Enumeration ejbFindAll()
    throws FinderException {

  Connection conn = null;
  PreparedStatement pstmt = null;
  ResultSet resultSet = null;
```

```
    try {
      conn = DriverManager.getConnection("jdbc:weblogic:jts:p2gPool");
      String select = "select u_p_name, u_p_size, u_i_name from units " +
        " order by u_p_name asc, u_p_size desc, u_i_name asc";
      pstmt = conn.prepareStatement(select);
      pstmt.executeQuery();

      resultSet = pstmt.getResultSet();
      Vector v = new Vector();
      PizzaUnitsEBPK primaryKey;

      while (resultSet.next()) {
        primaryKey = new PizzaUnitsEBPK();
        primaryKey.p_name = resultSet.getString("u_p_name");
        primaryKey.p_size = resultSet.getString("u_p_size");
        primaryKey.i_name = resultSet.getString("u_i_name");
        v.addElement(primaryKey);
      }

      resultSet.close();
      pstmt.close();
      conn.close();

      return v.elements();
    } catch (SQLException sqe) {
      throw new FinderException(sqe.getMessage());
    }
  }
}
```

The Remote Interface and Bean Implementation

The remote interface for the PizzaUnitsEB bean has the following methods:

- ❑ getPizza()
- ❑ getIngredient()
- ❑ setPizzaPrice()
- ❑ getPizzaPrice()
- ❑ setUnits()
- ❑ getUnits()
- ❑ setPizzaRemarks()
- ❑ getPizzaRemarks()
- ❑ setIngredientRemarks()
- ❑ getIngredientRemarks()

We are not going to look in detail at the implementation of these business methods. However, we will have a look into some of the lifecycle methods.

To recap, the lifecycle of the entity bean looks like this:

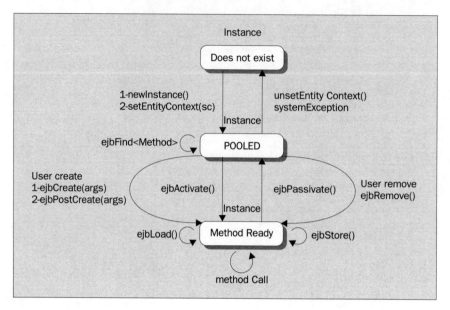

The methods we'll look at here are:

- ❑ ejbLoad()
- ❑ ejbStore()
- ❑ ejbRemove()

The other methods are default implementations, or empty.

The class fields used in these methods are:

Field	Description
p_name	Pizza name
p_size	Pizza size
i_name	Ingredient name
u_units	Ingredient units
p_base_price	Pizza price
p_remarks	Pizza remarks
i_remarks	Ingredient remarks

The `ejbLoad()` method has the following code:

```
/**
 * This method loads the data from the database.
 * @see #refresh(PizzaUnitsEBPK primaryKey)
 */
public void ejbLoad() {
  try {
    refresh((PizzaUnitsEBPK)ctx.getPrimaryKey());
  } catch (Exception e) {
    throw new EJBException(e.getMessage());
  }
}
```

The `ejbLoad()` method delegates the hard work to the `refresh()` method, just as we saw in the `findByPrimaryKey()` method.

The `ejbStore()` method updates the information of the bean to the three tables via JDBC:

```
/**
 * This method does the actual store of data to database.
 * The fields are saved in tables: <tt>units</tt>,
 * <tt>pizza</tt> and <tt>ingredient</tt>
 *
 */
public void ejbStore() {

  Connection conn = null;
  PreparedStatement pstmt = null;
  try {
    // Update units table
    conn  = DriverManager.getConnection("jdbc:weblogic:jts:p2gPool");
    pstmt = conn.prepareStatement("update units set u_units = ? " +
          "where u_p_name = ? and u_p_size = ? and u_i_name = ?");
    pstmt.setFloat (1, u_units);
    pstmt.setString(2, p_name);
    pstmt.setString(3, p_size);
    pstmt.setString(4, i_name);
    int i = pstmt.executeUpdate();
    if (i == 0) {
      throw new EJBException ("ejbStore: PizzaUnitsEB ("
          + p_name + "," + p_size + "," + i_name + ") not updated");
    }
    pstmt.close();

    // Update pizza table with new price or any remarks
    pstmt = conn.prepareStatement(
          "update pizza set p_base_price = ?, p_remarks = ? " +
          "where p_name = ? and p_size = ?");
    pstmt.setFloat (1, p_base_price);
    pstmt.setString(2, p_remarks);
    pstmt.setString(3, p_name);
    pstmt.setString(4, p_size);
    i = pstmt.executeUpdate();
```

```
            if (i == 0) {
              throw new EJBException ("ejbStore: PizzaUnitsEB ("
                    + p_name + "," + p_size + "," + i_name + ") not updated");
            }
            pstmt.close();

            // Update ingredient table with any remarks
            pstmt = conn.prepareStatement(
                    "update ingredient set i_remarks = ? " +
                    "where i_name = ?");
            pstmt.setString(1, i_remarks);
            pstmt.setString(2, i_name);
            i = pstmt.executeUpdate();
            if (i == 0) {
              throw new EJBException ("ejbStore: PizzaUnitsEB ("
                    + p_name + "," + p_size + "," + i_name + ") not updated");
            }
        } catch (SQLException sqe) {
          throw new EJBException (sqe.getMessage());
        } finally {
          try {
            pstmt.close();
            conn.close();
          } catch (Exception e) {
            throw new EJBException (e.getMessage());
          }
        }
    }
}
```

The `ejbRemove()` method performs a manual delete of the corresponding record in the database. The primary key has to be obtained from the context because it is possible to do a remove right after a find, and `ejbLoad()` may not have been called.

```
/**
 * This method removes the data of this EJB from the database.
 * The removed row is from table <tt>units</tt>.
 *
 * @exception javax.ejb.RemoveException
 */
public void ejbRemove()
    throws RemoveException {

  Connection conn = null;
  PreparedStatement pstmt = null;
  try {
    conn = DriverManager.getConnection("jdbc:weblogic:jts:p2gPool");
    PizzaUnitsEBPK primaryKey = (PizzaUnitsEBPK) ctx.getPrimaryKey();
    pstmt= conn.prepareStatement("delete from units where " +
      " u_p_name = ? and u_p_size = ? and u_i_name = ?");
    pstmt.setString(1, primaryKey.p_name);
    pstmt.setString(2, primaryKey.p_size);
    pstmt.setString(3, primaryKey.i_name);
    int i = pstmt.executeUpdate();
```

```
         if (i == 0) {
           throw new EJBException ("ejbRemove: PizzaUnitsEB ("
                 + primaryKey.p_name + "," + primaryKey.p_size + ","
                 + primaryKey.i_name + ") not found");
         }
     } catch (SQLException sqe) {
       throw new EJBException (sqe.getMessage());
     } finally {
       try {
         pstmt.close();
         conn.close();
       } catch (Exception e) {
         throw new EJBException (e.getMessage());
       }
     }
   }
 }
```

Finally, the ejbCreate() method does the same as ejbStore(), but instead of an update it inserts the necessary records in the three tables.

Client Use of the BMP Bean

The PizzaList.jsp page uses this bean to present the composition of each pizza in units of ingredients. The following code is from the PizzaList.jsp page and shows the detailed composition of the selected pizza:

```
<%
  sPName = request.getParameter("u_p_name");
  if (sPName != null){
%>
  <h2><center><%= sPName%></center></h2>

<table width="75%" border="1" align="center"
      cellpadding="0" cellspacing="0">
  <tr>
    <th colspan="2" bordercolor="#FFFFFF"></th>
    <th colspan="3">Units</th>
  </tr>
  <tr>
    <th colspan="2">Ingredient</th>
    <th>Small</th>
    <th>Medium</th>
    <th>Large</th>
  </tr>

<%
    try {
      // Get a handle to the PizzaServiceSL bean
      Context ctx = Util.getInitialContext();
      PizzaServicesSLHome pizzaServicesHome =
        (PizzaServicesSLHome)ctx.lookup("jsw.c05.PizzaServicesSL");
      pizzaServices = pizzaServicesHome.create();
      session.setAttribute("pizzaServices", pizzaServices);
```

```
      // Get a handle to the PizzaUnitsEB bean
      PizzaUnitsEBHome pizzaUnitsHome =
        (PizzaUnitsEBHome) ctx.lookup("jsw.c05.PizzaUnitsEB");
      Pizza pizza = new Pizza();
      pizza.setP_name(sPName);
      // Get all ingredients and units for pizza
      Enumeration ingredients = pizzaUnitsHome.findByPizzaName(pizza);

      String sParams = null;
      while(ingredients.hasMoreElements()) {
        PizzaUnitsEB pizzaUnits =
          (PizzaUnitsEB) ingredients.nextElement();
        %>
        <tr>
          <td colspan="2"><%= pizzaUnits.getIngredient() %></td>
          <% for(int i = 0; i < 3; i++) {%>
            <td><%= pizzaUnits.getUnits()%></td>
          <%   if (i < 2)
                  pizzaUnits = (PizzaUnitsEB) ingredients.nextElement();
              }%>
        </tr>
        <%
      }
```

```
      conn = DriverManager.getConnection("jdbc:weblogic:pool:p2gPool");
      String select = "select d_name, d_units from dough " +
        "where d_p_size <> 'Calzone' order by d_name desc, d_p_size desc";
      PreparedStatement pstmt = conn.prepareStatement(select);
      ResultSet resultSet = pstmt.executeQuery();
      boolean isFirst = true;
      while(resultSet.next()) {
        %>
        <tr>
          <%if(isFirst) {
              out.println("<td rowspan=\"2\">Dough</td>");
              isFirst=false;
          }%>
          <td><%= resultSet.getString("d_name")%></td>
          <% for(int i = 0; i < 3; i++) {%>
            <td><%= resultSet.getFloat("d_units")%></td>
          <% if(i < 2) resultSet.next();}%>
        </tr>
        <%
      }
      resultSet.close();
      pstmt.close();
      conn.close();
    } catch (Exception e) {
      System.err.print(e);
    }
  %>

  </table>

  <%
```

```
    } else {
%>
   (click on the name to see the detailed description)
<%
   }
%>
</body>
</html>
```

A nice side effect of this experiment is that this `PizzaUnitsEB` entity bean can be used for backend maintenance, something that allows the user to add pizzas, update the price of a pizza, or just edit the list of ingredients that make up a pizza.

Deploying the Applications

As the `PizzaUnitsEB` bean is of type BMP, only two files are needed for the deployment descriptor: `ejb-jar.xml` and `weblogic-ejb-jar.xml`. The third file, `weblogic-cmp-rdbms-jar.xml`, contains information about the container managed persistence, which is not used by this entity bean.

The following entries are in the file `weblogic-ejb-jar.xml`:

```
<weblogic-ejb-jar>
  <weblogic-enterprise-bean>
    <ejb-name>jsw.c05.PizzaUnitsEB</ejb-name>
    <caching-descriptor>
      <max-beans-in-cache>100</max-beans-in-cache>
      <idle-timeout-seconds>5</idle-timeout-seconds>
    </caching-descriptor>
    <persistence-descriptor>
    <delay-updates-until-end-of-tx>false</delay-updates-until-end-of-tx>
    </persistence-descriptor>
    <jndi-name>jsw.c05.PizzaUnitsEB</jndi-name>
  </weblogic-enterprise-bean>
</weblogic-ejb-jar>
```

Running the Entity Beans

As in the previous chapter, a `GNUmakefile` is provided to compile, deploy, and install the code for this chapter. Specific targets for the new entity EJBs are defined (`PizzaUnitsEB`, `OrderMasterEB`, and `OrderDetailEB`).

With these examples EJBs call each other, and so it is very important to understand the dependencies between them. The order in which they are deployed is critical. For the example in this chapter the order of dependency is (from the `weblogic.properties` file):

```
weblogic.ejb.deploy=\
   c:/wlsbook/srv/c05-srv/ejb/PizzaUnitsEBBean.jar,\
   c:/wlsbook/srv/c05-srv/ejb/OrderMasterEBBean.jar,\
   c:/wlsbook/srv/c05-srv/ejb/OrderDetailEBBean.jar,\
   c:/wlsbook/srv/c05-srv/ejb/PizzaServicesSLBean.jar,\
   c:/wlsbook/srv/c05-srv/ejb/OrderServicesSLBean.jar,\
   c:/wlsbook/srv/c05-srv/ejb/OutletServicesSLBean.jar,\
   c:/wlsbook/srv/c05-srv/ejb/OrderSFBean.jar
```

This is more or less straightforward. It becomes a little more complicated when you have circular dependencies. This is, when bean A calls bean B, which then uses bean A. For direct or indirect circular dependencies the solution is to place the beans involved in the same JAR file. In any case, it is highly recommended that you try to use JAR files as much as you can. They do make things a lot easier, more organized, and cleaner, and most important, allow for hot deployment.

The Controversy

After developing the code for this chapter, the Wonder Troops find themselves embroiled in a pretty lively controversy about the usage of entity beans. On one side of the table sits Mr Senior Developer and the majority of developers. They think that:

❑   Entity beans should only be used for queries when the enumeration or collection returned by a finder method is not more than a handful of records.

❑   Functions such as a listing of all the customers of Pizza2Go, which is bound to return a large number of records, should use JDBC directly. The argument is based on the fact that a large number of bean instances in the container will substantially diminish the performance of the server.

❑   They feel more comfortable using entity beans for updates and inserts to the persistence store, as well as for simple retrievals of information.

The opposition consists of Mrs Chief Architect and a few of the developers. Their view is that most of the access to the persistence store should be done solely through entity beans, except for queries that return a very large number of records. Direct JDBC access is the big no-no. The productivity gains possible during the development cycle through using entity beans far out-weigh any possible performance degradation, in their opinion.

The situation is reminiscent of historic fights where Assembler was pitted against FORTRAN or COBOL – execution efficiency against development and maintenance productivity.

However Mrs Chief Architect does not ignore the fact that this technology is relatively new and that there might be limitations on the implementations that are available today. This could potentially be the main performance issue.

Nobody seems to have a clear answer to the situation. Happily, for the parties involved, the performance of entity beans is one of the items that will be measured in Chapter 11, where the load capacity tests will hopefully resolve the controversy.

There is also a school of thought that container- and bean-managed beans should not be mixed in one system, as it makes design decisions too complex and maintenance too difficult. However, not enough work has yet been done with EJBs to know which approach is going to be the best.

The EJB 2.0 specification also introduces some significant changes, notably a much more sophisticated specification for beans using container-managed persistence, and it remains to be seen how much these will impact on EJB design. Since this book is concerned with proven development techniques, this has not been addressed here.

Summary

In this chapter, we've reviewed the lifecycle and development of entity beans, and seen how they can:

❑ Reduce the programming necessary to get and update data

❑ Hide database-specific code in entity beans, rather than scattering it throughout JSPs, servlets, and session beans

We've also seen something of the support that WebLogic provides for entity bean deployment and optimization.

In the next chapter, we'll return to user interface considerations, when we port an existing ASP site to JSP, interfacing its business functionality with the code we've built in the past two chapters, and making Internet ordering possible.

6

ASP Pizzas to JSP

Mr Yesman has lost no time. He witnessed how Mr Oldtimer was kicked out, so he felt compelled to bring some jewel to the attention of Mr Chairman of the Board. Where better to look than in the Silicon Valley, the Mecca of technology. Surely there has to be somebody using technology in a way that Pizza2Go can take advantage of.

The result of his research took him to a small outfit called E-Pizza. Although a relative newcomer to the pizza scene, they had something that Mr Yesman could not resist, a real web site that had been working for a while. Not only that, the web site looked a lot better that anything the Wonder Troops had done so far.

In conclusion, Pizza2Go purchases E-Pizza, now Mr Wonderboy has nice front end, but also faces a serious dilemma. That is, the system that E-Pizza has is written using Microsoft ASP, a direct competitor to JSP. The interface is much better looking than the one developed by the Wonder Troops in Chapter 3, but there are serious concerns about the ability to scale up to the increased level of business Pizza2Go has and also handle the growth plans. The concerns are based on the experiences of Mr Wonderboy's peers, who have experienced meltdowns of their previous ASP-based web sites when the load exceeded a few hundred simultaneous users. Another major disadvantage of using ASP is that web sites will only run on Microsoft platforms, whereas JSP-based sites will run on all the major platforms, including Microsoft ones.

In this chapter we will explore the ASP based web site and see how the Wonder Troops integrate it with the application they have developed so far. As we saw in Chapter 3, the look and feel of the application as developed so far is rather poor. The plan is to enhance it with the look and feel of the ASP based web site. They will also be adding new functionality that is present on the E-Pizza web site that does not exist on their current application, which will be discussed later.

The first step is to try to understand the E-Pizza web site. Mr Wonderboy is really interested to learn what the guys of E-Pizza have done and how different it is from the business model that Pizza2Go has today.

The setup instructions for the ASP site are provided at the end of the chapter.

The Tour

At first glance E-Pizza has exactly what the experiments of Pizza2Go are lacking so far, a good looking front end and a few concepts that the Wonder Troops have not even considered. Admittedly, they have only worked on experiments that were designed for use of the internal operators of Pizza2Go. The fundamental difference is that this is a true web site that can take orders over the Internet, and the more channels the better. The team decides to take a little tour of the web site and learn from it. They start from the home page, which can be seen in the following figure.

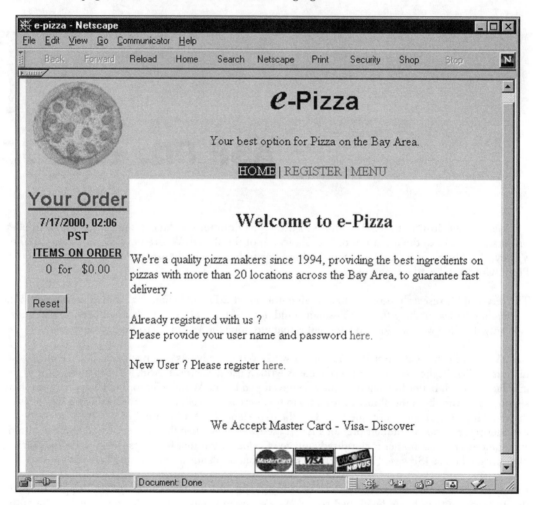

They first realize that in order to be able to do business with E-Pizza, the visitor is required to register by clicking the REGISTER link to move along. The following figure shows how they complete the registration operation:

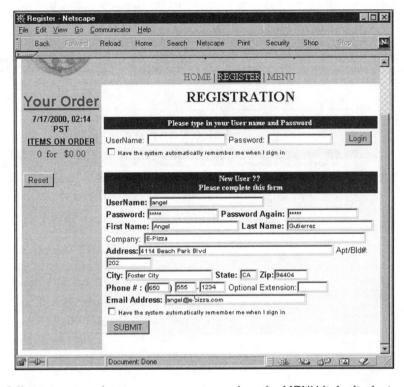

After successfully registering, the team moves on to explore the MENU link, displaying the standard range of pizzas. This is shown in the next screenshot:

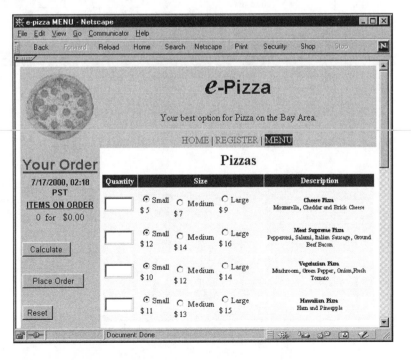

The Wonder Troops are surprised that as well as offering the standard pizzas, E-Pizza also allows the customer to create their own pizza by selecting from a variety of toppings, a real departure in comparison to the way Pizza2Go has done business so far. This procedure is illustrated in the following figure:

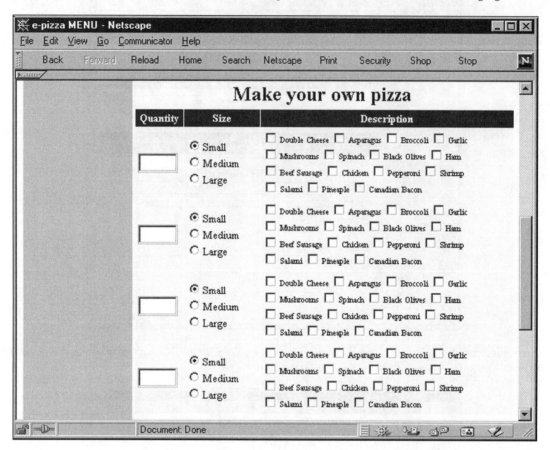

And if that was not enough, you can also choose a beverage to accompany the order, as is shown below:

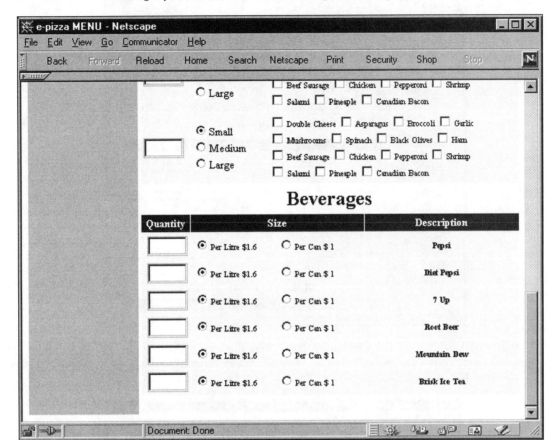

All functionality shown above is included within the same page and has the additional capability of calculating the price of the order as you go. After seeing this, the team is ready to place a test order. This order includes a standard pizza, a custom made one, and a beverage to wash down what so far has been described as second class pizza with a first class web site.

The order, which is composed of a medium cheese pizza, a medium pizza with garlic, mushrooms and chicken, and one liter of brisk ice tea totals $15.85, as calculated when the Calculate button is clicked on, shown in the figure overleaf:

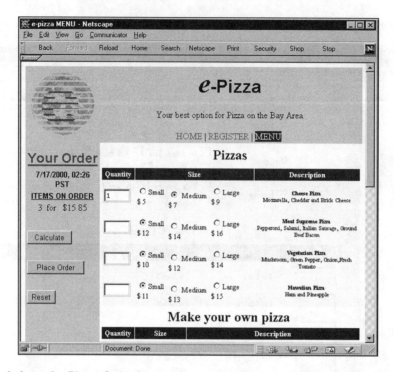

When they click on the **Place Order** button, the system presents them with the address where the pizza is going to be delivered and the actual order. The address is taken from the one used when registering. The customer has the option of modifying the address or the order, as shown below:

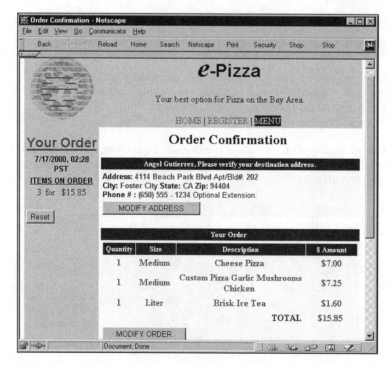

Additionally, on the same page they get to define the payment method:

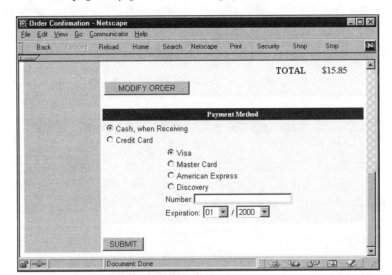

However, one problem was identified immediately. The absence of a Secure Socket Layer mechanism on the browser to secure the communication between browser and web site. A Secure Socket Layer mechanism is identified with a closed lock image at the bottom of the browser, which was absent from the page displaying important credit card information on E-Pizza's web site. In order to keep matters simple at present, support for the Secure Socket Layer mechanism will be discussed in Chapter 8.

When the Submit button is selected, the application sends the credit card number to the processing center for validation and approval of the transaction. If successful, they will get an order confirmation screen:

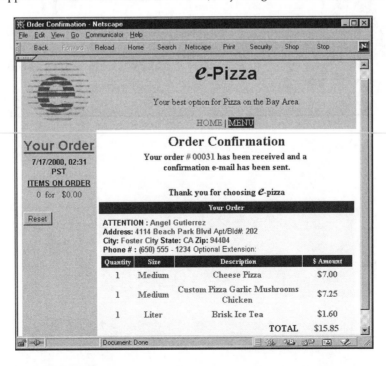

Internally what happens once the order has been confirmed is that it is assigned to the nearest outlet in the same fashion that the Pizza2Go application does. Once it is assigned, an e-mail message is sent with the order to the corresponding outlet. This is an improvement over the fax that Pizza2Go sends.

The next step for the team is to find out how the back-end or maintenance section of this system works. When logging in as administrator (password: pizza4me) they get a new menu option in the welcome page. That option is invoked by clicking the MANAGEMENT link, which allows them to view the queue of orders, as can be seen in the following figure.

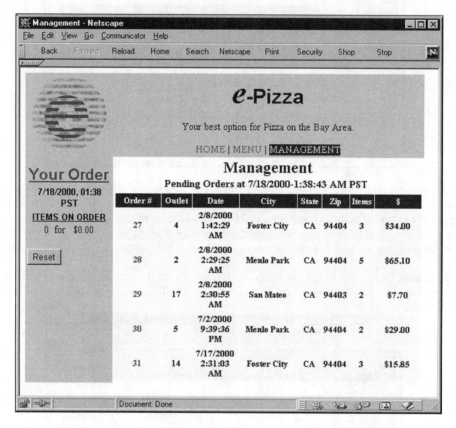

Just to test, they decide to click on order number 28, which then produces the following screen that contains the details of that order:

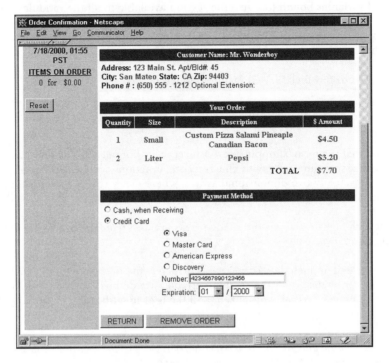

The only functionality offered in the maintenance section is the ability to remove an order from the queue.

The team is very impressed with the web site, especially when they continue the tests by forcing errors and seeing how it handles them.

Programming the Site

To better understand the internals of the system, Mrs Chief Architect and Mr Senior Developer travel to Silicon Valley to meet with the ASP Jockeys of E-Pizza. They start by getting a basic flow chart structure of the web site, as presented in the following diagram:

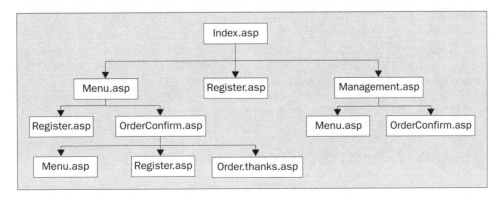

The basic architectural principle is that all the information related to the system is retrieved from the database, for example, the users, the pizzas, toppings, and pricing. The information needed for an order is stored as global variables bound to a specific session available to all the modules during execution.

Interestingly enough, the folks of E-Pizza have designed the application so that the orders are handled internally with three basic shopping carts:

- ❑ dpizzas_scart, which is used for pre-defined pizzas
- ❑ cpizzas_scart for custom made pizzas
- ❑ bev_scart for the beverages

It should be noted that the term 'shopping cart' is used very liberally in this sense as they are not conventional internet shopping carts with characteristic functions such as 'add to basket' or 'proceed to checkout'. They are actually two dimensional arrays, where every row is a vector that contains the necessary information associated to the corresponding shopping cart.

Additionally, the toppings for the custom made pizzas are also handled as a two dimensional array called cpizzas_toppings_scart.

The files used in the system include global.asa, which is the first page to be executed when the session with the server begins. In it, the session variables are defined, including the connection string to the database, the shopping carts are initialized, and the user identification is procured from the cookie, if there is one.

> *A cookie is a mechanism allowing the web server to remember the user and is used in session identification. Cookies will be explained further in Chapter 8.*

```
<SCRIPT LANGUAGE=VBScript RUNAT=Server>

Sub Session_OnStart
    Session("ConnString") = "DATABASE=epizza;DSN=epizza;" & _
                            "UID=epizza;Password=epizza;"
    Set epizza_conn = Server.CreateObject("ADODB.Connection")
    connstring = Session("connstring")
    epizza_conn.Open connstring


    ' Defining some User Variables
    Session("SessionActive") = "True"
    ' To validate if the Session is still active
    Session("UserLogIn") = False
    ' If the user has logged in
    Session("UserName") = ""
    Session("UserLevel") = 1


    ' Getting the UserID from the cookie
    UserCookie = Request.Cookies("UserInfo")("UserID")
    Session("Update_address") = False


    ' Flag to use the registration screen to update address information
    Session("Order_specified") = False
```

```
' Flag to use the menu screen to modify the order
Session("CookieFound") = False
If
    IsNull(UserCookie)
    Or IsEmpty(UserCookie)
    Or Len(Trim(UserCookie)) = 0 then
    Session("UserID") = 0

    ' If there's no cookie, then UserID will be 0
Else
    session("UserID") = Request.Cookies("UserInfo")("UserID")
    StrSQL = " Select * from Users where User_ID = " & _
            session("UserID")
    Set user_info = epizza_conn.Execute(strSQL)

    ' Validating the UserID from the cookie
    If not
        (user_info.EOF and user_Info.BOF) then
         Session("CookieFound") = True
        ' Session("UserLogin") = True
        Session("UserName") = user_info("Fname") & " " & _
                              user_info("Lname")
        Session("UserLevel") = user_info("UserLevel")
    Else
        Session("UserID") = 0
    End If
    Set user_info = nothing
End If

' Now defining variables for the Three Shopping Carts:
' Number of possible customizable pizzas to order
Session("Custom_Pizzas") = 4

' Getting the number of possible Toppings on the Database
strSQL = " Select number = Count (*) from toppings Where" & _
        " ActiveRecord = 1"
Set pizza_toppings = epizza_conn.Execute(strSQL)
Session("total_toppings") = pizza_toppings("number")
strSQL = "Select topping_ID from toppings where ActiveRecord = 1"
Set pizza_toppings = epizza_conn.Execute(strSQL)
```

```
' Creating the Shopping Cart for Pre-defined Pizzas
Session("OrderTotalDollars") = 0
Session("OrderTotalItems") = 0
ReDim dpizzas_scart(5,0)
' First dimension is the Item property (qty,size,id, etc).
' Second is the Item Index
Session("dpizzas_scart") = dpizzas_scart
Session("dpizzas_scart_Count") = 0

' Creating the Shopping Cart for Beverages
ReDim bev_scart(5,0)
' First dimension is the Item property (qty,size,id, etc).
' Second is the Item Index
Session("bev_scart") = bev_scart
Session("bev_scart_Count") = 0
```

```
      ' Creating the Shopping Cart for Custom Pizzas
      ReDim cpizzas_scart(5,Session("Custom_Pizzas"))
      ' This is a fixed cart (only for the maximum number of items)
      ReDim cpizzas_toppings_scart(Session("Custom_Pizzas"), _
                              Session("total_toppings"),5)
      ' To store the list of Toppings for every pizza
      For temp_counter0 = 1 to Session("Custom_Pizzas")
            pizza_toppings.MoveFirst
            For temp_counter1 = 1 to Session("total_toppings")
                  cpizzas_toppings_scart(temp_counter0,temp_counter1,1) = _
                           pizza_toppings("topping_id")
                  cpizzas_toppings_scart(temp_counter0,temp_counter1,2) = ""
                  ' We will use the qty field for the "selected"
                  pizza_toppings.MoveNext
            Next
      Next
      Session("cpizzas_toppings_scart") = cpizzas_toppings_scart
      Session("cpizzas_scart") =cpizzas_scart
End Sub

'EventName                Description
'Session_OnStart          Runs the first time a user runs any page in your
'                         application
'Session_OnEnd            Runs when a user's session times out or quits your
'                         application
'Application_OnStart      Runs once when the first page of your application
'                         is run for the first time by any user
'Application_OnEnd        Runs once when the web server shuts down

</SCRIPT>
```

Index.asp produces the default home page of the web site.

Register.asp is the module used for anything related to user registration. It starts by checking if the session is active. Then it defines a function to handle selected check box items.

```
<%
If
      Session("SessionActive") <> "True" then
      Response.Redirect  "Index.asp"
End If

Function conv_checkbox(ByVal this_item)
      If IsNull(this_item) or IsEmpty(this_item) or Len(this_item) = 0 then
            conv_checkbox = 0
      Else
            If this_item = 1 then
                  conv_checkbox = 1
            Else
                  this_item = 0
            End If
      End If
End Function
```

It continues by setting a connection to the database:

```
Set epizza_conn = Server.CreateObject("ADODB.Connection")
epizza_conn.Open Session("connstring")
```

Then the code initializes the necessary variables:

❑ When used with no parameters and there is a user identification (obtained from the cookie), only the password is requested

❑ In mode new, it is used to handle the registration of a new user

❑ In mode registered, it is used to obtain the information about a registered user either as a new connection or to allow switching users within a session

The main menu (menu.asp) is responsible for presenting all of the items the customer can select. It creates the contents of this page dynamically by reading all of the information from the database, namely the pizza, toppings, and beverages tables. This is done for every session:

```
<!--#include file="asp_functions.inc"-->
<%

If Session("SessionActive") <> "True" then
    Response.Redirect  "Index.asp"
End If

' Creating the Connection with the database
Set epizza_conn = Server.CreateObject("ADODB.Connection")
epizza_conn.Open Session("connstring")

' Retrieving the recordset with the list and prices of all the available
' pizzas
StrSQL = " Select Pizza_Id, ShortDesc, LongDesc, Sprice, Mprice," & _
        " LPrice from Pizza where ActiveRecord = 1"
Set pizza_info =epizza_conn.Execute(strSQL)

' Retrieving the recordset with the list and prices of all the available
' beverages
StrSQL = " Select  beverage_Id,Description,LiterPrice,CanPrice from" & _
        " beverages where ActiveRecord = 1"
Set beverage_info =epizza_conn.Execute(strSQL)

' Retrieving the recordset with the list and prices of all the available
' Toppings
StrSQL = " Select  topping_id,topping_description from toppings" & _
        " where ActiveRecord = 1"
Set topping_info =epizza_conn.Execute(strSQL)

' This variable defines the maximum number of customized pizzas available
custom_pizzas = Session("Custom_Pizzas")
```

If the action selected by the customer is to submit an order, then it goes through the list of pre-defined pizzas placing the selected ones in the corresponding shopping cart as can be seen in this code snippet:

```
If Request.Form("Action") = "submit_order" Then
    ' First, we're going through the list of pre-defined pizzas
    pizza_info.MoveFirst
    Do While Not pizza_info.EOF
        this_pizzaID = "pizzaID_" & pizza_info("Pizza_id")
        this_pizzaSize = "PizzaSize_" & pizza_info("Pizza_id")
        If Not (IsEmpty(Request.Form(this_pizzaID))
            or IsNull(Request.Form(this_pizzaID))
            or len(Request.Form(this_pizzaID)) = 0) Then
            If int(Request.Form(this_pizzaID)) > 0 Then
                Call AddToDPizza_Cart(pizza_info("Pizza_id"), _
                                      Request.Form(this_pizzaID), _
                                      Request.Form(this_pizzaSize), _
                                      pizza_info("ShortDesc"))

            End If
        End If
        pizza_info.MoveNext
    Loop
    pizza_info.MoveFirst

    ...
```

It does the same for the customized pizzas and the beverage list.

The HTML section of this module is used to display the pizzas and beverages. The following code fragment shows how the custom pizzas are displayed:

```
<%cpizzas_toppings_scart = Session("cpizzas_toppings_scart")%>

<p align="center"
   style="margin-left: 0; margin-top: 5; margin-bottom: 5">
   <b><font size="5">Make your own pizza</font></b>
</p>
<table border="0" cellspacing="1" width="100%" BGCOLOR="#660000"
       cellpadding="3">
   <tr>
       <td width="13%"  BGCOLOR="#660000" align=center>
          <p align="center"><font size="2" color="#FFFFFF">
          <b>Quantity</b></font></p>
       </td>
       <td width="20%"  BGCOLOR="#660000" align=center>
          <p align="center"><font size="2" color="#FFFFFF">
          <b>Size</b></font></p>
       </td>
       <td width="67%"  BGCOLOR="#660000" align=center>
          <p align="center"><font size="2" color="#FFFFFF">
          <b>Description</b></font></p>
       </td>
   </tr>

<%For custom_pizza_index = 1 to custom_pizzas
```

```
    ' To display the customizable pizzas. %>

    <%topping_info.MoveFirst%>
<%
    ' Searching for this Pizza on the Shopping Cart
    cpizzas_scart = Session("cpizzas_scart")

    If int(cpizzas_scart(Item_ID,custom_pizza_index)) > 0 Then
        'Getting the Values from the Shopping Cart
        ThisItemQTY =  cpizzas_scart(Item_Qty,custom_pizza_index)
        ThisItemSize = cpizzas_scart(Item_Size,custom_pizza_index)
    Else
        ' Getting the Default Values
        ThisItemQTY =   ""
        ThisItemSize = "Small"
    End If
%>
    <tr>
        <td width="13%" BGCOLOR="#ffffcc">
            <p align="center">
            <input type="text"
                    name="Qty_<%= custom_pizza_index %>"
                    size="5" onBlur="validate_number(this)"
                    value="<%= ThisItemQTY %>">
            </p>
        </td>

        <td width="20%" align="left" BGCOLOR="#ffffcc">
            <font size="2"><input type="radio" value="Small"
                                name="Size_<%= custom_pizza_index %>"
            <%If ThisItemSize = "Small" Then %> checked
            <%End If%> >Small</font><br>
            <font size="2"><input type="radio"
                                name="Size_<%=custom_pizza_index%>"
                                value="Medium"
            <%If ThisItemSize = "Medium" Then %>checked
            <%End If%>>Medium</font><br>
            <font size="2"><input type="radio"
                                name="Size_<%=custom_pizza_index%>"
                                value="Large"
            <%If ThisItemSize = "Large" Then %> checked
            <%End If%>>Large</font><br>
        </td>

        <td width="67%" BGCOLOR="#ffffcc"> <font size="1">
        <%Items_counter = 0
        ' Just for display purposes %>
        <%Do While not topping_info.EOF%>
            <%topping_index = SearchTopping(custom_pizza_index,
                                        topping_info("topping_Id"))%>
            <%Items_counter = Items_counter + 1%>
            <input type="checkbox"
                    name="Index_<%=custom_pizza_index%>_ID_
                                <%=topping_info("topping_Id")%>"
                    value="Checked"
```

221

```
            <%=cpizzas_toppings_scart
            (custom_pizza_index,topping_index,Item_Qty)%>>
            <%=topping_info("topping_Description")%>
            <%If Items_counter = 4 then%> <br>
                <%Items_counter = 0%>
            <%End If%>
            <%topping_info.MoveNext%>
        <%Loop%>
        </font>
        </td>
    </tr>

    <%Next %>
</table>
```

`OrderConfirm.asp` is the module that creates the page, presenting the order for confirmation, allowing for changing the address or the order. Additionally it obtains the payment method for the customer. The information presented on this screen is obtained by traversing the three shopping baskets and presenting their contents. Finally the order is committed to the database by calling the `PlaceOrder` function (part of the `asp_functions.inc` file), which can be seen here:

```
Function PlaceOrder(payment_type,cctype,ccnumber,ccexpdate)
    Set tmp_conn = Server.CreateObject("ADODB.Connection")
    tmp_conn.Open Session("connstring")
    Set cmd=Server.CreateObject("ADODB.Command")
    cmd.ActiveConnection=Session("connstring")

    ' Retrieving the recordset with the list and prices
    ' of all the available Toppings
    StrSQL = " Select topping_id, topping_description from toppings" & _
            " where ActiveRecord = 1"
    Set topping_info =tmp_conn.Execute(strSQL)

    ' First, Saving the Order Header
    cmd.CommandText="{call AddNewOrder(?,?,?,?,?,?,?)}"
    cmd(0)=0
    ' 0 to add a new Order,
    ' OtherWise it means the order has been delivered
    cmd(1)=Session("UserID")    ' UserID
    cmd(2)=Session("OrderTotalDollars")
    cmd(3)=payment_type
    cmd(4)=ccnumber
    cmd(5)=ccexpdate
    cmd(6)=cctype
    cmd.Execute
    Order_ID = cmd(0)            ' Getting the User_ID

    ' Now, Saving all the Items of the Order
    ' First, the predefined Pizzas:
    dpizzas_scart = Session("dpizzas_scart")
    For temp_counter = 1 to Session("dpizzas_scart_Count")
        cmd.CommandText="{call AddNewOrderItem(?,?,?,?,?,?,?,?,?)}"
        cmd(0)=0
        ' We don't need to know the Item_Id, only for customized pizzas
        cmd(1)=Order_ID
```

```
            cmd(2)=1

            ' 1:Predefined Pizzas, 2:Custom Pizzas,  3: Beverages
            cmd(3)=dpizzas_scart(Item_ID,temp_counter)
            cmd(4)=dpizzas_scart(Item_Size,temp_counter)
            cmd(5)=dpizzas_scart(Item_Qty,temp_counter)
            cmd(6)=dpizzas_scart(Item_Price,temp_counter)
            cmd(7)=0                        'Beverage_ID
            cmd(8)= dpizzas_scart(Item_Description,temp_counter)
            cmd.Execute
Next

' Second, the beverages
bev_scart = Session("bev_scart")
For temp_counter = 1 to Session("bev_scart_Count")
        cmd.CommandText="{call AddNewOrderItem(?,?,?,?,?,?,?,?,?)}"
        cmd(0)=0

        ' We don't need to know the Item_Id, only for customized pizzas
        cmd(1)=Order_ID
        cmd(2)=3

        ' 1:Predefined Pizzas, 2:Custom Pizzas,  3: Beverages
        cmd(3)=0
        cmd(4)=bev_scart(Item_Size,temp_counter)
        cmd(5)=bev_scart(Item_Qty,temp_counter)
        cmd(6)=bev_scart(Item_Price,temp_counter)
        cmd(7)=bev_scart(Item_ID,temp_counter)
        cmd(8)= bev_scart(Item_Description,temp_counter)
        cmd.Execute
Next

' Finally, Save the Customized Pizzas
cpizzas_scart = Session("cpizzas_scart")
cpizzas_toppings_scart = Session("cpizzas_toppings_scart")
custom_pizzas = Session("Custom_Pizzas")
For custom_pizza_index = 1 to custom_pizzas
    ' To parse the customizable pizzas
    If int(cpizzas_scart(Item_Qty,custom_pizza_index)) > 0 Then
        cmd.CommandText="{call AddNewOrderItem(?,?,?,?,?,?,?,?,?)}"
        cmd(0)=0
        ' We don't need to know the Item_Id,
        ' only for customized pizzas
        cmd(1)=Order_ID
        cmd(2)=2
        ' 1:Predefined Pizzas, 2:Custom Pizzas,  3: Beverages
        cmd(3)=0
        cmd(4)=cpizzas_scart(Item_Size,custom_pizza_index)
        cmd(5)=cpizzas_scart(Item_Qty,custom_pizza_index)
        cmd(6)=cpizzas_scart(Item_Price,custom_pizza_index)
        cmd(7)=0
        cmd(8)=cpizzas_scart(Item_Description,custom_pizza_index)
        cmd.Execute
        ThisItem_ID = cmd(0)
        ' Now Saving the Toppings for this pizza.
```

```
                topping_info.MoveFirst
                Do While not topping_info.EOF
                    topping_index = SearchTopping _
                    (custom_pizza_index,topping_info("topping_Id"))

                    If
                        cpizzas_toppings_scart _
                        (custom_pizza_index,topping_index,Item_Qty) = "checked"
                    Then
                        cmd.CommandText="{call AddNewOrderCPizza(?,?,?)}"
                        cmd(0)=ThisItem_ID
                        cmd(1)=topping_info("topping_Id")
                        cmd(2)=cpizzas_toppings_scart _
                                (custom_pizza_index,topping_index,Item_Price)
                        cmd.Execute
                    End If
                    topping_info.MoveNext
                Loop
            End If
        Next
    PlaceOrder = Order_ID
End Function
```

The `Order.Thanks.asp` module is responsible for presenting the order after it has been committed to the database. This includes the confirmation number. This fragment of code shows how it goes to the database to obtain the user information:

```
<!--#include file="asp_functions.inc"-->

<%
If Session("SessionActive") <> "True" then
    Response.Redirect   "Index.asp"
End If


' Getting the User's information
Set epizza_conn = Server.CreateObject("ADODB.Connection")
epizza_conn.Open Session("connstring")
StrSQL = "Select Address, Apartment, City, State, Zip, " & _
        "PhoneAreaCode, PhonePrefix, PhoneSuffix, PhoneExt " & _
        "from Users where User_ID = " & Session("UserID")
Set user_info =epizza_conn.Execute(strSQL)

%>
```

After that there is the HTML code, responsible for presenting the order as it is contained in the shopping carts, and finally it resets them by calling the `ResetCarts` function.

The `management.asp` module establishes a connection with the database and issues a query looking for all the orders that are still open:

```
<%
If Session("SessionActive") <> "True" then
    Response.Redirect  "Index.asp"
End If
' Getting the Order's information
Set epizza_conn = Server.CreateObject("ADODB.Connection")
epizza_conn.Open Session("connstring")

StrSQL = " select Order_ID, OrderDate,TotalAmount,City,State,Zip, "
StrSQL = StrSQL & " (Select Count(Item_ID) from OrderItems Where
OrderItems.Order_ID = Orders.Order_ID) as TotalItems "
StrSQL = StrSQL & " From Orders,Users Where "
StrSQL = StrSQL & " Orders.User_ID = Users.User_ID And " & _
                    OrderStatus = 0 Order by Order_ID"
Set order_info = epizza_conn.Execute(strSQL)
%>
```

Following this code is the HMTL necessary to present it on the browser.

There is a library of functions in `asp_functions.inc` that is included by `menu.asp`, `Order.Confirm.asp`, and `Order.Thanks.asp`. The functions are listed in the following table:

Function	Description
AddToDPizza_Cart	Adds a pre-defined pizza to the corresponding shopping cart. It also updates the total price of the order by adding the price of the pizza just added.
AddToCPizza_Cart	Adds a custom pizza to the corresponding shopping cart. Price is updated when toppings are added.
AddToppingToCPizza	Adds a topping to the active custom pizza and increases the price by the price of the topping.
AddToBeverages_Cart	Adds a beverage to the corresponding cart, updating the total price of the order
SearchTopping	Searches on the cart for a specific topping.
IsIDonDPizza_Cart	Searches for a specific pizza ID on the shopping cart.
IsIDonBev_Cart	Searches for a specific beverage ID on the shopping cart.
PlaceOrder	Commits the order information to the database.
ResetCarts	Resets all the shopping carts.

The Database

The database is quite simple. It contains seven tables, which are described in the following diagram.

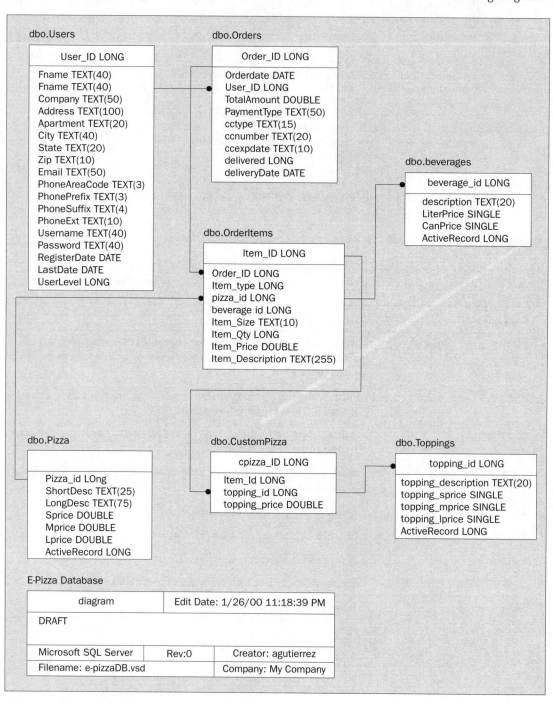

A quick look at the diagram shows that there is a `Users` table containing all the relevant information about the user and the primary key is the user ID. The `Order` table contains the necessary information about the order and points to the `OrderItems` table, which describes every item making up the order. Three additional tables handle the three kinds of items: standard pizzas, custom pizzas, and beverages. One last table handles the toppings of the custom pizzas. The connection to the database will be established later on in the chapter.

The Metamorphosis

It was a nice surprise to find that the E-Pizza system had been designed in such a way that the presentation layer was substantially removed from the business logic. As far as this code merger was concerned, this allows for easier integration with the existing system. The issue the Troops are wrestling with is how to integrate both systems.

As you can see, the architecture of the ASP based system is very similar to the one developed in Chapter 4 using the stateful session bean. Basically the initial information is brought from the database and as the order is being built, its state is kept in the global session variables until it is committed, when it is written to the database.

Mrs Chief Architect states that the objective of this exercise is to use the look and feel of the ASP site and add the functionality missing with the current system, namely, the ability for the customer to create their own pizza and offer beverages. What this boils down to is that all the HTML code of the ASP system will be used as the new front end. This front end will then call the business logic as developed in Chapter 5. Some changes will need to be made to the J2EE code to add the new functionality from the ASP application.

There are currently no rules or programs with which to convert ASP to JSP. It is basically a tedious and laborious job, involving reading every single line of ASP code and converting it. As stated previously, this means that every ASP module has to be checked so that the HTML part remains pretty much the same and any calls to business logic are changed to call the appropriate servlet or EJB. The business logic will be provided by the `OrderSF`, `PizzaServicesSL`, `OrderServicesSL`, and `OutletServicesSL` beans. The data access will be provided by `OrderMasterEB` and `OrderDetailEB` beans as well as through JDBC.

We'll be using the existing business logic; there will now only be one shopping cart instead of four. The shopping cart will be the stateful session bean, `OrderSF`, and all the other pages that make reference to the matrix based shopping carts have to be changed to use the stateful session bean.

The Troops start with `global.asa` and the first decision has to be made. As we saw earlier, this file contains all the functions needed when a session is initialized. The question is whether this functionality should be translated to a servlet or to a JSP page. After much pondering Mr Senior Developer decides that it will be translated to a JSP page. The reasoning for this is based more on practicality than perceived performance.

Using a servlet would probably be more efficient, and would ensure that the presentation logic is kept separate from the business logic as far as possible, but it does complicate things a little more than desired at this stage. By using a JSP page, the conversion process gets closer to a *literal translation*. This effort is a lot easier to coordinate. In a more general sense, it is recommended that servlets be used in these situations.

The *literal translation* in itself is not difficult, it's just a time consuming process. For example, whereas in the ASP code you define a session-wide user variable like this:

```
Session("UserLogIn") = False   ' If the user has logged in
```

In a JSP page it is done like this:

```
session.setAttribute("UserLogIn", "false");    // If the user has logged in
```

The next decision the troops made was to defer anything related to user, user registration, and other security matters to a future set of experiments related to security. This will be covered in Chapter 8. So all the code that is related to checking the cookie is discarded and a test user with fake information is defined and hard coded into the application.

The ASP code that follows in global.asa is used to initialize the shopping carts. This code was seen earlier in this chapter and is unnecessary because the shopping cart functionality is now handled by OrderSF.

Compared with VBScript, Java is a strongly typed language requiring all variables to be initialized before they are used. Because of this the following code has to be added to the JSP page:

```
float totalDollars = 0.0f;
session.setAttribute("OrderTotalDollars",
                     Util.formatToString(totalDollars));
```

> *Admittedly, it would be better to just assign the string "0.00" to OrderTotalDollars, but for consistency the formatToString() utility function is used to convert a float to a formatted string.*

Now the troops review the asp_functions.inc file. As we saw earlier, this file is included by a number of ASP files and provides common functions related to the handling of the shopping carts. As it contains functionality that is all offered by OrderSF this file will no longer be needed.

The next file under scrutiny is index.asp. For this one, the conversion effort is minimal, as this file is pure HTML. Nothing has to change, except for calling JSP pages instead of ASP pages. For example, the following line from the ASP file:

```
<p align="center">
  <A href="index.asp">
  <FONT style="BACKGROUND-COLOR: #660000" color="#ffffff">HOME</font></a>
  | <A href="register.asp">REGISTER</a>
  | <A href="menu.asp">MENU</a>
```

Becomes the following in the JSP page file:

```
<p align="center">
  <A href="index.jsp">
  <FONT style="BACKGROUND-COLOR: #660000" color="#ffffff">HOME</font></a>
  | <A href="Register.jsp">REGISTER</a>
  | <A href="Menu.jsp">MENU</a>
```

`Menu.jsp` is next to change. The original ASP file is rather simple. It has two parts:

- ❑ In the first one it goes to the database to obtain the information about all the pizzas and beverages

- ❑ In the second part there is HTML code to display the information

Even though the translation is more or less direct, a big philosophical change is about to be made. Every time `main.asp` is executed, it opens a database connection and maintains it open for the duration of the session. Then it queries the database for the pizza and beverage information. This happens every single time. If you look at the ASP code presented earlier in this chapter there are no statements to close the connection to the database. Supposedly this happens automatically when the page finishes execution, but it is rather suspicious.

The big change in `Menu.jsp` is that there is a check to verify that the pizza and beverage information has already been retrieved from the database. If it has not, then it proceeds to use a connection pool and obtain the information and store it in vectors such as `predefinedPizzas`, `toppings`, and `beverages`, which are then kept for the duration of the session as session variables.

```
Vector predefinedPizzas =
                    (Vector)session.getAttribute("predefinedPizzas");
if (predefinedPizzas == null) {
  Class.forName("weblogic.jdbc.pool.Driver").newInstance();
  conn = DriverManager.getConnection("jdbc:weblogic:pool:p2gPool");
  predefinedPizzas = new Vector();
  java.util.Date date = new java.util.Date();
  stmt = conn.createStatement();
  select = "select distinct p_name from pizza";
  stmt.execute(select);
  resultSet = stmt.getResultSet();
  while(resultSet.next()){
    // Fill out the predefinedPizzas vector with information
    ...
  }
  session.setAttribute("predefinedPizzas", predefinedPizzas);
  resultSet.close();
  stmt.close();
}
```

Even though the Wonder Troops had decided to stick to literal translations, this improvement was too obvious to let go. They had already seen in Chapter 3 that JDBC connection pools are incredibly efficient; what's more, minimizing access to the database by storing results of queries in memory was even more efficient. However, caching results in this way must only be used in specialized circumstances because when the database data changes the whole session needs to be destroyed and restarted.

When submitting an order, the following Java code is used to go through the list of pre-defined pizzas:

```
// First, we are going through the list of pre-defined pizzas
String this_pizzaID    = null;
String this_pizzaSize  = null;
String this_pizzaDough = null;
Pizza pizza = null;
enu = predefinedPizzas.elements();
```

```
while(enu.hasMoreElements()) {
  pizza = (Pizza)enu.nextElement();
  this_pizzaID    = "PizzaID_"    + pizza.getP_name();
  this_pizzaSize  = "PizzaSize_"  + pizza.getP_name();
  this_pizzaDough = "PizzaDough_" + pizza.getP_name();
  String sID   = request.getParameter(this_pizzaID);
  String sSize = request.getParameter(this_pizzaSize);

  if ((sID != null) && (sID.length()>0) &&
    (sSize != null) && (sSize.equals(pizza.getP_size()))) {
    int quantity = Integer.parseInt(sID);
    String dough = request.getParameter(this_pizzaDough);
    OrderDetail orderDetail = new OrderDetail();
    Pizza selectedPizza = new Pizza();
    selectedPizza.setP_name(pizza.getP_name());
    selectedPizza.setP_size(pizza.getP_size());
    orderDetail.setOd_pizza(selectedPizza);
    orderDetail.setOd_quantity(quantity);
    orderDetail.setOd_dough(dough);
    currentOrder.addOrderDetail(orderDetail);
  }
}
```

The new arrangement determines that the state of the order is maintained alternately between the form and the `OrderSF` bean. The form is used to take the order, calculate the price, and update the form. When the order is confirmed, the bean contains the information about the order, uses it to show the confirmation, and delivers the order.

Additions to this JSP page include calling the `PizzaServicesSL` bean so that it can obtain the special of the day, which was not a functionality that E-Pizza had available. It also retrieves the number of custom pizzas to be displayed from the `weblogic.properties` file:

```
int custom_pizzas =
            Integer.parseInt(System.getProperty("jsw.customPizzas", "4"));
```

The default is four pizzas. This is a nice enhancement, as in the ASP code it is set as a fixed value within the code.

Next in line for surgery is `Order.Confirm.asp`. This one falls into the literal translation category. Let us have a more detailed look into some of the translations. For example, listing the pre-defined pizzas in ASP is done with the following code:

```
<%dpizzas_scart = Session("dpizzas_scart")%>
<%For temp_counter = 1 to Session("dpizzas_scart_Count")%>
    <tr>
        <td width="13%" BGCOLOR="#ffffcc">
            <p align="center"><font color="red"><b>
            <%= dpizzas_scart(Item_Qty,temp_counter) %>
            </b></font></p>
        </td>
        <td width="16%" BGCOLOR="#ffffcc">
            <p align="center"><font color="red"><b>
```

```
                    <%= dpizzas_scart(Item_Size,temp_counter) %>
                    </b></font></p>
            </td>
            <td width="51%" BGCOLOR="#ffffcc">
                <p align="center"><font color="red"><b>
                <%= dpizzas_scart(Item_Description,temp_counter) %>
                </b></font></p>
            </td>
            <td width="20%" BGCOLOR="#ffffcc">
                <p align="center"><font color="red"><b>
                <%=FormatCurrency(dpizzas_scart(Item_Price, temp_counter),2)%>
                </b></font></p>
            </td>
        </tr>
<%Next%>
```

The corresponding translation into a JSP page uses the following code:

```
        <%// First displaying the pre-defined Pizzas %>
        <%
        Vector orderDetails = null;
        If (currentOrder != null)
            orderDetails = currentOrder.getOrderDetail();
        Else
            orderDetails = null;
        If (orderDetails != null) {
            For (int vi = 0; vi < orderDetails.size(); vi++) {
                OrderDetail orderDetail = (OrderDetail)
                orderDetails.elementAt(vi);

                If (orderDetail.getOd_type() == OrderDetail.PREDEFINED) {
        %>
                    <tr>
                    <td width="13%" BGCOLOR="#ffffcc">
                      <p align="center">
                      <font color="red"><b>
                      <%= orderDetail.getOd_quantity() %>
                      </b></font></p>
                    </td>

                    <td width="13%" BGCOLOR="#ffffcc">
                      <p align="center">
                      <font color="red"><b>
                      <%= orderDetail.getOd_pizza().getP_size() %>
                      </b></font></p>
                    </td>

                    <td width="13%" BGCOLOR="#ffffcc">
                      <p align="center">
                      <font color="red"><b>
                      <%= orderDetail.getOd_dough() %>
                      </b></font></p>
                    </td>
```

```
                    <td width="41%" BGCOLOR="#ffffcc">
                     <p align="center">
                     <font color="red"><b>
                     <%= orderDetail.getOd_pizza().getP_name() %>
                     </b></font></p>
                    </td>

                    <td width="20%" BGCOLOR="#ffffcc">
                     <p align="center">
                     <font color="red"><b>
                     $<%= Util.formatToString(orderDetail.getOd_price()) %>
                     </b></font></p>
                    </td>
                    </tr>
        <%
                }
            }
        }
        %>
```

The differences can be broken down in two parts. First, they verify that there is a vector containing the order detail. Then, embedded in the HTML code there is an actual reference to the order detail:

```
<%= orderDetail.getOd_pizza().getP_name() %>
```

The last ASP victim is Order.Thanks.asp. The procedure is the same as with the previous ASP file.

During a break the Troops decide to have a conversation with their peers at E-Pizza and share some of the experiences.

❑   The first thing that comes up is the pain of having to declare every single variable in Java, which is not necessary in ASP, although it is considered good practice to do so by using the Option Explicit mode.

❑   Another issue that the ASP Jockeys brought up was the pain in handling the cache of ASP, especially in pages with different operational modes. This does not seem to be an issue when working with JSP.

❑   The final problem was the fact that Java is case sensitive, whereas ASP does not really care about the case of variable names, and getting used to a case sensitive language after being familiar with a more relaxed one can be difficult at first. On the bright side, the nice thing is that both technologies offer predefined objects with similar names that reference the same entities, for example session and request.

They all had to agree that JSP is a rather new and immature technology. When they compared Visual InterDev with the tools the Wonder Troops were using to develop the JSP pages, there was a difference.

At the time of writing, Macromedia DreamWeaver is one of the few tools that offer the capability of being a JSP editor, but in general it was felt that Visual InterDev was a more mature product.

Forte for Java: Community Edition is another useful tool for editing and debugging JSP pages. Another advantage is that it can be freely downloaded from the Sun site at http://www.sun.com/forte/ffj/ce/.

The annoyance with the case sensitivity and data types was so painful that the Wonder Troops had to create a new target in their makefile that would compile the JSP pages. They did this so that they could detect all the compilation errors without having to wait to execute and compile the page to find them.

Back to work. There are still some more adjustments that need to be made before getting the application to work. The OrderDetail class had to be modified by adding one field to specify the kind of detail it contains. They decided to use constants, in the OrderDetail class, to represent this:

❑   OrderDetail.PREDEFINED for pre-defined pizzas

❑   OrderDetail.CUSTOM for custom pizzas, which then includes a vector with the ingredients that compose it

❑   OrderDetail.BEVERAGES for beverages

A new class, Beverage, was created for handling the beverages. The updatePrice() method of the PizzaServicesSL bean was changed to handle the cases of custom-made pizzas and beverages. This was done by adding the following switch statement:

```
String location = System.getProperty("jsw.location", "US");

float price = 0.0f;

switch(orderDetail.getOd_type()) {

  case OrderDetail.PREDEFINED:
    price = getPrice(orderDetail.getOd_pizza(), location, date,
                     orderDetail.getOd_dough());
    break;

  case OrderDetail.CUSTOM:
    price = getCustomPizzaPrice(orderDetail.getOd_pizza(),
                                location, date,
                                orderDetail.getOd_dough(),
                                orderDetail.getOd_toppings());
    break;

  case OrderDetail.BEVERAGE:
    price = getBeveragePrice(orderDetail.getOd_beverage(),
                             location, date);
    break;
}

price *= orderDetail.getOd_quantity();

try {
  price = Util.format(price);
} catch(ParseException pe) {
  throw new P2GException(Util.getStackTraceAsString(pe));
}

orderDetail.setOd_price(price);
```

Note that the system property `location` is retrieved to calculate the price correctly depending on the country.

Since the ASP system presents the number of items in an order, a new method, `getNumItems()`, is added that will calculate the number of items in a order. These can be the same as or more than the number of order details.

One more change. The `deliverOrder()` method in the `OrderServicesSL` bean is changed to handle the custom pizzas and the beverages, as well as to include the proper inventory management of these new items.

Finally, some tables have to be modified. The following figure presents the new schema structure:

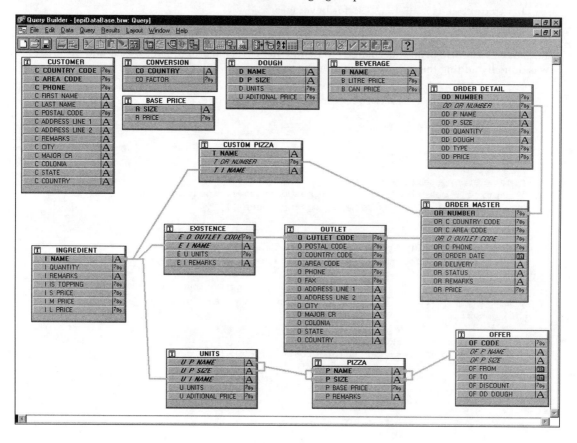

Setting up the Examples

This section will provide you with the instructions to set up the ASP based web site as well as the Java web site with the improved front end.

The ASP Web Site

The requirements for the ASP web site are the following:

- ❑ NT server 4.0 Service Pack 6a
- ❑ IIS 4 Installed (from the NT Option Pack 4)
- ❑ MS SQL server 7.0 Service Pack 1

The installation of the ASP web site involves four steps:

- ❑ Setting up the application on IIS
- ❑ Setting up the database
- ❑ Setting up the database connection (ODBC connection)
- ❑ Setting up the main administrator user

These four steps are described next.

To set up the application on IIS you must follow these instructions:

- ❑ Unzip the file epizza.zip on the directory C:\inetpub\wwwroot (the home directory for IIS)
- ❑ Go to the IIS Service Manager (Start | Programs | Windows NT 4.0 Option Pack | Microsoft Internet Information Server | Internet Service Manager), expand the Default Web Site, select the directory called epizza, right-click and select Properties.

  If using Windows 2000 Professional, you may first need to add IIS to the list of services using Control Panel; Add/Remove Programs and click on Add/Remove Windows Components. The Internet Service Manager can be started from Start | Programs | Administrative Tools | Internet Services Manager.

- ❑ Under the Directory tab, on Application Settings, click on Create
- ❑ Under the Documents tab, set index.asp as the default document
- ❑ Click on Apply and OK

The database is set up as follows:

- ❑ Create a new Database called epizza, using the SQL Server 7.0 Enterprise Manager (Start | Programs | Microsoft SQL Server 7.0), right-click on Databases and select New Database.
- ❑ Execute the script epizza.sql, to create the tables and stored procedures. Select the new database epizza and then SQL server Query Analyzer, opening the SQL script and executing it by pressing *F5* on the keyboard or the green arrow icon on the console.

❑   Returning to the Enterprise Manager, you need to create a new Login called epizza, with password epizza. To do this, select Security | Logins and right-click for New Login. Put epizza both in the Username box and the password box. You will also need to specify the Database as epizza.

❑   Click on the Database Access tab, check the Permit box that is next to epizza. This will allow the new login to access the database.

Follow these instructions to set up the database connection:

❑   Go to the ODBC Data Source Administrator (Settings | Control Panel | ODBC Data Sources), click on System DSN, and select Add

   For Windows 2000, look under Administrative Tools in the Control Panel.

❑   As a driver, Select SQL server and click on Finish

❑   Set Name to epizza, Description to epizza, and Server to (local), and click on Next

❑   Select With SQL server authentication, set Login ID to epizza, Password to epizza, and click Next

❑   Check the box that says: Change the default database to: and select epizza, click Next

❑   Click Finish

❑   Click on OK to finish setting up the ODBC Connection (Optional: Click on Test Data Source to test it)

And finally, to set up the main administrator user:

❑   Using the SQL Server Enterprise Manager again, edit the table Users for the epizza database and manually change the value for the administrator user on the column UserLevel to 0.

The Java Web Site

The source code for the application in Chapter 6 is under the directory c:\wlsbook\src\c06. This directory also contains the file GNUmakefile, which is ready to be used to compile and deploy the code.

The application is deployed under the directory c:\wlsbook\srv\c06-srv, and the file weblogic.properties is set up to start the WebLogic server with the E-Pizza application.

As usual, you can open a command shell, run the setEnv and the startWls scripts to begin using the application in this chapter.

```
C:\> cd \wlsbook
C:\wlsbook> setenv 6
------------------------------------------------------------
Setting environment for chapter 6
------------------------------------------------------------
Current settings:
     Java Home = c:\jdk1.3
  WebLogic Home = c:\weblogic
   Project Home = c:\wlsbook
      CLASSPATH =
c:\weblogic\lib\weblogic510sp5boot.jar;c:\weblogic\classes\boot;c:\weblogic\lib\we
blogic510sp5.jar;c:\weblogic\license;c:\weblogic\classes;c:\weblogic\lib\weblogica
ux.jar;c:\wlsbook\srv\c06-srv\serverclasses

C:\wlsbook> startwls
```

Open the browser and point it to the usual URL (http://localhost:7001), and the site should look just like the ASP site.

Summary

In this chapter we have seen how the Wonder Troops created a new front end for the system they have been developing. They took the look and feel of the ASP based web site and added it to their system. They also added new functionality that did not exist in their original system, namely the ability to order custom-made pizzas and beverages over the internet.

In the next chapter, we will introduce the Java Message Service (JMS). This will be used to improve the communication of orders between the Pizza2Go centers and the pizza outlets. Currently Pizza2Go just sends a fax to the outlet and E-Pizza sends an e-mail message. These mechanisms will be enhanced using JMS point-to-point messaging. Plus JMS publish-and-subscribe will give us the opportunity to create an interesting example of a loyalty scheme.

7

Java Message Service

In this chapter we will be reviewing the basic concepts of messaging and the Java Message Service (JMS) API. We will then review two examples that use JMS and enhance the application that has been developed in the previous chapters.

Messaging Basics

Messaging is generally considered to be a mechanism that allows communication between two or more computer programs. Under this definition, pretty much anything can be considered a messaging system, from a simple exchange of TCP/IP packets to the communication between a client program and a database.

Rather than creating a specific messaging mechanism for every situation that arises, a number of software vendors have created systems that allow passing messages between different applications in a generic fashion. These systems are called Message Oriented Middleware (MOM). They define a message structure and the protocol by which the applications send and receive messages.

One of the advantages of a MOM system is that it decouples the message producers from the message consumers; in this way they can operate independently of each other. One side effect of this is that this architecture can scale more than one where producers and consumers are communicating directly.

Another important feature offered by MOM systems is the concept of Guaranteed Message Delivery (GMD) where, at the price of decreased performance, the messages are stored in a database before being delivered to the consumers. This way, if the consumer is not available for whatever reason, they can receive the messages when they become available.

There are two different models in which MOM systems can handle messages.

Point-To-Point Messaging

The first model is called Point-To-Point or PTP. Here one client can send messages to another client. These messages can go one-way or in both directions, meaning that there can be a response from the consumer to the producer.

PTP systems are typically implemented in such a way that there is a queue in which multiple producers can place their messages and then multiple consumers can take them. The queue handles the messages in a serial fashion and generally follows the First In First Out (FIFO) algorithm. Only one consumer can take a message from the queue; once a message has been taken from the queue it is no longer available to other consumers. The following figure offers an example of the PTP model:

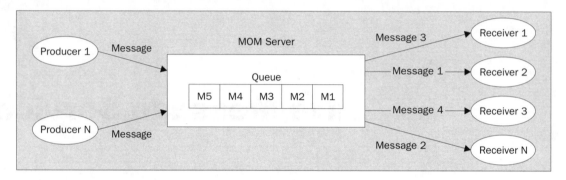

It can be said that a PTP model is based on a one-to-one relationship between the producer and the consumer of the message. A good example of a PTP application is sending a pizza order to an outlet. In this example the message contains the order, which is created at the central location of Pizza2Go (the producer) and sent to one unique outlet (the consumer).

Publish and Subscribe Messaging

The second model is called Publish and Subscribe (Pub/Sub), also known as event driven messages. This is because the messages are usually produced as the consequence of an event. In this case the producer is the publisher and the consumer is the subscriber since the client will only receive the message if it has subscribed to a specific event that triggers the message.

Pub/Sub systems are implemented using a mechanism called a topic, which can be considered similar to a queue. Publishers can place messages on a topic and these will be delivered to all the consumers who have subscribed to the event that triggered the message. Here we see an example of this model.

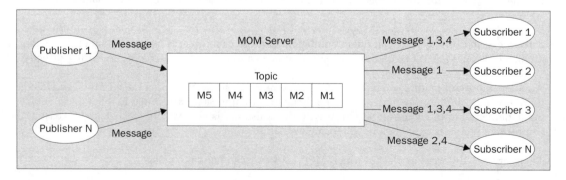

It can then be said that the Pub/Sub model is based on a one-to-many relationship between consumer and producer. For example, suppose a topic is defined for each stock traded on a stock exchange. One consumer may subscribe to any trade of a particular stock whereas another consumer may subscribe to a different event, which only triggers a message when the price of a trade is greater then a specific value.

JMS

JMS is not a MOM system but a specification of the different interfaces that should be used to send messages between producers and consumers as well as the different message formats. The WebLogic server is a MOM system that implements the JMS specification. Additionally, JMS is fully integrated with all the other APIs implemented in WebLogic. This is akin to way that JDBC, as provided by Sun, is largely a set of interfaces, and third party database vendors provide implementations of these interfaces that developers can then use while still coding to the interfaces.

In general it can be said that a JMS application is one or more clients that exchange messages. Currently JMS does not address how to handle non-Java clients. In a similar fashion, the JMS implementation in WebLogic does not handle non-Java clients.

The JMS specification defines both the Point-To-Point and Publish and Subscribe models. From the programming standpoint, almost everything is similar between both models. The basic distinction is the **destination**, which can be a queue or a topic. Other than that, most of the methods are similar in both models.

The concept of Guaranteed Message Delivery is handled in JMS as persistent or non-persistent messages. Persistent messages are stored in a database before they are sent over to the consumer(s). In WebLogic, the database is connected using a JDBC connection pool to the database of your choice.

Connections

JMS clients communicate with the server by means of a connection. Connections are created by a **Connection Factory** obtained with a JNDI lookup. A connection factory is an **Administered Object** that encapsulates a set of connection parameters. The messaging model (PTP or Pub/Sub) is defined depending on the type of connection factory called.

JMS defines administered objects as objects that contain JMS configuration information that is created and managed by a JMS administrator. This effectively separates the development from the deployment. In the case of WebLogic, an administered object can be handled by the WebLogic console and the `weblogic.properties` file.

Sessions

A client can have one or more sessions within a connection. A session can communicate with different destinations. Within a session there can be one or more Message Producer and Message Consumer objects. Each one of these objects can communicate to only one destination.

A client can request that messages be delivered synchronously or asynchronously. If synchronous, the client calls a `receive()` method and the Message Consumer does nothing more than wait until a message arrives. If messages are delivered asynchronously, the client provides an implementation of the JMS `MessageListener` interface. When a message arrives, the `onMessage()` method of that implementation is called to receive the message. This allows the client to process other work while waiting for a message.

JMS can participate in transactions with other J2EE services such as EJB. In addition to this capability, JMS can also provide transactional support within a JMS session. When JMS participates in a transaction that goes beyond the scope of a JMS session, the transactional support of JMS cannot be used since the whole transaction is handled by the Java Transaction API (JTA).

A JMS transaction is one that is considered a single unit from the moment a message is produced to when it is consumed. Transacted messages are buffered until committed. For messages that have been consumed, an acknowledgement will not be issued until a commit has occurred. For messages that are produced, they will not be sent to the WebLogic server until the transaction commits. Transactions can rollback. If this happens, the consumed messages are recovered and the produced messages are destroyed.

When a rollback is performed a session is recovered. That is, a session will be stopped and restarted with the first unacknowledged message. Transactions in JMS transacted sessions are chained; once a transaction has been committed or rolled back, another transaction begins automatically.

When a session is transacted, message acknowledgement is automatic. If a session is not transacted there are three options that define the condition under which the session will acknowledge the receipt of a message to the JMS server:

- ❑ DUP_OK_ACKNOWLEDGE – The session will acknowledge the delivery of messages, but it is lazy. If the JMS server fails there is a possibility of delivering some duplicate messages. Use this option only if the consumer can handle duplicate messages. This is the option with the lowest overhead, as the session does not have to work on preventing duplicates.

- ❑ AUTO_ACKNOWLEDGE – The session will automatically acknowledge the receipt of the message when the consumer has completed the execution of the `receive()` method, in the synchronous case, or the asynchronous message handler.

- ❑ CLIENT_ACKNOWLEDGE – The client is responsible for acknowledging the receipt of a message. The client uses the `acknowledge()` method of the message object to do this. Calling this method will acknowledge *all* consumed messages that have not been acknowledged.

When talking about producers and consumers, there are a couple of special cases that have to be considered in the Publish and Subscribe model. Topic Subscribers can be durable or non-durable. A non-durable Topic Subscriber will only receive messages sent when its session is active; the subscriber will never see any other messages. A durable Topic Subscriber will receive all the messages it is subscribed to, even those that are sent while its session is not active. The latter will be received when the session becomes active again. The WebLogic server stores messages in a database until the message has been delivered to all durable subscribers or it has expired according to the predefined lifetime of the message.

A special note has to be made regarding multithreading. When using JMS API the session, message producer, and message consumer objects cannot be used concurrently. JMS Connections, connection factories, and destinations can be used in a multithreaded fashion.

Client Setup

To summarize, the steps required for a client to set up a connection with a JMS server are the following:

- ❑ Use JNDI to locate a `Connection Factory` object.
- ❑ Use the `Connection Factory` to create a `Connection` to the server.
- ❑ Use the `Connection` to create one or more `Sessions`.
- ❑ Use JNDI to locate one or more `Destination` objects.
- ❑ Use the `Sessions` and `Destinations` to create the Message Producers and Message Consumers as needed.

Messages

Independent of which model is used, within JMS the messages are the same. A JMS message consists of three parts: Header, Property Fields, and Body.

Headers

All JMS messages have exactly 10 header fields that must always be present:

Header Field	Description
JMSMessageID	A unique message identifier, assigned by WebLogic.
JMSDestination	The MOM specific name of a queue or topic where the message will be delivered.
JMSDeliveryMode	Persistent or Non-Persistent. See explanation below.
JMSTimeStamp	The time the message was transferred to the JMS Server. *Not* the time the message was produced.
JMSCorrelationID	Designed to link or correlate messages. See explanation below.
JMSReplyTo	The destination that a reply should be sent to.
JMSRedelivered	This will inform a consumer if the server considers this message to be unacknowledged.
JMSExpiration	Lifetime of the message. When 0, the message does not expire.
JMSType	Message type identifier specified by the producer. Not used by WebLogic.
JMSPriority	Not implemented by WebLogic. See explanation below.

The message delivery mode is probably one of the most powerful features of JMS. Messages can be non-persistent, which can be lost if there is a server failure. This mode is very cheap regarding performance, as there is no overhead of logging the message into a database. These kinds of messages are delivered *at-most-once*. That is, the message can be lost, but not delivered twice. This makes sense with time sensitive information, such as stock quotes where it usually does not make sense to resend the information if it is lost.

Persistent messages are written to a database, and are not considered delivered until they have been committed in the database. These messages are delivered *once-and-only-once*. The message cannot be lost and cannot be delivered twice. WebLogic uses a JDBC connection pool to store the persistent messages in the relational database of your choice.

The message correlation number is a field that can be used in many useful ways. One example is where a message consumer replies to the producer with a different message, but places the message ID of the original message in this field to correlate the messages. Another useful feature is that the field can contain an application-specific string, or a native byte array.

The JMS specification does not require that the priority feature be implemented. WebLogic has chosen not to implement it for the time being. This means that messages of higher priority will not travel or be processed faster.

Property Fields

Property fields are the standard name/value pairs. The most interesting feature of these fields is that they can be examined by **message selectors**. When a consumer connects to the server, it can define a message selector. This message selector can examine the header and property fields of a message in a specified queue or topic. A message selector cannot examine the body of a message, so the property fields are typically used to summarize the content of the body of the message in the form of an index or keywords.

Message selectors can be used to filter out unwanted messages. As these selectors execute on the server, one of the net effects is that, when used correctly, performance could increase by diminishing the use of network bandwidth by not sending over the wire unwanted messages from the server to the consumer.

Selectors are based on SQL92 syntax, so the tests look like SQL queries. For example:

```
outlet = 214 or zip_code = 94403
product like 'WebLogic%' and version > 4.5
```

Message Body

The body of the message can be any of the following types:

Body Type	Description
Stream	A stream of Java primitive values
Map	Name/value pairs, where the name is a string and the value is a primitive Java type
Text	Plain text (type string)
Object	A single serializable Java object, or a collection of objects if using JDK 1.2+
Bytes	A stream of uninterrupted bytes

JMS does not have a specific XML message type, so such a message would be sent as a text message.

Hasta La Vista Fax

After learning all this about JMS, the Wonder Troops found the PTP model to be a natural fit to send orders from the Operation Center to the corresponding outlets. Not only did it seem natural but also quite simple and more solid then the current fax method. The e-mail method used by E-Pizza was good, but a system based on JMS could be extended to send messages back from the outlet to the central location. As you might remember, the outlets send inventory information at the end of the day related to the walk-in orders. Because of this they decide to use JMS PTP for communication between the Operations Center and the outlets.

The initial experiment is based on sending an order to the corresponding outlet. To do this they will require a programmatic or fat client on the outlet. This client will contain the message consumer and logic to present the order in the outlet. As it is an experiment, it will only display the order for now.

Obviously, it is critical for the operation of the Pizza2Go outlets to receive all the orders, so it is decided to use the Guaranteed Message Delivery feature. This way they can be sure that the order will eventually get to the outlet. However, because an outlet can go offline and not connect with the central location in a decent period of time, they also decide to use the JMSReplyTo feature, so that every time the outlet receives an order an acknowledgement is sent back to the Operations Center. This way they know whether the outlet has received the order and also what time the order was received.

This particular experiment is relatively simple. Just replace the function that prints the fax with a call to a JMS producer that will create a message for the specified outlet and will consume a reply from the outlet. The outlet has a client that consumes the message and sends a reply back to the producer.

The next order of business is deciding the type of message. Here we find another confrontation between Mrs Chief Architect and Mr Senior Developer. Thinking of the future, she wants to use XML to describe a customer order. An example of a line item in an XML based order would be:

```
<order-detail>
  <detail-type> pre-defined pizza </detail-type>
  <pizza>
    <pizza-name> Margherita </pizza-name>
    <pizza-size> Large </pizza-size>
    <dough> Classic </dough>
  </pizza>
  <quantity> 3 </quantity>
</order-detail>
```

In essence the whole order would be represented in XML using a syntax defined by the Wonder Troops that would enable them to represent an order. This XML based order would then be sent to the outlet as a text type message. This message would then have to be parsed and converted to something that could be used by the client-side application.

Mr Senior Developer does not particularly want to complicate issues by having to modify the order into XML, which later has to be specially parsed and processed at the receiving end. Additionally, he abhors the aesthetics of an unbelievable amount of <tag> and </tag> pairs which make the text almost unreadable. The simplicity of just sending an object down the wire and letting WebLogic deal with all the transport issues seems unbeatable.

This time the argument is won by Mr Senior Developer. It was not possible to justify the additional time in creating an XML syntax for describing an order and all the coding associated with processing it.

The general feeling of the troops was that XML was better suited for communicating with external systems, such as the ones used for Business to Business (B2B) where the different partners do not have full control of the systems outside their company or the clients are non-Java. For this purpose XML is well suited. XML provides the grammar, but the parties using it have to agree on the words to be used and their meaning. For example, what one company calls customers another calls clients. In a message these two words are different. This is where efforts such a BizTalk from Microsoft , ebXML, and RosettaNet are focusing on defining a business language based on the XML grammar that all parties can agree on.

As all the information contained in the order comes from objects, the easiest thing to do is to use a message type object. This object will be a hash table that is composed of the Customer JavaBean, which contains all the information associated to the customer, the destination outlet number, the OrderMaster JavaBean and a vector with all the OrderDetail JavaBeans included in the order.

The next order of business is to design the actual queue architecture. The issue to consider here is whether there should be one queue per outlet or a single queue for all the outlets. Whereas at first it might seem more efficient to have one queue per outlet, in reality it is not so. Queues are expensive resources and having many of them can have a negative impact on performance. If one single queue for all the outlets is used, then all that has to be done is to define the outlet number as a message property. This way the message selectors of every message consumer (the actual outlet) can check if the message matches their outlet, in which case the message is sent down the wire to the corresponding outlet.

The architecture is simple, but one thing has to be pointed out. At first glance it seems as if there will be only one producer and as many consumers as outlets. But, since the producer is a session bean, there will be as many producers as session beans are instantiated. This is not a problem in itself, as every instance will have its own connection and session, but it is important to understand that this is happening.

The Message Producer

As these are a series of experiments, there is no real fax being sent to the outlet. If there was, however, it would be done from the deliverOrder() method of the OrderServicesSL bean. It would be logical to change the hash table and then call another method that will be the actual JMS message producer. The first change in deliverOrder() is adding the code that places the Customer object, the outlet number and the orderMaster() object in the hash table:

```
//c07
Hashtable messageContent = new Hashtable();
...
//c07
messageContent.put("customer", findCustomer(orderMaster));
messageContent.put("outletNumber", new Long(outletNum));
messageContent.put("orderMaster", orderMaster);
Vector orderDetailsVector = null;
```

The order details will be stored in a vector. This is done within the `while` loop that handles the order detail inventory update with the following statements:

```
//c07
if (orderDetailsVector == null) {
  orderDetailsVector = new Vector();
}

orderDetailsVector.addElement(orderDetail);
```

Once the inventory has been updated the vector that contains the order details is placed in the hash table and the method `sendOrderFax()` is called:

```
//c07
if (orderDetailsVector != null) {
  messageContent.put("orderDetail", orderDetailsVector);
}

sendOrderFax (messageContent);
```

The `sendOrderFax()` method is the actual producer of the message:

```
/**
 * The name of the JMS queue connection factory.
 */
public final static String JMS_FACTORY =
                           "javax.jms.QueueConnectionFactory";

/**
 * The name of the "order" queue.
 */
public final static String QUEUE = "jsw.orderQueue";

/**
 * This method sends a JMS message with the details of an order.
 *
 */
protected void sendOrderFax(Hashtable messageContent)
    throws P2GException {

QueueConnectionFactory qConnFactory;
QueueConnection qConn;
QueueSession qSession;
QueueSender qSender;
Queue queue;
ObjectMessage message;
```

The first two lines define the names of the administered objects: the `Connection Factory` for the queue and the JMS queue. The first line specifies the name of the default Queue Connection Factory provided by WebLogic. The second line specifies the name of the "order" JMS queue created by WebLogic at startup. It is declared in the `weblogic.properties` file as follows:

```
weblogic.jms.queue.order=jsw.orderQueue
```

The first step is to get the JNDI context and a queue factory:

```
try {
    Context context = new InitialContext();
    qConnFactory = (QueueConnectionFactory) context.lookup(JMS_FACTORY);
```

Next, the connection is created:

```
qConn = qConnFactory.createQueueConnection();
```

As well as a session:

```
qSession = qConn.createQueueSession(false,
                            Session.AUTO_ACKNOWLEDGE);
```

Here the session is created with the AUTO_ACKNOWLEDGE mode set to false. If it is set to true, the session will automatically acknowledge the receipt of the message when the database has committed the message. In this case, the Wonder Troops are not necessarily interested in this, as the priority is to know if the outlet was the one that received it, not the database. Since the message is defined as persistent, they would much rather get a reply from the outlet than from the database.

For code robustness, they verify that the queue already exists. If it does not exist, they create it.

```
try {
    queue = (Queue) context.lookup(QUEUE);
} catch (NamingException ne) {
    queue = qSession.createQueue(QUEUE);
    context.bind(QUEUE, queue);
}
```

Next, the sender is created:

```
qSender = qSession.createSender(queue);
```

The sender is made to create persistent messages:

```
qSender.setDeliveryMode(DeliveryMode.PERSISTENT);
```

And a message type object is created:

```
message = qSession.createObjectMessage();
```

Because every connection is in the stopped state when created, it has to be started:

```
qConn.start();
```

Now the message is prepared and sent:

```
        message.setLongProperty("outletNumber",
                    ((Long)messageContent.get("outletNumber")).longValue());

        message.setObject(messageContent);

        qSender.send(message);
```

And everything is closed down:

```
        qSender.close();
        qSession.close();
        qConn.close();
```

The Message Consumer

As mentioned earlier, the program running on the client side is a programmatic or fat client. It is a standalone Java program that starts with two arguments, the URL of the JMS server and the number of the outlet. This program consists only of two methods. The `run()` method starts a receiver and initializes it for the corresponding queue with the message selector that specifies the outlet:

```
package jsw.c07.fax;

import java.util.*;
import javax.naming.*;
import javax.jms.*;
import jsw.c07.*;

/**
 * This class is a Java application that receives Orders from the
 * Operations Center.
 * This application is a JMS PTP client that receives JMS messages with
 * orders and prints them out on the console.
 * <pre>
 * usage: java -Djsw.serverURL=url jsw.c07.fax.Client outletNumber
 * </pre>
 * @see jsw.c07.fax.OrderReceiver
 */
public class Client {

  /**
    * This is the application's entry point.
    * It retrieves the parameters from the environment and from the
    * calling arguments and starts execution.
    */
  public static void main(String args[]) {

    if (args.length != 1) {
      System.err.println(
        "usage: java -Djsw.serverURL=url jsw.c07.fax.Client outletNumber");
      return;
    }
```

```
    Client client = new Client();
    try {
      client.outletNumber = Long.parseLong(args[0]);
      client.url = System.getProperty("jsw.serverURL",
                                       "t3://localhost:7001");
    } catch(Exception e) {
      System.err.println(e);
      return;
    }
    client.run();
  }


/**
 * The application main loop.
 * The application will receive orders and print them out.
 */
public void run() {
  try {
    orderReceiver = new OrderReceiver();
    Context context = Util.getInitialContext(url);
    orderReceiver.init(context,
                       OrderReceiver.QUEUE,
                       "outletNumber = " + outletNumber);
```

The next step is critical. A synchronized block is started on the order receiver. When the `orderReceiver.wait()` method is called, the main thread of execution is blocked waiting for the order receiver to return control. When it does so, and it is not a quit, it retrieves the objects from the message and calls the `saveOrder()` method:

```
        while (true) {
          synchronized(orderReceiver) {
            try {
              orderReceiver.wait();
              if (orderReceiver.quit)
                break;
              else {
                System.out.println(
                              "New order received in jsw.c07.fax.Client");

                Customer customer =
                      (Customer)orderReceiver.hashTable.get("customer");

                OrderMaster orderMaster =
                    (OrderMaster)orderReceiver.hashTable.get("orderMaster");

                Vector orderDetails =
                      (Vector)orderReceiver.hashTable.get("orderDetail");

                saveOrder(customer, orderMaster, orderDetails);
              }
            }
          catch (InterruptedException ie) {
            System.err.println(ie);
          }
        }
      }
```

The second method is `saveOrder()`. For the purposes of this experiment, this method only displays the objects that make up the order on the console where the WebLogic server was started. For any practical application this method should contain the logic to handle the actual order.

The Order Receiver

This class is similar to the order producer. The `init()` method defines the connection factory, creates the connection and the session, and verifies that there is a queue to listen to. Then it creates the actual receiver and starts to listen:

```java
package jsw.c07.fax;

import java.rmi.RemoteException;
import javax.naming.*;
import javax.jms.*;
import java.util.*;

/**
 * This class implements the MessageListener Interface to asynchronously
 * receive JMS messages with orders.
 *
 * @see jsw.c07.fax.Client
 */
public class OrderReceiver
    implements MessageListener {

  /**
   * The name of the JMS queue connection factory.
   */
  public final static String JMS_FACTORY =
                               "javax.jms.QueueConnectionFactory";

  /**
   * The name of the "order" queue.
   */
  public final static String QUEUE = "jsw.orderQueue";

  protected QueueConnectionFactory queueConnectionFactory = null;
  protected QueueConnection queueConnection = null;
  protected QueueSession queueSession = null;
  protected Queue queue = null;
  protected QueueReceiver receiver = null;
  public boolean quit = false;
  public Hashtable hashTable = null;

  /**
   * This method initializes all the objects.
   */
  public void init(Context ctx, String queueName, String selector)
      throws NamingException, JMSException, RemoteException {

    queueConnectionFactory =
                     (QueueConnectionFactory) ctx.lookup(JMS_FACTORY);
    queueConnection = queueConnectionFactory.createQueueConnection();
    queueSession = queueConnection.createQueueSession(false,
                                     Session.AUTO_ACKNOWLEDGE);
```

```
      try {
        queue = (Queue) ctx.lookup(queueName);
      } catch(NamingException ne){
        queue = queueSession.createQueue(queueName);
        ctx.bind(queueName, queue);
      }
      receiver = queueSession.createReceiver(queue, selector);
      receiver.setMessageListener(this);
      queueConnection.start();
      System.out.println("OrderReceiver: JMS conection opened");
  }

  /**
   * This method closes all the objects.
   */
  public void close()
      throws JMSException {
    receiver.close();
    queueSession.close();
    queueConnection.close();
    System.out.println("OrderReceiver: JMS conection closed");
  }
```

Once the message has arrived, the onMessage() method is called:

```
  /**
   * This is a call-back method.
   * This method is called when a message is received with an order.
   */
  public void onMessage(Message msg) {
    String msgText = "";
    quit = false;
    try {
      if (msg instanceof ObjectMessage) {
          hashTable = (Hashtable)((ObjectMessage)msg).getObject();
          System.out.println("msg received!");
      }
      else {
        msgText = msg.toString();
      }
    } catch(Exception e){
      System.err.println(e);
    }

    if (msgText.equalsIgnoreCase("quit")) {
      synchronized(this) {
        quit = true;
      }
    }

    synchronized(this) {
      this.notifyAll();
    }
  }
}
```

The body of the message is retrieved into a hash table and a message is displayed. The synchronized call returns the control to the main thread.

Setting Up The Example

As the WebLogic server uses a relational database for persistency, some special tables have to be created to store the messages. This has already been done within the script setDB.cmd provided and executed in Chapter 2. In this script a call is made to the program supplied by WebLogic called utils.Schema. As the Troops are using Oracle, the command line to use is:

```
C:\jdk1.3\bin\java utils.Schema jdbc:weblogic:oracle \
                weblogic.jdbc.oci.Driver \
                -s %DBSERVER% -u %DBUSER% -p %DBPASS% -verbose \
                c:\weblogic\classes\weblogic\jms\ddl\jms_oracle.ddl
```

In the weblogic.properties file, a JDBC connection pool is defined for JMS use, as well as the queue for the orders:

```
weblogic.jms.connectionPool=p2gPool
weblogic.jms.queue.order=jsw.orderTopic
```

Different types of client can use the same JDBC connection pool (JSP, servlets, EJBs, and JMS).

The message producer is in the new version of the OrderServicesSL bean that is deployed at server startup by specifying the JAR file name in the weblogic.properties file:

```
weblogic.ejb.deploy=\
    c:/wlsbook/srv/c07-srv/ejb/OrderMasterEBBean.jar,\
    c:/wlsbook/srv/c07-srv/ejb/OrderDetailEBBean.jar,\
    c:/wlsbook/srv/c07-srv/ejb/TicketServicesSLBean.jar,\
    c:/wlsbook/srv/c07-srv/ejb/PizzaServicesSLBean.jar,\
    c:/wlsbook/srv/c07-srv/ejb/OrderServicesSLBean.jar,\
    c:/wlsbook/srv/c07-srv/ejb/OutletServicesSLBean.jar,\
    c:/wlsbook/srv/c07-srv/ejb/OrderSFBean.jar
```

The message producer can be used in the same way as in the previous chapter. By placing a new order through the JSP pages, the `OrderServicesSL` bean will send a new message with the order. A new order was created in the following example:

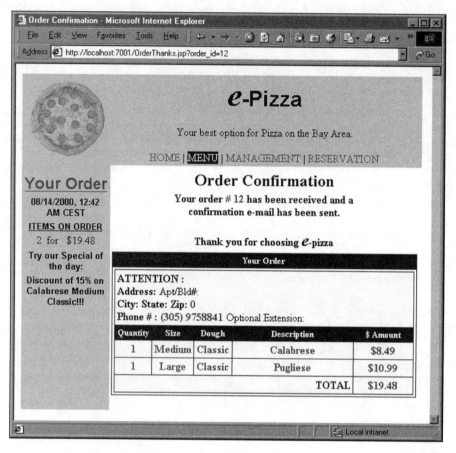

The message consumer is a java application that must be run in the command line. To run it, just start a new command window, change to the `c:\wlsbook` directory, and run the `setEnvCli.cmd` script with the argument 7 (the chapter). This script sets the client environment to run this and other java applications. After setting the client environment, run the application by typing the following command:

```
c:\wlsbook>java -Djsw.serverURL=t3://localhost:7001 jsw.c07.fax.Client 0
```

The `jsw.serverURL` property specifies the URL of the WebLogic server, and the program argument (in this case is the number 0) specifies the outlet number to receive orders. These steps and the results are shown as follows:

```
c:\wlsbook>setenvcli 7
------------------------------------------------------------
Setting CLIENT environment for chapter 7
------------------------------------------------------------
Current settings:
      Java Home = c:\jdk1.3
   WebLogic Home = c:\weblogic
    Project Home = c:\wlsbook
       CLASSPATH =
c:\weblogic\lib\weblogic510sp4boot.jar;c:\weblogic\classes\boot;c:\weblogic\lib\we
blogic510sp4.jar;c:\weblogic\license;c:\weblogic\classes;c:\weblogic\lib\weblogica
ux.jar;c:\wlsbook\srv\c07-srv\clientclasses;c:\wlsbook\srv
\c07-srv\serverclasses;c:\wlsbook\srv\c07-srv\ejb\TicketServicesSLBean.jar


c:\wlsbook>java -Djsw.serverURL=t3://localhost:7001 jsw.c07.fax.Client 0
OrderReceiver: JMS connection opened
msg received!
New order received in jsw.c07.fax.Client
Mon Aug 14 00:42:02 CEST 2000: order received:
++++++++++++++ begin order ++++++++++++++
>>>Order:          [Order number = 12][Country code = 1][Area code = 305]
[Phone = 9758841][Outlet code = 0][Order date = 2000-08-14 00:41:59.0]
[Delivery = Address][Status = Ordering][Remarks = null][Price = 19.48]
>>>Customer:       [Country code = 1][Area code = 305][Phone = 9758841]
[First name = Juancho][Last name = Otaola][Postal code = 33180][Address line 1 =
24 Doral Blvd.][Address line 2 = null][Remarks = null][City = Miami][Major
Crossroads = null][Colonia = null][State = FL][Country = USA]
>>>Order detail: [Order detail number = 16][Order master number = 12][type =
predefined pizza][Pizza name = Calabrese][Pizza size = Medium][Dough =
Classic][Quantity = 1][Price = 8.49]
>>>Order detail: [Order detail number = 17][Order master number = 12][type =
predefined pizza][Pizza name = Pugliese][Pizza size = Large][Dough =
Classic][Quantity = 1][Price = 10.99]
++++++++++++++ end order ++++++++++++++
```

An interesting exercise is to have a look at the server by using the WebLogic Console. The WebLogic Console can be started in a new command window, by changing to the c:\wlsbook directory, setting the environment (setenv 7), and typing "java weblogic.Console". The screenshot overleaf shows the user "guest" connected to the server and a JMS session (1) with one message received. All this information is related to the message consumer application (jsw.c07.fax.Client) previously started, which is connected to the server.

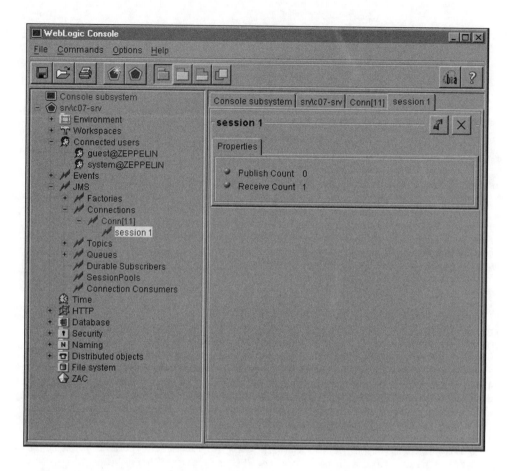

A Message-Driven Reservation System

As part of the push to create more revenue, Mrs Marketroid created a program for frequent pizza eaters, just like the airlines and their 'air mile' schemes. With the Pizza Gobbler Program you get points for purchases at Pizza2Go, which can then be redeemed for more pizzas or other items. The idea was that people could not only redeem their points for pizzas, but also tickets to sports events such as baseball, football, basketball, or ice hockey games.

This marketing idea inspired the Wonder Troops to find out the requirements for an experiment to test the Publish and Subscribe messaging features of JMS. The experiment will be a reservation system. This system will allow the operators of Pizza2Go to reserve a seat or group of seats at a venue for a specific sports event.

There can be many operators working on the same sports match. When one makes a reservation, the others need to know that those seats are no longer available, on a real-time basis.

This can be easily modeled using JMS Publish and Subscribe. The reservation system acts as the producer, and every operator working on a specific sports match is a subscriber to that event. Every time a seat is taken by the reservation system, a message is sent to the clients subscribed to the corresponding sports match.

The sports match is the topic. A client can produce a message, a reservation or cancellation of seats, and all the clients that are subscribed to that topic will receive an update with the new status of the seats. Notice that a client can be both a producer and a subscriber to the same topic. This is one of the features of JMS Pub/Sub.

The Implementation

This experiment is a standalone system, unrelated to the current application the Wonder Troops have been developing. The architecture is based on a server-side module that receives requests for reserving (buying) or canceling seats on specific sports matches. It performs the required operation on the database and then notifies all the subscribers. The client side presents the venue information for the selected sports match and allows the operator to choose a seat or group of seats and request an operation (purchase or cancel) to the server-side module. The client also presents any changes to the venue as per the messages it receives.

On the database front, only two tables are needed. One contains the information related to the sports matches and the other contains the information of the sold seats. The structure of the tables can be seen in the following figure. The Troops have also created the corresponding JavaBeans to represent them, `match` and `ticket`.

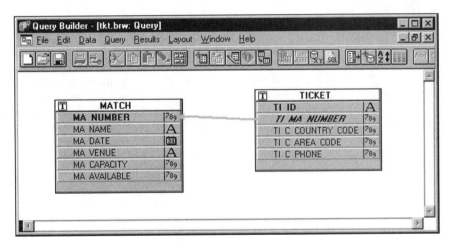

For the server-side module they decide to create a stateless session bean called `TicketServicesSL`, which offers the functionality to buy one or more tickets, or cancel a ticket for a match.

```
package jsw.c07;

import java.util.*;
import java.sql.*;
import java.rmi.RemoteException;
import javax.ejb.*;
import javax.naming.*;
import javax.jms.*;
import javax.jts.*;
```

```
/**
 * This class is the Bean Implementation for the Stateless Session EJB
<tt>TicketServicesSL</tt>.
 *
 * @see        jsw.c07.TicketServicesSLHome
 * @see        jsw.c07.TicketServicesSL
 */
public class TicketServicesSLBean implements SessionBean {
  private SessionContext ctx;

  /**
   * This is the static initializer,
   * executed the first time this class is referred to.
   * It makes sure the JDBC JTS driver is loaded.
   */
  static {
    try {
      Class.forName("weblogic.jdbc.jts.Driver");
    } catch(Exception e) {
      System.err.println(e);
    }
  }
```

The buy() method in this bean is the core of the subsystem. When it is called, it inserts a row in the seat table, if it's available for purchase, with the corresponding information. Then it updates the number of available seats on the match table. This method has two arguments, a vector that contains the seats to be purchased and a mode for the purchase. There are two modes available, the ALL_OR_NOTHING mode, meaning that either all the seats requested are purchased or none. The second mode is named AS_MANY_AS_POSSIBLE, which tries to get as many seats as possible from the seats requested. These modes are defined as constants in the TicketServicesSL remote interface as follows:

```
package jsw.c07;

import javax.ejb.*;
import java.rmi.RemoteException;
import java.util.Date;
import java.util.Vector;

/**
 * This is the Remote Interface for the Stateless Session EJB
<tt>TicketServicesSL</tt>.
 *
 * @see        jsw.c07.TicketServicesSLHome
 * @see        jsw.c07.TicketServicesSLBean
 */
public interface TicketServicesSL extends EJBObject {

  /**
   * Will try to buy or cancel all the tickets or none.
   */
  public static final int ALL_OR_NOTHING = 1;

  /**
   * Will try to by or cancel as many tickets as possible.
   */
  public static final int AS_MANY_AS_POSSIBLE = 2;
```

The `buy()` method in the `TicketServicesSL` bean implementation:

```
/**
 * Buys a group of tickets. It can be all or nothing.
 *
 * @param     tickets a Vector with tickets.
 * @param     mode TicketServicesSL.ALL_OR_NOTHING,
 *               TicketServicesSL.AS_MANY_AS_POSSIBLE.
 * @return    the number of tickets actually bought.
 */
public int buy(Vector tickets, int mode)
    throws P2GException {

  java.sql.Connection conn = null;
  String sqlStatement = "";
  PreparedStatement pstmt = null;
  Vector vNotify = null;
  int nSeats = 0;
  try {
    conn = DriverManager.getConnection("jdbc:weblogic:jts:p2gPool");
    if ((tickets == null) || (tickets.size() == 0))
      throw new P2GException("nothing to buy");
    Match match = getMatch((Ticket)tickets.firstElement());
    nSeats = match.getMa_available();
```

The `getMatch()` method is called to ensure that the sports match where the seats are requested actually exists. As all the code in the `buy()` method is in a `try` loop, if the `getMatch()` method fails, the exception is caught, the database connections are closed, and control is returned to the caller.

```
    sqlStatement = "insert into ticket values (?, ?, ?, ?, ?)";
    for (int i = 0; i < tickets.size(); i++) {
        Ticket ticket = (Ticket)tickets.elementAt(i);
        pstmt = conn.prepareStatement(sqlStatement);
      pstmt.setString   (1, ticket.getTi_id());
      pstmt.setLong     (2, ticket.getTi_ma_number());
      pstmt.setInt      (3, ticket.getTi_c_country_code());
      pstmt.setInt      (4, ticket.getTi_c_area_code());
      pstmt.setLong     (5, ticket.getTi_c_phone());
      try {
        int res = pstmt.executeUpdate();
        if (res == 0) {
          throw new P2GException("nothing updated");
        }
        decAvailableSeats(match);
        if (vNotify == null) {
          vNotify = new Vector();
        }
        vNotify.addElement(ticket);
```

The vector of requested seats is processed one seat at a time. If the insert statement fails, it can only be because the seat is taken (it can be also because the database failed, etc. but bear with us on this one). This failure will throw an exception, which will be caught in the following code:

```
    } catch(Exception e) {
    String msg = "the following ticket could not be inserted: " +
                ticket.getTi_id() + ", due to: " + e.toString();
    System.err.println(msg);

    switch (mode) {
      case TicketServicesSL.ALL_OR_NOTHING:
        throw new P2GException(msg);
      case TicketServicesSL.AS_MANY_AS_POSSIBLE:
        continue;
    }

    }
    finally {
      try {
        pstmt.close();
      } catch(Exception w) {
        System.err.println("Warning: " + w);
      }
    }
```

The beauty of this is that the exception is processed by asking if the mode is ALL_OR_NOTHING, in which case a new exception is thrown and the request is completed. If, however, the mode is AS_MANY_AS_POSSIBLE, the exception is ignored and the processing continues to the next seat in the vector.

An extremely important requirement of the system is that a customer cannot purchase a seat that has already been sold. The reason we bring it up is that this is probably the most important feature of a reservation system like this. Using other technologies, the development required to achieve this result is a big effort. By using JTS in this session bean, the Wonder Troops do not have to worry about developing any code for this. All they have to do is define the bean to be a TX_REQUIRED transaction and the isolation level to SERIALIZABLE.

When the transaction has been inserted successfully, the total count of available seats is updated and the seat is added to a vector that will be used later when producing the message to the subscribers.

```
    match = getMatch((Ticket)tickets.firstElement());
    notify(match, vNotify, "sold");
    nSeats -= match.getMa_available();
  } catch(Exception e) {
    throw new P2GException(e.toString());
  }
  finally {
    try {
      pstmt.close();
      conn.close();
    } catch(Exception w) {
        System.err.println("Warning: " + w);
    }
  }
  return nSeats;
}
```

After calling the `notify()` method to send the message to the topic, the `buy()` method returns the number of seats actually purchased to the caller, in this case the client that requested the reservation. This is calculated by storing the number of available seats the first time `getMatch()` is called, and subtracting the number of available seats after all the inserts have been done (also provided by calling `getMatch()`).

The `decAvailableSeats()` method connects to the database searching for the appropriate sports match. The available seat count is decreased with the following SQL statement:

```
sqlStatement = "update match " +
               "set (ma_available) = (ma_available - 1) " +
               "where (ma_number = ?)";
```

This method only has to decrease the seat count by one because it is called within the loop that processes each individual seat request.

The `getMatch()` method in itself is very simple. Since the vector that contains the seat requests also contains the sports match number, all this method does is query the database for a sports match given a seat. The query is done using JDBC. It could also use an entity bean, but the Wonder Troops have chosen not to do so as they are afraid that a sold out sports event in a large stadium could produce too many entity beans for the container to handle in an efficient manner.

The `cancel()` method is left as an exercise for the reader.

The Message

The seats are identified by section, row, and seat number. This is handled as a string to accommodate all naming possibilities of the different venues. A seat number in this system would be represented in a comma delimited list, for example: 7,18,5 or A,27,H2.

As a purchase can be made for one or more seats the issue to debate is whether a message should be used for only one seat or should be able to handle a group of seats. The gut feeling indicates that one message per seat is inefficient, so it is decided that a message can have one or more seats concatenated by the "&" sign. For example:

```
7,18,5&7,18,6&7,18,7&5,1,10&5,1,11
```

In this example the message has 5 seats: section 7, row 18, seats 5, 6 and 7 and section 5, row 1, seats 10 and 11.

Should there be as many topics as sport matches, or should there be just one topic? Once again gut feeling leans towards only one topic; the more topics there are, the more resources are used in the server. It seems as if the ideal solution to this system is to use only one topic and then have the sports match as a message property field. This way a client can view the desired messages by using a message selector on this field.

Seats can be either sold or canceled, and the client needs to know this in order to handle the reservations correctly. Please note that 'reserving' and 'purchasing' a seat mean the same in this context. The client also benefits by knowing the number of available seats.

Now the question is which type of message should be used. The options to be considered for this particular message are object, text, and map. An object message would mean that all the clients would need to have access to the object in order to be able to instantiate it. That means that the object has to travel down the wire, creating unwanted traffic.

If text type messages are used, then some parsing routines have to be created to process the message. This is inconvenient.

Using a map message seems to be the most suitable. The following list presents the pairs of names and values selected to represent the message:

Name	Value
availableSeats	An integer with the available seat count
seats	A string as described earlier
type	A string, either `sold` or `cancelled`

A graphic of the message is presented in the following figure:

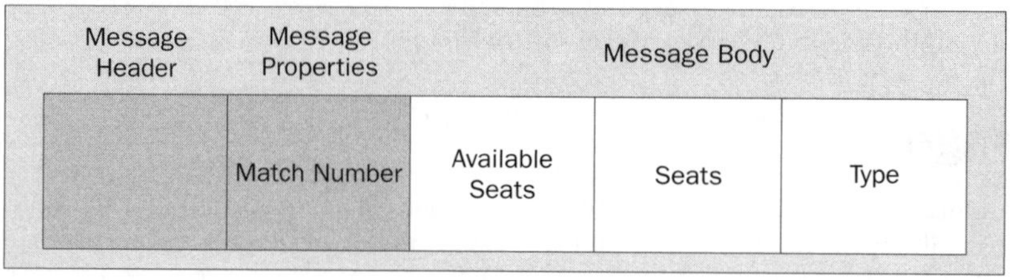

The Notifier

The `notify()` method in the `TicketServicesSL` bean sets up the appropriate JMS infrastructure in a similar fashion to the PTP example seen earlier in this chapter in the `OrderServicesSL` bean. The structures of the two systems are very similar, but entirely different interfaces are being used so it is important not to confuse them; the main visible difference is that instead of using the word *queue* it uses *topic*.

```
/**
 * The name of the JMS topic connection factory.
 */
public final static String JMS_FACTORY =
                               "javax.jms.TopicConnectionFactory";

/**
 * The name of the "ticket" topic.
 */
public final static String TOPIC = "jsw.ticketTopic";

/**
 * Notifies subscriptors of a ticket selling.
 *
 * @param      match the match.
 * @param      tickets a Vector with tickets.
 * @param      type notification type, values: "sold", "cancelled".
 */
```

```
protected void notify(Match match, Vector tickets, String type)
    throws P2GException {

  TopicConnectionFactory tConnFactory;
  TopicConnection tConn;
  TopicSession tSession;
  TopicPublisher tPublisher;
  Topic topic;
  MapMessage message;

  try {
    Context context = new InitialContext();
    tConnFactory = (TopicConnectionFactory) context.lookup(JMS_FACTORY);
    tConn = tConnFactory.createTopicConnection();
    tSession = tConn.createTopicSession(false,
                                        Session.AUTO_ACKNOWLEDGE);
    try {
      topic = (Topic) context.lookup(TOPIC);
    } catch (NamingException ne) {
      topic = tSession.createTopic(TOPIC);
      context.bind(TOPIC, topic);
    }
    tPublisher = tSession.createPublisher(topic);
```

The type of message is defined by instantiating the corresponding class:

```
message = tSession.createMapMessage();
```

Now that the setup is complete, the connection is started:

```
tConn.start();
```

The message property field with the match number is set with:

```
message.setLongProperty("matchNumber", match.getMa_number());
```

The message body is filled first with the number of available seats:

```
message.setInt("availableSeats", match.getMa_available());
```

Then with the seats, using the following loop:

```
StringBuffer ticketString = null;
Enumeration enum = tickets.elements();

while (enum.hasMoreElements()) {
    if (ticketString == null)
      ticketString = new StringBuffer("");
    else
      ticketString.append("&");
    ticketString.append(((Ticket)enum.nextElement()).getTi_id());
}

message.setString("tickets", ticketString.toString());
```

Finally, the type of operation on the tickets (sold or cancelled) is stored:

```
        message.setString("type", type);
```

After this, the message is published:

```
        tPublisher.publish(message);
```

And everything is closed:

```
        tPublisher.close();
        tSession.close();
        tConn.close();
    } catch(Exception e) {
        System.err.println(e);
        throw new P2GException(e.toString());
    }
}
```

The Fat JMS Client

Now that the server-side module has been completed, the Troops set off to create a client that can request reservations and subscribe to the server module. This experiment will be done with a Java-based programmatic client that will run standalone. It could also be done with an applet, but they prefer to use a standalone program.

This client will handle the basketball match between Miami Heat and Boston Celtics in the Miami Arena, which for the purposes of this experiment has 8 sections, each with 300 seats. The client uses the Swing classes and uses the *all or nothing* mode for the purchases. To simplify the experiment, all the purchases will be done by the same customer, whose data is hard-coded in the program. As there are plenty of good books about the Swing classes we will not be describing the methods and classes that are related to the graphic interface. This client is intended for the use of the Pizza2Go operators. As such, the Java code can be delivered to every machine used by the operators and maintained up to date by means of the Zero Administration Client (ZAC) of WebLogic.

The main method is simple. It defines the match it wants to work with, connects to the WebLogic server and calls the run() method.

```
package jsw.c07.reservation;

import java.awt.*;
import java.awt.event.*;
import javax.swing.*;
import javax.swing.border.*;
import javax.naming.*;
import javax.ejb.*;
import java.util.*;
import java.text.*;
import javax.jms.*;
import java.sql.*;
import jsw.c07.*;
```

```
/**
 * This class is a Java application that receives messages from the
 * Operations Center.
 * This application is a JMS Pub/Sub client that receives JMS messages
 * with tickets and updates a venue graphical display. It also
 * supports ticket selling by using the <tt>TicketServicesSL</tt> bean.
 * <pre>
 * usage: java -Djsw.server=host jsw.c07.reservation.Client matchNumber
 * </pre>
 * @see jsw.c07.TicketServicesSL
 */
public class Client
    implements ActionListener {

  /**
   * This is the application's entry point.
   * It retrieves the parameters from the environment and from the
   * calling arguments and starts execution.
   */
  public static void main(String args[]) {

    if (args.length != 1) {
      System.err.println (
"usage: java -Djsw.server=host jsw.c07.reservation.Client matchNumber");
      return;
    }

    Client client = new Client();
    try {
      client.matchNumber = Long.parseLong(args[0]);
      client.url = "t3://" + System.getProperty("jsw.server", "localhost")
                 + ":7001";
    } catch(Exception e) {
      System.err.println(e);
      return;
    }
    client.run();
  }
```

The `run()` method first calls the `createdFrame()` method, which conducts the Swing elements and presents a view of the venue as shown here:

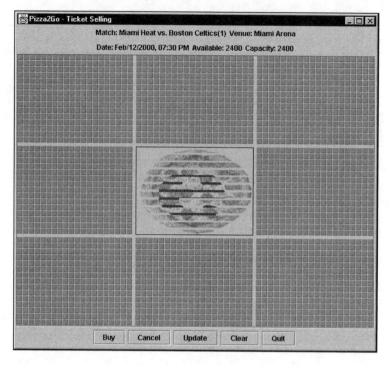

Every little green box is an available seat. The actual basketball court is where the logo of E-Pizza is. The buttons at the bottom provide the basic operational functionality. The operator can:

❑ **Buy** a seat (or seats)

❑ **Cancel** a purchased seat (not implemented in this experiment)

❑ **Update** the screen by reading all the purchased seats from the database

❑ **Clear** a selected seat (or seats)

❑ **Quit** the application

Next, the `run()` method will start the listener and subscribe to the topic with a selector that will choose the desired match:

```
/**
 * The application main loop.
 * The application will receive "ticket messages" and will update
 * the venue display.
 */
public void run() {
  createFrame();
  try {
    ticketReceiver = new TicketReceiver();
    Context context = Util.getInitialContext(url);
    ticketReceiver.init(context,
                        TicketReceiver.TOPIC,
                        "matchNumber = " + matchNumber);
```

Then the `loadSeats()` method is called to bring all the existing sold seats from the database. Note the order of the sequence. You need to activate the listener and subscribe to the topic before loading the sold seats so that you don't lose any real-time information.

```
loadSeats();
while(true) {
  synchronized(ticketReceiver) {
    try {
      ticketReceiver.wait();
      if (ticketReceiver.quit)
        break;
      else {
        int status = 0;
        if (ticketReceiver.type.equals("cancelled"))
          status = Seat.AVAILABLE;
        if (ticketReceiver.type.equals("sold"))
          status = Seat.SOLD;
        etAvail.setText("Available: " + ticketReceiver.available);
        venue.updateSeats(ticketReceiver.tickets, status);
      }
    } catch (InterruptedException ie) {
    }
  }
}
```

The following figure presents the view of the venue after it has loaded the sold seats. In reality you will not actually see the screen as presented previously. This is because the operation is so fast that you will only really see the screen as shown here.

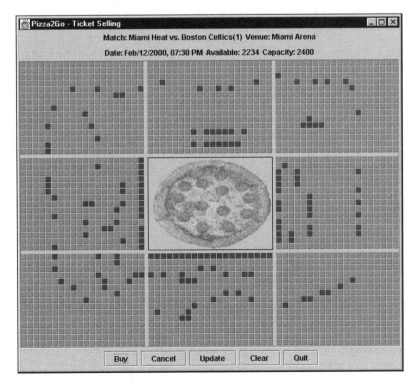

Now comes the tricky part. The next diagram shows how all these things interrelate. It might not be an accurate picture as far as the internal workings of the JVM goes, but it will provide a good understanding of the scenario.

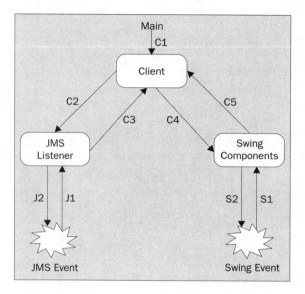

Thread number 1, denoted by the arrows C1, C2 and C3, is started by the `main()` method of the client. Arrow C2 of the main thread is where it synchronizes with the JMS listener and then waits for a message to arrive. This thread is now blocked at the listener. Liberation comes when the following statement is executed in the `onMessage()` method of the listener:

```
synchronized(this) {
    this.notifyAll();
}
```

Thread number 2 is from the JMS world. It is denoted by arrows J1 and J2. When arrow J1 gets a message gets to the listener, a hand over occurs in the `onMessage()` method:

```
/**
 * This is a call-back method.
 * This method is called when a message is received with tickets.
 */
public void onMessage(Message msg) {
    String msgText = "";
    quit = false;
    try {
        matchNumber = msg.getLongProperty("matchNumber");
        if (msg instanceof MapMessage) {
            available = ((MapMessage)msg).getInt("availableSeats");
            tickets   = ((MapMessage)msg).getString("tickets");
            type      = ((MapMessage)msg).getString("type");
        }
        else {
            msgText = msg.toString();
```

```
      }
    } catch(JMSException jmse) {
      jmse.printStackTrace();
    } catch(Exception e) {
      System.err.println(e);
    }

    if (msgText.equalsIgnoreCase("quit")) {
      synchronized(this) {
        quit = true;
      }
    }

    synchronized(this) {
      this.notifyAll();
    }
  }
}
```

After the listener unblocks the main thread it goes back to the `Client` object, arrow C3. After the handover, the JMS thread goes back to the JMS world, arrow J2.

When the main thread returns to the `Client` object, arrow C3, it calls the `venue.updateSeats()` method in the Swing world with the seats and status obtained from the message, arrow C4, and returns to the client, arrow C5. Here the loop starts again, by going to the listener and waiting for a message, arrow C2.

Thread number 3, depicted with arrows S1 and S2, is from the Swing world. When a Swing event happens, arrow S1, it is sent over to the corresponding object.

In this case, if it is a `mouseEvent` triggered by selecting a seat, it is sent over to the `mousePressed()` method of the `Seat` object. This method just marks the seat with an X and repaints the venue. If the event is an `actionEvent` created by clicking on a button, the event is sent to the `actionPerformed()` method of the `Client` object. Here it will perform the function that was chosen by the button.

When the Buy button has been clicked, the `buySeveral()` method is called with a string that contains all the selected seats. The `TicketServicesSL` bean is then created as well as a vector of seats. Then the `buy()` method of the bean is called to perform the actual purchase of the seats.

```
/**
 * This method buys tickets.
 */
protected int buySeveral(String seats, int mode) {
  int n = 0;
  if (seats == null)
    return n;
  try {
    Context context = Util.getInitialContext(url);
    TicketServicesSLHome ticketServicesHome =
      (TicketServicesSLHome) context.lookup("jsw.c07.TicketServicesSL");
    TicketServicesSL ticketServices = ticketServicesHome.create();
    Vector tickets = new Vector();
    Ticket ticket = null;
```

269

```
        StringTokenizer stringTokenizer = new StringTokenizer(seats, "&");
        while(stringTokenizer.hasMoreTokens()) {
          String seat = stringTokenizer.nextToken();
          ticket = new Ticket();
          ticket.setTi_id(seat);
          ticket.setTi_ma_number(matchNumber);
          ticket.setTi_c_country_code(1);
          ticket.setTi_c_area_code(305);
          ticket.setTi_c_phone(9758841);
          tickets.addElement(ticket);
        }
        n = ticketServices.buy(tickets, mode);
        ticketServices.remove();
      } catch(Exception e) {
        e.printStackTrace();
      }
      return n;
  }
```

The snippet of code above shows how the information about the customer who purchases the seat is fixed for all purchases.

The next figure shows another interesting screenshot of the venue. It presents the screen with seats that have been selected for a button action, and also, in a call out box, you can see that it presents the actual seat information of the seat it is pointing to.

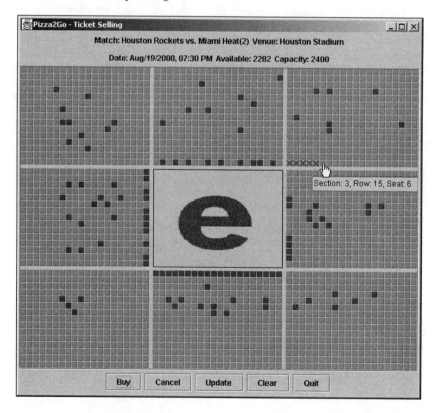

Exercises

- ❑ An interesting exercise for the reader is to add the code that will purchase the seat for a customer chosen by the operator.

- ❑ One of the nice things to add to this screen is a message area. This message area can be used to confirm a purchase or inform the operator that a purchase did not happen. This last case is a distinct possibility, as another operator can have selected the same seats and clicked on the buy button a short time before the first one did so.

- ❑ An additional exercise for the reader is to implement the cancel functionality.

The Browser Client

The fat client was a nice experiment, but unrealistic for practical use on the Internet. If this application were to be released, a browser client would make more sense. The main problem with this type of client would be that presenting the entire venue in the browser would be highly impractical. It would therefore be likely that the browser would not be able to handle a large venue. So it is decided that instead of displaying the whole venue, they will present one section at a time. To make the navigation easy, a list of links to the other sections will be available from each page.

The next issue is the selection of seats. HTML is rather primitive, so there is only one limited option to get a similar functionality to that in the programmatic client, where you can select a group of seats and then purchase them. This option is using check boxes, but it is very likely the browser will not be able to handle that number of check boxes. The solution is that every seat in the section is a link to execute a purchase of that specific seat. So in this interface you will only be able to buy one seat at a time. In this experiment the cancel functionality will not be implemented.

As HTML is not really a push technology, this interface will not refresh automatically. These are the constraints under which the client will be developed. The implementation is based on three JSP pages. The first one, `TicketReservation.jsp`, presents the list of sport matches available. The output of this page is presented in the following screenshot overleaf.

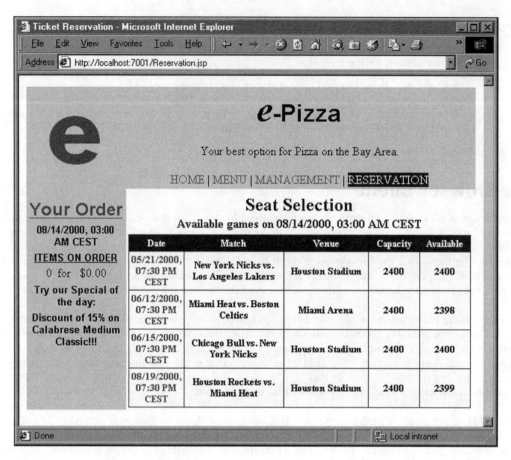

This JSP page queries the database and retrieves all the games from the match table. It then builds a list with links using the statement within a loop:

```
<a href="Venue.jsp?match_id=<%=resultset.getLong("ma_number")%>">
```

This link points to the Venue.jsp page with the appropriate argument. The initial page generated by the venue JSP page is presented opposite.

Here you can see how the Wonder Troops solved the problem of presenting the links to the various sections of the venue. Venue.jsp will first go to the database to get a count of sold seats and then calculate the actual available seats for every section with the following piece of code:

```
long matchNumber = 0;
try {
  matchNumber =(new Long(request.getParameter("match_id"))).longValue();
} catch(Exception e) {
  System.err.println("no match specified: " + e);
}
String section = null;
section = request.getParameter("section_id");
int sectionsNum = 8;
int sectionCapacity = 300;
int availableSeats[] = new int[sectionsNum];
Vector soldSeats = null;

try {
  conn = DriverManager.getConnection("jdbc:weblogic:pool:p2gPool");
  for (int i = 1; i <= sectionsNum; i++){
    sqlStatement = new StringBuffer("select count(*) from ticket ");
    sqlStatement.append("where ti_ma_number = ? and ti_id like '");
    sqlStatement.append(i + ",%'");
    pstmt = conn.prepareStatement(sqlStatement.toString());
    pstmt.setLong(1, matchNumber);
    resultSet = pstmt.executeQuery();
    if(resultSet.next()) {
      availableSeats[i-1] = sectionCapacity - resultSet.getInt(1);
    }
    resultSet.close();
    pstmt.close();
  }
```

If no section has been specified, then the message presented in the previous screenshot is displayed. Otherwise, the database is queried to obtain all the information for the requested section:

```
if (section != null) {
  sqlStatement = new StringBuffer("select ti_id from ticket ");
  sqlStatement.append("where ti_ma_number = ?  and ti_id like '");
  sqlStatement.append(section + ",%' order by ti_id");
  pstmt = conn.prepareStatement(sqlStatement.toString());
  pstmt.setLong(1, matchNumber);
  resultSet = pstmt.executeQuery();
  while(resultSet.next()) {
    if (soldSeats == null)
      soldSeats = new Vector();
    soldSeats.addElement(resultSet.getString("ti_id"));
  }
  resultSet.close();
  pstmt.close();
}
```

Then the method displaySection() is called to show a representation of the section. This method is actually defined in the JSP page, which is something the Wonder Troops had not done before. The resulting display is shown here:

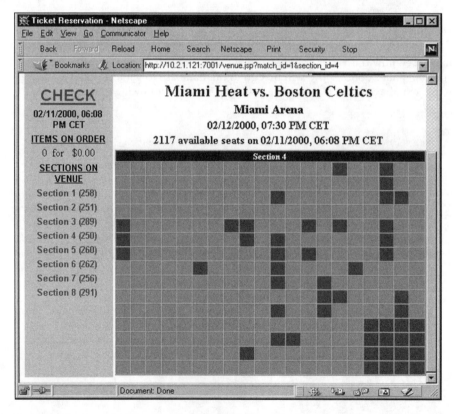

When the Internet Explorer browser is used (version 4.0 or higher), there is a slightly different behavior on this screen. The seat over which the mouse is pointing will change color.

This fact that this behavior is not seen in the Netscape browser can be attributed to the fact that it is not correctly processing the cascading style sheets. The following fragment contains the offensive code:

```
A:hover
{
  BACKGROUND: #660000;
  COLOR: #FFFFFF;
  TEXT-DECORATION: none
}
```

The seat JSP page contains only the method `buySeveral()` that was used for the programmatic client.

The Netscape Bonus

The Wonder Troops found out that if a document is defined as a multi-part MIME document, the socket used to communicate with the web server is kept open until the document is finished. Out of curiosity they decided to develop another interface that takes advantage of this. In order to obtain this behavior, it is better to work with a servlet than a JSP page, as it will be easier to define all the needed arguments as the document type. While the browser client is working with the servlet the document will remain open. The effect of this is that any update to the seating map will be automatically presented on this browser. No refresh or reloads are necessary.

The big disadvantage of using this option is that it will consume resources that are considered expensive and scarce. When doing this remember that not only the socket will remain open, but also a thread is blocked for exclusive use of the browser.

The new `VenueNetscapeS` servlet tests if the browser is Internet Explorer, and if so it redirects execution to the venue JSP page:

```
public void service(HttpServletRequest request,
                    HttpServletResponse response)
   throws ServletException, IOException {

  try {
    String userAgent = request.getHeader("User-Agent");
    if (userAgent.indexOf("MSIE") != -1) {      //Microsoft
      String sURL = response.encodeRedirectURL("Venue.jsp");
      ServletContext context = getServletContext();
      RequestDispatcher requestDispatcher;
      requestDispatcher = context.getRequestDispatcher(sURL);
      try {
        requestDispatcher.forward(request, response);
      } catch (ServletException e) {
        System.err.println(e);
      }
    }
  }
```

The rest of the servlet pretty much replicates the functionality of the fat client and uses some of its code. It starts by defining the document type and setting the boundary of the parts to the word End:

```
try {
  response.setContentType("multipart/x-mixed-replace;boundary=End");
} catch(Exception e) {
  System.err.println(e);
}
PrintWriter out = null;
try {
  out = response.getWriter();
  out.println();
  out.println("--End");
  out.flush();
} catch(Exception e) {
  System.err.println(e);
}
```

The other change is that it uses the initSession() method instead of the loadSeats() method. The reason for the change is because the servlet has to be thread-safe. Whereas loadSeats() uses objects to handle the seat information, initSession() uses session values:

```
TicketReceiver ticketReceiver = null;

try {
  long matchNumber = (new
                  Long(request.getParameter("match_id"))).longValue();
  ticketReceiver = new TicketReceiver();
  Context context = Util.getInitialContext();
  ticketReceiver.init(context,
                  TicketReceiver.TOPIC,
                  "matchNumber = " + matchNumber);

  initSession(request); // equivalent to loadSeats() in the fat client
```

The Troops lifted the synchronize code from the fat client and copied it with only one change. Instead of calling the Swing object to display the screen, they call another method that will do the equivalent for HTML.

Before the synchronize block, but as part of the loop, the following statements are executed:

```
int n = 0;
do {
  out.println("Content-Type: text/html");
  out.println();

  displayHtmlPage(request, response, out);

  out.println();
  out.println("--End");
  out.flush();
  n++;
```

```
      synchronized(ticketReceiver) {
        try {
          ticketReceiver.wait();
          if (ticketReceiver.quit) {
            break;
          }
          else {
            int status = 0;
            if (ticketReceiver.type.equals("cancelled")){
              status = Seat.AVAILABLE;
            }
            if (ticketReceiver.type.equals("sold")) {
              status = Seat.SOLD;
            }
            updateAvailableSeats(request,
                                 ticketReceiver.tickets,
                                 status);
          }
        } catch (InterruptedException ie) {
          System.err.println("Interrupted: " + ie);
          if (ticketReceiver != null) {
            ticketReceiver.close();
          }
        }
      }
    }
  while(n < 1000); //load limit
```

Note: The loop has been purposely limited to only 1000 refreshes or receipts of messages, so as to not cause problems with system resources.

As stated earlier, this servlet is generally pretty much the same as the fat client, with the main differences being that the output is designed for HTML and includes the changes to make it thread-safe.

Also worth mentioning is the `displayHtmlPage()` method. This is the perfect example of **clever laziness**. In a servlet the HTML statements are sent using the `out.print()` method. This implies that all the HTML code of the venue JSP page had to be rewritten for use in the servlet. Instead of doing this, the Wonder Troops compiled the venue JSP page with the `-keepgenerated` option. This option keeps the generated HTML code in a file. Having done this, the troops proceeded to cut and paste from this file to `out.print()` statements.

Putting It All Together

There are two new elements in this section that are registered in the `weblogic.properties` file: the `ticket` topic and the `VenueNetscapeS` servlet. They are registered as follows:

```
weblogic.jms.topic.ticket=jsw.ticketTopic

weblogic.httpd.register.VenueNetscapeS=\
        jsw.c07.VenueNetscapeS
```

The server can be started as usual from a command line and the environment pointing to Chapter 7 (`setenv 7`).

The new java application, `jsw.c07.reservation.Client`, must be started from the command line, following these instructions:

- ❑ Start a command line session
- ❑ Change to directory `c:\wlsbook`
- ❑ Execute the client environment setup script `setEnvCli.cmd` specifying the chapter number (7):

```
c:\wlsbook>setenvcli 7
-----------------------------------------------------------
Setting CLIENT environment for chapter 7
-----------------------------------------------------------
Current settings:
      Java Home = c:\jdk1.3
   WebLogic Home = c:\weblogic
   Project Home = c:\wlsbook
      CLASSPATH = c:\weblogic\lib\weblogic510sp4boot.jar;c:\weblogic\classes\
boot;c:\weblogic\lib\weblogic510sp4.jar;c:\weblogic\license;c:\weblogic\classes;c:
\weblogic\lib\weblogicaux.jar;c:\wlsbook\srv\c07-srv\clientclasses
;c:\wlsbook\srv\c07-srv\serverclasses;c:\wlsbook\srv\c07-srv\ejb\TicketSer
vicesSLBean.jar
```

- ❑ Execute the Client program with the following parameters:

```
C:\wlsbook> java -Djsw.server=localhost jsw.c07.reservation.Client 2
```

The last command will start the Client program connected to the server at localhost and displaying the specified venue (2).

EJBs and Publish/Subscribe

The 1.0.1 specification of JMS does not consider the special case where an EJB can be subscribed to a Pub/Sub event. Because of the nature of stateless session beans and entity beans it generally does not make sense for them to be subscribed to a Pub/Sub event. However, it makes sense for a stateful session bean to do this. This particular case is a problem because the bean will not receive a message when it has been passivated.

Version 2.0 of the EJB specification defines a new kind of bean called a message-driven bean that provides a formal way of interacting EJBs with JMS. A message-driven bean is a special class of EJB designed to be called by the container when a message arrives. It is special because this kind of bean does not have a home or remote interface and their instances have no conversational state.

The stated goal of these beans is to make developing an enterprise bean that is asynchronously invoked to handle the processing of incoming JMS messages as simple as developing the same functionality in any other JMS MessageListener. A further goal of the message-driven bean model is to allow for the concurrent processing of a stream of messages by means of container-provided pooling of message-driven bean instances.

At the moment of this writing BEA Systems has a beta quality implementation of EJB 2.0 that includes message-driven beans.

A Special Note on JNI

Java Native Interface is a special API that allows Java programs to communicate with native programs, typically C or C++. Our experience has been that when these native programs produce an error that makes them crash it will usually crash the Java Virtual Machine it interacts with. This will cause everything running on this particular instance of the JVM to be lost. This is an undesirable effect, and one way of minimizing this is to isolate the execution of the native code to a separate JVM. The issue is how to communicate from one JVM to the other.

We feel that the JMS Point-To-Point model provides a superb mechanism for this. The abstraction would be such that the producer of the message is the entity that wants to use JNI, and the object to be executed is the actual message. The consumer of the message, the JMS client, is the isolated process that interacts with the native code. If the native code produces an error that causes the JVM to crash, it will only affect that JVM and not the one where the application is running.

In older JVMs the JNI interface was suspected of creating high instability when a large amount of threads were created and destroyed. A proposed technique to reduce the instability is based on a thread pool, which can be created with a fixed number of available threads that will be created only once, at the beginning of the process. None of the threads should be destroyed until the end of the process. This is similar to a JDBC connection pool or a JMS session pool, but without the ability to increase or shrink the size of the pool. After all, this was exactly what was to be avoided. The pool of threads should then have some methods to reserve, execute, and release a thread that provide some decent management capabilities for the pool.

Although this technique was initially created to tackle the instability problems, it has the side effect of creating an efficient and disciplined method of handling requests to native code. When combining this technique with a JMS Point-To-Point message model you have a highly efficient way of dealing with the issues related to native calls. We call this **disciplined isolation**.

The heart of the system is the client that listens to the queue. When a message arrives, it verifies that a thread is available. If there is a thread available, it consumes the message, takes the object to be executed from the body of the message and assigns it for execution to the selected thread. If there are no threads available, the client does not consume the message until a thread has been released. The response of the native code is then sent back as another message. All the issues surrounding the management of the queue are taken care of by JMS. All the developer has to do is 'piggy back' on this infrastructure.

The Disciplined Isolation model provides a loosely coupled arrangement that can minimize the instability produced by JNI. This same model can be extended so it can be used in other cases. If JNI is not the target, then dynamic pool size reconfiguration is relatively easy to add.

This model can also be used to handle native calls from EJBs. The current specification does not allow making JNI calls from EJBs. Even though the current version of WebLogic (5.1) does not enforce this, meaning that you can call JNI directly from an EJB, we suggest that you consider using this model. The next version of WebLogic will enforce this restriction, but you will be able to disable it with a property.

Summary

In this chapter we have learned about messaging systems, Java Message Service, and the two messaging models Point-To-Point and Publish and Subscribe. One experiment was done to test the Point-To-Point model in which the pizza order is now sent to the outlet as a message, and another experiment was done to demonstrate the details of the Publish and Subscribe model. With this we covered the Java Message Service and now we are ready to move into the security aspects in the next chapter.

8
Security

Security is a very important matter that cannot be ignored, although unfortunately it is an afterthought in many projects. There are many definitions and ever more interpretations about security and many different ways to implement it. This chapter will concentrate on the security mechanisms offered by J2EE and the WebLogic server, specific to the areas of authentication and authorization.

In this context, **authentication** is used by the various clients to determine that the web site actually is what it claims to be. In some cases it is also used to verify that the client is who they claim to be. **Authorization** is the mechanism used to enforce the laws of execution within the application, for example, who can access what information. Some of these mechanisms also offer additional security functionality, such as data protection, data encryption, and integrity during communications.

In the figure overleaf you will see the typical architecture of a web site. Internet clients will have to go through a firewall in order to get to the web server. In some cases the web server lives in a demilitarized zone (DMZ), residing between two firewalls, effectively separated from the applications by an additional firewall.

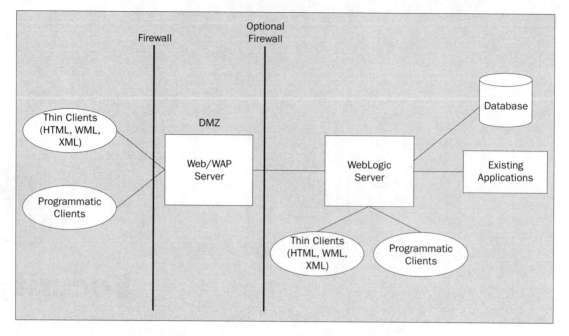

A firewall is a combination of hardware and software that restricts the type of information that can pass through it, checking known methods of attack. This generally means that communications are limited to HTTP, typically on port 80 and secure HTTP on port 443.

When the web server is located in a DMZ, the rules for the second firewall are a little more relaxed. In this case there is a better chance of convincing a network administrator to open a port that will only be used for specific communications between the web server and the WebLogic server (for example port 7001).

As an alternative, complementing the second firewall, there can also be secure communications between the web server and WebLogic.

The bottom line is that when you have Internet clients, thin or programmatic, you want to protect the applications and data. In this context security is based on protecting the web site from unwanted usage of the applications and unauthorized access to sensitive data.

From the perspective of a person who is doing business with a web site over the Internet, security has a different aspect. In this case the visitor wants to make sure that the web site they are interacting with is the same one that it claims to be. The visitor or customer also wants the information that has been submitted to the web site to be unavailable to unauthorized parties. Additionally, the user also wants the information to travel over the network in a secure fashion so unscrupulous third parties cannot intercept it.

Let us now have a look at the various mechanisms available for authorization and authentication.

Authentication

There are four main authentication mechanisms, and many other less popular ones. Not all can be considered secure, but they are useful to achieve different objectives, as we will see next.

HTTP Authentication

HTTP 1.0 includes a very basic authentication system, which is thoroughly described in RFC 2617. There are two flavors of the authentication. One is called **basic** and the other is called **digest**, and both are based on a challenge response mechanism, in this particular case using a login password. The fundamental difference between basic and digest is the way that the password is transmitted from the browser to the server. In basic authentication it is transmitted as a string of clear text encoded as Base64. The digest authentication is encrypted using the MD5 hash or message digest.

The Base64 encoding method transforms 8 bit characters into 6 bit characters giving the impression that the text is encrypted. A message digest or cryptographic hash function is a function that will generate a fixed size string or digest that is unique for any message. MD5 is one of the available message digest functions.

The WebLogic server only offers the basic HTTP authentication. We do not recommend the use of this as a security mechanism because it is very lightweight. It is used more as a deterrent to prevent access to certain areas of a web site in a friendly environment; basic authentication is often used as a precursor to more advanced security, only enabled when the user actually wants to do something sensitive. The other popular use for this mechanism is to monitor the usage statistics of an Intranet.

The advantage of using HTTP authentication is that the developer does not have to code anything to obtain and verify the user name and password. It is all done automatically. In the case of WebLogic, users and their passwords are defined in the `weblogic.properties` file.

```
weblogic.password.helen=jbond007
weblogic.password.john=shaft2000
```

In this case the user Helen has been defined with password `jbond007` and user John with password `shaft2000`. As you can see, the passwords are stored in the properties file in clear text. This is a basic security flaw in itself, although this problem can be avoided by using secure layer protocol, which will be discussed later. Now you see one of the reasons for not recommending this as a security mechanism.

When a client wants to access WebLogic, they will be prompted with the following dialog requesting the authentication of their identity.

The request from the browser will include the user name and password as part of the header to be sent to the web server. In the case of WebLogic, it will grant access only if it can identify the user with the appropriate password in the properties file.

From within the servlet or JSP page it is possible to retrieve information about the authenticated user with the following statements:

```
<p>Remote User: <%= request.getRemoteUser() %></p>
<p>Authorization Scheme: <%= request.getAuthType() %></p>
```

Forms-Based Authentication

There are cases when the developers prefer to write their own HTML forms and do their own authentication, usually against a database table that is part of the application. This gives the developers the flexibility to create a more complex authentication system, which is directly related to the application and not the web server. This mechanism is used by the new front end that we created in Chapter 6.

`Register.jsp` contains the forms-based custom login for the application, which then verifies the user and password against the user table in the database.

Cookies

A cookie is a piece of information that contains a set of name/value pairs that is exchanged between a browser and a web server. Netscape designed the cookie mechanism to overcome the limitations associated with the statelessness of the HTTP protocol. It is used so that a web server can remember the user and maintain the illusion of a session (a collection of multiple stateless pages). This is called the session identification (SessionID).

Because of the generic nature of cookies, they can be used for pretty much anything. They are flexible enough that their names and values can be arbitrary and set or deleted during a session.

Cookies also have properties, and probably the most useful one is the lifetime of the cookie, which can be set to be anything from just a few minutes up to a designated year. Typically they last for the duration of an HTTP session, but when the lifetime of a cookie is defined to exceed the duration of a session, the cookie is stored at the client side by the browser, if the browser allows it.

It is this last characteristic that makes some people extremely uncomfortable. By virtue of being able to store a name/value pair in their machine and later being able to retrieve this piece of information you have the basic infrastructure for tracking the Internet habits of a user. The textbook example of this invasion of privacy is doubleclick.com. Although you might not have visited this web site, chances are that you have a cookie from them in you browser files. Many web sites subscribe to doubleclick.com to present advertisement. In order to know the kinds of things that you prefer and present a piece of advertising that might be of interest to you, doubleclick.com tracks your visits to members of their advertising network. All this is done by means of a very simple cookie.

Although cookies are generating very strong controversy, this book will not concern itself with taking sides. Instead we will limit ourselves to presenting them as an authentication mechanism. In any case the user has the option to deny cookies (a very simple operation in the web browser). Additionally, many web sites are now alerting users that they can choose not to use cookies. Depending on your position in the cookie argument you should consider building your web site so that it does not rely on them.

Using cookies to automatically access user accounts on web sites is popular with portals such as Yahoo and Excite, but they are not the best security mechanism. You have to consider that the computer being used by the client can be shared, thus enabling direct access to the user account from a public machine. The other thing to consider is that not all users know or understand what a cookie is, so when proposing the use of one, ask the user a clear question related to the intended use and effect of the cookie.

When dealing with sensitive information always ask for an additional password so as to add a level of security to the possible conditions previously described.

URL Rewriting

If the browser does not allow for cookies, an alternative mechanism called URL rewriting can be used. It is so called because instead of keeping the HTTP session identification in a cookie, it appends it to the end of the URL. For example, the following URL:

```
http://localhost:7001/sample.jsp
```

Would be converted to:

```
http://localhost:7001/sample.jsp?WebLogicSession=large_string
```

To enable this feature the following properties must be set as shown when WebLogic is started:

```
weblogic.httpd.session.enable=true
weblogic.httpd.session.URLRewriting.enable=true
weblogic.httpd.session.cookies.enable=true
```

This mechanism is particular useful when working with WAP devices, as the micro-browsers in WAP telephones do not allow cookies. The problem is that the session ID created as a default by WebLogic is too large for a WAP phone. Most of these devices are limited to 128 characters for a URL. In these cases, the `weblogic.httpd.session.sessionIDLengthURL` property can be changed to specify the generation of smaller session IDs.

Pizzas and Cookies

The Wonder Troops are ready to try out the cookies. They decide to do so with the code that was developed in Chapter 6, where they converted the front end from the ASP web site of E-Pizza.

Taking into consideration all the things they have learned, they decide to compromise with the use of the cookies. A cookie will be used only to remember the user identification in the application. The user will still be prompted for a password to gain access to the web site.

To do this, the troops create `Register.jsp`, which handles:

- ❑ User registrations
- ❑ Changes of identity
- ❑ User authentication

This JSP page verifies that the user wants to have a cookie enabled, in which case a cookie with a lifetime of 1 year is sent to the browser. If the user does not desire this, a cookie with a lifetime of zero is sent to the browser. A lifetime of zero means that the cookie will be available only for the session. If the user had a "persistent" cookie this will invalidate it. This is done with the following code:

```
//remove the cookie by default
int age = 0;

if (isChecked(request, "remember")) {
  //add the cookie
  System.out.println("adding the cookie");
  age = (60 * 60 * 24 * 365);
}
else {
  //remove the cookie
  System.out.println("removing the cookie");
}

Cookie thisCookie = new Cookie("EPizza",
                       (String)session.getAttribute("UserID"));

thisCookie.setPath("/");
thisCookie.setMaxAge(age);
response.addCookie(thisCookie);

/*
//cookie trace:
System.out.println("Cookie added: "+ thisCookie);
System.out.println("name: "         + thisCookie.getName());
System.out.println("value: "        + thisCookie.getAttribute());
System.out.println("age: "          + thisCookie.getMaxAge());
System.out.println("path: "         + thisCookie.getPath());
System.out.println("domain: "       + thisCookie.getDomain());
*/

session.setAttribute("UserIsNew", "true");
response.sendRedirect("index.jsp");
return;
```

The isChecked() method is declared at the beginning of this page as follows:

```
<%!
    protected boolean isChecked(HttpServletRequest request,
                          String checkbox) {

    return ((request.getParameter(checkbox) != null) &&
           (request.getParameter(checkbox).equals("1")));
    }
%>
```

The `Customer` table in the database and the `Customer` class were modified to add the following fields (from `Customer.java`):

```
    ...
 *     c_uname            VARCHAR(20),
 *     c_password         VARCHAR(20),
 *     c_company          VARCHAR(20),
 *     c_phone_ext        VARCHAR(10),
 *     c_apt              VARCHAR(10),
 *     c_user_level       NUMBER(3),
 *     c_email            VARCHAR(30),

    ...

    public String c_uname          = "";
    public String c_password       = "";
    public String c_company        = "";
    public String c_phone_ext      = "";
    public String c_apt            = "";
    public int    c_user_level     = 0;
    public String c_email          = "";
```

With all these changes done, when a visitor connects to the web site for the first time there is no E-Pizza cookie present in the browser, so they are presented with the standard welcome screen.

If the visitor registers, they activate the remember option, basically telling the application to send a cookie to the browser. If the user has selected the browser option that will alert them every time, and a web site wants to deposit a cookie, they will get a dialog screen as shown here:

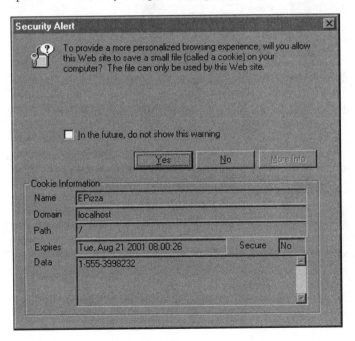

In this screenshot we can see that the structure of the cookie is very simple. It has a name, EPizza, a domain (the server sets the domain on the cookie), the path of the application, the expiration (one year from the moment it is created) and a value. The value of the cookie corresponds to the primary key of the customer table, which identifies this customer. The primary key is constructed from the telephone country code, the area code, and the actual telephone number.

Once the cookie has been written to the browser, the user is welcomed to the system with the personalized welcome page. The next time the customer with the cookie enabled comes back to the web site, they will be properly identified and asked for a password, as can be seen in here. However, in some portal sites, the user can check an option for an automatic logon when the cookie is set; there is an option which says "that's not me" if an unauthorized customer is using the browser.

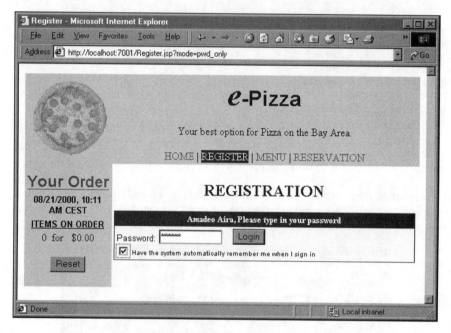

The information about the authenticated customer is used throughout the session, for example to deliver the order and to reserve tickets.

Finally, a new JSP page has been included, `Logout.jsp`, to handle the end of a session. The code of this page is quite simple:

```
<%
   //invalidate current session
   session.invalidate();

   response.sendRedirect("index.jsp");
%>
```

As you can see, using cookies is not difficult and you can add an ease-of-use feature to your web site without compromising the security of it.

Secure Socket Layer (SSL)

SSL is probably the most popular mechanism for offering secure communications between clients and web sites. It is a protocol proposed by Netscape that handles authentication, encryption, and data integrity over the communication channel. More recently, TLS 1.0 (Transport Layer Security) has been developed, allowing client-server applications to communicate in a way that is designed to prevent eavesdropping, tampering, or message forgery.

Authentication is the act of verifying that the communicating parties are who they claim to be. In the case of SSL you can have one-way or two-way authentication. One-way is the client verifying that the server is who it claims to be. Two-way authentication involves the client and server verifying each other.

Authentication in SSL is based on the use of Digital Certificates. These certificates are based on a standard called X.509. It is not necessary to go into the details of the standard, but we need to understand the concept of a Certificate Authority (CA) such as VeriSign or EnTrust. A CA is a trusted organization that issues digital certificates to companies and people. There are different types of certificates and they vary depending on the degree to which the holder has been verified.

Another important component of security is encryption, which is nothing more than encoding a message in such a way that only those that have rights over the message can properly decode it. For the purposes of explaining SSL, we will say that messages are encoded and decoded using a secret key. This key is the same for encoding as for decoding, in other words it is symmetric. Therefore both parties must know the secret key. The safe distribution of secret keys is a very big challenge from a security and logistic standpoint.

SSL solves this challenge by using public key cryptography to establish a shared secret key. It also uses public key cryptography for authentication. This method of cryptography has two keys. One, the public key, is known to everybody, and the other, a private key, is known only to the owner of the pair of keys. If you want to send a private message to John, you encrypt it using his public key. The only way that it can be decrypted is when John uses his private key for this operation. This process is shown in the following figure:

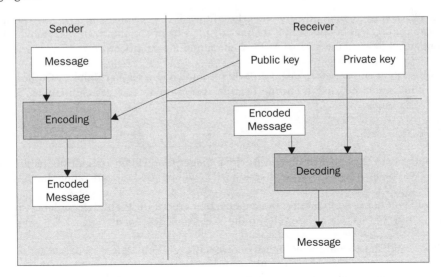

Messages in SSL are sent in what is known as a digital envelope. A digital envelope has three parts:

- ❑ A secret key, which is encoded using the public key of the intended receiver
- ❑ The message itself, encrypted using the secret key
- ❑ A message digest or digital signature, which is a unique fixed size summary of the message itself

The next diagram presents a graphic depiction of a digital envelope:

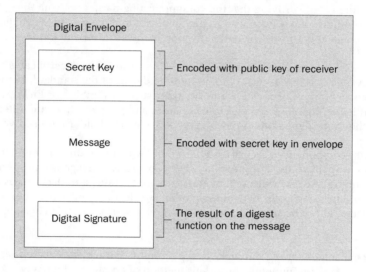

The reason messages are not encoded using public keys is because these algorithms are slow (they have to deal with large prime numbers, typically 512 bits in size). It is preferable to encode messages with what are called bulk encryption algorithms such as DES (Data Encryption Standard) and its variants based on secret keys.

Digital signatures exist to guarantee the integrity of the message. Since a message digest produces a unique signature, this will be different if the message has been tampered with. Moreover, browsers are usually configured to warn the user when they encounter a corrupt certificate.

SSL allows the client and server to negotiate what is known as a **Cipher Suite**. A Cipher Suite describes which algorithms are to be used to encode/decode every one of the three components of a digital envelope. For example:

`RSA_WITH_RC4_128_MD5`

specifies that the RSA (Rivest, Shamir, and Adelman) algorithm will be used for the public key, RC4 with a 128 bit key will be used for the bulk cipher and MD5 will be used for generating the message digest.

In general you will not need to modify the defaults that are set on WebLogic, unless you will be using strong encryption. In this case please refer to the WebLogic documentation.

Using public keys leads to extremely intensive calculations. WebLogic uses native code instead of Java on most platforms to accelerate these calculations. If your platform does not have this support, it will default to Java for these calculations. The next version of WebLogic will also have support for hardware devices that perform these calculations.

With this knowledge we can now define Digital Certificates a little bit more. A Digital Certificate is a document containing the public key belonging to the holder and states that it really is the public key of who the holder claims to be. This is the reason we can use public key cryptography for authentication. The certificate has a digital signature from the CA, which can be verified with the public key of the CA.

> *The big issue about domestic and export strength encryption has to do with the size of the keys of the cryptographic algorithms. At the time of writing any public key algorithm with a key bigger than 512 bits and any symmetric cryptographic algorithm (basically the bulk and stream ciphers) with a key bigger than 40 bits cannot be legally exported from the United States. This is called strong encryption. The US government has declared that it will relax these export restrictions.*

> *BEA offers the WebLogic server with both export and strong (or domestic) encryption. By default the product you get contains export strength encryption. If you want strong encryption you will have to do a full reinstall of WebLogic. Please contact a BEA salesperson for more information on how to obtain a strong encryption version of WebLogic.*

Having said this, you need to procure a digital certificate from a certificate authority such as Verisign or Entrust.net so that you can get into business. To request a certificate you can use a servlet that is part of the WebLogic distribution. From a browser just go to the following URL:

http://localhost:7001/Certificate

Replace localhost with the name of the server running WebLogic and make sure that it is running on port 7001; otherwise change it in this instruction. This servlet will assist you in procuring a Digital Certificate from any CA that produces certificates in the DER or PEM format. When you receive the certificate check the WebLogic documentation for installation information.

While you are going through that process, which can take a couple of weeks, you can use the demo certificate that is included in the distribution of WebLogic. As this certificate is already installed nothing has to be done to be able to use it.

One-Way SSL with a Browser Client

This is the WebLogic server default setting; the server is required to present a certificate to the client, but the client is not required to present a certificate to the server.

This is probably the most popular of all the configurations used for e-commerce. Specifically when sensitive information, such as a credit card number, will be transmitted to a web site.

The intention here is to provide a mechanism to encrypt the communication channel between the client (browser) and the server when the payment is to be done. This way the customer will be sure that their credit card number cannot be used, even if the communication is tampered with.

The Troops get ready to test this by adding the following statements to the `weblogic.properties`:

```
weblogic.security.ssl.enable=true
weblogic.system.SSLListenPort=7002

weblogic.security.certificate.server=democert.pem
weblogic.security.key.server=demokey.pem
weblogic.security.certificate.authority=ca.pem
```

The X.509 certificate of the server is in file democert.pem. The file demokey.pem contains the corresponding private key. The file ca.pem holds the X.509 root certificate of the certificate authority.

In the OrderConfirm.jsp page the following statements are added to establish a secure HTTP communication (HTTPS) to the server secure port (the default secure port of WebLogic is 7002). First, two strings are initialized with the corresponding URL information:

```
String urlWithoutSSL = "http://" + request.getServerName() + ":" +
                        System.getProperty("weblogic.system.listenPort",
                                            "7001") + "/";

String urlWithSSL    = "https://" + request.getServerName() + ":" +
                        System.getProperty("weblogic.system.SSLListenPort",
                                            "7002") + "/";
```

Then, the urlWithSSL string is used to construct the final destination in the form tag:

```
<form method="Post"
      action="<%=urlWithSSL%>OrderConfirm.jsp"
      id="form2" name="form2">
```

When the customer wants to pay for the pizza order, the server executes the servlet with the SSL protocol. If the browser has been configured to announce it, then a confirmation dialog as shown here will be presented to the customer:

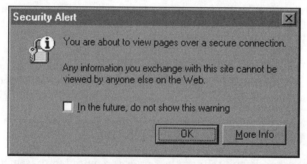

Next, the server will notify the browser about possible problems with the X.509 certificate of the server.

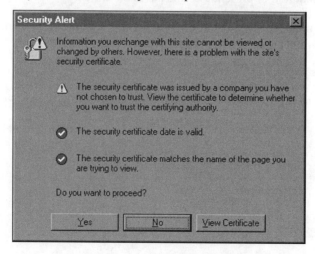

By choosing to view the certificate, you can learn, in more detail, which are the specific issues:

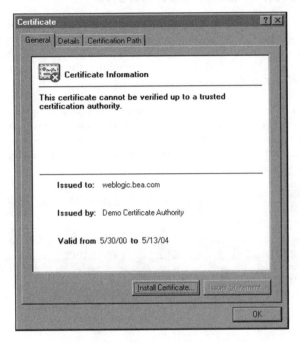

Once `OrderConfirm.jsp` processes the request using SSL, it redirects the browser to the confirmation page using normal HTTP instead of HTTPS.

```
if (finish_order) { //Conclude the Order?
  currentOrder.deliverOrder();
  response.sendRedirect(urlWithoutSSL +
                  "OrderThanks.jsp?order_id=" +
                  currentOrder.getOrderMaster().getOr_number());

  return;
}
```

This fires a new confirmation dialog in the browser after which the order confirmation screen is presented to the user.

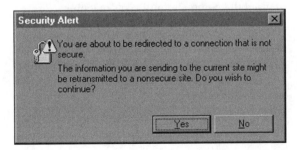

295

Two-Way SSL with a Browser Client

This mechanism is becoming quite popular within corporations as a more practical authentication system than the login/password pair. This scheme assumes that the users are working on a computer with an operating system that requires a login password pair for access (such as Unix, Linux, or NT). As the user has already been authenticated on the local machine, the client certificates in the browser are used to authenticate the user from that point on.

To do a two-way SSL communication, a certificate has to be installed in the browser. You can see the certificate in the browser by calling upon the functionality from your browser. In the following screenshot a certificate is displayed from Internet Explorer. This is done by selecting the **Tools** button, then **Internet Options...**, and here you choose the **Content** tab and under the certificates area you will be able to choose what you want to see.

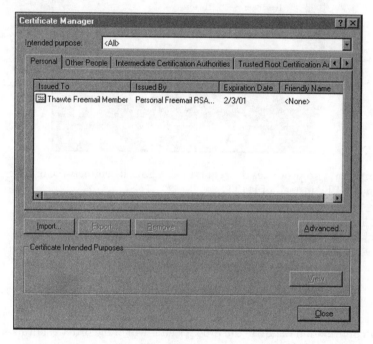

You can also obtain detailed information by using the keytool application included in the JDK. This is the output we got when we used the command on Paco's machine:

```
C:\wlsbook\private\cert>keytool -file paco.cer -printcert
Owner: EmailAddress=paco.gomez@terra.com, CN=Thawte Freemail Member
Issuer: CN=Personal Freemail RSA 1999.9.16, OU=Certificate Services, O=Thawte,
L=Durbanville, ST=Western Cape, C=ZA
Serial number: 20ccc
Valid from: Fri Feb 04 15:07:25 CET 2000 until: Sat Feb 03 15:07:25 CET 2001
Certificate fingerprints:
        MD5:   10:64:17:2B:CB:3B:33:D7:3B:CE:F8:5C:73:BD:48:22
        SHA1: E9:92:B0:06:9B:F4:F1:21:EA:3D:CC:A2:36:96:8B:C0:72:A6:8F:74
```

This certificate certifies the owner, as specified in the field Owner, that he is who he claims to be and that there is no other person with such data certified by the Certification Authority (CA). In this case the owner is paco.gomez@terra.com and the CA a company called Thawte in South Africa (a subsidiary of VeriSign).

The Wonder Troops define this experiment to test that only users with a valid certificate and with the right user level can access the management section of the application. The user is identified in the table by their e-mail address. To achieve this, the following steps have to be taken:

❏   Install an X.509 certificate in the browser (already done)

❏   Install the certificate of the CA in the WebLogic server

❏   Force the server to request a certificate from the browser when an HTTPS session is active

❏   In the page that handles the management functionality, make sure that the user has been authenticated, that is, has presented a valid certificate, and that the user has the appropriate authorization to manage the orders

The certificate of the CA is installed in the server. This contains the public key. In this particular case the file thawte.cer contains the following information:

```
C:\wlsbook\private\cert>keytool -file thawte.cer -printcert
Owner: EmailAddress=personal-freemail@thawte.com, CN=Thawte Personal Freemail CA,
OU=Certification Services Division, O=Thawte Consulting, L=Cape Town, ST=Western
Cape, C=ZA
Issuer: EmailAddress=personal-freemail@thawte.com, CN=Thawte Personal Freemail CA,
OU=Certification Services Division, O=Thawte Consulting, L=Cape Town, ST=Western
Cape, C=ZA
Serial number: 0
Valid from: Mon Jan 01 01:00:00 CET 1996 until: Fri Jan 01 00:59:59 CET 2021
Certificate fingerprints:
        MD5:  1E:74:C3:86:3C:0C:35:C5:3E:C2:7F:EF:3C:AA:3C:D9
        SHA1: 20:99:00:B6:3D:95:57:28:14:0C:D1:36:22:D8:C6:87:A4:EB:00:85
```

In the weblogic.properties file, the following properties have to be defined:

```
#Two-Way SSL Authentication: (set to "true" or "false" as required)
weblogic.security.enforceClientCert=true
weblogic.security.clientRootCA=thawte.cer
```

The link in the menu is changed to conduct an HTTPS connection to the secure port of the WebLogic server:

```
        <%if ((session.getAttribute("UserLevel") != null) &&
            (session.getAttribute("UserLevel").equals("0"))) {%>
      | <A href="<%=urlWithSSL%>Management.jsp">
          <FONT style="BACKGROUND-COLOR: #660000" color="#ffffff">
          MANAGEMENT
          </font></a>
      <%}%>
```

As this page will be accessed through HTTPS, the rest of links in the menu should point to HTTP as follows:

```
        <a href="<%=urlWithoutSSL%>index.jsp">HOME</a>
      | <a href="<%=urlWithoutSSL%>Register.jsp">REGISTER</a>
      | <a href="<%=urlWithoutSSL%>Menu.jsp">MENU</a>
```

In `Management.jsp`, the troops make sure that the user has connected by means of SSL and presents a valid X.509 certificate:

```
<%
    weblogic.security.X509 certs [] = (weblogic.security.X509 [])
                request.getAttribute("javax.net.ssl.peer_certificates");

    if (certs == null) {
%>
<p>Not using SSL or client certificate not required in
    weblogic.properties.</p>
<p>Please, activate client certificate in order to manage orders.</p>
<%
    }
```

If the JSP page can retrieve the certificate presented by the user, it means that the user has been positively identified. The next step is to obtain the name and e-mail address from the user certificate and show them on the page. This information could be used to verify the user level and the authorization to manage orders through a specific table in a database or a LDAP server. For this experiment the current customer is retrieved from the HTTP session and the user is authorized if the user level equals 0. The user level is retrieved from the database table `customer` and stored in the Customer field `c_user_level`.

```
    else {
      X509 x509 = certs[0];
      X500Name x500Name = (X500Name)x509.getHolder();
%>
      <p align="center"
        style="margin-left: 0; margin-top: 3; margin-bottom: 5">
        The following user has been authenticated through a X.509
            certificate:
      </p>

      <p>holder CN: <%= x500Name.getName() %>
        email: <%= x500Name.getEmail() %></p>

      <p>issuer: <%= (X500Name)x509.getIssuer() %></p>

<%

    Customer currentCustomer = (Customer)
                            session.getAttribute("currentCustomer");

    boolean authorized = currentCustomer.c_user_level == 0;

    if (! authorized) {
      %>
        <p align="center"
          style="margin-left: 0; margin-top: 3; margin-bottom: 5">
          This user is not authorized to manage orders.
        </p>
      <%
    }
    else {
%>
        <p align="center"
          style="margin-left: 0; margin-top: 3; margin-bottom: 5">
          This user is authorized to manage orders.
        </p>
```

It is left as an exercise for the reader to implement the function `hasManagementPermission (String email)`.

From the user's standpoint what happens is the following: When the user tries to access the management function, the dialog presented here is displayed, asking which certificate is to be used.

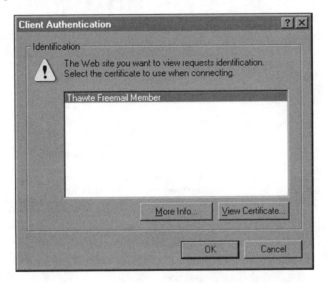

The browser will then inform the user that the information to be transmitted to the server will be signed using his private key as can be seen here:

Finally, the server will present the user with the management page shown in the following screenshot overleaf. Note that the padlock image on the bottom of the browser is locked, meaning that there is secure communication with the server.

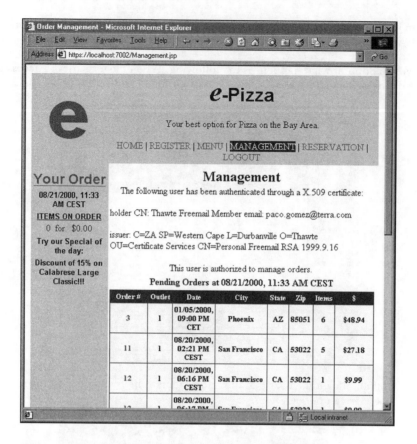

One-Way SSL with A Programmatic Client

You will not always have a browser as a client, so this example will show you how to set up a secure communication using SSL from a Java client. Here the Troops decide to use the existing client on the pizza outlet, which was developed in Chapter 7. As you might remember, this client receives the orders via JMS and then displays them.

For one-way SSL, no changes have to be made to the original program since the URL of the server is given as a property when starting the client:

```
-Djsw.serverURL=protocol://host:port
```

This WebLogic client can establish an SSL connection just by changing the specification of the protocol and the port. So instead of using t3://localhost:7001 it can use t3s://localhost:7002. T3s is the secure version of the t3 protocol.

Before running the client, the WebLogic server must be set up not to require client authentication, in the weblogic.properties file, and restarted.

```
#Two-Way SSL Authentication: (set to "true" or "false" as required)
weblogic.security.enforceClientCert=false
```

Then, the fax client can be run. In a new command shell, run the `setEnvCli.cmd` script and then the program itself:

```
c:\wlsbook>setenvcli 8
------------------------------------------------------------
Setting CLIENT environment for chapter 8
------------------------------------------------------------
Current settings:
      Java Home = c:\jdk1.3
   WebLogic Home = c:\weblogic
    Project Home = c:\wlsbook
      CLASSPATH =
c:\weblogic\lib\weblogic510sp4boot.jar;c:\weblogic\classes\boot;c:\weblogic\lib\we
blogic510sp4.jar;c:\weblogic\license;c:\weblogic\classes;c:\weblogic\lib\weblogica
ux.jar;c:\wlsbook\srv\c08-srv\clientclasses;c:\wlsbook\srv
\c08-srv\serverclasses;c:\wlsbook\srv\c08-srv\ejb\TicketServicesSLBean.jar

           PATH = c:\wlsbook\bin;c:\jdk1.3\bin;c:\orant\bin;C:\WINNT\
system32;C:\WINNT;c:\weblogic\bin;c:\weblogic\bin\oci815_8

c:\wlsbook>java -Djsw.serverURL=t3s://localhost:7002 jsw.c08.fax.Client 1
OrderReceiver: JMS connection opened
msg received!
New order received in jsw.c08.fax.Client
Mon Aug 21 11:47:19 CEST 2000: order received:
++++++++++++++ begin order ++++++++++++++
>>>Order:          [Order number = 25][Country code = 1][Area code = 305]
[Phone = 5552000][Outlet code = 1][Order date = 2000-08-21 11:47:13.0]
[Delivery = Address][Status = Ordering][Remarks = null][Price = 9.99]
>>>Customer:       [Country code = 1][Area code = 305][Phone = 5552000]
[First name = Heidi][Last name = Funai][Postal code = 53022][Address line 1 = 10
Pinar][Address line 2 = null][Remarks = null][City = San Francisco]
[Major Crossroads = null][Colonia = null][State = CA][Country = USA][User Name =
][User Password = ][Company = ][Phone Extension = ][Apt # = ][User Level =
0][Email Address = ]
>>>Order detail: [Order detail number = 35][Order master number = 25][type =
predefined pizza][Pizza name = Calabrese][Pizza size = Medium][Dough =
Classic][Quantity = 1][Price = 9.99]
++++++++++++++ end order ++++++++++++++
```

The client code obtains the initial context from the URL passed as a property (if it is not present, the `getProperty()` method will return the second parameter passed):

```
client.url = System.getProperty("jsw.serverURL", "t3://localhost:7001");
...
     else {
       context = Util.getInitialContext(url);
     }

     orderReceiver = new OrderReceiver();
     orderReceiver.init(context,
                     OrderReceiver.QUEUE,
                  "outletNumber = " + outletNumber);
```

And the JMS objects are initialized from the SSL connection obtained:

```
...
queueConnectionFactory = (QueueConnectionFactory) ctx.lookup(JMS_FACTORY);
queueConnection        = queueConnectionFactory.createQueueConnection();
queueSession           = queueConnection.createQueueSession(false,
                           Session.AUTO_ACKNOWLEDGE);
...
```

Using the WebLogic Console, the Troops can verify that the JMS client has established a secure connection using the t3s protocol as shown in the following figure:

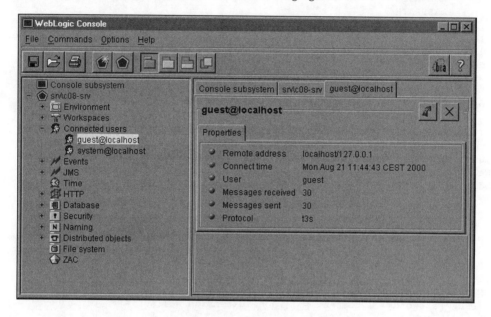

Two-Way SSL with a Programmatic Client

When the server forces clients onto a two-way SSL communication, the Java client can also present an X.509 certificate similar to the way that the browser does. The Troops decided to augment the fax client to connect a two-way SSL link with the server by adding the following property:

```
-Djsw.clientCertDir=c:/wlsbook/src/c08/cert
```

This property specifies a directory where the X.509 client certificate resides. Along with the certificate, the root CA certificate and the private key must also be present in that directory. For the experiment, the troops will use the certificates and key provided by WebLogic, files `democert.pem`, `demokey.pem`, and `ca.pem`.

The certificates and private key files are read by the client application as `InputStream` objects and included in the properties of the t3s connection to the server. This is done by calling the method `setSSLClientCertificate()`. The method expects an array of `InputStream` objects, the first of them being the client's private key and the rest the certificate chain. The certificate chain begins with the client's certificate and ends with the root CA's certificate. As the program reads the files in alphabetical order, the files were renamed to `0demokey.pem`, `1democert.pem`, and `2ca.pem`. The complete code is shown opposite:

```
    try {
      Context context = null;

      String caDir = System.getProperty("jsw.clientCertDir");
      if (caDir != null) {
        Environment env = new Environment();
        env.setProviderUrl(url);
        env.setInitialContextFactory(
                         "weblogic.jndi.WLInitialContextFactory");

        String certFiles[] = new File(caDir).list();
        InputStream[] chain = new InputStream[certFiles.length];
        for (int i = 0; i < certFiles.length; i++) {
          try {
            File file = new File(caDir, certFiles[i]);

            System.out.println("reading file: " + file.getAbsolutePath());
            InputStream is  = new FileInputStream(file.getAbsolutePath());

            if (file.getAbsolutePath().toLowerCase().endsWith(".pem")) {
              is = new PEMInputStream(is);
            }
            chain[i] = is;

          } catch (Exception e) {
            e.printStackTrace();
            System.out.println("Couldn't read file " +
                           caDir + certFiles[i]);
          }
        }
        env.setSSLClientCertificate(chain);
          context = new InitialContext(env.getProperties());
      }
      else {
        context = Util.getInitialContext(url);
      }

      orderReceiver = new OrderReceiver();
      orderReceiver.init(context,
                      OrderReceiver.QUEUE,
                    "outletNumber = " + outletNumber);
```

In order to test this new functionality, the server must be set up again to require client certification. The root CA certificate is also added to the list of client root certificates (WebLogic allows up to four client root certificates).

```
#Two-Way SSL Authentication: (set to "true" or "false" as required)
weblogic.security.enforceClientCert=true
weblogic.security.clientRootCA=thawte.cer
weblogic.security.clientRootCA2=ca.pem
```

Note that ca.pem is also used by the server's certificate by using the property:

```
weblogic.security.certificate.authority=ca.pem
```

After these changes, the improved fax client is run with the following results:

```
c:\wlsbook>java -Djsw.serverURL=t3s://localhost:7002
               -Djsw.clientCertDir=c:/wlsbook/src/c08/cert
               jsw.c08.fax.Client 1

reading file: c:\wlsbook\src\c08\cert\0demokey.pem
reading file: c:\wlsbook\src\c08\cert\1democert.pem
reading file: c:\wlsbook\src\c08\cert\2ca.pem

OrderReceiver: JMS connection opened
msg received!
New order received in jsw.c08.fax.Client
Mon Aug 21 13:30:52 CEST 2000: order received:
+++++++++++++ begin order +++++++++++++
>>>Order:        [Order number = 31][Country code = 1][Area code = 305]
[Phone = 5552000][Outlet code = 1][Order date = 2000-08-21 13:30:35.0]
[Delivery = Address][Status = Ordering][Remarks = null][Price = 9.99]
>>>Customer:     [Country code = 1][Area code = 305][Phone = 5552000]
[First name = Heidi][Last name = Funai][Postal code = 53022][Address line 1 = 10
Pinar][Address line 2 = null][Remarks = null][City = San Francisco]
[Major Crossroads = null][Colonia = null][State = CA][Country = USA][User Name =
][User Password = ][Company = ][Phone Extension = ][Apt # = ][User Level =
0][Email Address = ]
>>>Order detail: [Order detail number = 41][Order master number = 31][type
=predefined pizza][Pizza name = Calabrese][Pizza size = Medium][Dough =
Classic][Quantity = 1][Price = 9.99]
+++++++++++++ end order +++++++++++++
```

Authorization

Authorization is done by means of a mechanism called Access Control Lists, or ACLs as they are better known. In WebLogic the ACLs are implemented using the JavaSoft ACL standard (java.security.acl), which represents users, groups, and the ACL itself.

An ACL protects a resource, which can be a service, an object or a method running on WebLogic. An ACL grants permission on a resource or class of resources to a list of users or groups.

In WebLogic a user represents an authenticated user of an application running on the server. When the user requests a resource, the ACL is tested to see if they have the necessary permissions to do so. A group is a named list of users.

As seen earlier, users are defined as follows in the weblogic.properties file:

```
weblogic.password.victoria=guapisima
weblogic.password.luis=elgranjefe
weblogic.password.carlos=puesnada
```

Here we have defined a set of three users: Victoria, Luis, and Carlos with their corresponding passwords. In a similar fashion you can define groups:

```
weblogic.security.group.madrid=victoria,luis,carlos
weblogic.security.group.helsinki=ari,matti,mika
```

In this particular case we defined a group named *Madrid*, which contains the three users we defined earlier, and another group with the *Helsinki* users.

There is one user that must always be present, and that is system, which is the WebLogic administrator. The system name can be changed by editing the properties file, but this will affect the ACLs because a lot of them explicitly refer to the system user.

Permissions vary according to the resource. WebLogic has predefined ACLs for some of the resources. The following table presents a list of some of these predefined ACLs and their associated permissions:

Resource	Permissions
Servlets	Execute
JDBC Connection Pools	Reserve
	Reset
	Shrink
JMS Destination	Send
JNDI Resource	Lookup
	Modify
	List

Permissions are defined in the properties file using the weblogic.allow property. When no permissions are defined they default to granting all permissions to everyone. Following a priority order, user permissions override group permissions. Generally speaking, if an ACL entry is defined more than once, the latest definition is the one that is obeyed.

The following example defines an ACL for a JNDI context named applications:

```
weblogic.allow.lookup.weblogic.jndi.applications=peter,madrid,helsinki
weblogic.allow.modify.weblogic.jndi.applications=administrator
weblogic.allow.list.weblogic.jndi.applications=peter,madrid,helsinki
```

A permission on a servlet is defined as follows:

```
Weblogic.allow.execute.weblogic.servlet.CustomerList=p2gGroup
```

Wildcards can also be used. There are two wildcard characters that can be used to modify how permissions are applied to directories: asterisk (*) and dash (-). The asterisk is used to signify any file in the specified directory. The dash is used to signify any files or subdirectories below the specified directory. The following ACL defines that the Helsinki group can execute any JSP page:

```
weblogic.allow.execute.weblogic.servlet.*.jsp=helsinki
```

When the resource is an Enterprise JavaBean, the ACLs are configured in the access control properties of the bean's deployment descriptor. In this case there are no predefined permissions as they can be granted on individual methods of a bean. There is a big difference from the permissions we have seen so far, and that is that permissions are granted to *roles* instead of users or groups. Roles, defined in the EJB deployment descriptor, should be mapped to WebLogic groups.

Currently WebLogic does not implement the Java Authentication and Authorization Service (JAAS). This will be done in a future release. The Java Development Kit (JDK) provides access control based on where the code originated and on who signed the code. JAAS adds the ability to enforce access control based on who runs the code.

URL-Based ACLs

There is an additional security access check designed specifically for servlets. The `UrlAcl` security policy goes beyond the usual ACL explained earlier, as it grants or denies principal permissions on specific files or directories served by the WebLogic server.

When using `UrlAcl` you have to specify all the users you want to grant access to, as the default is to deny all access. The policy file uses the following syntax:

```
grant_or_deny Principal Principal_Class "Principal_Name" {
    Permission Permission_Class "Permission_name", "Target";
};
```

The following example will grant permission to all the members of the group `southafrica` to all files except those under the directory `finance`. This directory is only available to `Ken` and `Rick`.

```
grant Principal weblogic.security.acl.GroupImpl "southafrica" {
    Permission weblogic.security.acl.URLAcl "weblogic.url", "-";
};

deny Principal weblogic.security.acl.GroupImpl "southafrica" {
    Permission weblogic.security.acl.URLAcl "weblogic.url", "/finance/-";
};

grant Principal weblogic.security.acl.User "ken"
    Principal weblogic.security.acl.User "rick" {
    Permission weblogic.security.acl.URLAcl "weblogic.url", "/finance/-";
};
```

User-Defined ACLs

When the resource you want to use does not have a predefined ACL in WebLogic, you can define your own. This can be a rather simple procedure, as the Troops will illustrate in the following example.

Using the code developed in Chapter 7 for the reservation system, the Wonder Troops want to restrict The ability of purchasing tickets to just a few people. The actual purchase operation is done using the `buy()` method of the `TicketServicesSL` bean. In the deployment descriptor the troops specify an ACL that will only allow some of the users to purchase a ticket. In the following example, the members of the `p2gGroup` and `outlets` groups can only execute the `buy()` method. The role and permission are defined in file `ejb-jar.xml` as follows:

```
<security-role>
  <description>This role allows buy tickets</description>
  <role-name>buyer</role-name>
</security-role>
<method-permission>
  <description></description>
  <role-name>buyer</role-name>
  <method>
    <ejb-name>jsw.c08.TicketServicesSL</ejb-name>
    <method-name>buy</method-name>
  </method>
</method-permission>
```

Then the role-principal mapping is done in the file `weblogic-ejb-jar.xml` as shown below:

```
<security-role-assignment>
  <role-name>buyer</role-name>
  <principal-name>outlets</principal-name>
  <principal-name>p2gGroup</principal-name>
</security-role-assignment>
```

The EJB Deployer Tool can set up all these properties graphically. The following screenshot shows how to create roles and assign them to WebLogic groups:

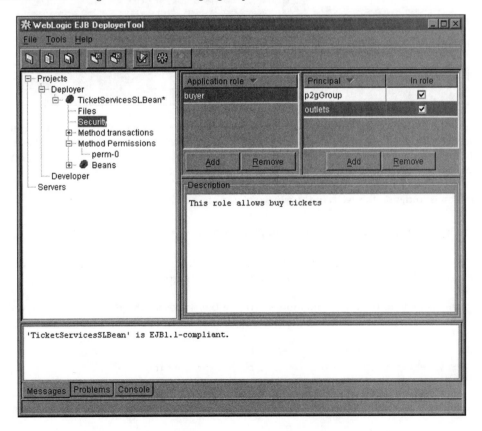

The next figure shows how to set up method permissions with the EJB Deployer Tool:

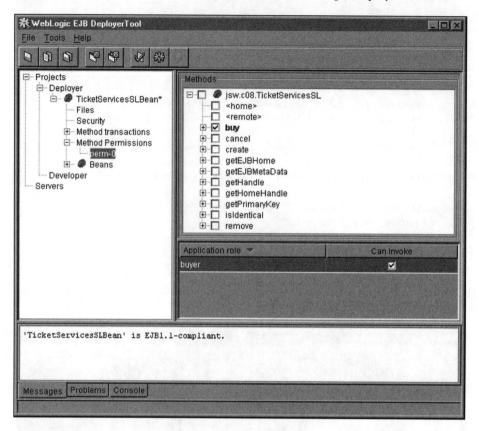

This was rather simple, so the Troops decide to create a custom ACL that will restrict the permission to purchase when there are more than 5 tickets per reservation. That is, only some users will have the ability to purchase more than 5 tickets per attempt. To do this you have to add the ACL to the properties file and then check for permissions during run time by calling certain methods in the ACL package.

The first step is to define the ACL in the `weblogic.properties` file:

```
weblogic.allow.buyMoreThan5.jsw.c08.TicketServicesSL=outlets,helen
```

This ACL defines a permission called `buyMoreThan5` for the `TicketServicesSL` bean, which can only be executed by Helen and the members of the `outlets` group.

The next step is done in the `buy()` method where the `buyMoreThan5` permission is retrieved and processed as can be seen in the following code fragment:

```
/**
 * Buys a group of tickets. It can be all or nothing.
 * If the number of tickets to buy is more than 5,
 * then a security check is done.
 *
```

```
 * @param     tickets a Vector with tickets.
 * @param     mode TicketServicesSL.ALL_OR_NOTHING,
 *                  TicketServicesSL.AS_MANY_AS_POSSIBLE.
 * @return     the number of tickets actually bought.
 */
public int buy(Vector tickets, int mode)
    throws P2GException {

  if (tickets.size() > 5) {
    try {
      //check permission to buy more than 5

      User user = Security.getCurrentUser();
      BasicRealm realm = Realm.getRealm("weblogic");
      Acl acl = realm.getAcl("jsw.c08.TicketServicesSL");

      if ((acl == null) || !
          (acl.checkPermission(user,
                             realm.getPermission("buyMoreThan5")))) {

        Security.logAndThrow("buyMoreThan5" +
                           " denied for user " +
                           user);
      }
      System.out.println("user " + user + " could " +
                        "[buyMoreThan5]" + " on " +
                        "[jsw.c08.TicketServicesSL]");
    } catch(Exception e) {
      throw new P2GException(e.toString());
    }
  }
```

On the client side (jsw.c08.reservation.Client), a user and password have to be obtained and used to establish a connection:

```
/**
 * This is the application's entry point.
 * It retrieves the parameters from the environment and from the
 * calling arguments and starts execution.
 */
public static void main(String args[]) {

  if (args.length != 3) {
    System.err.println("usage: java -Djsw.server=host " +
                "jsw.c08.reservation.Client matchNumber user password");
    return;
  }

  Client client = new Client();
  try {
    client.matchNumber = Long.parseLong(args[0]);
    client.user = args[1];
    client.password = args[2];
    client.url = "t3://" + System.getProperty("jsw.server", "localhost")
                + ":7001";
```

```
        } catch(Exception e) {
          System.err.println(e);
          return;
        }
        client.run();
    }
    ...


    /**
     * The application main loop.
     * The application will receive "ticket messages" and will update the
     * venue display.
     */
    public void run() {
        createFrame();
        try {
          ticketReceiver = new TicketReceiver();
          Context context = Util.getInitialContext(url, user, password);

          ticketReceiver.init(context, TicketReceiver.TOPIC,
                            "matchNumber = " + matchNumber);
          loadSeats();
```

This way, a user without the correct permissions will not be allowed to purchase more that 5 tickets. If an unauthorized user attempts to do this, the system throws the following exception:

```
c:\wlsbook>java -Djsw.server=localhost jsw.c08.reservation.Client 1 john shaft2000

TicketReceiver: JMS connection opened
jsw.c08.P2GException: java.lang.SecurityException: buyMoreThan5 denied for user
john
```

However, users that are authorized will succeed, and the console will show the following message:

```
user helen could [buyMoreThan5] on [jsw.c08.TicketServicesSL]
```

Security Realms

A **realm** is a Java class that provides access to a place where the definitions of users, groups, and ACLs are stored. In WebLogic the default realm is the `weblogic.properties` file, which is read every time the WebLogic server is started. This is a disadvantage as it makes the information static. Whenever you modify a user, group, or ACL you must restart WebLogic so that it will take effect.

There are, however, alternative realms that allow access to security-related information in other places such as LDAP servers, Unix, or Windows NT. Most of these alternative realms are dynamic in the sense that if the data changes, the realm retrieves the updated values without the user having to restart the server.

This may lead to overhead when looking for updated information. WebLogic can cache the results that have been retrieved from the alternative realm to avoid this. Surprisingly enough this is implemented in the Caching Realm. When you use an alternative realm, WebLogic first calls into the Caching Realm, which then calls the alternative realm.

When a lookup fails in an alternative realm it will be retried in the default realm, the `weblogic.properties` file. This behavior can be modified so that you can use various alternative realms and delegate lookup failures to other realms. Please consult the documentation to learn more about the details of how to do this.

Caching Realm

The caching realm is used every time an alternative realm is defined, but it is not used for the default realm as the information contained in the `weblogic.properties` file is placed in memory at startup time.

This realm caches the results of alternative realm lookups, successful or not. It manages separate caches for users, groups, permissions, ACLs, and authorizations, which can be selectively enabled depending on the alternative realm that will be used. You can also define the size of these caches. When changes are made in the alternative realm the caching realm will not recognize them until after a certain period of time has elapsed. The default is 60 seconds.

LDAP Realm

The LDAP realm provides authentication from a Lightweight Directory Access Protocol (LDAP) server. Instead of defining users and groups in the `weblogic.properties` file, you define them in an LDAP server. At the moment there are only three LDAP servers supported, namely, the Netscape Directory Server, Microsoft Site Server, and Novell NDS.

A limitation of this realm is that authorization still has to be done by defining the ACLs in the `weblogic.properties` file.

This realm has two modes of authentication:

- ❑ **Simple**: where the user name and password are sent to the LDAP server for authentication.

- ❑ **Strong**: when SSL is used the realm obtains the user name from the X.509 certificate and verifies its existence in the LDAP server.

SSL can be used for communications between WebLogic and the LDAP server.

To set up this realm the `ldaprealm.properties` file has to be modified to define the following information:

- ❑ The network location of the LDAP service

- ❑ Whether to use SSL for LDAP connections

- ❑ Name and credentials (password or certificate) of the user for LDAP connections

- ❑ Type of authentication to use for LDAP connections

- ❑ User schema: attributes that locate unique users in the LDAP directory

- ❑ Group schema: attributes that locate groups and their members in the LDAP directory

Please consult the WebLogic documentation to obtain the details of the setup, as they change depending on the LDAP server being used.

Unix Realm

As with the LDAP Realm, this realm is limited to authenticated users and groups on the Unix system. Authorization still has to be defined in the `weblogic.properties` file.

WebLogic Server executes a small native program, `wlauth`, to look up users and groups, and to authenticate users given UNIX login names and passwords. On some platforms, `wlauth` uses PAM (Pluggable Authentication Modules), which allows you to configure authentication services in the operating system without altering applications that use the service. On platforms where PAM is not available, `wlauth` uses the standard login mechanism, including shadow passwords, where supported.

Please consult the WebLogic documentation for the appropriate setup of your specific Unix system.

NT Realm

Similar to the LDAP and Unix realms, this realm is limited to authenticated users and groups on a Windows NT Primary Domain Controller. Authorization still has to be defined in the properties file of WebLogic.

The WebLogic documentation offers all of the details for the setup of this security realm.

RDBMS Realm

This realm is based on an example provided with the WebLogic documentation. It reads user, group, and ACL information from a relational database, thus offering both authentication and authorization from a database.

All the code for this custom-made realm is available in the examples section of the documentation. You can use it as is, or modify it to suit your particular needs.

Securing the WebLogic Server

We will assume that you have taken care of the physical security of the computers that are running the WebLogic server, as well as setting up the operating system, file systems, and network to the desired levels of security.

The WebLogic server is controlled by the properties file. As it ships, there are many properties that can leave some gaps regarding security. We will list some of the properties that should be reviewed in order to secure the server before being placed in production.

`weblogic.password.system`: Be sure to set this password to something that would not be easy to guess. For example, selecting 'password' or something equally unoriginal would not be a good choice, as the user `system` is entitled to perform any operation on the WebLogic server.

`weblogic.security.disableGuest`: Make sure that this property is set to `true`. When set to `false` WebLogic enables a `guest` user with password `guest`.

`weblogic.system.listenport`: This property describes on which port the WebLogic server will listen for connections. You should coordinate the use of a firewall with this port and explicitly open ports that you want to allow through while disallowing all other ports.

`weblogic.system.SSLListenPort`: This property defines the port that will be used to secure communications. Again, you should coordinate this value with your firewall.

`weblogic.security.ssl.enable`: Setting this value to `true` enables the SSL port. If you want WebLogic to do only SSL communications with external clients, allow only this port to pass through your firewall.

`Digital Certificates for SSL`: Do *not* use the demo certificates for production environments. The digital certificates included in the WebLogic server are for demonstration and developmental purposes only. You will need to get your own digital certificate specific to your deployment environment and domain name.

`Administration Servlets`: If you plan on using the administration servlets then make sure that the ACLs are restricted to be used only by authorized people. Otherwise disable these servlets.

`Servlets`: Make absolutely sure that you set the permissions of the servlets to match your goals and expected audience. Servlets that handle sensitive information should only be executed by people that are authorized to do so. You must make sure that this is the case. Review every ACL associated to a servlet.

`weblogic.system.enableSetUID`: This property is only used on Unix systems. It allows the WebLogic server to assume the identity of root for a short period of time in order to bind to port 80 during startup. Once it has bound to this port, WebLogic reverts to normal user mode for the rest of the execution. This is not a security threat, but you need to understand what happens when this property is set to `true`.

Other Security Items

There are many other security items that can be handled with the WebLogic server. These are all well covered in the documentation. However, some of them are worth a special mention:

- ❑ Certificate-based user authentication
- ❑ The ability to perform audits
- ❑ Filtering network communications

Certificate-Based User Authentication

When having a two-way SSL communication, WebLogic has the possibility of using the information on the client's certificate to authenticate the remote user, thus removing the need for the client to explicitly provide a username and password.

Setting the following property enables this feature:

```
weblogic.security.realm.certAuthenticator
```

The property must point to the name of a class implementing the `weblogic.security.acl.CertAuthenticator` interface. The `authenticate()` method in this interface receives the certificate chain, giving the implementing class the opportunity to search for information inside and search a LDAP directory or RDBMS table to match that information. It returns an authenticated user or `null` if authentication failed.

Auditing

In WebLogic you can create a pluggable auditing service for security-related events such as when a user attempts to authenticate, when a permission is tested, or when an invalid user certificate or root CA certificate is presented.

Using the `weblogic.security.audit` package you create a class that implements the `AuditProvider` interface, and install it in WebLogic by setting the `weblogic.security.audit.AuditProvider` property to the name of your class. Your `AuditProvider` class will receive all the events and then you can process them as you deem necessary.

Filtering Network Communications

With the WebLogic server you have the ability to accept or reject connections based on criteria determined by your security policies. You could, for example, deny any communication originating from outside your firewall, or accept it only if it is SSL-based.

To do this, set the `weblogic.security.net.ConnectionFilter` property to the name of the class that implements the `weblogic.security.net.ConnectionFilter` interface.

When a client connects, WebLogic constructs a `ConnectionEvent` and passes it to the `accept()` method of your `ConnectionFilter` class. The event includes the remote IP address, as a `java.net.InetAddress`, the remote port number, the local WebLogic server port number, and a `String` containing the protocol (HTTP, HTTPS, T3, T3S, or IIOP).

Now, based on your criteria, you can accept the connection or throw a `FilterException`.

Summary

In this chapter we have seen how authentication and authorization are handled in the WebLogic server. We covered examples on how to code using cookies and SSL with examples of one and two way secure communications using a browser, as well as one way and two way secure communications using a Java client. We reviewed ACLs and realms and closed by checking the `weblogic.properties` file before deploying an application.

9

The Wireless Pizzas

From the business perspective, Mr Chairman of the Board considered the e-commerce incursion a done deal. The next step was to conquer Europe, so a research trip was in order. London, Paris, Frankfurt, and Rome were the compulsory stops. The big surprise for Mr Chairman of the Board was that everybody in Europe seemed to have a mobile phone. It is ubiquitous. Not only that, the same phone in the UK worked seamlessly in France, Germany, Italy, and the rest of Europe. As if it were not enough, coverage also reached South Africa, Australia, and China, to mention but few.

This is in stark contrast to the USA, which seems to be a couple of years behind Europe on this front. This is mainly due to the fact that there are many different standards of transmission used by the mobile operators creating a fragmented market, which becomes even more fragmented because the operation licenses are granted by regions rather than countrywide. In Europe the governments decided and imposed the GSM standard on the mobile operators and then granted countrywide licenses.

The other major difference is that whereas in the USA calls to mobile phones are paid by the person receiving the call, in Europe the calls are paid by the person initiating the call. This is the reason why in Europe mobile phone numbers have separate and distinctive area codes. You would think that this is a deterrent for making calls to mobile phones, but the Europeans already have to pay for local calls, which are metered and charged by time. In the USA the basic monthly package includes unlimited local calls with no time limit. This has fueled the success of the Internet in the USA.

The bottom line is that the rate of adoption and growth of mobile telephones in Europe has been incredible. From taxi drivers in Athens to 10 year olds in Helsinki, everybody seems to have a mobile phone. No longer it is a fashionable must-have object, but a true necessity of life. Just spend a few minutes at the business lounge of any European airport and you will see how many people are chatting to their business partners and sending text messages, this revolution is set to continue with the use of the new WAP technology.

After experiencing this first hand, Mr Chairman of the Board found out that the biggest uptake of WAP so far has been among financial institutions, followed by businesses dealing in travel, hotels, retail, and entertainment. Currently it is only the most up-to-the-minute users who actually use WAP, although this is expected to rise and eventually it will have the same social usage as normal mobile phones. Mr Chairman of the Board knew that using WAP phones as an additional channel to order pizzas was going to be a business differentiator that would provide Pizza2Go with a good marketing tool with which to penetrate Europe. The call was made and Mr Wonderboy got his marching orders. A WAP front end was needed for the Pizza2Go system.

Wireless Application Protocol

This protocol, widely known as WAP is designed to allow small portable devices to access the Internet. The most popular implementation of WAP has so far been on mobile telephones, although it has also been used on pagers.

The WAP standard is maintained by an organization called the WAP Forum (www.wapforum.org). The founding members of the WAP Forum are Ericsson, Motorola, Nokia, and Phone.com (previously known as Unwired Planet). Currently in use is the WAP 1.1 version of the specifications, which will be described in this chapter. Version 1.2 has been defined, but at the moment of this writing it is preliminary. The major feature of version 1.2 is the push capability. This allows an application to push information to a WAP device without the user of the device having to initiate the call; this may be useful for telling users when they have new e-mail, rather than having to connect to download it.

WAP is a set of protocols that allow the development of applications and services for mobile phones and other mobile devices. The WAP Forum chose to design the standards by mimicking the current Internet standards. The process can be described as taking the existing Internet standards and modifying them to meet the very specific needs of these devices and networks.

However, WAP is not the only group proposing an alternative standard for handling mobile devices, Lightweight and Efficient Application Protocol or LEAP proposes a standard that seems to be technically more sophisticated and efficient than WAP, but does not have the support of the of the large companies in this market, thus its future is unknown. More information about LEAP can be found at http://www.LeapForum.org/leap/index.html. Additionally, you can find a very detailed and critical article on WAP from Rohit Khare at http://www.4k-associates.com/IEEE-L7-WAP-BIG.html.

Another technology, soon to be available in 2001 and already making waves, is GPRS. This changes the way mobile phones connect to the carrier from a per call basis to a permanent connection where the billing occurs based on the number of packets transmitted (packet switched). GPRS will also increase the bandwidth to 64K from the current GSM data bandwidth of 9.6K; the maximum bandwidth available is 115k, although this has not been implemented anywhere yet.

The combination of both WAP 1.2 and GPRS will fuel the growth and usage of WAP devices still further.

There are however, currently a few problems with the wireless networks, specifically, less bandwidth, more latency, less connection stability and unpredictable availability. Another very major concern is security – only the Nokia 7110 currently supports certificates, so most WAP sites are not inherently secure. The first point that comes to mind is to increase the bandwidth, but this is not easy. As you increase the bandwidth, the power consumption is also increased, and as you may already know, these devices do not have too much power to spare.

A mobile phone is not a personal computer. The CPU is a joke, substantially less powerful than that of a PC and has a laughable amount of memory (typically 48K). The power consumption factor is always a problem, and the limited availability of power is a major factor when dealing with these devices. However, the most important limitation is that the mobile does not have a keyboard or mouse, and the display typically averages 4 lines of text. The WAP standard tries to deal with these limitations.

As an example it is possible to translate every plain text header of HTTP into binary code which decreases the amount of data to send, allowing sessions to be resumed and suspended very easily, without any overhead. Of course, this is just a sample of the things that are done to handle the situation under the existing constraints.

In trying to leverage as much as possible from the Internet, WAP has an equivalent structure. The following figure shows a comparison of the Internet and WAP architectures, in other words, the IP Stack and the WAP Stack.

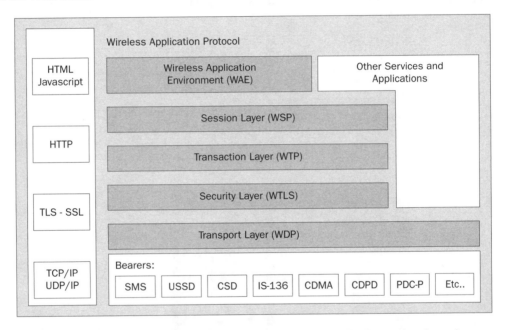

As you can see, the figure is arranged as a hierarchical system; on the lowest level are the bearers, defined as the different transmission standards available for mobile telephony. You may have heard a few of these names, CDMA, CSD, GMS, SMS, etc. They are the equivalent to the wire in a normal telephone line. On top of that there is the Wireless Datagram Protocol (WDP). This is the Transport Layer of the WAP Stack, equivalent to User Datagram Protocol (UDP), a fast but unreliable protocol needed to deliver data between any two applications in the world. Security is taken care of by the Wireless Transport Layer Security. This works in much the same way TLS (Transport Layer Security) and SSL (Secure Socket Layer) do for the Internet world. Then there is Wireless Transaction Protocol, roughly equivalent to Transmission Control Protocol (TCP), which is a slower, but more reliable protocol than UDP but carries out a similar function. Finally Wireless Session Protocol is the network protocol that performs the equivalent functionality to HTTP (Hypertext Transport Protocol).

To develop a WAP application that can take advantage of your existing J2EE based system, you use the Wireless Application Environment (WAE), which includes:

❑   Wireless Mark-up Language (WML).

❑   WMLS, which is a scripting language derived from ECMAScript.

In order to become familiar with WAP, all you need to know is WML, which is essentially the wireless equivalent of HTML. WML is an XML based language that is specifically designed to interface with the micro-browsers that exist in the WAP enabled devices.

Before we go into the detail of WML, let us understand how all this integrates with an existing WebLogic server-based application. In the figure below you can see how simple it is. All you need is for your servlets and JSP pages to generate WML. This is what is sent to the WAP Gateway, which encodes the information and converts it to Binary WML (which optimizes WML for transmission based on tokens) and sends it over the air.

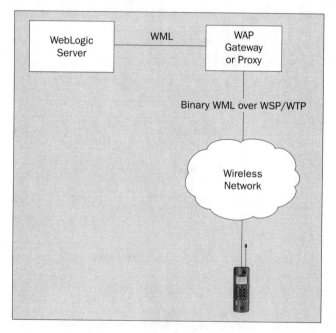

There is also the possibility of generating HTML and then translating it to WML. The problem with this is that many people think that translating HTML to WML will also take care of the presentation issues. The translators do not take care of this, so it is generally not recommended to directly translate an HTML page designed for web browsers into WML as the results will usually look rather odd on a 4 line screen.

The Mobile Operators

Currently in Europe there are two radically different positions that have been taken by the mobile operators. On one side of the equation there are what are called the **closed operators**. The WAP gateway, the portal, and all the content is their property and they have full control of it. If you are a third party trying to place content you will have to reach an agreement with the operator in order to be able to either link or publish in their portal. The way these operators enforce this despotic position is by selling WAP phone kits that have the URL and IP numbers of their portal burned in the phone, thus eliminating the possibility of the user going to another gateway or portal. This is equivalent to buying a PC that can only communicate with one ISP and there is no chance of changing this, so watch out when buying a WAP phone.

The **open operator**, on the other hand, offers a gateway that allows the user to connect to the Internet acting as an ISP for your WAP phone. In most cases these operators also have a portal.

It is also possible for the role of the mobile operator to be reduced to handling the data call, if a company has its own WAP gateway, which can be connected to the Internet or have its very own bank of modems. In this case the WAP user can access the gateway via an ISP or by calling directly the bank of modems. This architecture is depicted in the next figure. This is becoming attractive as there are some mobile operators that offer a cheaper rate for data calls, in some cases as little as only 25% of the cost of a voice call.

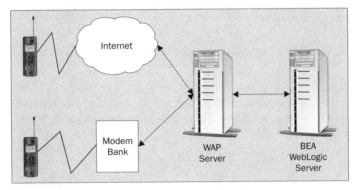

Nokia has been marketing its WAP Server product as a corporate WAP gateway. This is an option that many companies are using to implement WAP solutions. For example, imagine an electric company, where the electricity meter reader enters the information using a WAP phone. The WAP phone runs an application that collects the meter readings. This is more efficient than writing readings down and later having to digitize and process them.

This particular example could work as follows:

❑   The meter reader calls the modem bank of the electric company with a WAP phone, establishes a connection and executes the URL of the application that will handle this data.

❑   The meter reader introduces the meter number and the application verifies that the meter exists and returns the address where it is installed to confirm the location.

❑   Now the actual number presented by the meter is entered through the WAP phone. The application performs some basic verifications, like making sure the number is greater than for the last reading, etc.

When this cycle is completed the person moves on to the next electricity meter and restarts the process. As you can see there are orders of magnitude to be gained in such a simple process that currently is done by hand.

Design Considerations

If the web site is a public one, one of the issues that needs to be addressed is whether there will be separate entry points for WAP devices and normal HTML browsers or if all will use the same URL. There are some cases related to firewalls where the latter is not an option. For the first case is it simple to offer the standard www.company.com for the HTML browsers and a wap.company.com for WAP devices. Each of these has a different home page that will then use specific JSP pages or servlets depending on the device.

In the second case, there is a unique URL and all the home page does is ask which browser is being used by the visitor. It then continues execution of the corresponding servlets and JSP pages according to the device. The first check should be which MIME type of documents the browser explicitly accepts. This is done on the server by checking the special HTTP request header with the name `Accept`. The second check is the browser identification. Because the various WAP phones produce so many different responses to the inquiry for which browser is being used, the strategy is to test whether the browser is either Netscape or Internet Explorer and assume that if it is not one of these, it must be a micro browser from a WAP device. The forthcoming WAP 1.2 will include a more sophisticated way of countering this problem, including UA-PROF that allows each browser to state its personal identity after it makes a request. The browser sends its type to the server in a particular HTTP request header with the name `User-Agent`, (`Request.getHeader("User-Agent")`). Some examples of actual values of this header follow:

Microsoft Internet Explorer version 5:

```
User-Agent: Mozilla/4.0 (compatible; MSIE 5.0; Windows NT; DigExt)
```

Netscape version 6:

```
User-Agent: Mozilla/5.0 (Windows; U; WinNT4.0; en-US; m17) Gecko/20000807
            Netscape6/6.0b2
```

Nokia 7110:

```
User-Agent: Nokia7110/1.0 (04.78)
```

The following code snippet illustrates how to determine the type of browser from a servlet or JSP page on the server:

```
String browser = request.getHeader("User-Agent");

if (browser.indexOf("MSIE")      != -1){
...
}else
if (browser.indexOf("Netscape")  != -1){
...
}else
if (browser.indexOf("Nokia7110") != -1){
...
}
```

It has been suggested that by using XSL (eXtensible Style Language) you can avoid having to deal with the type of device on the client side. An application can have the JSP pages and servlets generate XML and then the XSL style sheets will translate the content to something suitable for the corresponding browser (on a PC or a mobile device). The reality is that writing the style sheets of such dramatically different devices is impractical and requires more work than just handling them separately. Just remember that a normal HTML browser can address a typical display of 800 by 600 pixels, whereas the WAP micro-browser will deal with screen sizes that typically have only 4 lines by 12 characters. Despite this however, it is possible to write style sheets to render information across different WAP phones.

It makes more sense to use Style Sheets to handle the difference between micro-browsers as well as between the sizes of displays and features offered by the various WAP phones. For example, the Nokia 7110 has a pixel display of 96 by 65 pixels, which is considered large in comparison to normal mobile phones. This translates into four lines of about 12 characters long of main text, plus a header text line and an area for the two soft keys. The Ericsson R380s, based on the Palm Pilot, has a screen of 360 by 120 pixels and handles proportional font with three type sizes and bold face. This gives you a work area of about 7.5 lines for the small type down to 5 lines for the large type size. As the font is proportional, a typical average line size is 54 characters. Additionally it has a touch sensitive screen. The Siemens C35i has 6 lines of text plus a header line, and the bonus is that it can handle 6 colors.

Because of this, it makes sense to use style sheets if you want to take advantage of the specific characteristics and features that a mobile phone can have. You also have to be aware that even if two different mobile phones have the same display size, the applications can have different results when presenting the same WML instructions. However, if you want to read more about XSL, then visit: http://www.w3schools.com/xsl/xsl_resources.asp.

The last and most important design consideration related to the usability of the application is that you have to keep in mind that WAP devices do not have a keyboard. Therefore you have to try to minimize the amount of information the user has to provide the application with. Filling in a large form, like the registration to a web site, might be a functionality offered on a WAP phone, but probably seldom used by visitors because of the amount of effort required to input the required information using a telephone keypad.

One trick to minimize input by the visitor is to guess what they want and present that information by default. Usually this guess can be pretty close to reality in a well defined business processes. For example, if you visit the WAP site of your bank, there is a high probability that you are interested in knowing the balance of the account. So the trick is to present this information by default. If the visitor did want this information it is already presented with no effort on their part. If not, they can go to the menu to select the desired option, which adds only one keystroke to reach the option menu.

Another example, a little more complex, can be an airline that offers various services via WAP. The defaults can be context sensitive. For example, if a passenger for a flight has already checked in and is accessing the WAP site of the airline before the departure time, then it is very likely that they are interested in knowing the gate number and if the flight is still on time. By using this guess as the default information to be presented the site will give the likely desired information without effort. Again, if this was not the desired information, the menu option is only one keystroke away.

Once again, the objective is to minimize the number of keystrokes a visitor needs to move around a WAP site. The other objective is to minimize the amount of information presented on the screen. This is a lot harder to achieve, but keep in consideration the following: do not use abbreviations. It is better to scroll down to read a message than to try to figure out a cryptic message that fits in one display. The other thing is that bitmap images that are small enough to fit in one of these displays are cheap to transmit and process on the mobile phone. As they say, a graphic is worth a thousand words. Use them but do not abuse them.

One way of minimizing the keystrokes a user has to issue is to use cookies to remember information about the user. The problem is that the micro-browsers in WAP devices do not support cookies. The alternative is to use a mechanism called URL rewriting, which basically tags the session ID to the end of the URL.

When an HTTP session is created on the server, the server assigns a session identifier. The subsequent requests, if related to the session just created, should include the session ID in order to allow the server to recover the corresponding session from its ID. The browser can include the session ID appended to the URL as a GET parameter or in the request as a POST parameter.

The question is: 'How does the browser know the session ID if it doesn't accept cookies?' If the server cannot store the session ID as a cookie, the only solution is that the session ID appears "hard coded" on the page the browser receives from the server.

The server thus forces all the requests from the browser with the session ID included. If the request is made with the GET command, all the links should be encoded to include the session ID as a GET parameter. The WebLogic implementation of the encodeRedirectURL() method does include the current session ID. In WML, the go element indicates navigation to a URL, indicated by the href field. Instead of writing the href links as simple strings:

```
<go href="/wthanks.wml">
```

They must be rewritten as follows:

```
<go href="<%=response.encodeRedirectURL("/wthanks.wml")%>">
```

If the request is done by a POST command, then the WML postfield element (WeblogicSession) must be used to include the session ID as a POST parameter. For example:

Another alternative is to use a WML postfield element in combination with any WML go element. The go element in WML indicates navigation to a URL and a postfield element can be used to handle the session ID.

```
<go href="wloginS" method="post">
  <postfield name="UserName" value="$(UserName)"/>
  <postfield name="UserPassword" value="$(UserPassword)"/>
  <postfield name="WebLogicSession" value="<%= session.getId() %>"/>
</go>
```

This example will cause an HTTP POST to the URL wloginS and will pass the session ID as the value of the WebLogicSession parameter. From within the wloginS servlet, the session ID is transparently retrieved using the request.getSession() method call.

In both cases (GET or POST) the session ID is included in the page in all the required places so the browser can safely send this ID back to the server.

There is one last concern. The session ID is rather lengthy and can easily exceed 128 characters, which in many WAP devices is a limit for URL strings. The ID is even larger when using WebLogic in a clustered mode. To solve this problem you can change the length of the session ID with the weblogic.httpd.session.sessionIDLength property, by specifying a number equal to or larger than 10.

Wireless Markup Language (WML)

As mentioned earlier, this is all you really need to know for any development in WAP. If you have experience with HTML, it should only take you a couple of hours to familiarize yourself with WML. If we compare the HTML world with WML, the biggest difference is the abstraction used for a WML document.

A WML document is a collection of one or more **Cards** called a **Deck of Cards**. Each Card is both a well defined unit of interaction, and a service. The general rule of thumb is that a Card carries enough information to fit in one screen of a mobile device. Therefore, the size of the card is determined by the size of the screen.

How you divide your application into Decks depends on the logic of it. But you should be aware that a deck is the smallest download unit, that is, information is downloaded to the WAP device in Decks, not Cards. A Deck can contain as few as one Card and as many as you want, but it is strongly suggested to avoid Decks with large amounts of Cards. Remember that there is a limitation in the size of memory on these devices. A WML Card looks like this (from `wtest.wml`):

```
<?xml version="1.0"?>
<!DOCTYPE wml PUBLIC "-//WAPFORUM//DTD WML 1.1//EN"
"http://www.wapforum.org/DTD/wml_1.1.xml">

<wml>

   <card id="test_card" title="Title of Card">
     <p>
        Test text
     </p>
   </card>

</wml>
```

Using a Nokia 7110 WAP phone emulator, the output of this Card is:

Using an Ericsson R320s emulator, the output is:

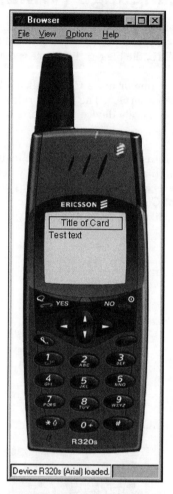

And using an Ericsson R380s emulator, the output is:

You can navigate from card to card very easily. All you have to do is use the `href` directive:

```
<go href="#card3" />
```

This will send control to a card called `card3` in the same deck. If you want to send control to another deck:

```
<go href="deck2.wml" />
```

This will default to the first card of that deck. If you want to send control to a specific card in another deck:

```
<go href="deck2.wml#card4" />
```

A lot of WAP is very similar to HTML, but there is quite a bit more WML specific content, to be touched upon later in the chapter. There are some other important differences between the two, but as this book is only touching upon the WAP world briefly, it will not be discussed in any great detail. For a more detailed explanation of WAP and WML, readers may wish to refer to *Professional WAP* from Wrox Press (*ISBN 1-861004-04-4*).

Terve Maailma

None of Wonder Troops had heard about WAP, but they were enthusiastic from the beginning. The instructions were very simple: A customer should be able to place a pizza order from a WAP device.

The first step of the Troops was to go to all the appropriate web sites to find information. They found the best quality in the following:

- ❑ http://www.wapforum.com
- ❑ http://www.ericsson.com
- ❑ http://www.nokia.com
- ❑ http://www.phone.com

Not only did they find a large amount of information on the subject, but also mobile phone emulators, WAP Toolkits, and design guidelines for WAP applications.

The next step was to write a test application, the typical `Hello World`. The Wapplication is rather simple: it presents a list of language options, and then displays "Hello World" in the selected language. To do this the Wapplication is broken down into four cards in one deck. The first card contains the initial menu offering the options with the available languages. Then there is a card for each of the possible three languages that presents the Hello World message (from `whello.wml`).

```
<?xml version="1.0"?>
<!DOCTYPE wml PUBLIC "-//WAPFORUM//DTD WML 1.1//EN"
"http://www.wapforum.org/DTD/wml_1.1.xml">

<wml>
```

```
<card id="MainCard" title="Wapplication" newcontext="true">
  <p>
    Select a language:
  </p>
  <p align="center">
    <a href="#Finnish">Suomi</a>
    <a href="#English">English</a>
    <a href="#Spanish">Espa&#xF1;ol</a>
  </p>
</card>

<card id="Finnish" title="Suomi">
  <p align="center">
    Terve Maailma
    <do type="accept" label="Go to Start"><go href="#MainCard"/></do>
  </p>
</card>

<card id="English" title="English">
  <p align="center">
    Hello World
    <do type="accept" label="Go to Start"><go href="#MainCard"/></do>
  </p>
</card>

<card id="Spanish" title="Espa&#xF1;ol">
  <p align="center">
    Hola Mundo
    <do type="accept" label="Go to Start"><go href="#MainCard"/></do>
  </p>
</card>

</wml>
```

By now you may have figured out that 'Terve Maailma' means 'Hello World' in the Finnish language. As a curious note, 'maa' means ground and 'ilma' means air, but put together it means world. On the following screenshots you can see the main menu and the result of selecting Finnish using the Nokia 7110 emulator.

Using the Ericsson R320s emulator, you can see the main menu and the result of selecting English as the language:

And finally, using the Ericsson R380s emulator, the following screenshots present the main menu and the result of selecting Spanish as the language:

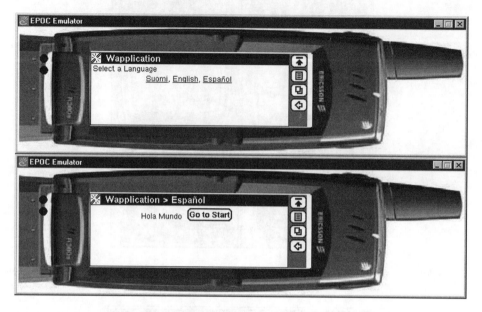

The Pizza WAPplication

To keep this experiment as simple as possible, the Troops decide to offer minimal functionality to the visitor of the WAP site. Basically a home page requesting a login and password, the menu of pizzas, which will be restricted to the pre-defined pizzas, and the ability to place an order for these pizzas only.

As part of the objective to minimize the input from the visitor, the troops decide to present the last order the person has placed, if there is one available, and ask if they want to repeat the order. If the response is negative, the WAPplication will send them to the pizza menu.

Also, the Troops decide to use the separate URL strategy to handle the WAP requests. This way a WAP visitor will work with wap.pizza2go.com where the default page is index.wml.

There are no rules regarding which cards are to be placed in which deck of cards. The objective is to achieve a decent size deck to have a fast download time and try to minimize jumping from one deck to another as this implies that a new deck has to be downloaded. Usually it is very difficult to have the decks execute sequentially, as there will be some going back and forth from one deck to another. The best is to start the design trying laying out all the cards in a sequential fashion and choosing which ones will make up the decks. Once this has been done they will probably no longer be in order. When this happens you have to start rearranging the cards in such a way that you minimize jumping from one deck to the other. As there are no rules, this can only be trial and error. After going through this process, the Troops arrive at a design that uses four decks of cards and a servlet, which will be explained next. The complete map of the WAP site is shown in next figure:

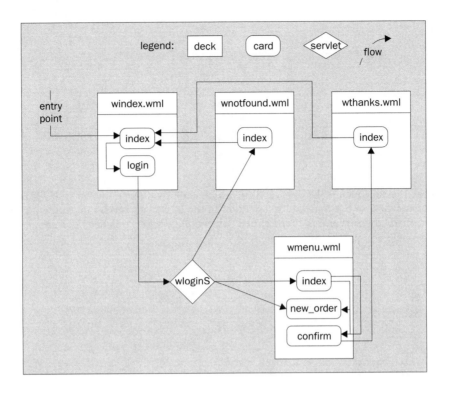

windex.wml

This is the entry point to the system. It is a JSP page, but it generates WML. It is very important to note the first lines of the page:

```
<?xml version="1.0"?>
<!DOCTYPE wml PUBLIC "-//WAPFORUM//DTD WML 1.1//EN"
                    "http://www.wapforum.org/DTD/wml_1.1.xml">

<%@ page contentType="text/vnd.wap.wml"%>
```

First, and most importantly, without leaving any blank space or adding any character(s) you must define the XML tag to identify the page. By default, the JSP servlet will generate HTML. As WAP devices work with WML, we need to specify the appropriate MIME type that has to be generated, as declared in the last line.

The first card in this deck is the index card. It shows a small welcome logo (a wireless bitmap). It also declares a timer that will trigger a timer event five seconds after the card is loaded. The trigger event will cause the browser to show the login card. If the user is not patient enough, an explicit jump to that card can be made with the action labeled Login. The page initiates a new context on the WAP browser, resetting any state the browser could have.

```
<wml>

  <card id="index" title="thE-Pizza" newcontext="true" ontimer="#login">
    <timer value="50"/>
    <do type="accept" label="Login">
      <go href="#login"/>
    </do>
    <p align="center">
      <img src="epizza.wbmp" alt="E-Pizza logo"/>
    </p>
  </card>
```

The second card in this deck is the `login` card, which is equivalent to a form in HTML. It just obtains the login and password of the user and sends them to the `wloginS` servlet for authentication. It also sends the session ID the server has "hard coded" on the page when this has been served.

```
<card id="login" title="Login">
  <do type="accept" label="Login">
    <go href="wloginS" method="post">
      <postfield name="UserName" value="$(UserName)"/>
      <postfield name="UserPassword" value="$(UserPassword)"/>
      <postfield name="WebLogicSession" value="<%= session.getId() %>"/>
    </go>
  </do>
  <do type="prev" label="Back">
    <prev/>
  </do>
  <p>
    user name: <input name="UserName"/>
    password: <input name="UserPassword" type="password"/>
  </p>
</card>
</wml>
```

The dollar signs are used to specify WAP state variables, and will be explained further in this section.

wloginS

This servlet does not generate WML. It plays the well-known servlet role in the Model 2 architecture described in Chapter 3, that is it acts as a switchboard for the client request and the response. It accesses the database to authenticate the user and forwards the execution to `wmenu.wml`, the corresponding WML page. If the user is not authenticated `wnotfound.wml` is invoked instead.

When the user is found, the information is stored in session values of the servlet so it can be easily available to other Decks and Cards:

```
session.setAttribute("UserLogIn", "true");
session.setAttribute("currentCustomer", customer);
session.setAttribute("UserName", customer.c_first_name + " " +
                     customer.c_last_name);
session.setAttribute("UserID", "1-" + customer.c_area_code + "-" +
                     customer.c_phone);
```

Given the limitations of a wireless channel it is highly recommended to redirect control to another Deck using the `forward()` method instead of the `sendRedirect()` method. For example:

```
...
        destinationURL = response.encodeRedirectURL("/wmenu.wml");
      }
      else{
        destinationURL = response.encodeRedirectURL("/wnotfound.wml");
      }
...
      ServletContext context = getServletContext();
      RequestDispatcher requestDispatcher;
      requestDispatcher = context.getRequestDispatcher(destinationURL);

      requestDispatcher.forward(request, response);
```

The reason for doing this is very simple. When using the `forward()` method, the client is not aware there was a redirection as it happens on the server side. When the `sendRedirect()` method is used, the client receives a response from the server indicating it has to access another card or deck to continue processing, which forces the client to make a request to the server. Also, using a `sendRedirect()` forces all the information to be sent as part of the URL. As we saw, this can be a problem because of the length restrictions for the URL string in WAP devices. Thus by using a `forward()` method you can both economize bandwidth as there are less trips between the device and the server and avoid problems with potentially large URLs. One potential problem is that this may cause problems in bookmarking pages, for example, the menu page, as the actual URL will point to the servlet, even though the `menu.wml` page is displayed.

This code also shows how a URL must be encoded with `encodeRedirectURL()` to force the addition of the session ID to the original URL. If a `forward()` method has been used and any content has been written back to the user agent then an `IllegalStateException` may be thrown.

wnotfound.wml

This deck only contains one card, `index`, which is shown when the user is not found or not authenticated by the calling the servlet `wloginS`:

```
<?xml version="1.0"?>
<!DOCTYPE wml PUBLIC "-//WAPFORUM//DTD WML 1.1//EN"
                     "http://www.wapforum.org/DTD/wml_1.1.xml">

<%@ page contentType="text/vnd.wap.wml" %>

<wml>

  <card id="index" title="User not found">
    <do type="prev" label="Back">
      <prev/>
    </do>
    <p align="center">
      Please register at our WebSite.<br/>
      <a href="/windex.wml">[home]</a>
    </p>
  </card>

</wml>
```

This time the destination URL (`href="/windex.wml"`) is not encoded as there no interest in continuing with the same session when the main page (`windex.wml`) is reached.

wmenu.wml

This page is used so that the customer can place an order. This page uses JDBC and EJBs to access the information about the available pizzas and customer information (personal data and previous orders).

This page takes advantage of a really nice feature that WML has, the WAP device state variables. WML specifies a state model, which includes variables. These variables are parameters that can be used to change the characteristics and content of a WML Deck or Card. WML variables can be used in place of strings and are substituted at run-time with their current value.

Variables are used in this page to configure the pizza order. For example:

```
<wml>

<%
  String lastOrder = (String)session.getAttribute("lastOrder");
  if (lastOrder != null){
    OrderDetail orderDetail =
              (OrderDetail)session.getAttribute("lastOrderDetail");
%>

  <card id="index" title="Menu">
    <p align="center">
      Hi, <%=session.getAttribute("UserName")%>, Welcome back.
      Did you enjoy the <%= lastOrder %>?
      <do type="accept" name="repeat" label="Repeat Order">
        <go href="#confirm">
          <setvar name="pizza"
                  value="<%= orderDetail.getOd_pizza().getP_name() %>"/>
          <setvar name="size"
                  value="<%= orderDetail.getOd_pizza().getP_size() %>"/>
          <setvar name="dough"
                  value="<%= orderDetail.getOd_dough() %>"/>
          <setvar name="quantity"
                  value="<%= orderDetail.getOd_quantity() %>"/>
        </go>
      </do>
      <do type="accept" name="new" label="New Order">
        <go href="#new_order">
        </go>
      </do>
    </p>
  </card>
<%}%>
```

In this card, if a previous order by the same customer is found, it is stored in WML variables using the setvar directive. In the next step, the confirm card retrieves these values to build the order:

```
<card id="confirm" title="Order Confirm">
  <p>
    <%=session.getAttribute("UserName")%>, please confirm your order:
    $(quantity)x$(pizza), $(size), $(dough)<br/>
    <do type="confirm" label="Confirm">
      <go href="<%=response.encodeRedirectURL("/wthanks.wml")%>"
          method="post" >
        <postfield name="pizza" value="$(pizza)"/>
        <postfield name="size" value="$(size)"/>
```

```
                <postfield name="dough" value="$(dough)"/>
                <postfield name="quantity" value="$(quantity)"/>
            </go>
        </do>
        <do type="prev" label="Edit">
            <prev/>
        </do>
    </p>
</card>
```

Using the $(variable_name) you gain access to the variable. This way the order is built to be sent to the wthanks.wml, which will actually process the order using the corresponding EJB.

If there is no previous order found for the current customer, or if the customer wants a different order, the new_order card is shown. This card shows a form with the available pizzas and sets the WML variables after submitting it.

```
<card id="new_order" title="New Order">
    <p>
        <%if (session.getAttribute("lastOrder") == null){
            %>Hi, <%=session.getAttribute("UserName")%>,
                Welcome back.<br/><%}%>
        Select your pizza:<br/>
        <select name="pizza" title="Pizza">
<%
    //' First, we're going through the list of pre-defined pizzas
    Vector pizzas = (Vector)session.getAttribute("predefinedPizzas");
    String this_pizzaID = null;
    Pizza pizza = null;
    Enumeration enum = pizzas.elements();
    while(enum.hasMoreElements()){
    pizza = (Pizza)enum.nextElement();
%>
        <option value="<%=pizza.getP_name()%>">
            <%=pizza.getP_name()%>
        </option>
<%
    }
%>
        </select>
        <select name="size" title="Size">
            <option value="Small">Small</option>
            <option value="Medium">Medium</option>
            <option value="Large">Large</option>
        </select>
        <select name="dough" title="Dough">
            <option value="Thin Crust">Thin Crust</option>
            <option value="Classic">Classic</option>
        </select>
        <input type="text" title="Quantity" name="quantity" format="*N"
                value="1"/>
        <a href="#confirm">[continue]</a><br/>
        <do type="prev" label="Back">
            <prev/>
        </do>
    </p>
</card>
```

wthanks.wml

The last deck, wthanks.wml displays the confirmation message once the order has been placed. This is really the card that makes the order happen if it was reached from the wmenu.wml JSP page (from card confirm) with the correct parameters. These parameters identify the desired order (and the session ID!). In this case a stateful session EJB (OrderSF) is created to handle the order and retrieve the confirmation number.

```
<?xml version="1.0"?>
<!DOCTYPE wml PUBLIC "-//WAPFORUM//DTD WML 1.1//EN"
                     "http://www.wapforum.org/DTD/wml_1.1.xml">

<%@ page contentType="text/vnd.wap.wml"
         import="java.util.*, javax.naming.*;"%>

<wml>

  <card id="index" title="Thanks!">

<%
  String message = "";
  Customer customer = (Customer)session.getAttribute("currentCustomer");
  if (customer != null){
   try{
    Context ctx = Util.getInitialContext();
    OrderSFHome orderHome = (OrderSFHome) ctx.lookup("jsw.c09.OrderSF");
    OrderSF currentOrder = orderHome.create(customer);
    OrderDetail orderDetail = new OrderDetail();
    Pizza pizza = new Pizza();
    pizza.setP_name(request.getParameter("pizza"));
    pizza.setP_size(request.getParameter("size"));
    orderDetail.setOd_pizza(pizza);
    orderDetail.setOd_quantity(
                       Integer.parseInt(request.getParameter("quantity")));
    orderDetail.setOd_dough(request.getParameter("dough"));
    currentOrder.addOrderDetail(orderDetail);
    currentOrder.deliverOrder();
    message = "Your order # " +
               currentOrder.getOrderMaster().getOr_number() +
               " has been received!";
    currentOrder.remove();
   }
   catch(Exception e){
     System.err.println(e);
     message = "Your order could not be processed!";
   }
  }
  else{
    message = "Your order could not be processed! ";
  }
%>
    <p align="center">
      <%= message %><br/>
      <a href="/windex.wml">[home]</a>
    </p>
  </card>

</wml>
```

Setting It Up

The WebLogic server already includes the MIME type that handles WML in the
`weblogic.properties` file:

```
# MIME types
weblogic.httpd.mimeType.text/vnd.wap.wml=wml
weblogic.httpd.mimeType.image/vnd.wap.wbmp=wbmp
weblogic.httpd.mimeType.application/vnd.wap.wmlc=wmlc
weblogic.httpd.mimeType.text/vnd.wap.wmlscript=wmls
weblogic.httpd.mimeType.application/vnd.wap.wmlscriptc=wmlsc
```

Then the first step is to register the `.wml` extension so that the JSP pages with this extension will be
processed by the servlet responsible for compiling the JSP pages (`weblogic.servlet.JSPServlet`):

```
weblogic.httpd.register.*.wml=\
        weblogic.servlet.JSPServlet

weblogic.httpd.initArgs.*.wml=\
        pageCheckSeconds=0,\
        packagePrefix=jsw.c09,\
        compileCommand=c:/jdk1.3/bin/javac.exe,\
        workingDir=c:/wlsbook/srv/c09-srv/classfiles,\
        keepgenerated=true,\
        verbose=true

weblogic.allow.execute.weblogic.servlet.*.wml=everyone
```

This way, when a WAP device requests a WML page from the WebLogic server, it will compile it into a
servlet, load it into the virtual machine and execute it to generate the WML code. This is done in pretty
much the same way that it would be for generating a JSP page that generates HTML. This servlet,
`weblogic.servlet.JSPServlet` can be registered as many times as needed, so the registration of
the JSP pages (`.jsp`) can be handled simultaneously.

The parameters related to the HTTP session must be also set up as follows:

```
weblogic.httpd.session.cookies.enable=true
weblogic.httpd.session.URLRewriting.enable=true
weblogic.httpd.session.sessionIDLength=10
```

Finally, the new servlet must be registered:

```
weblogic.httpd.register.wloginS=jsw.c09.wloginS

weblogic.allow.execute.weblogic.servlet.wloginS=everyone
```

To summarize, the application in Chapter 9 is composed of all the code of the Chapter 8 plus the JSP
pages and servlet that generate the WML code (and the logo!). Thus the new application can be
accessed from either an HTML browser or a WML browser, allowing for both Web and WAP access.

Execution

The application compilation and deployment processes are identical to the ones in previous chapters. The WebLogic server also can be started in the same way.

The new task is to start the WAP browser to connect to the WebLogic server showing the application. In the case of the Nokia 7110, after installing the Nokia WAP Toolkit version 2.0, the user can start the application by using Start | Programs | Nokia Wap Toolkit 2.0 | WAP toolkit. Alternatively, open a command-line window and type the following:

```
C:\>cd \"Program Files"\Nokia\WAP_Toolkit_2.0

C:\Program Files\Nokia\WAP_Toolkit_2.0>java -jar toolkit.jar
In cCreateProc

cCreateProc name: javaw -classpath
"lib\wapminisrv.jar;lib\activation.jar;lib\jsdk.jar;lib\mail.jar;toolkit.jar" -
DPATH="lib\i386" com.nokia.wap.gw.manager.MiniServerManager
cCreateProc dir: ServerSimulator
cCreateProc set new PATH to be lib\i386;C:\WINNT\system32;C:\WINNT succeeded:
 id: 370 hdl: 724
```

You may need to specify the path before typing `java -jar toolkit.jar`, *for example, if using JDK 1.3, the the default correct command to start the application would be* `C:\JDK1.3\bin\java -jar toolkit.jar`.

Then select the Nokia 7110 device as shown in the following screenshot:

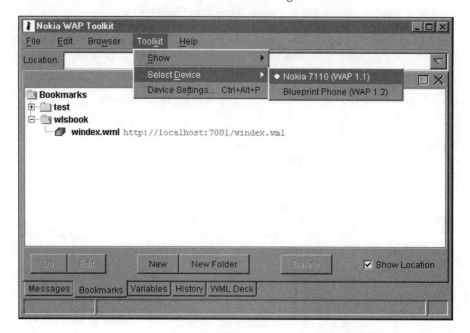

The toolkit comes with an abridged version of the Nokia gateway. A gateway is defined as a bridge between the Internet (IP network) and the wireless data network. It is required because the two platforms differ in underlying technology, therefore in a basic sense, a gateway is just software that supports both WAP and IP, converting information across the two different protocols. The gateway is automatically started in the background, allowing access by the Nokia 7110 to the WebLogic server.

In the Bookmarks section, create a new bookmark with the application URL: http://localhost:7001/windex.wml. Click on the Go button to start loading the page. The result is shown in the next image:

After a few seconds, the phone shows the login form. Here the user is requested to provide their user name and the password. For this, the user has to already be registered at the web site:

And then the user must select the login option to gain access to the system:

If the user cannot be authenticated, the following message will be displayed:

If the user is accepted, their name will be displayed and the system searches for their last order. If the user has placed an order previously, it is presented to them and will be asked if they liked it. This way the user can repeat the order or create a new one:

If the user has no previous orders, they are sent directly to the creation of a new order:

The dialog to choose between repeating an order and creating a new one is the following:

If the user wants to create a new order they will have to select the type, size, dough type, and quantity. After this the system requests confirmation and the order is filled returning an order number, just as on the HTML version of the web site. This sequence is illustrated in the following screenshots:

Summary

This chapter has demonstrated how easy it is to add support for a WAP device to an existing application. All the developer needs to do is remember the basic design considerations, minimize the amount of user input and try to offer shortcuts based on educated guesses of what the visitor to the WAP site will want to do.

Mr Wonderboy was very impressed with how easy it was to implement, and now the Pizza2Go site is ready to take orders form WAP devices all over. After creating what they feel is a pretty solid web site, the Troops are now ready to test it under conditions with simultaneous users.

10

Stress Testing

In the previous chapters we have seen how the Wonder Troops have successfully developed both the web and WAP versions of the E-Pizza portal. Now that the developments are going into production there are some questions floating in the air:

❑   How long will pages take to be loaded into the browser?

❑   What is the relationship between the number of connected users and the response time?

❑   For a given Quality of Service (response time and percentage of errors), what is:

   ❑   The maximum number of users supported by a given configuration?

   ❑   The minimum configuration for an expected number of users?

❑   How can the platform be tuned (hardware, operating system, application server, and application deployment) to optimize the response time of the whole system?

The load test (or stress testing) phase aims to answer these and other related questions. In this chapter, we'll look at the design of the Grinder, the application that performs the actual testing.

The Grinder

After searching the market for commercial products useful for stress testing, the Wonder Troops found very powerful tools enabling stress testing of HTTP-based applications. A tool of this kind can typically simulate concurrent users' activity accessing the web server and requesting the HTML pages that make up the application. From the server point of view, the activity from these load generators is indistinguishable from that created by real users. These tools also provide fine control capabilities on the number of simulated users. They collect performance data and make statistical analyses and reports from the collected data (both graphical and numerical). However, these stress-testing tools are quite expensive. The price issue and the fact that the team is very enthusiastic to develop solutions using Java means that they decide to develop an in-house stress-testing tool, which they call The Grinder.

The Grinder is not designed to replace commercial products in this field, but it can be used to start load testing applications and obtain a pretty good idea of how an application performs under a given user load. The Grinder can simulate simultaneous HTTP clients accessing the web server. It also records the response time of each request. The Grinder has a number of parameters that can be configured, the most important of which are the following:

❑ The number of simultaneous clients

❑ The URLs visited by the clients

❑ The string used to validate the response from the server

❑ The 'thinking time', or the time interval between requests

❑ The number of iterations of the URLs to be made

Other parameters are used to tune the Grinder itself. These are, among others:

❑ The number of threads in each virtual machine and the number of virtual machines to run

❑ The heap size of the virtual machine that executes the Grinder

❑ Other virtual machine arguments

The Grinder can be extended by creating what the troops call a 'plugin'. The HTTP test is a particular case of 'plugin'. Other plugins can be developed, for example to load test EJBs, or n-tier applications with a Java-based user interface.

The Grinder can be run on one machine or on several, and being a pure Java application means it can run on different platforms.

Getting Started

A basic example is provided in this section to help you start using the Grinder. The example is based on a web application, composed of three JSP pages:

❑ login.jsp starts a new servlet session and stores a user name in it, which is retrieved as a parameter from the HTTP request

❑ status.jsp checks the existence of the user name in the servlet session

❑ logout.jsp also checks the user name in the session. If it exists then it invalidates the current session

The following listing shows the first page, `login.jsp`:

```
<% System.out.println("Trace: login"); %>
<html>
<body>

<%
  String user = request.getParameter("user");
  if ((user == null) || (user.equals(""))) {
    user = "default";
  }
  session.setAttribute("user", user);
%>

<p>User <b><%= user %></b> logged in!</p>

<a href="status.jsp">status</a>

</body>
</html>
```

Grinder Properties

We are interested in knowing the download time of each of the three pages for different numbers of concurrent users. The download time of a page is also referred to as the response time, that is, the response time of the request for the page. The Grinder configuration is established in a properties file called `grinder.properties`, which must be present in the JVM classpath.

We set up the properties for the Grinder to request the URLs of the JSP pages, including the request parameters, as shown in this excerpt from the `grinder.properties` file:

```
grinder.cycleParams= \
  [keepSession]true,\
  [logHtml]false,\
  [url0]http://localhost:7001/login.jsp?user=fofito&password=bond007,\
  [url1]http://localhost:7001/status.jsp,\
  [url2]http://localhost:7001/logout.jsp,\
  [ok0]User <b>fofito</b> logged in!,\
  [ok1]User <b>fofito</b> in session,\
  [ok2]User <b>fofito</b> logged out!
```

The `grinder.cycleParams` property holds the URLs of the JSP pages in strings delimited between the [url*n*] string and the comma. The property also has other parameters such as the validation string, the session, and the log. These and other properties will be fully explained in the next few sections.

Two other properties, `grinder.jvms` and `grinder.threads`, configure the number of users. The result of multiplying both properties gives the number of concurrent users simulated by the Grinder.

The length of the test is set up with the `grinder.times` property. This property indicates the number of times the Grinder will iterate through the URLs.

347

The time between requests is specified in the `grinder.sleepMillis` property. This property improves the mimicking of the browser user accessing the URLs, and is also known as 'user think time'.

The properties just described have the following values in the properties file provided:

```
grinder.jvms=2
grinder.threads=3
grinder.times=5
grinder.sleepMillis=5000
```

These define the execution of two instances of the Grinder, each with three threads, effectively simulating six users. Each thread will execute the test script five times with a think time of five seconds.

The steps for running the WebLogic server with the JSP pages and the Grinder are described next. Both programs will be started in their own command windows.

1. Open two command line windows. The first will run the WebLogic server with the sample JSP pages, while the second will run the Grinder.

2. In the Grinder window, change directory to the source for Chapter 10, and set the environment:

```
C:\> cd \wlsbook\src\c10

C:\wlsbook\src\c10> setenv
------------------------------------------------------------
Current settings:
      Java Home = c:\jdk1.3
   WebLogic Home = c:\weblogic
    Grinder Home = c:\wlsbook\src\c10
      CLASSPATH = .;c:\weblogic\lib\weblogic510sp5boot.jar;c:\weblogic\
classes\boot;c:\weblogic\lib\weblogic510sp5.jar;c:\weblogic\license;c:\weblogic\cl
asses;c:\weblogic\lib\weblogicaux.jar;c:\wlsbook\src\c10\lib\grinder1_6_0.jar

          PATH = c:\wlsbook\bin;c:\jdk1.3\bin;C:\WINNT\system32;C:\WINNT

C:\wlsbook\src\c10>
```

3. Staying in the Grinder window, deploy the Web application to the server directory by typing the following:

```
C:\wlsbook\src\c10> make all
...
C:\wlsbook\src\c10> make deploy
deploying JSPs...
xcopy /E c:\wlsbook\src\c10\jsp\\*.jsp c:\wlsbook\srv\c10-srv\public_html
C:\wlsbook\src\c10\jsp\login.jsp
C:\wlsbook\src\c10\jsp\logout.jsp
C:\wlsbook\src\c10\jsp\status.jsp
3 File(s) copied
copy c:\wlsbook\src\c10\ejb\\*.jar c:\wlsbook\srv\c10-srv\ejb
c:\wlsbook\src\c10\ejb\\ejb_basic_statelessSession.jar
        1 file(s) copied.
```

4. In the WebLogic window, change to the `wlsbook` directory, set the environment for Chapter 10 and start the server as in the previous chapters, by typing the `startwls` command:

```
C:\> cd \wlsbook
C:\wlsbook>setenv 10
------------------------------------------------------------
Setting SERVER environment for chapter 10
------------------------------------------------------------
Current settings:
      Java Home = c:\jdk1.3
  WebLogic Home = c:\weblogic
   Project Home = c:\wlsbook
        CLASSPATH = c:\weblogic\lib\weblogic510sp5boot.jar;c:\weblogic\classes\boot;
c:\weblogic\lib\weblogic510sp5.jar;c:\weblogic\license;c:\weblogic\classes;c:\webl
ogic\lib\weblogicaux.jar;c:\wlsbook\srv\c10-srv\serverclasses

        PATH = c:\wlsbook\bin;c:\jdk1.3\bin;c:\orant\bin;C:\WINNT\
system32;c:\weblogic\bin;c:\weblogic\bin\oci815_8

C:\wlsbook>startwls
Sun Sep 10 11:20:08 CEST 2000:<I> <WebLogicServer> Read global properties
c:\wlsbook\weblogic.properties
...
```

5. Back to the Grinder window, change to the `examples\HttpClient` directory and start the Grinder as shown below:

```
C:\wlsbook\src\c10> cd examples
C:\wlsbook\src\c10\examples>cd httpclient
C:\wlsbook\src\c10\examples\HttpClient>java com.ejbgrinder.Grinder
Sun Sep 10 11:26:45 CEST 2000: Grinder (v1.6.0) started with the following
properties:
 grinder.mx: 32
 grinder.ms: 16
 grinder.cycleParams:
[keepSession]true,[logHtml]false,[url0]http://localhost:7001/login.jsp?user=fofito
&password=bond007,[url1]http://localhost:7001/status.jsp,[url2]http://localhost:70
01/logout.jsp,[ok0]User <b>fofito</b> logged in!,[ok1]User <b>fofito</b> in
session,[ok2]User <b>fofito</b> logged out!
 grinder.reportToConsole: false
 grinder.mx.arg: -mx
 grinder.jvms: 2
 grinder.appendLog: false
 grinder.times: 5
 grinder.console.multicastAddress: 228.1.1.2
 grinder.cycleMethods: init,url0,url1,url2,end
 grinder.multicastPort: 1234
 grinder.sleepMillis: 5000
 grinder.multicastAddress: 228.1.1.1
 grinder.ms.arg: -ms
 grinder.initialWait: false
 grinder.cycleClass: com.ejbgrinder.grinder.plugin.HttpBmk
 grinder.hostId: 0
```

349

```
grinder.jvm.args: -classpath .;c:/wlsbook/src/c10/lib/grinder1_6_0.jar
grinder.jvm.path: c:/jdk1.3/bin/java
grinder.fileStats: true
grinder.logDir: log
grinder.initialSleepTimes: 2
grinder.console.multicastPort: 1234
grinder.threads: 3
Sun Sep 10 11:26:46 CEST 2000: [c:/jdk1.3/bin/java -classpath
.;c:/wlsbook/src/c10/lib/grinder1_6_0.jar -ms16m -mx32m -Dgrinder.jvmId=0
com.ejbgrinder.grinder.GrinderProcess] [Started]
Sun Sep 10 11:26:46 CEST 2000: [c:/jdk1.3/bin/java -classpath
.;c:/wlsbook/src/c10/lib/grinder1_6_0.jar -ms16m -mx32m -Dgrinder.jvmId=1
com.ejbgrinder.grinder.GrinderProcess] [Started]
```

6. The Grinder is now running. In the WebLogic window, the trace messages show that the server is receiving requests:

```
Sun Sep 10 11:20:48 CEST 2000:<I> <ListenThread> Listening on port: 7001
Sun Sep 10 11:20:48 CEST 2000:<I> <SSLListenThread> Listening on port: 7002
<NT Performance Pack> NATIVE: created IoCompletionPort successfully.
IoPort=0x00000378
Sun Sep 10 11:20:49 CEST 2000:<I> <WebLogicServer> WebLogic Server started
Sun Sep 10 11:25:18 CEST 2000:<I> <NT Performance Pack> Allocating: '2' NT reader
threads
Sun Sep 10 11:25:21 CEST 2000:<I> <ServletContext-General> *.jsp: init
Sun Sep 10 11:25:21 CEST 2000:<I> <ServletContext-General> *.jsp: param verbose
initialized to: true
Sun Sep 10 11:25:21 CEST 2000:<I> <ServletContext-General> *.jsp: param
packagePrefix initialized to: jsw.c10
Sun Sep 10 11:25:21 CEST 2000:<I> <ServletContext-General> *.jsp: param
compileCommand initialized to: c:/jdk1.3/bin/javac.exe
Sun Sep 10 11:25:21 CEST 2000:<I> <ServletContext-General> *.jsp: param
srcCompiler initialized to weblogic.jspc
Sun Sep 10 11:25:21 CEST 2000:<I> <ServletContext-General> *.jsp: param superclass
initialized to null
Sun Sep 10 11:25:21 CEST 2000:<I> <ServletContext-General> *.jsp: param workingDir
initialized to: C:\wlsbook\srv\c10-srv\classfiles
Sun Sep 10 11:25:21 CEST 2000:<I> <ServletContext-General> *.jsp: param
pageCheckSeconds initialized to: 0
Sun Sep 10 11:25:21 CEST 2000:<I> <ServletContext-General> *.jsp: initialization
complete
Trace: login
Trace: login
Trace: login
Trace: login
Trace: login
Trace: login
Trace: status
Trace: status
Trace: status
Trace: status
Trace: status
Trace: status
Trace: logout
Trace: logout
Trace: logout
Trace: logout
Trace: logout
Trace: logout
Trace: login
```

7. When all the iterations are done, the Grinder shows the following messages:

```
Sun Sep 10 11:28:13 CEST 2000: [c:/jdk1.3/bin/java -classpath
.;c:/wlsbook/src/c10/lib/grinder1_6_0.jar -ms16m -mx32m -Dgrinder.jvmId=1
com.ejbgrinder.grinder.GrinderProcess] [Exit Status: 0]
Sun Sep 10 11:28:13 CEST 2000: [c:/jdk1.3/bin/java -classpath
.;c:/wlsbook/src/c10/lib/grinder1_6_0.jar -ms16m -mx32m -Dgrinder.jvmId=0
com.ejbgrinder.grinder.GrinderProcess] [Exit Status: 0]

C:\wlsbook\src\c10\examples\HttpClient>
```

Interested in the test results? The next section will explain how to decipher them.

Viewing the Results

The test results are stored in three files:

❑   The standard output produced by the test, stored in a file with extension `.out`

❑   The standard error produced by the test, stored in a file with extension `.err`

❑   The response time of every request made, stored in a file with extension `.dat`

These files are located in the `log` directory, below the current directory, that is, `c:\wlsbook\src\c10\examples\HttpClient\log`. The test we've just executed has produced two files of each type, one for each virtual machine started by the Grinder.

The summarized results can be found in the output file. The file `grinder_log_0_0.out` holds the output from the first virtual machine started by the Grinder. At the end, it shows some summary statistics from the test on this JVM:

```
Final statistics for this JVM: [hostId=0,jvmId=0]
     (TST=Total Successful Transactions)
     (TPT=Total Processing Time (milliseconds))
     (ART=Average Response Time (seconds))
     (TPS=Transactions Per Second)
     (TUT=Total Unsuccessful Transactions)
     per method:
     url0, TST:15, TPT:322, ART:0.02, TPS:46.58,  TUT:0
     url1, TST:15, TPT:112, ART:0.01, TPS:133.93, TUT:0
     url2, TST:15, TPT:100, ART:0.01, TPS:150.00, TUT:0
total TST=45
total TPT=534
total ART=0.04
total TUT=0
Sun Sep 10 11:41:15 CEST 2000: Grinder process finished
```

The following table contains the same results but in a more readable form:

URL	Successfully completed transactions	Total processing time (milliseconds)	Average response time (seconds)	Transactions per second	Unsuccessfully completed transactions
url0	15	322	0.02	46.58	0
url1	15	112	0.01	133.93	0
url2	15	100	0.01	150.00	0
Sum	45	534	0.04		0

The response time for each request is recorded in the file `grinder_log_0_0.dat`. The file uses a comma-delimited format with the identification of each request and the response time in milliseconds. The first lines of the file are the following:

```
hostId,jvmId,threadId,timesId,methodId,millis
0,0,0,0,url0,131
0,0,1,0,url0,121
0,0,2,0,url0,10
0,0,0,0,url1,0
0,0,1,0,url1,10
```

The `.dat` file can be used for graphical and more detailed statistical analysis of performance data. The following chart was created using the data from the test, by importing it into an Excel spreadsheet and creating a PivotChart report. The chart represents the average response time of the request, grouped by URL.

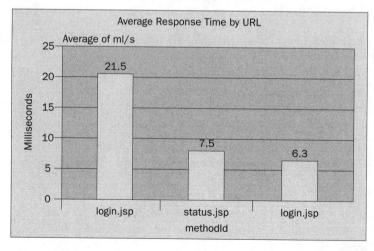

It is important to note that the requests recorded in the `.dat` file are always successfully completed requests. The requests that ended with errors of any kind are not present in this file. We will explain later what the Grinder considers successfully completed requests (or transactions).

Finally, the err file, `grinder_log_0_0.err`, contains the error messages that may occur. If this file is empty, then the test finished without any errors. When running HTTP tests, HTML files can also be generated. These files are generated when the response from the server is not what was expected. They contain the response received from the server and allow you to determine the cause of the error.

The Grinder considers the response to be wrong in several situations, for example, not having connected with the server. Assuming the Grinder connects to the server and receives an HTML page, it will search the page for a string matching the validating string. If it is found, the page is considered valid. If there is no such string, the Grinder will report an error in the err file, save the page and leave out the rest of requests in the current iteration, jumping to the next one. The name of the page fully identifies the client and the request that caused the wrong answer. For example, the file `page-0-1-3-5-2.html` is the wrong response from the request identified by:

- ❏ Host ID = 0
- ❏ JVM ID = 1
- ❏ Thread ID = 3
- ❏ Iteration number = 5
- ❏ URL ID = 2

The validation string is in the `grinder.cycleParams` property, specified by the strings delimited between the [ok*n*] string and the comma (or end of the line). The ok string is associated with the url string by the number suffix.

The Grinder Properties

This section will describe in more detail the Grinder properties that affect the generated workload and its characteristics. As we've shown, the properties can be set in a `grinder.properties` file for the HTTP client, which is on the JVM classpath. They can also be specified on the command line, as a system property, with the –D JVM option:

```
java -Dgrinder.jvms=1 -Dgrinder.times=10 com.ejbgrinder.Grinder
```

Workload

The test in the first section was run with six simultaneous users, which is a relatively small number. As explained above, the Grinder parameters relating to the number of clients are the number of virtual machines to run and the number of threads started on each one. The test run in the previous section can be described by the following diagram:

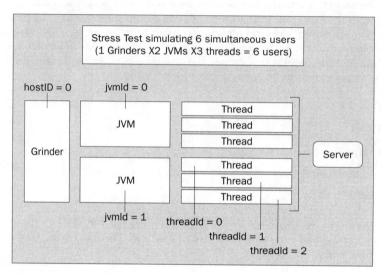

The diagram also illustrates the naming convention for each simulated client:

❏   The host ID, one per Grinder instance

❏   The Java virtual machine ID

❏   The thread ID

❏   The iteration number

The number of simulated users can be increased by modifying the grinder.jvms parameter and/or the grinder.threads. More grinder instances can also be started on the same machine or in others. But what should we increase, the number of Grinders, JVMs, or threads? When testing HTTP applications, all parameters can be increased. This is not true when testing EJBs with WebLogic. When several WebLogic clients run in one JVM, they only use one socket to communicate with the server, even if they have several distinct logical connections with the server, as this optimizes performance. In order to better simulate real EJBs clients, multiple JVMs must be started, with only one thread each.

In our HTTP test case, let's suppose we want to simulate 50 simultaneous users and have a significant amount of performance data. We could set up the following parameters:

```
grinder.jvms=2
grinder.threads=25
grinder.times=10
```

A simple multiplication of these three numbers shows that this test scenario will generate 500 requests per URL.

There are two other parameters that also help to better simulate the workload from real users – `grinder.sleepMillis` and `grinder.initialSleepTimes`.

`grinder.sleepMillis` is the time that a thread waits in between requests; as we saw earlier, this is best thought of as 'think time'. The response time is recorded from the instant the request is started to the time the response is completed, not taking into account the think time. The think time allows the Grinder to simulate concurrent HTTP clients, as this situation is similar to real life.

The `grinder.initialSleepTimes` property allows for a smooth beginning of the test. If all the clients start accessing the server at the same time, it can overload the server, which does not correspond to a real-life situation. The Grinder starts all the threads at the same time, but each one will wait a number of milliseconds before its first request. This number is a random one between 0 and the result of multiplying `grinder.sleepMillis` by `grinder.initialSleepTimes`. If we take a look at the output file we can see the resulting initial random number as follows:

```
jvmId=0: started at Sun Sep 10 19:35:58 CEST 2000
<I> <CycleThread-run> Random initial wait (millis)=7357 current=[0,0,0]
<I> <CycleThread-run> Random initial wait (millis)=1634 current=[0,0,1]
<I> <CycleThread-run> Random initial wait (millis)=2713 current=[0,0,2]
<I> <CycleThread-run> Random initial wait (millis)=518 current=[0,0,3]
```

The numbers between brackets are the host ID, JVM ID, and thread ID, identifying the simulated client. The test can be run again increasing the think time. Common values for this property range between 5 and 25 seconds. By increasing the `grinder.initialSleepTimes` property, a smoother start can be obtained. This property introduces randomness without compromising the correctness of the recorded performance data.

Specifying Transactions

There are three main properties for specifying the type of work the Grinder has to perform:

- ❑   `grinder.cycleClass`
- ❑   `grinder.cycleMethods`
- ❑   `grinder.cycleParams`

The `grinder.cycleClass` property indicates the plugin class that will be executed by each thread. For HTTP tests, the class provided, `com.ejbgrinder.grinder.plugin.HttpBmk`, will satisfy most testing requirements. Other plugin classes (`SimpleBmk` and `SimpleEJBBmk`) are also provided with this chapter's source code. Writing plugins is described in the next sections.

The `grinder.cycleMethods` property indicates the Java methods of the previous class that the Grinder will call on each step of the cycle. The first and the last are always `init` and `end`, respectively. The rest can be `url0`, `url1`, `url2`, and so on up to `url50`. These methods are present in the class `com.ejbgrinder.grinder.plugin.HttpBmk`. There must be at least as many methods as the number of URLs you request in each cycle. In the example there are three URLs to visit, so the property is defined as:

```
grinder.cycleMethods=init,url0,url1,url2,end
```

The `grinder.cycleParams` property is passed by the Grinder to the plugin during its initialization. In the case of the `HttpBmk` plugin, which makes the HTTP tests, it contains the following information:

❑ Whether the plugin should keep and resend cookies sent by the web server in its response. The relevant cookie here is the one that keeps the servlet session identifier. The parameter is `[keepSession]true`.

❑ Whether the plugin must write the response to an output file. This is set up mainly for debug purposes, using the parameter `[logHtml]false`.

❑ The URLs to be requested by each of the methods previously defined, in the desired order. The parameter follows the pattern `[urln]http://....` The number (n) associates the URL with the method in the `grinder.cycleMethods` property.

❑ The string to validate the response from the web server. The parameter follows the pattern `[okn]validating-string`. The number (n) associates the string with the corresponding URL.

As a reminder, the value of this property in the previous example is shown here:

```
grinder.cycleParams= \
   [keepSession]true,\
   [logHtml]false,\
   [url0]http://localhost:7001/login.jsp?user=fofito&password=bond007,\
   [url1]http://localhost:7001/status.jsp,\
   [url2]http://localhost:7001/logout.jsp,\
   [ok0]User <b>fofito</b> logged in!,\
   [ok1]User <b>fofito</b> in session,\
   [ok2]User <b>fofito</b> logged out!
```

The URLs can include a request string. In the example, the first URL, `url0`, has two parameters in the request string, `user=fofito` and `password=bond007`. The Grinder will request the URL as specified, including the request string.

In Chapters 11 and 12 these properties will be configured to load-test the programs of the previous chapters.

Index of Properties

The following table lists all the Grinder properties, with their meanings, and default values:

Property	Meaning	Default value
`grinder.hostId`	An identifier for this Grinder instance	`grinder.hosted=0`
`grinder.cycleClass`	The Java class with which to grind the application	`grinder.cycleClass= com.ejbgrinder. grinder.plugin. SimpleBmk`
`grinder.cycleMethods`	The methods in the class to be called by the Grinder	`grinder.cycleMethods= init,methodA,methodB, methodC,end`
`grinder.cycleParams`	The parameters to pass to the class	`grinder.cycleParams= [paramA]a,[paramB]500, [paramC]10.2`

Property	Meaning	Default value
`grinder.jvms`	The number of JVMs to start	`grinder.jvms=1`
`grinder.ms`	The minimum heap size of the JVM to start, in megabytes	`grinder.ms=16`
`grinder.mx`	The maximum heap size of the JVM to start, in megabytes	`grinder.mx=32`
`grinder.threads`	The number of threads to create in each JVM	`grinder.threads=2`
`grinder.times`	The number of times to repeat each method call in order	`grinder.times=3`
`grinder.initialWait`	Whether the Grinder should wait at the beginning for a signal from the Console	`grinder.initialWait=false`
`grinder.multicastAddress`	The multicast IP address on which the Grinder will expect Console commands	`grinder.multicastAddress=228.1.1.1`
`grinder.multicastPort`	The port to which the Grinder will listen for Console commands	`grinder.multicastPort=1234`
`grinder.logDir`	The directory to save log and statistics data to	`grinder.logDir=.`
`grinder.appendLog`	If the log and data are to be appended or not to the existing file.	`grinder.appendLog=false`
`grinder.fileStats`	If the Grinder will save performance data to a file for statistical analysis	`grinder.fileStats=true`
`grinder.reportToConsole`	If the Grinder is to send performance data to the Console	`grinder.reportToConsole=false`
`grinder.console.multicastAddress`	The multicast IP address to which the Console will listen for data from the Grinder	`grinder.console.multicastAddress=228.1.1.2`
`grinder.console.multicastPort`	The port to which the Console will listen for data from the Grinder	`grinder.console.multicastPort=1234`
`grinder.ms.arg`	The name of the ms parameter in the virtual machine, which specifies the initial size, in bytes, of the memory allocation pool	`grinder.ms.arg=-ms`
`grinder.mx.arg`	The name of the mx parameter in the virtual machine, which specifies the maximum size, in bytes, of the memory allocation pool	`grinder.mx.arg=-mx`

Table continued on following page

Property	Meaning	Default value
`grinder.jvm.path`	The absolute path of the binary to start the virtual machine	`grinder.jvm.path=` `c:\jdk1.2.2\bin\java`
`grinder.` `sleepMillis`	The time to wait between two consecutives method invocations	`grinder.sleepMillis=0`
`grinder.` `initialSleepTimes`	Used to calculate the random amount of time to wait before the first method invocation	`grinder.` `initialSleepTimes=0`

We'll see what the Console is in a few sections time.

Extending the Grinder

The Grinder application can be extended to suit the needs of your own application. In order to do this effectively, you need to know something of its design, which is what we'll cover here.

The Grinder Architecture

While most of the tests planned by the Wonder Troops concern HTTP applications, they decided to design the Grinder with an open architecture allowing other kinds of applications to be tested. By designing the testing tool in a generic way, they could test, for example, the applications of Chapter 7, which have a Java-based user interface.

Basically, they come up with an architecture composed of two parts:

❑ A central part responsible for iterations, instances, and registration of execution time

❑ A variable part providing the code to be iterated. Each element here is called a **plugin**

The following UML class diagram shows all the classes and interfaces that make the Grinder, as well as the relationship between them.

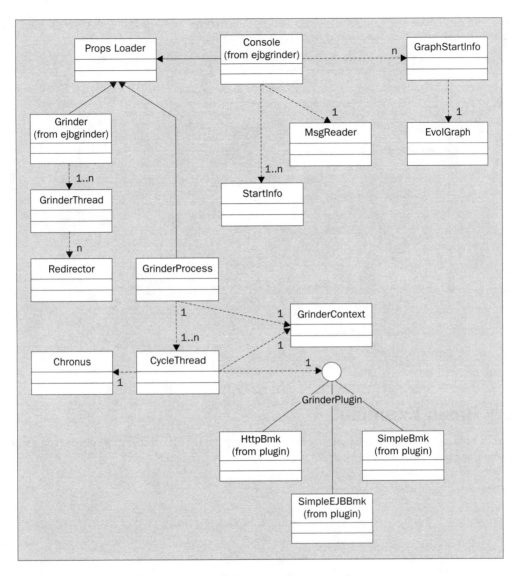

The plugin part of the Grinder is the set of classes implementing the
com.ejbgrinder.grinder.GrinderPlugin interface. Any classes implementing this interface can
be specified in the grinder.cycleClass property.

The role of each class and interface is described in the corresponding Javadoc documentation. The architecture can be better understood from the following figure:

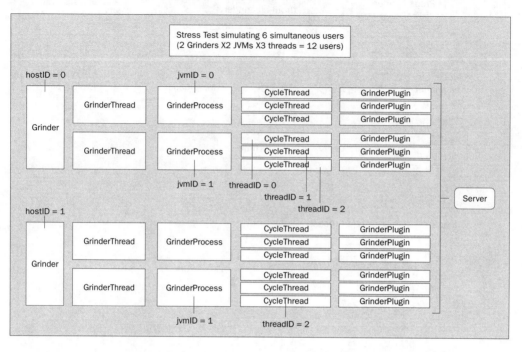

A Very Basic Example

A Grinder plugin is a class implementing the com.ejbgrinder.grinder.GrinderPlugin interface. This interface is defined as follows:

```
package com.ejbgrinder.grinder;

/**
 * The interface a valid Grinder plugin must implement.
 */
public interface GrinderPlugin {

  /**
   * This method is executed the first time the plugin is
   * loaded. It is executed only once. It allows the
   * plugin initialization passing the GrinderContext
   * from the Grinder to the plugin.
   */
  public void init(GrinderContext grinderContext);

  /**
   * This method is executed at the end of the iterations.
   * It is executed only once. It allows the plugin
   * finalization.
   */
  public void end();

}
```

Obviously, a Grinder plugin should include more than these two methods (init() and end()). The following valid plugin, SimpleBmk.java, defines three more methods: methodA(), methodB(), and methodC():

```java
package com.ejbgrinder.grinder.plugin;

import com.ejbgrinder.grinder.GrinderContext;
import com.ejbgrinder.grinder.GrinderPlugin;

/**
 * Simple Java application benchmark.
 *
 */
public class SimpleBmk implements GrinderPlugin {

  public void init(GrinderContext gc) {
    System.out.println("calling init");
    _paramA = gc.paramAsString("paramA");
    _paramB = gc.paramAsInt("paramB");
    _paramC = gc.paramAsDouble("paramC");
  }

  public void methodA() {
    System.out.println("calling methodA. paramA=" + _paramA);
  }

  public void methodB() {
    System.out.println("calling methodB. paramB=" + _paramB);
  }

  public void methodC() {
    System.out.println("calling methodC. paramC=" + _paramC);
  }

  public void end() {
    System.out.println("calling end");
  }

  String _paramA = "";
  int _paramB = 0;
  double _paramC = 0.0;
}
```

The SimpleBmk plugin doesn't really do anything interesting, but illustrates two other important rules of a plugin:

❑ The iteration methods must be declared public, returning no value and without parameters

❑ The initialization parameters of a plugin are passed from the Grinder to the plugin within an object of class com.ejbgrinder.grinder.GrinderContext, passed as an argument in the init() method.

The parameter `gc` of class `GrinderContext` allows the plugin to retrieve the parameters from the `grinder.cycleParams` as values of a given type. The properties for this example are in the `grinder.properties` file in the directory `c:\wlsbook\src\c10\examples\basic`. It is worth having a look at the following properties in this file:

```
grinder.cycleClass=com.ejbgrinder.grinder.plugin.SimpleBmk
grinder.cycleMethods=init,methodA,methodB,methodC,end
grinder.cycleParams= \
  [paramA]a,\
  [paramB]500,\
  [paramC]10.2
```

Load Testing EJBs

A third example illustrates a plugin designed to test an EJB. The EJB to test is a stateless session EJB, the `Trader`, which comes as a basic EJB example with the WebLogic server.

> *The EJB is inside the file `ejb_basic_statelessSession.jar`, which was deployed with the `make deploy` command at the beginning of this chapter. In order to run this example, the WebLogic server must be up and running.*

If we take a look at the `grinder.properties` file in the `c:\wlsbook\src\c10\examples\EjbClient` directory, we can see the plugin class used in the test, the order of execution of its methods, and the initialization parameters:

```
grinder.cycleClass=com.ejbgrinder.grinder.plugin.SimpleEJBBmk
grinder.cycleMethods=init,connect,buy,sell,buy,disconnect,end
grinder.cycleParams= \
  [serverURL]t3://localhost:7001,\
  [stock]BEAS,\
  [buy]100,\
  [sell]25
```

The initialization parameters are retrieved in the plugin `init()` method (from `SimpleEJBBmk.java`):

```
public void init(GrinderContext gc) {
  System.out.println("calling init");
  _gc = gc;
  _serverURL = gc.paramAsString("serverURL");
  _stock     = gc.paramAsString("stock");
  _sell      = gc.paramAsInt("sell");
  _buy       = gc.paramAsInt("buy");
}
```

The parameters are stored in fields for later use. The fields are defined as follows:

```
String _serverURL   = "";
String _stock       = "";
int    _sell        = 0;
int    _buy         = 0;

protected Trader          _trader = null;
protected Context         _ctx    = null;
protected GrinderContext  _gc     = null;
```

The server is contacted and the EJB is instantiated in the connect() method:

```
public void connect() {
  System.out.println("calling connect");
  try {
    _ctx = Util.getInitialContext(_serverURL);
    TraderHome brokerage = (TraderHome)
                          _ctx.lookup("statelessSession.TraderHome");
    _trader = brokerage.create();

    System.out.println("SimpleEJBBmk: EJB contacted");
  } catch(Exception e) {
    System.err.println("SimpleEJBBmk: an exception has occurred when " +
                       "trying to contact JNDI:");
    System.err.println("SimpleEJBBmk: " + e);
    e.printStackTrace(System.err);
    _gc.setErrorIteration(true);
    _gc.setStopIteration(true);
  }
}
```

The buy() EJB business method is called in the buy() plugin method:

```
public void buy() {
  System.out.println("calling buy");
  try {
    TradeResult tr = _trader.buy(_stock, _buy);
    System.out.println("SimpleEJBBmk: EJB buy invoked: " + _stock + ", "
                       + _buy);
  } catch(Exception e) {
    System.err.println("SimpleEJBBmk: an exception has occurred:");
    System.err.println("SimpleEJBBmk: " + e);
    e.printStackTrace(System.err);
    _gc.setErrorIteration(true);
    _gc.setSkipIteration(true);
  }
}
```

Then sell() EJB business method is then called in the sell() plugin method:

```
public void sell() {
  System.out.println("calling sell");
  try {
    TradeResult tr = _trader.buy(_stock, _sell);
    System.out.println("SimpleEJBBmk: EJB sell invoked: "
                       + _stock + ", " + _sell);
  } catch(Exception e) {
    System.err.println("SimpleEJBBmk: an exception has occurred:");
    System.err.println("SimpleEJBBmk: " + e);
    e.printStackTrace(System.err);
    _gc.setErrorIteration(true);
    _gc.setSkipIteration(true);
  }
}
```

Finally, there is a call to the EJB's `remove()` method in the `disconnect()` plugin method:

```
public void disconnect() {
  System.out.println("calling disconnect");
  try {
    _trader.remove();
    System.out.println("SimpleEJBBmk: EJB removed.");
  } catch(Exception e) {
    System.err.println("SimpleEJBBmk: an exception has occurred when " +
                       "trying to close an EJB conection:");
    System.err.println("SimpleEJBBmk: " + e);
    e.printStackTrace(System.err);
    _gc.setErrorIteration(true);
    _gc.setStopIteration(true);
  }
}
```

Special use of the `GrinderContext` parameter is made in this plugin, with the methods `setErrorIteration(boolean)` and `setSkipIteration(boolean)`. These methods instruct the Grinder to log an error and jump to the next iteration, passing over the execution of the rest of methods in the current iteration. This feature is introduced to reduce the number of errors produced. For example, if the `connect()` method cannot instantiate the EJB, then the rest of methods will also generate supporting errors, so there is no point in executing the `buy()`, `sell()`, and `disconnect()` methods, and it's better to jump to the next iteration.

The Grinder Console

The Grinder console is another program that the Troops developed. It is a basic tool for control and monitoring of one or several Grinder instances.

The console can coordinate the synchronized start of several Grinders instances. By setting the property `grinder.initialWait` to `true`, the Grinder instance will wait until a signal from the Console arrives to start execution. To start the Console you need to change the directory on the host machine to `c:\wlsbook\src\c10` and type `setenv`. This will put the necessary files into the classpath. To initiate the console from here type the `java com.ejbgrinder.Console` command. To send the start signal from the Grinder console, just press the **StartGrinder** button on the console itself.

The Grinder instances can send performance data to the Console while they are running. If the property `grinder.reportToConsole` is set to `true`, the instances will send this information to be displayed by the console, as shown in the next figure:

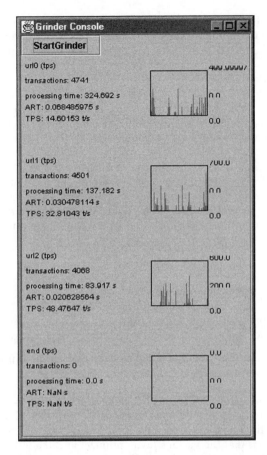

The Wonder Troops are pretty happy with the resulting test load application as it provides them with a free tool with which to test their application under stressful conditions. They are aware that a lot can be improved in this application, particularly in the area of defining the test script. They hope and expect readers to contribute their improvements and place them in the public domain.

A Testing Methodology

Now that we have a tool, we need to have a consistent method to be able to test the behavior of the applications correctly. The most important thing here is to be consistent across all the measurements. For example, it does not matter if you state that a 2 foot ruler is actually 1 meter, as long as you always use that ruler for all your measurements.

The Business Transaction

The first step is to define a **business transaction**. This is a collection of URLs (in the case of an HTTP-based application) or methods (in the case of a Java-based client) that models the expected behavior of a typical visitor to your web site or application. The intention is to talk about the performance of the application being measured in terms of the business transaction.

For example, in the case of an e-commerce web site, a typical visitor will search the catalog a few times, place a couple of goods in the shopping basket, order them, and check out. In some cases, where there are various very well defined profiles of visitors, you can have more than one business transaction.

The business transaction does not have to exercise all the URLs or code of the application; it just has to replicate a typical usage of the application as closely as possible. This means for example, that you should try to avoid the use of the same customer if this is used as a key for a critical database search. Another example is not to place the same product in the shopping basket if the catalog is rather large, since this could be buffered in memory and produce a less realistic performance number by avoiding an actual database search.

The only thing that can safely be altered from a real customer's interaction is the think time. It is logistically impractical to define think times of 2 or 3 minutes in a stress test, which is the case when some forms have to be filled. The recommendation is to reduce these times to anywhere between 5 and 25 seconds, which will still do the trick by creating a necessary pause between the usage of URLs or methods.

Performance

Performance numbers are used for two main reasons.

❑ The first and probably the most important reason is to make sure that the response times of the URLs or methods of the application are within the defined ranges

❑ The second reason is to create a behavior pattern that can help predict where the application no longer performs adequately

In both cases a specific number of interactions has to be defined. This is the number of times a client will execute the business transaction. You want to choose a large enough number to give you a good statistical sample, but small enough so that your test runs don't take hours. Another reason for having a fair number of interactions is that the various Java optimizers need a few interactions to improve the performance of the code. Stress tests usually have 3 to 10 iterations of the business transaction.

In the first case, you have to analyze the individual response times of each URL or method and verify that the response time falls within the defined range. Some companies define as an adequate response that an application should present an HTML screen within two seconds from the moment it was requested. This is the limit for human beings before they perceive the application as being too slow. Whatever the time period, it can usually be broken down into:

❑ A processing component
❑ A transmission component
❑ A display component

Since the clients of a stress test are not real browsers, the display component cannot really be measured. The transmission component will not be very accurate either, as these tests typically happen on an isolated network, which does not have additional traffic competing for bandwidth.

Usually, though, the actual performance measured under stress-test conditions is dominated by the processing component. In most companies the unspoken rule of thumb is a 'sub-second' response time. Whatever your defined response is, you need to verify that each individual URL or method falls within that expected range.

For the second case, the creation of a pattern, the total response time of the business transaction is used instead of the individual URLs or methods, mostly for simplicity.

The pattern is started with a baseline case.

Baseline Case

Now that you have defined the ruler you will use for your application, that is, the business transactions, the number of interactions, and the ranges of acceptable response times, you are ready to start measuring performance. It is best to start with a small discrete number of simultaneous clients and understand how the application behaves under normal conditions. This will be called the **baseline case**.

By using the baseline case on different JVMs, operating systems, or combinations of hardware, you should get a good idea of how your application will behave by just looking at the total response time of the business transaction. You can always review the individual response times to better understand the more expensive operations of your application.

The objective of the baseline case is to be able to make a statement like, "With X simultaneous users the application had an average response time of Y milliseconds for a typical usage. The highest response time was for URL Z with T milliseconds."

Typically baseline cases are defined with something like 50 users, five interactions of the business transaction, and one second of maximum response time for any given URL or method. Your case may well be different, especially if you expect many thousands of simultaneous users, when 1000 users will produce a more meaningful baseline case.

Stress Tests

Now that you have a fair idea of the performance of your application under calm conditions, you are ready to start really stressing it. This has to be done in an orderly manner for it to make sense. The idea is to increase the user load while all the other parameters remain the same. The business transaction, the number of interactions, the WebLogic Server, the JVM and its arguments, the operating system, the hardware configuration, etc. remain the same.

The increase in the load should be stepped in such a way that a meaningful performance chart can be drawn. Admittedly this is a case of trial and error at first, but the more you run the stress tests, the more familiar you will become with your application and its behavior. For example, if you start with 50 users and then increase the load to 100 users and notice a significant degradation in performance, you will be better off by increasing the load in 10s of users starting at 50 to understand what happens in between. On the other hand, in the same example, if you notice no impact in the response time, you might venture to increase the user load to 200 and analyze the results to define the next stress test.

Once you have reached the limits of the application, that is, when the response times no longer fall within the acceptable ranges you have defined, you can start analyzing the reasons for this. The next step is to look for ways of optimizing the various components (WebLogic Server properties, JVM parameters, database tuning, OS tuning, etc.) that relate to the application. For every change you should have a new run with the baseline case to understand the impact of the change. Once you feel comfortable with the change and its impact, you can start stress testing the application again.

When the fine-tuning is complete, you should have a very good idea of when the application will reach its limits and can start planning for this event.

Summarizing, the proposed methodology is the following:

- ❏ Define the business transaction
- ❏ Define the number of interactions, and acceptable ranges of response times for the individual URLs or methods
- ❏ Define and execute the baseline case
- ❏ Increase the user load in a meaningful fashion until you exceed the acceptable ranges of performance
- ❏ Analyze the reasons for exceeding those limits. If there are any changes, redo the stress test starting with the baseline case

Summary

In this chapter we have introduced the need for and solution to the workload test phase. This stage can be very useful for several goals including:

- ❏ Preventing unexpected runtime situations before going into production
- ❏ Identifying the performance of the application
- ❏ Performance tuning the application and platform
- ❏ Identifying architectural or implementation pitfalls in the application
- ❏ Identifying potential sources of improvement in the application
- ❏ Capacity planning

We presented the Grinder, a tool to load-test applications. We saw how to set up and run HTTP-based load tests with the Grinder, as well as how to analyze the results obtained. We also learned how to load-test server-side EJBs and how to extend the Grinder by creating customized plugins. Finally, we presented a methodology for stress testing the application.

The final two chapters will load-test the different versions of the Pizza2Go web site using the Grinder. The Wonder Troops will be looking at how the different versions react under stressing and comparing them, to find out which one is the best bet.

Pizza2Go

11

Grinding the Pizzas

In this chapter the Wonder Troops will be conducting a series a load tests using the Grinder to understand how the different versions of their experiments work under stress conditions. The first step is to set up the testing environment and prepare the Grinder to create the appropriate stress loads. The tests to be performed are the following:

- ❑ Selecting a Java Virtual Machine
- ❑ Testing the application developed in Chapter 3
- ❑ Testing the stateless session beans version developed in Chapter 4
- ❑ Testing the stateful session bean version developed in Chapter 4
- ❑ Testing the entity bean version developed in Chapter 5
- ❑ Testing the JMS Point-to-Point application developed in Chapter 7
- ❑ Testing the JMS Publish and Subscribe application developed in Chapter 7

The Test Environment

The test environment for these experiments is composed of various machines organized as shown in the diagram below.

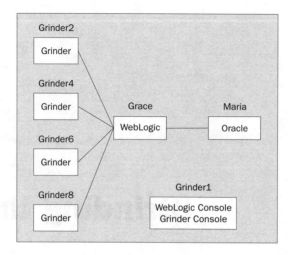

The specification details for the machines are presented in the following table:

Name	CPU	Clock Speed	Memory	O/S
Grace	Pentium III	450MHz	256MB	NT Workstation 4.0 SP5
Maria	Pentium III	500MHZ	256MB	NT Workstation 4.0 SP5
Grinder1, Grinder2, Grinder4, Grinder6, Grinder8	Pentium II	350MHZ	256MB	NT Workstation 4.0 SP5

All of these machines have 100Mb Ethernet cards and are connected to a Compaq 100BASE-TX Hub (model HB2122).

The WebLogic server running on Grace is version 5.1.0 with Service Pack 4. For all the tests in this chapter WebLogic will also be acting as the web server. The Oracle database running on Maria is version 8.1.5. Oracle is used just as it would come out of the box, as no alterations are made. Maria will also be used as a central file store repository to pick up the applications and deposit the results of the tests.

The Business Transaction

The first thing that needs to be done is to define a typical business transaction for Pizza2Go. This will be used as the main unit of measurement. It is decided that placing an order with three different pizzas will represent a typical transaction.

The next step is to represent this transaction in the `grinder.properties` file. The Grinder does not have a recording mechanism, so the model business transaction will have to be created manually by replicating the actions of an operator when interacting with the browser.

The first thing the operator does is to execute the main menu of the host machine. This is defined in the `grinder.properties` file by replacing the `localhost` with the name of the host machine; in this case the name of the host is `Grace`.

```
[url0]http://localhost:7001/index.jsp,\
```

This is changed to:

```
[url0]http://grace:7001/index.jsp,\
```

The `url0` specifies that it is the first URL of the business transaction or grinder cycle. What follows is a normal statement of execution of the `index.jsp` running on the server named Grace on port 7001. Notice that the line finishes with a comma to signify that another URL continues, and a backslash to tell the Grinder that there are more lines after this one.

The next step is where the operator selects the customer search button. When this button is selected the `CustomerSearch.jsp` is executed. To mimic this operation the following statement is defined:

```
[url1]http://grace:7001/CustomerSearch.jsp,\
```

Next, the operator needs to provide a phone number to search for that specific customer. Since the actual search will be done by the `CustomerSearchS` servlet, this is what has to be called by the Grinder. This servlet also requires some arguments so the resulting Grinder statement is:

```
[url2]http://grace:7001/CustomerSearchS?c_country_code=1&\
                          c_area_code=305&\
                          c_phone=9758841,\
```

This searches for a customer with a telephone number with country code 1, area code 305 and phone number 975-8841. The problem with this statement is that every order will be from the same customer, and therefore would not be a particularly realistic stress test for real-life situations.

The ideal way to resolve this issue is to have the ability to generate a different telephone number for every order. A simple algorithm for this is:

```
555 + Grinder ID Number + Grinder JVM ID Number + Grinder Thread Number
```

This information is available in the Grinder and is defined in the properties file. For a Grinder with ID number 2, running on 2 JVMs with 25 threads (meaning 50 simultaneous users), the sequence of telephone numbers is 555-2000 through 555-2024 for the first JVM, and 555-2100 through 555-2124 for the second JVM.

To achieve this, the troops hack the Grinder plug-in: `HttpBmkWlsBook`. This plug-in is a specialized version of the `HttpBmk` plug-in described in Chapter 10, so that when a keyword is found it is replaced by the result of running the algorithm. The keyword chosen is `$GRINDER_VARIABLE`, and the final statement for the Grinder is the following:

```
[url2]http://grace:7001/CustomerSearchS?c_country_code=1&\
                          c_area_code=305&\
                          c_phone=$GRINDER_VARIABLE,\
```

So that the Grinder knows that it will have to parse the URLs looking for this variable, a property is added at the beginning of the properties file:

```
grinder.transformURL=true
```

When the previous statement is executed and the customer exists in the database, the screen presents the information about that customer. Now we want to add an order. When the 'add order' button is clicked, the `OrderMaintenanceS` servlet is executed and requires an argument to specify the action of adding an order:

```
[url3]http://grace:7001/OrderMaintenanceS?command=Add%20Order,\
```

Notice that the argument to be passed contains a space. To handle this, the hexadecimal representation of the ASCII value of the space character (%20) is used. You also have to make sure that upper and lower cases of the arguments are respected, otherwise this will generate problems.

Now the first pizza is added to the order with the following statement:

```
[url4]http://grace:7001/OrderMaintenanceS?Pizza=Calabrese&\
                                          Size=Medium&\
                                          Dough=Classic&\
                                          Quantity=1&\
                                          command=Add,\
```

As are the additional two pizzas:

```
[url5]http://grace:7001/OrderMaintenanceS?Pizza=Margherita&\
                                          Size=Large&\
                                          Dough=Classic&\
                                          Quantity=1&\
                                          command=Add,\
[url6]http://grace:7001/OrderMaintenanceS?Pizza=Napolitana&\
                                          Size=Small&\
                                          Dough=Thin%20Crust&\
                                          Quantity=1&\
                                          command=Add,\
```

The next step in the sequence is to update the order. Here the servlet needs to know if the order is for delivery or pickup and any possible remarks. For these tests it is chosen to be a home delivery with no remarks:

```
[url7]http://grace:7001/OrderMaintenanceS?Delivery=Address&\
                                          Remarks=&\
                                          command=Update%20order,\
```

Finally, the order is set for delivery:

```
[url8]http://grace:7001/OrderMaintenanceS?command=Deliver,\
```

The Grinder has the capability of verifying the response of every URL defined. If the response is not the expected one, the Grinder skips the rest of the cycle and starts a new one from the beginning. If it is the expected response, it continues with the execution of the next URL.

This verification is done with a Grinder OK statement. An OK statement defines a string, any string that will be present in the HTML page given with a successful response. In the case of URL0 the OK statement is:

```
[ok0]Pizza2Go Main Menu,\
```

The rest of the OK statements for the URLs previously defined are:

```
[ok1]Search,\
[ok2]Existing customer,\
[ok3]New order succesfully created,\
[ok4]Pizza succesfully added,\
[ok5]Pizza succesfully added,\
[ok6]Pizza succesfully added,\
[ok7]Order succesfully updated,\
[ok8]Pizza2Go Order
```

Now that the script has been defined, there are a few other parameters that have to be defined in the `grinder.properties` file. The first one defines that the test will be based on an HTML client and therefore it should use the corresponding plug-in. This is done with the following statement, which is placed before the script we defined earlier:

```
grinder.cycleClass=jsw.c11.HttpBmkWlsBook
```

Next, the Grinder needs to know how many URLs the test script contains. This is done as follows:

```
grinder.cycleMethods=init,url0,url1,url2,url3,url4,url5,url6,url7,url8,end
```

The actual test script is defined with the following statement:

```
grinder.cycleParams=\
```

Since the test is HTML, the Grinder offers a couple of options for the script. The first one denotes whether we want to keep the test script in the same HTTP session. This is defined with:

```
[keepSession]true,\
```

The other option is to specify whether we want the Grinder to generate a log of the HTML that is generated. This option is useful to debug the test script.

```
[logHtml]true,\
```

After this comes all the test script with its URL and OK statements.

Another parameter that can be defined in the Grinder is the time to 'sleep' between executing the different URLs of the test script. This adds a degree of realism to the tests, since in the real life not all the URLs are executed immediately one after another. For these tests a sleep of 10 seconds will be used:

```
grinder.sleepMillis=10000
```

Now that the basic test script is done, the troops will give it a test to see if it works correctly. For this they enable the option to log HTML, and define that the test will run only once, on one JVM with one thread:

```
grinder.hostId=2

grinder.jvms=1
grinder.threads=1
grinder.times=1
```

This test is run like the previous tests in Chapter 10. Just open two command line consoles, one for the WebLogic server and another for the Grinder, and follow these instructions:

1. On the Grinder window, change to the source for Chapter 11 directory, and set the environment:

```
C:\> cd \wlsbook\src\c11

C:\wlsbook\src\c11>setenv
------------------------------------------------------------
Current settings:
      Java Home = c:\jdk1.3
   WebLogic Home = c:\weblogic
    Grinder Home = c:\wlsbook\src\c10
      CLASSPATH =
.;c:\weblogic\lib\weblogic510sp4boot.jar;c:\weblogic\classes\boot;c:\weblogic\lib\
weblogic510sp4.jar;c:\weblogic\license;c:\weblogic\classes;c:\weblogi
caux.jar;c:\wlsbook\src\c10\lib\grinder1_6_0.jar;
c:\wlsbook\src\c11\classes

           PATH = c:\wlsbook\bin;c:\jdk1.3\bin;C:\WINNT\system32;C:\WINNT

C:\wlsbook\src\c11>
```

2. On the WebLogic window, change to the `wlsbook` directory, set the environment for Chapter 3 and start the server by using the `startwls` command:

```
C:\> cd \wlsbook

C:\wlsbook>setenv 3
------------------------------------------------------------
Setting SERVER environment for chapter 3
------------------------------------------------------------
Current settings:
      Java Home = c:\jdk1.3
   WebLogic Home = c:\weblogic
    Project Home = c:\wlsbook
      CLASSPATH = c:\weblogic\lib\weblogic510sp4boot.jar;c:\weblogic\classes\boot;
c:\weblogic\lib\weblogic510sp4.jar;c:\weblogic\license;c:\weblogic\classes;c:\webl
ogic\lib\weblogicaux.jar;c:\wlsbook\srv\c03-srv\serverclasses

           PATH = c:\wlsbook\bin;c:\jdk1.3\bin;c:\orant\bin;C:\WINNT\
system32;c:\weblogic\bin;c:\weblogic\bin\oci815_8

C:\wlsbook>startwls
Sun Sep 10 11:20:08 CEST 2000:<I> <WebLogicServer> Read global properties
c:\wlsbook\weblogic.properties
…
```

3. Back to the Grinder window, change to the `test\c03` directory and start the Grinder:

```
C:\wlsbook\src\c11> cd test

C:\wlsbook\src\c11\test>cd c03

C:\wlsbook\src\c11\test\c03 >java com.ejbgrinder.Grinder
Sun Sep 10 11:26:45 CEST 2000: Grinder (v1.6.0) started with the following
properties:
...
```

4. The Grinder is now running. When all the iterations are done, the results are stored in the directory `c:\wlsbook\src\c11\test\c03\log`.

The test failed when the order was being updated, but the reason was not obvious. After some research, they found that the `OrderMaintenanceS` servlet was expecting the parameter `or_o_outlet_code`, even though it does nothing with it. So to please it, the parameter was set to a value of 99, although it could have been any number:

```
[url7]http://grace:7001/OrderMaintenanceS?Delivery=Address&\
                             Remarks=&\
                             or_o_outlet_code=99&\
                             command=Update%20Order,\
```

Another test with the modification in the script proved successful, so the HTML logging was turned off.

Analyzing the Results

The Grinder provides three kinds of files that are useful to analyze the numeric results of the test runs:

❑   The `.out` file that contains a log of the run and includes summary information of the response times of the run.

❑   The `.dat` file that contains the response times of every URL executed.

❑   The `.err` file that contains any error that occurred during the run.

These files are created with the following naming convention: `grinder_log_GID_JID.ext` where GID is the Grinder ID number as defined in the properties file and JID is the JVM ID number. If a Grinder run specifies that there will be 2 JVMs, there will be two sets of files, one with JID 0 and another with JID 1.

It is important to note that none of the timings collected by the Grinder include the sleep time between the executions of URLs.

The `.out` file can be used to get a quick glance at the performance of the run for that particular Grinder/JVM run. For example, the following is the summary information that will be found at the end of this file:

```
Final statistics for this JVM: [hostId=2,jvmId=0]
     (TST=Total Successful Transactions)
     (TPT=Total Processing Time (miliseconds))
     (ART=Average Response Time (seconds))
```

```
        (TPS=Transactions Per Second)
        (TUT=Total Unsuccessful Transactions)
        per method:
        url0, TST:90,     TPT:1191,     ART:0.01,     TPS:75.57,     TUT:0
        url1, TST:90,     TPT:930,      ART:0.01,     TPS:96.77,     TUT:0
        url2, TST:90,     TPT:4329,     ART:0.05,     TPS:20.79,     TUT:0
        url3, TST:90,     TPT:6119,     ART:0.07,     TPS:14.71,     TUT:0
        url4, TST:90,     TPT:5731,     ART:0.06,     TPS:15.70,     TUT:0
        url5, TST:90,     TPT:5556,     ART:0.06,     TPS:16.20,     TUT:0
        url6, TST:90,     TPT:5251,     ART:0.06,     TPS:17.14,     TUT:0
        url7, TST:90,     TPT:4849,     ART:0.05,     TPS:18.56,     TUT:0
        url8, TST:90,     TPT:5826,     ART:0.06,     TPS:15.45,     TUT:0
  total TST=810
  total TPT=39782.00
  total ART=0.44
  total TUT=0
  Wed Jul 12 01:53:42 CEST 2000: Grinder process finished
```

The `.dat` file contains detailed information on the execution of every URL in the following format:

```
hostId, jvmId, threadId, timesId, methodId, millis
```

The data in this file can be used to feed a spreadsheet and obtain custom summary information.

Selecting a JVM

The first set of tests will be conducted to try various JVMs. The idea is to select the one with the best performance as the JVM to be used for the rest of the tests.

It is decided that this set of tests will be done using the code developed in Chapter 4, where the stateless session beans are used. It is felt that this will cover a wide variety of the J2EE specifications: servlets, JSP, JDBC, JNDI, and the basic stateless session EJBs.

The test will be done by having 100 simultaneous users execute the business transaction. This will be achieved by running the Grinder on 1 JVM and 25 threads on 4 computers. Each user will execute the business transaction three times.

The test script developed earlier in this chapter is designed for the application developed in Chapter 3 therefore some changes need to be made. The main difference is that there is a logout function that will be called at the end of every business transaction or Grinder cycle. The required changes revolve around adding a new URL:

```
grinder.cycleMethods=init,url0,url1,url2,url3,url4,url5,url6,\
                     url7,url8,url9,end

[url9]http://grace:7001/Logout.jsp,\

[ok9]Session successfully ended
```

The script was tested and worked successfully. This test also helped by compiling the JSP pages, this way the actual test runs do not take up compilation time in the first instance in which the JSP pages are called.

To have all 4 Grinders synchronized from the beginning, the test run will be started using the Grinder console. Additionally, no reporting will be done on the console so that no unwanted traffic is traveling on the network.

```
grinder.initialWait=true
grinder.reportToConsole=false
```

Finally the logs are enabled and placed in the desired directory.

```
grinder.logDir=d:/chapter11/results
grinder.appendLog=false
grinder.fileStats=true
```

On the server side, the `weblogic.properties` file is only modified to change the number of execute threads to 30 and the JDBC connection pool to start with 50 connections, up to a maximum of 150 with increments of 5. A discussion on these parameters will be presented later in this chapter. The rest of the values are left with their defaults.

A special note on a parameter generally known as Performance Pack: The performance pack is basically where the WebLogic server has a pool of sockets bypassing the usage of the sockets of the JVM and directly accessing the sockets of the operating system. The performance will increase depending on how much input/output the application does. The performance pack can be enabled or disabled with the following property:

```
weblogic.system.nativeIO.enable=boolean
```

Test 11.1.1 – Sun JDK 1.1.7B

To run this test it is necessary to open three command-line consoles. The third one is for starting the Grinder console. The `grinder.properties` file used here is in directory `c:\wlsbook\src\c11\test\c04a`. To start the console, just follow these instructions:

1. On the Grinder console window, change to the source to the Chapter 11 directory, and set the environment (`setEnv`).

2. Then change to the `test\c04a` directory and start the Grinder console:

```
C:\wlsbook\src\c11> cd test

C:\wlsbook\src\c11\test>cd c04a
C:\wlsbook\src\c11\test\c04a>java com.ejbgrinder.Console
```

The run executed flawlessly in just under six minutes. No errors were detected either by the Grinder or by manually counting the order master and order detail records in the database.

The figure overleaf shows a screenshot of the CPU usage of Grace, the machine running the WebLogic server. It clearly shows the three cycles that each user performs, reaching 100% during the peaks of those cycles.

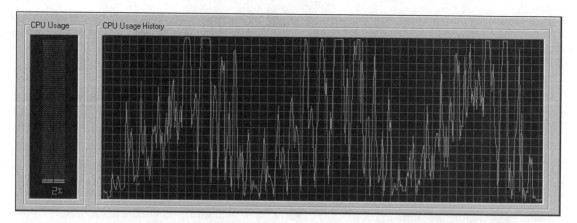

In the following figure you can see a screenshot of the CPU usage of Maria, the machine running the Oracle database. It also shows the three cycles of the business transaction that each user performs.

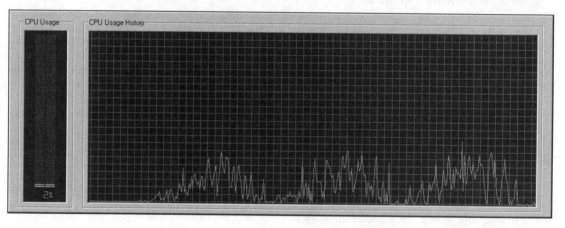

The next figure shows the WebLogic console. There are three points of important information:

❑   The first graph showing the usage of the heap by the application, in this case you can see that the maximum usage was about 75% of the 128MB defined. The see-saw pattern observed in this graph is the result of the garbage collector doing its job clearing memory.

❑   The second graph offers a view of the execute queue length. This is basically a view of the processes that have to wait for a thread of execution. In this case there is a brief moment that there were 8 threads waiting for execution. This little spike can be considered normal and nothing to worry about.

❑   The third graph presents a view of the throughput of the execute threads. It gives an idea of how many tasks per second the WebLogic server is completing. In this case you can see that it is averaging about 30 tasks per second and it peaks up to 60, which is pretty good.

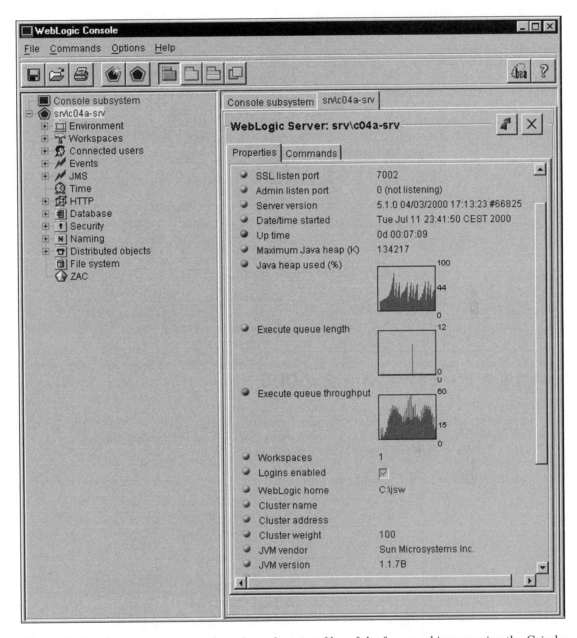

The results for this run are averaged out from the `.dat` files of the four machines running the Grinder, and are presented as the average response time (ART) of the WebLogic server for every URL (in milliseconds), and transactions per second (TPS) calculated as 1/ART in the table overleaf. The totals at the bottom of the table are the sum of the ART column and the corresponding TPS.

Test 11.1.1	ART	TPS
url0	61.69	16.21
url1	13.30	75.21
url2	73.60	13.59
url3	129.20	7.74
url4	202.73	4.93
url5	426.56	2.34
url6	644.29	1.55
url7	768.79	1.30
url8	615.15	1.63
url9	34.25	29.19
Total	**2969.56**	**0.33**

The total average response time for executing the business transaction is close to 3 seconds. Obviously, this number does not include the 10 seconds sleep time between the execution of every URL. It is interesting to learn that with 100 simultaneous users running on a Pentium 3 at 450 MHz the WebLogic server can achieve 153 business transactions (model pizza orders) per second.

Test 11.1.2 – Sun JDK 1.2.2-005

This run was done with Hot Spot disabled since it is not supported by WebLogic on the NT platform. Again, it lasted just under six minutes and again there were no errors detected. The CPU usage of Grace and Maria are pretty much the same as on the previous runs. The information presented in the WebLogic console is also very similar to the previous run.

The results of this run are presented in the following table:

Test 11.1.2	ART	TPS
url0	48.83	20.48
url1	11.28	88.68
url2	78.79	12.69
url3	170.68	5.86
url4	280.47	3.57
url5	512.92	1.95
url6	844.29	1.18
url7	1081.45	0.92
url8	1083.80	0.92
url9	56.21	17.79
Total	**4168.72**	**0.24**

These results came as a surprise. Even though the transactions per second are roughly equivalent, the average response time is about 40% higher than the previous test. The ART was expected to be lower. The troops checked all the properties files from WebLogic and the Grinder and found nothing that could have produced such a significant difference. They even went through the exercise of running this and the previous test again, and obtained similar results.

Test 11.1.3 – Sun JDK 1.3.0-C

One of the interesting claims of this JVM is that it has a code optimizer based on usage statistics gathered while the application is executing. In order to see if this is true the troops decided to run this test twice. The first time will be considered a "warm up" for the optimizer (HotSpot). Then, resetting the database but without resetting WebLogic, the Grinders will execute the test for a second time.

This run lasted about the same amount of time as the previous ones and had one error. The error described in the file `grinder_log_4_0.err` is the following:

```
<E> <HttpBmkWlsBook-proccessUrl> [4,0,15,url=6] error: java.net.SocketException:
Socket closed
Grinder: the plugin reports an error. This method is logged as an
error...(current=[4,0,15,0,url16])
Grinder: the plugin wants to skip this iteration. Jumping to the next
iteration...(current=[4,0,15,0,url16])
```

From this log we can deduce that the error occurred in the WebLogic server by closing the socket that was being used by thread 15. The result is that one pizza order was not processed completely. If this error had happened with an operator interacting with the system, the order would have to be started over from the beginning.

In the corresponding `.out` file the error is presented in the TUT column:

```
url16, TST:74,    TPT:30636,  ART:0.41, TPS:2.42,      TUT:1
```

Let us have a look at the results of this run:

Test 11.2.3.1	ART	TPS
url0	54.67	18.29
url1	12.05	83.01
url2	64.44	15.52
url3	109.67	9.12
url4	164.45	6.08
url5	329.29	3.04
url6	427.10	2.34
url7	431.54	2.32
url8	366.80	2.73
url9	50.20	19.92
Total	**2010.20**	**0.50**

The results are impressive, about half the time of JDK 1.2.2 and substantially less time than JDK 1.1.7B. Also the TPS have increased by about 5%. The figure below shows the CPU usage of Grace:

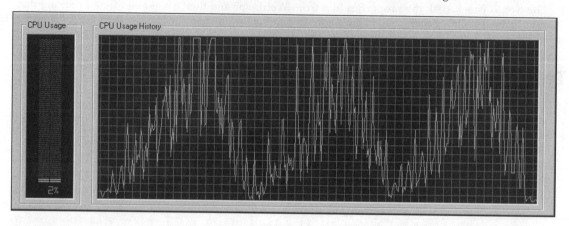

The CPU usage of Maria also presents a smoother curve, shown below:

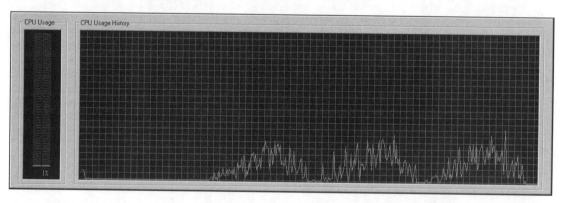

Looking at the console in the following figure we can see also a different graph for the usage of the heap. It appears that the garbage collector (GC) is only called once. This could be because the GC combined with HotSpot is more efficient in the use of memory. We can also see that at no point in time was there a task waiting for an execution thread. All in all it seems that this JVM is more efficient.

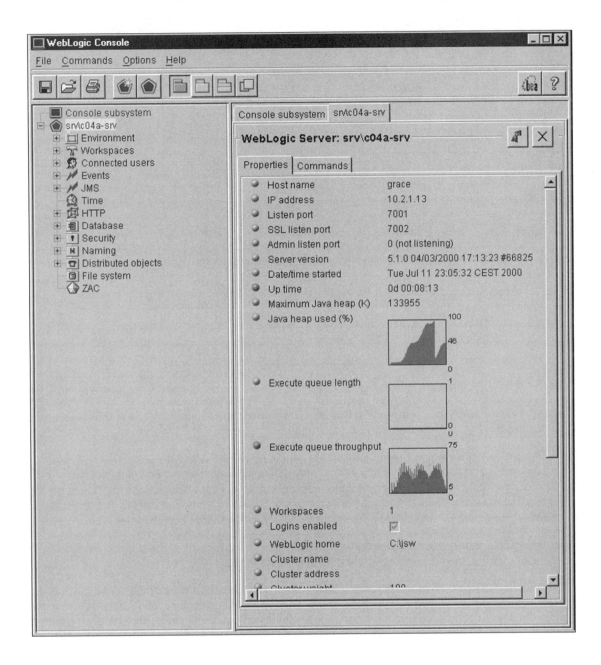

As explained earlier, the second test of this JVM is done by just resetting the database and starting the Grinder processes again. This time there were no errors. The results follow:

URL	ART	TPS
url0	55.77	17.93
url1	12.47	80.17
url2	43.21	23.14
url3	75.87	13.18
url4	151.05	6.62
url5	260.15	3.84
url6	328.37	3.05
url7	370.11	2.70
url8	305.92	3.27
url9	15.91	62.84
Total	**1618.84**	**0.62**

This is even more impressive. The HotSpot optimizer really works. The response time is about 20% better than that obtained during the "warm up" run. The TPS also improved by about 33%. The CPU usage on Grace and Maria was pretty much the same as on the previous run. The graphs presented in the WebLogic console were also similar.

Obviously a run of six cycles would have yielded a different result, which probably would be close to the average of these two runs. A run of 12 cycles would yield a number closer to that of the second test run. The more cycles there are, the more the curve improves up to a point where it stabilizes. The objective of the tests in this chapter is to measure the performance of the application developed in the book, and not to do a study on the performance of HotSpot. This would be a nice exercise for the reader.

To prevent the runs being so time consuming, it is decided that the rest of the test runs in this chapter will be of 3 cycles, even though a 6 cycle run will present better numbers.

The Wonder Troops tried to run the tests with the Microsoft Virtual Machine (Build 3234), but a bug in WebLogic did not allow them to deploy the EJBs. They also tried using the IBM JVM 1.1.8, but at the time of this writing it was unsupported, and trying it therefore produced a large amount of error messages.

Test 11.1.4 – JRockit 1.1.1

This is a very interesting JVM produced by a company in Sweden called Appeal. It is not supported by WebLogic, but the Troops decided to give it a try. The people at Appeal claim that this JVM has been designed specifically for server-side processing and it works in conjunction with the Sun JRE 1.2.2 or 1.3.0. You can find more information on their web site (www.appeal.se).

At the time of writing, JRockit does not fully support native calls. Since the troops were working with the type 2 Oracle JDBC driver from WebLogic that uses native calls to the Oracle OCI library, the test would not be possible. However, trying to satisfy their curiosity, they replaced the JDBC driver of WebLogic with the type 4 JDBC driver provided by Oracle (also known as the thin driver). Since this one does not use native calls, as it is 100% Java, there would be no problems.

Obviously, because of the change of JDBC drivers, this run was not going to be a fair comparison with the previous ones, so this test was conducted out of interest more than anything else.

Because of their success with JDK 1.3.0, the troops decided to use JRE 1.3.0 for the tests with JRockit. Having learned that HotSpot really works, they also did two tests. The first one was a HotSpot warm-up, and the second one only re-initializing the database. The results can be seen side by side in the following table:

Test 11.1.4	Run 1	Run 1	Run 2	Run 2
	ART	TPS	ART	TPS
url0	120.96	8.27	33.32	30.02
url1	21.96	45.53	6.11	163.67
url2	83.78	11.94	37.67	26.54
url3	299.21	3.34	104.87	9.54
url4	306.70	3.26	181.78	5.50
url5	436.59	2.29	263.00	3.80
url6	684.75	1.46	336.33	2.97
url7	804.79	1.24	382.32	2.62
url8	798.15	1.25	795.04	1.26
url9	6.57	152.21	6.48	154.32
Total	**3563.47**	**0.28**	**2146.91**	**0.47**

The results are interesting. You can see that the URLs using the database are slower compared with the other runs. However, the URLs not using JDBC are substantially faster. Because of this we obtain 0.47 TPS on the second run.

In talking with the engineers of Appeal we were told that full JNI support is close to being released. We look forward to testing it as it shows a lot of promise.

Conclusion

When comparing the three JVMs we formally tested in this section, it is obvious that JDK 1.3.0 is better, so this will be used for the rest of the tests in this chapter and the next.

Testing the Servlets

The objective of this set of tests is to understand the upper limit of simultaneous users running the application developed in Chapter 3. This application is based on servlets and JSP pages calling the Oracle stored procedures and accessing the database directly with JDBC calls.

Before we review the `weblogic.properties` file you must be aware of an important property, the number of execution threads. As work enters the WebLogic server, it is placed on an execution queue while waiting to be performed. This work is then assigned to an execution thread to perform the task. This effectively defines the number of simultaneous operations that can be performed by the WebLogic server.

Adding more threads does not necessarily imply that you will be able to process more work. Setting the number of threads too high will cause too much context switching, which will lead to cache thrashing and a higher memory usage. This variable is more dependent on your computer and operating system than on WebLogic.

For this set of tests the number of execute threads is left with its default value of 15.

The WebLogic server is using all the default values in the properties file. Only two modifications have been made. The first one defines the number of milliseconds that WebLogic will wait for a client login request to fail before timing out the socket. The default value is 5,000 milliseconds. This is brought up to 15,000 milliseconds with the following statement:

```
weblogic.login.readTimeoutMillis=15000
```

The reason for this change is that in preliminary tests many errors were produced where the connections were rejected after the default 5 seconds.

The other change is in the JDBC connection pool, which was redefined to start with 15 connections up to a maximum of 150 with increments of 5.

Test 11.2.1 – 60 Users

To have a nice starting point the Troops decide to do the first test with 60 simultaneous users. This is achieved by running the Grinders on 1 JVM with 15 threads on 4 machines. The results are presented in the following table:

Test 11.2.1	ART	TPS
url0	13.91	71.91
url1	8.11	123.29
url2	48.32	20.69
url3	68.57	14.58
url4	63.49	15.75
url5	56.74	17.62
url6	57.29	17.45
url7	50.84	19.67
url8	53.31	18.76
Total	**420.58**	**2.38**

It is interesting to see that such a small machine can easily handle 60 simultaneous users running an application that is pretty close to a real one. The CPU of Grace, the machine running WebLogic, is relaxed as can be seen below. Its highest peak is at 40%, but there are surges at the beginning of the graph, which are due to WebLogic starting up.

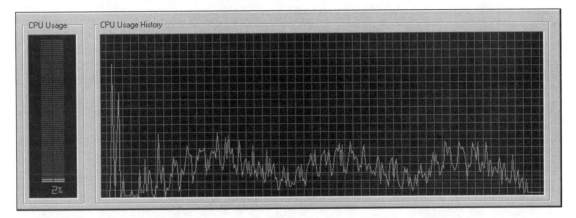

In a similar fashion, the CPU usage of Maria, which runs the Oracle database, is very low as shown below. The highest peak is of 15%, but again, there are surges at the beginning of the graph. These surges are due to the database being re-initialized.

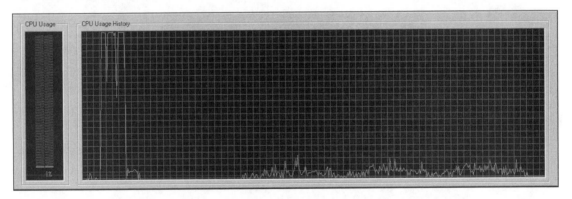

The WebLogic console presents the heap usage to a maximum of 35% and no garbage collection. Interestingly enough the maximum simultaneous usage of the JDBC connection pool was 1 connection; this shows how efficient the use of a connection pool is. Under the 2-tier architecture every client would require a connection, in this case 60 connections. Using a 3-tier architecture augmented with a connection pool we only use 1 connection. The figure overleaf presents a screenshot of the WebLogic console.

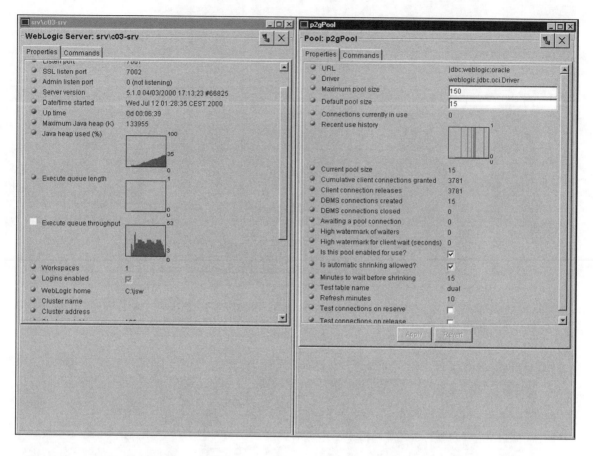

Test 11.2.2 – 120 Users

The next step is to test with 120 simultaneous users. The Grinders are set to run on 4 machines, each with 1 JVM using 30 threads. The results are presented on the following table:

Test 11.2.2	ART	TPS
url0	11.71	85.43
url1	8.57	116.73
url2	43.82	22.82
url3	62.98	15.88
url4	65.16	15.35
url5	65.86	15.18
url6	62.88	15.90
url7	57.58	17.37
url8	60.79	16.45
Total	**439.32**	**2.28**

Here we can see that doubling the user load has not had much of an impact. The TPS remain roughly the same and the response time has increased a negligible 4%. Basically, Grace is holding pretty well with a load of 120 users. The CPU usage has increased with a maximum peak of about 75%, which shows a healthy usage of CPU as shown below:

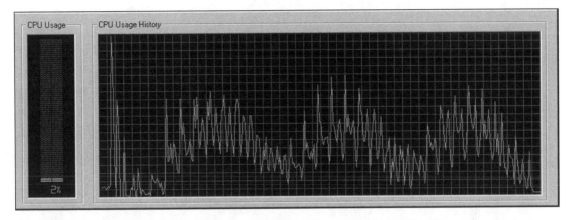

The CPU usage of Maria has also incremented proportionally, but still presents a low usage. The WebLogic console shows the heap at 71% by the end of execution with no garbage collection. It also shows that there was one moment during the first half of the execution that 2 connections were used from the JDBC pool. Other than that, only one connection was used for the rest of the execution.

Test 11.2.3 – 160 Users

Now the load is increased to 160 simultaneous users. The Grinders are set to execute on the 4 machines with 2 JVMs each running 20 threads. The results follow:

Test 11.2.3	ART	TPS
url0	20.53	48.72
url1	11.11	90.02
url2	50.61	19.76
url3	84.19	11.88
url4	89.81	11.13
url5	89.60	11.16
url6	85.90	11.64
url7	81.65	12.25
url8	73.97	13.52
Total	**587.36**	**1.70**

Here we can see degradation in performance. The response time increased by about 34% and the TPS decrease by about 28%. The WebLogic console reveals a heap usage of 96% at the end of the run with no garbage collection. There is a peak of 3 connections used from the JDBC pool, but mostly 1 connection. The CPU usage of Grace is higher, but the peaks still do not reach 100%, as shown below. The CPU usage of Maria is a little higher, but not much.

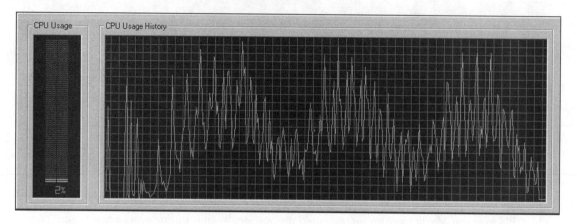

Test 11.2.4 – 200 Users

Let us see how much performance degradation there will be by increasing the load to 200 simultaneous users. The Grinders are set on the 4 machines each with 2 JVMs and 25 threads. The results follow:

Test 11.2.4	ART	TPS
url0	20.89	47.87
url1	13.26	75.41
url2	68.28	14.65
url3	114.24	8.75
url4	134.97	7.41
url5	137.05	7.30
url6	122.83	8.14
url7	93.83	10.66
url8	85.16	11.74
Total	**790.49**	**1.27**

The degradation is about 17% for the TPS and about 35% on the response time. The CPU usage graph of Grace looks more or less similar to the previous run, but the peaks are a little more frequent, as shown above opposite.

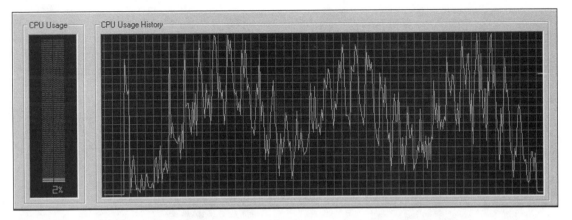

The CPU usage of Maria shows a similar pattern to the previous run, however it becomes more obvious that the CPU usage increases from cycle to cycle, as shown below:

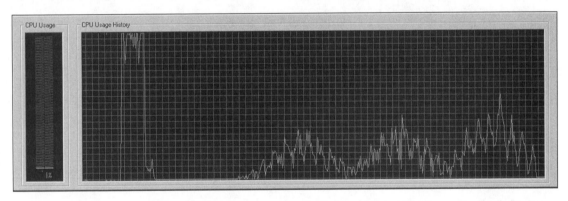

A screenshot of the WebLogic console is presented overleaf. Here you can see that the garbage collector worked during the execution of this test. You can also see that for a couple of brief moments there were 4 tasks waiting for a thread of execution. On the JDBC connections you can see that twice the number of simultaneous connections peaked to around 12.

This screenshot of the console also includes a view of the usage of the `CustomerSearchS` servlet. The graphs just present a count of the times the servlet has been used. With 200 users running 3 cycles of the business transaction you can see a nice incremental curve.

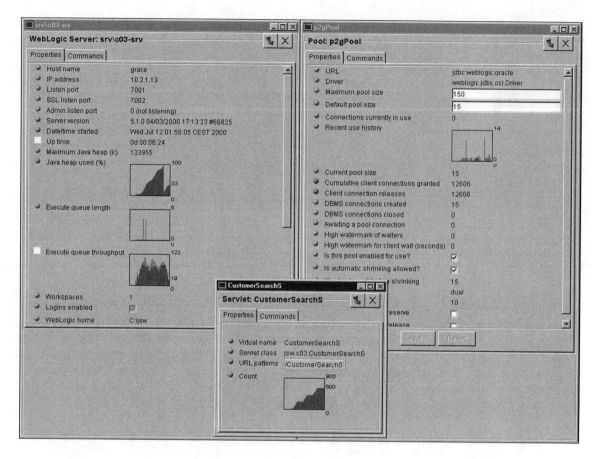

Test 11.2.5 – 240 Users

Now running the Grinders on the usual 4 machines, each with 2 JVMs and 30 threads, the results are the following:

Test 11.2.5	ART	TPS
url0	18.70	53.48
url1	12.09	82.74
url2	72.81	13.73
url3	128.21	7.80
url4	162.05	6.17
url5	200.51	4.99
url6	201.59	4.96
url7	188.60	5.30
url8	146.50	6.83
Total	**1131.05**	**0.88**

The performance degradation for the response time is 43% and for the TPS is 3%. The CPU usage of Grace is now peaking quite often on 100% as seen below:

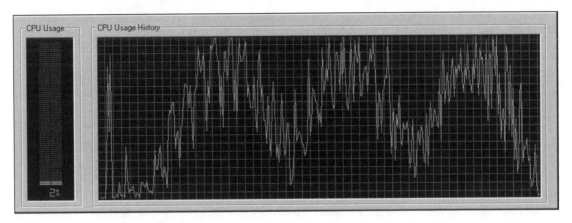

The CPU usage of Maria is proportionally higher presenting a similar pattern to that which it has so far. The WebLogic console reveals a few more peaks in the usage of connections, but not exceeding 12 simultaneously.

Test 11.2.6 – 280 Users

Increasing the load a little more, the Grinders are set to execute on the 4 machines with 2 JVMs each with 35 threads. The results are:

Test 11.2.6	ART	TPS
url0	21.46	46.59
url1	13.26	75.42
url2	122.00	8.20
url3	272.53	3.67
url4	349.43	2.86
url5	462.73	2.16
url6	463.55	2.16
url7	335.25	2.98
url8	259.91	3.85
Total	**2300.11**	**0.43**

The response time is roughly double than the previous run. It seems that we are starting to reach some limits. The CPU chart of Grace shows that the peaks at 100% are lengthy on each cycle, as shown here:

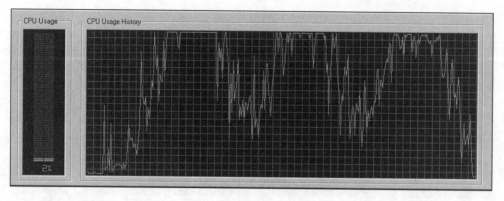

The CPU usage of Maria slightly increases with in the expected pattern, and the WebLogic console shows that the garbage collector kicks in twice during the run. The execution threads are keeping busy at an average of 70 tasks per second and there are substantially more instances of the JDBC connections: the peak number of simultaneous connections is 15.

Test 11.2.7 – 320 Users

This test is prepared by setting the Grinders to run on the 4 machines, each with 4 JVMs and 20 threads. This run produced a number of errors of the kind:

```
<W> <ListenThread> Connection rejected: 'Login timed out after: '15000' ms on
socket: 'Socket[addr=GRINDER8/10.2.1.63,port=4094,localport=7001]''
```

Obviously a limit had been reached, where the connections were timing out after 15 seconds. In an effort to improve this, the number of execution threads was increased to 30 and the test was ran again.

During the second run 15 new JDBC connections were added to the pool, and a large number of errors like that shown above were produced.

It seemed that changing the number of execute threads did not have any effect on the execution and that a hard limit had been reached. Looking at the CPU usage chart of Grace shown below you can see how saturated the system is.

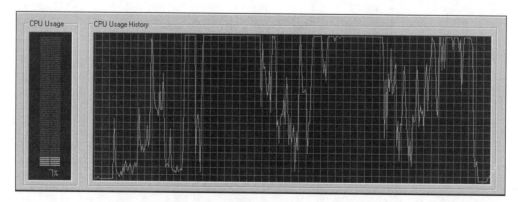

Conclusion

It is interesting to go through the experience of steadily increasing the load on the application and learning how it behaves. The two charts presented beneath show how the response time increases as the load increases and how the TPS decreases as the load increases. In analyzing these charts it seems that it would be safe to run the application with up to 240 simultaneous users. We know that the system can handle 280 users pretty well, but anything beyond that has a high potential to create problems.

The recommendation would be that this application runs on the tested hardware and operating system with an average load of 240 and a peak safely up to 280 users.

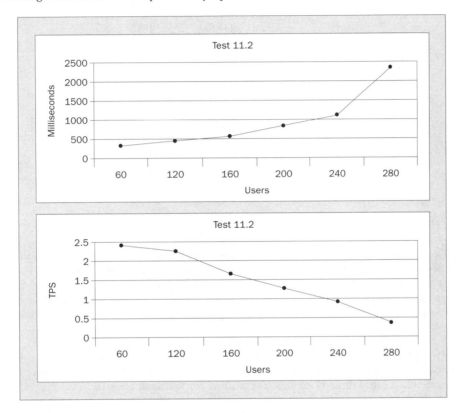

Testing the Stateless Session Beans

This set of test runs will follow the same methodology as the tests in the previous section. Here the troops will be testing the application developed in the first part of Chapter 4, which builds on the application developed on Chapter 3. The Oracle stored procedures have been replaced by stateless session beans.

As the troops do not know how the EJBs will behave, they decide that they will increase the number of execute threads from 15 to 45 for this set of tests. After seeing the efficient way the JVM handles memory they feel confident that this will not have a negative impact on the performance.

Test 11.3.1 – 60 Users

To keep in step with the previous set of runs, here the tests start with 60 users. Because the use of the JDBC connections was so efficient in the last set of test, the troops decide to decrease the initial size of the connection pool to 5 connections. The results are the following:

Test 11.3.1	ART	TPS
url0	17.58	56.87
url1	243.13	4.11
url2	2842.90	0.35
url3	2525.24	0.40
url4	2924.81	0.34
url5	529.81	1.89
url6	422.18	2.37
url7	339.81	2.94
url8	240.68	4.15
url9	8.06	124.14
Total	**10094.21**	**0.10**

This is quite a disappointing surprise. However, checking the WebLogic log file they notice that 25 new JDBC connections have been created. Obviously the behavior with the stateless beans is different from when using straight servlets. The response time is so high because WebLogic waits one second between establishing connections. The length of time WebLogic waits can be defined with the loginDelaySecs property when defining the connection pool; the default is 1 second. This property exists because WebLogic can overrun the database server when it requests many new connections at the same time.

So how many JDBC connections should be defined? The general rule of thumb is that it should be equal to the number of execution threads plus a couple more to make sure that there is always a connection available even when other threads are blocked waiting for the database.

When using transactions it gets a little trickier. In this case connections are allocated one per transaction. If the transactions are long lived then they could block a connection for a long time – this also needs to be taken into consideration.

Test 11.3.2 – 60 Users, Again

After experiencing the price that has to be paid for establishing a JDBC connection during execution, the Troops set out to calculate a good initial number of connections for the pool. Following the recommendations given earlier, the number seems to be 45. It is suggested that they add a few more and they want to round up, so they decide that the initial number should be 50. However, they are now working with transactions, so they do not know what is going to happen. Just to be on the safe side, they decide to make the initial number of connections 80. After the tests they can determine a more optimal number with the aid of the WebLogic console.

The results of this run are the following:

URL	ART	TPS
url0	83.79	11.93
url1	9.11	109.76
url2	62.51	16.00
url3	116.59	8.58
url4	166.22	6.02
url5	247.63	4.04
url6	225.28	4.44
url7	244.59	4.09
url8	213.91	4.67
url9	14.11	70.89
Total	**1383.73**	**0.723**

This seems a better result, about 15% of the response time from the previous run. The CPU of Grace is quite busy, but it does not reach 100% usage as shown below:

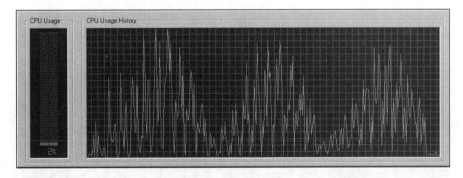

The database on Maria does not seem to be working too hard, as can be observed here:

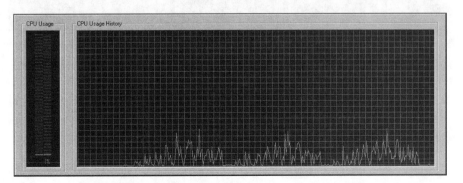

Test 11.3.3 – 120 Users

Now there are no added JDBC connections and no errors, the Troops are ready to increase the load to 120 users. The results are the following:

Test 11.3.3	ART	TPS
url0	55.84	17.91
url1	11.04	90.61
url2	81.26	12.31
url3	147.33	6.79
url4	313.13	3.19
url5	662.48	1.51
url6	1258.84	0.79
url7	1251.13	0.80
url8	1385.73	0.72
url9	27.02	37.01
Total	**5193.78**	**0.193**

There are no errors in this run, but the degradation in performance is large in comparison to the previous set of tests. The response time is almost 4 times bigger, and the TPS decreased by about 73%. The CPU of Grace is now hitting the 100% usage mark for steady periods, shown below.

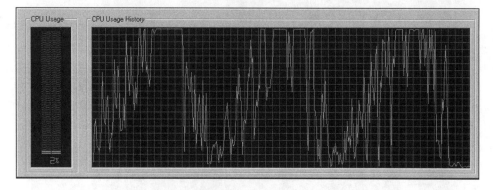

The CPU usage of Maria has increased slightly and the WebLogic console shows that the garbage collector is working twice. No tasks are waiting for execution threads, which are averaging about 45 tasks per second.

Test 11.3.4 – 160 Users

Increasing the load one more notch, the run had no errors and produced the following results:

Test 11.3.4	ART	TPS
url0	99.33	10.07
url1	13.47	74.23
url2	145.66	6.87
url3	341.78	2.93
url4	887.59	1.13
url5	2752.30	0.36
url6	4874.67	0.21
url7	5205.24	0.19
url8	6119.59	0.16
url9	148.47	6.74
Total	**20588.11**	**0.049**

It seems that a pattern is appearing in this set of runs. Once again the response time is about 4 times the previous one. Below you can see the CPU usage of Grace with a pattern that is easier to explain by highlighting the dips from 100%.

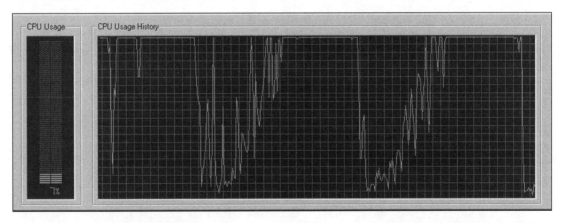

The CPU of Maria keeps a similar pattern with a slight increase in comparison to the previous run. Overleaf is a screenshot of the WebLogic console. In it you can see that at certain moments there have been up to 55 tasks waiting for an execution thread. These threads are averaging about 50 tasks per second. The JDBC connection pool has seen up to 40 simultaneous connections in use.

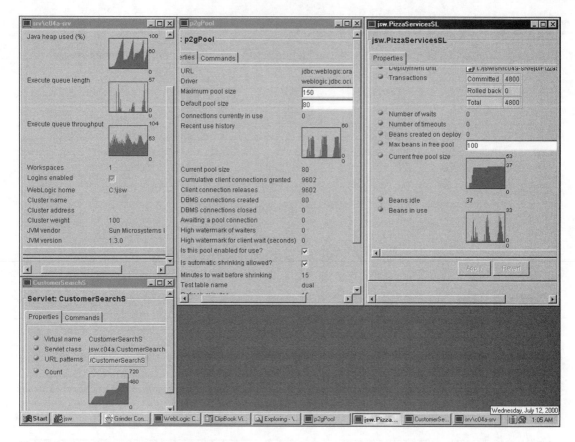

Next, there is a window that provides information on the PizzaServicesSL bean. It shows us that there have been 4800 transactions with no rollbacks during this test. It also indicates that from a maximum of 100 beans available in the free pool, only 37 are present, and the maximum number of beans created during this test is about 30.

Test 11.3.5 – 200 Users

The Troops are getting close to saturation, but nothing has broken yet. So they decide to give it another try with 200 users. This run has many errors; the servlets are failing and because of this 7 transactions are lost. There is also an error related to a closed socket. The results are:

Test 11.3.5	ART	TPS
url0	120.32	8.31
url1	29.65	33.73
url2	162.30	6.16
url3	557.60	1.79
url4	2228.74	0.45
url5	5279.85	0.19
url6	8128.44	0.12
url7	7908.34	0.13
url8	8840.10	0.11
url9	523.28	1.91
Total	**33778.62**	**0.030**

Saturation has been reached as you can see in the following figure, where the CPU of Grace spends even more time at 100% usage than during the previous run. The CPU usage of Maria has increased proportionally, but still does not exceed 45%.

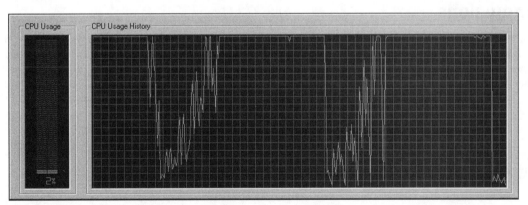

The WebLogic console pictured overleaf tells us that the garbage collector worked 4 times. The number of tasks waiting for an execute thread was high, sometimes getting to 100. The JDBC connection pool was heavily used averaging about 45 simultaneous connections.

The `PizzaServicesSL` bean was well behaved. It kept about 30 instances of the bean in the free pool and used about 30 of them simultaneously.

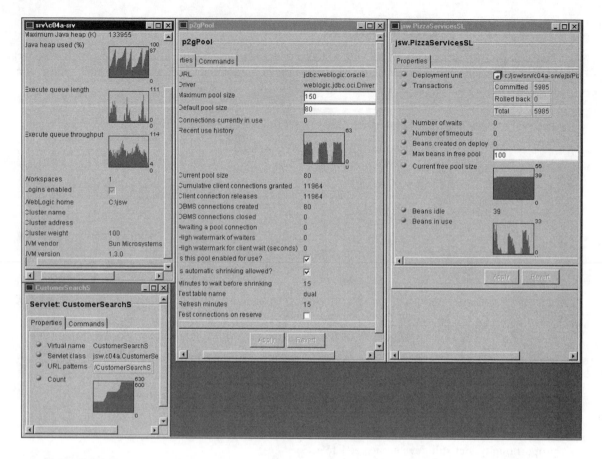

Conclusions

In general the results are disappointing. If we look closely at where the time is being spent it is in the URLs that access the database. The time is significantly higher than in the previous set of tests because now it is using the JTA driver and every access to the database is a transaction. As the transaction has been defined with an isolation level of `serializable`, which is the highest, this means that every access to the database has to be done on a serial fashion, therefore every request has to wait until the database is available.

Opposite are the charts presenting the combined results of this set of test runs. It seems that it would be safe to run this application with about 120 simultaneous users with peaks of up to 140 users. Beyond that the chances of getting in trouble are very high.

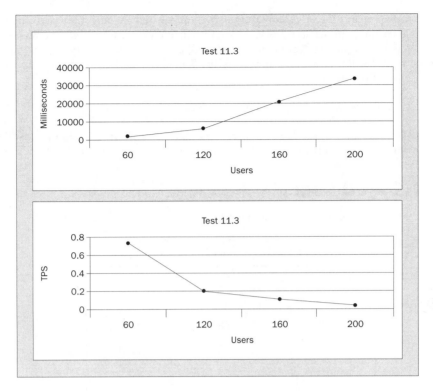

A comparison between this set of tests and the previous one (servlets) is shown later in this chapter.

Testing the Stateful Bean

The next set of tests will use the code developed in the second half of Chapter 4. The application tested in the previous section was enhanced by adding a stateful session bean. This will build and maintain the pizza order in memory rather than constantly going to the database.

A quick test of the Grinder script shows that it does not seem to be working correctly. After a little research the Troops find that the problem is the same as when they were moving from the servlet test to the stateless session beans test. Because now the stateful session bean is handling the order, it also expects the or_o_outlet_code variable when the deliver button is clicked, even if it will do nothing with it. So the statement in the Grinder script is changed to:

```
[url8]http://grace:7001/OrderMaintenanceS?Delivery=Address&\
                               Remarks=&\
                               or_o_outlet_code=99&\
                               command=Deliver,\
```

The Troops decide to leave the number of execution threads at 45, but decrease the number of initial JDBC connections to 70.

With stateful session beans there is a configurable parameter that can affect the performance of the application. This is the number of beans to be kept in the memory cache. If the number is too small, the beans will be passivated (moved from memory to disk), thus paying a penalty in performance. If the number is too high it will use memory unnecessarily. The ideal number will be one that minimizes or avoids passivation of the bean.

For these tests the troops decide to leave the size of the cache to its default value of 100.

The Oracle default value for the number of processes allowed is 59. If you find that that this is not enough when running these tests, increase the value (200 is suggested) in the `init.ora` file.

Test 11.4.1 – 60 Users

Starting with this base line, the results are the following:

Test 11.4.1	ART	TPS
url0	64.42	15.52
url1	9.74	102.62
url2	68.93	14.51
url3	103.04	9.70
url4	58.14	17.20
url5	70.34	14.22
url6	62.49	16.00
url7	54.38	18.39
url8	207.01	4.83
url9	11.67	85.67
Total	**710.17**	**1.41**

These results are surprisingly good. Much better than using only stateless session beans, but more expensive than the application that uses only servlets. This reflects the price of using the EJB infrastructure.

Notice that the most expensive URLs are number 3, where the stateful session bean is created and number 8 where the pizza order is committed to the database.

The CPU usage graph of Grace now presents a slightly different pattern where the peak of the cycle is closer to the end instead of the middle where it was previously. This is because most of the work is done on URL number 8. This graph is presented in the figure above opposite.

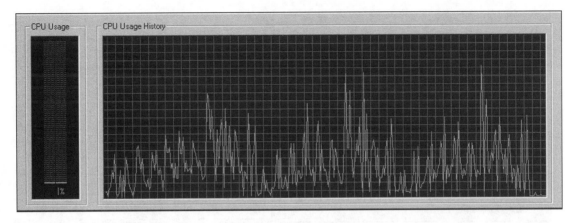

The CPU usage of Maria also shows a different pattern. The first part of the cycle shows about half as much CPU usage as the second part, as can be seen in the figure below. The spikes at the beginning of the graph are caused by the re-initialization of the database and the activity that follows it is the WebLogic server establishing the JDBC connections for the pool.

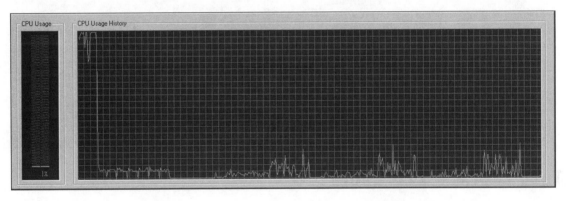

Overleaf is another screenshot of the WebLogic console. It shows that the heap gets to a maximum of 44% with no garbage collection. The connection pool is barely used, with a maximum of 2 connections being used simultaneously.

The new piece of information is related to the OrderBeanSF stateful session bean. Here we can see that out the maximum of 100 beans in the cache it only uses about 60 at most. The other useful piece of information is that there has not been any passivation of this bean during the test.

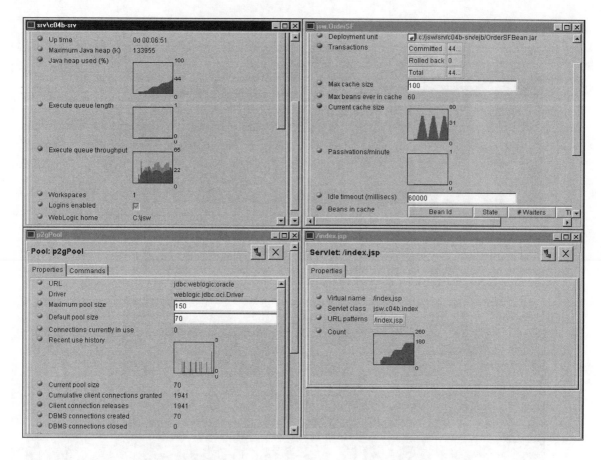

Test 11.4.2 – 120 Users

Continuing with the increase in user load, the results with 120 users are the following:

Test 11.4.2	ART	TPS
url0	22.73	44.00
url1	8.81	113.53
url2	59.33	16.86
url3	80.34	12.45
url4	69.21	14.45
url5	135.70	7.37
url6	173.69	5.76
url7	138.39	7.23
url8	790.67	1.26
url9	32.17	31.09
Total	**1511.04**	**0.66**

408

The degradation of performance is high, with about double the response time and half the TPS. The CPU usage of Grace is greater, reaching 100% at the peaks of the cycles as can be seen here:

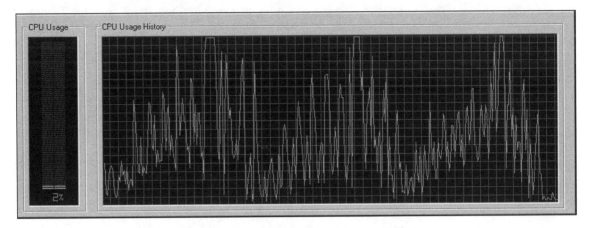

The CPU usage of Maria is higher on the second half of the cycle. In the figure below we can see a screenshot of the WebLogic console. It is interesting to observe that the cache is fully used. There is also a lot of passivation activity happening, up to 200 per minute. This is a sure sign that the cache size needs to be increased.

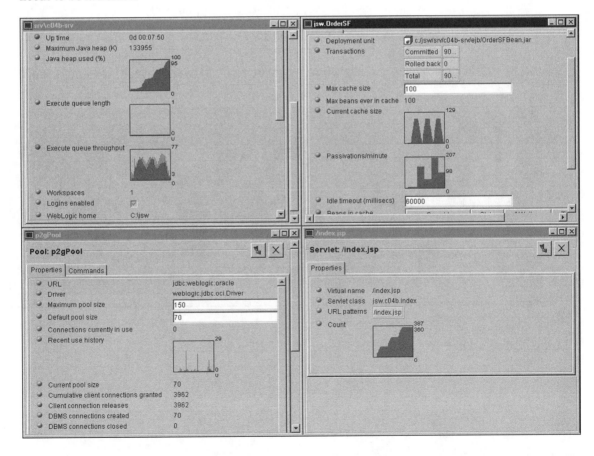

Test 11.4.3 – 160 Users

Even though it is obvious that the cache size has to be increased for the stateful bean, the Troops decide to leave it at 100 to better understand the behavior of the cache. The results of this run are:

Test 11.4.3	ART	TPS
url0	25.77	38.80
url1	12.19	82.05
url2	98.93	10.11
url3	191.67	5.22
url4	258.32	3.87
url5	387.43	2.58
url6	534.14	1.87
url7	537.17	1.86
url8	1308.95	0.76
url9	85.56	11.69
Total	**3440.12**	**0.29**

Again the degradation is high, not only more than doubling the response time, but also substantially decreasing the TPS. The CPU of Maria now spends more time at 100% usage, as can be seen here:

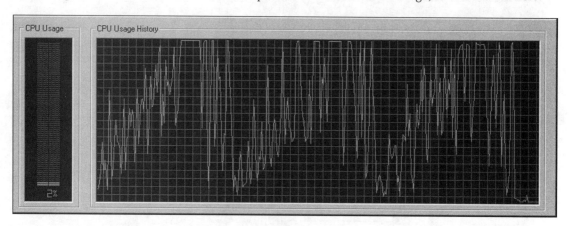

The database in Maria continues to show the same pattern of CPU usage presented previously, but slightly higher usage. The passivations are now at the order of 450 per minute.

Test 11.4.4 – 200 Users

Stubbornly the Troops decide to leave the cache size still at 100. The results are:

Test 11.4.4	ART	TPS
url0	95.21	10.50
url1	54.81	18.24
url2	98.16	10.19
url3	285.71	3.50
url4	386.97	2.58
url5	671.77	1.49
url6	1022.55	0.98
url7	1080.86	0.93
url8	4249.90	0.24
url9	204.50	4.89
Total	**8150.44**	**0.12**

Once again the performance degradation manages to double the response time. The TPS also take a significant hit. As can be seen in the figure below, the CPU usage of Grace spends even more time at 100%.

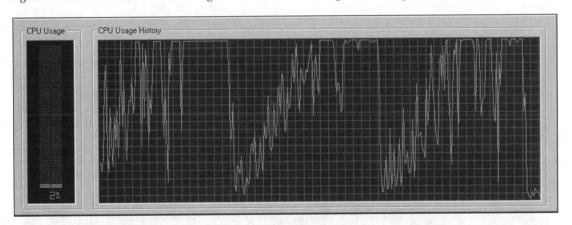

The database on Maria continues to present the same pattern with the expected higher usage. The console shows that there are signs of the processes in the execution queue and the passivations increase to 812 per minute.

Test 11.4.5 – Increase Bean Cache Size

Finally the Troops decide to increase the size of the cache to 500. The results are the following:

Test 11.4.5	ART	TPS
url0	72.94	13.71
url1	14.54	68.80
url2	84.37	11.85
url3	124.54	8.03
url4	114.75	8.71
url5	173.41	5.77
url6	252.11	3.97
url7	247.93	4.03
url8	1940.79	0.52
url9	49.83	20.07
Total	**3075.19**	**0.33**

Now we can see a remarkable improvement by just increasing the size of the stateful bean cache. The figure below shows the CPU usage of Grace. It still spends a fair amount of time at 100%, but now there are no passivations at all. The maximum amount of beans used in the cache is 200. Interestingly enough the memory usage is normal with the garbage collector working twice. The troops suspect that they have hit a limit driven by the hardware they are using.

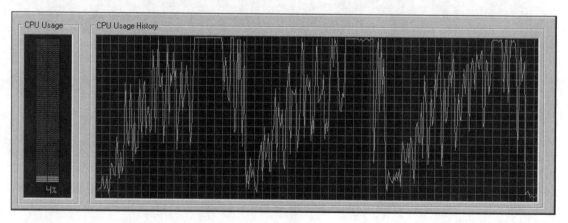

Conclusion

If there is one lesson to be learned from this set of tests it is that when dealing with stateful session beans, the size of the cache is extremely important. In this particular case it seems that the ideal number would have been somewhere between 250 and 300. With 500 there was not a visible impact on memory.

Testing the Entity Beans

This set of tests will use the application developed in Chapter 5. The application tested in the previous section using the stateful session bean is augmented by using one entity bean for all the database operations related to the order master table, and another entity bean for all the operations related to the order detail table.

No changes have to be made to the Grinder test script. In the `weblogic.properties` file, the Troops cautiously decide to increase the initial size of the JDBC connection pool to 80 as they do not know what to expect from the entity beans. They also decide to give both entity beans a cache size of 1000.

Test 11.5.1 – The Transactional Surprise

Starting from the baseline of 60 users, the troops conduct the first test. During this run a few exceptions appeared on the WebLogic console:

```
<EJB> Transaction: '950493805916_60' rolled back due to EJB exception:
jsw.c04b.P2GException: jsw.c04b.P2GException: The order could not be
delivered at jsw.c04b.OrderBean.deliverOrder(OrderBean.java:376)
```

The explanation of this message is that the transaction is being rolled back by JTS and the exception is being thrown from the `deliverOrder()` method in the stateful `OrderBeanSF` bean, although this method only calls the `storeOrder()` method and sets the status of the order. It is in the `storeOrder()` method that the actual database commit happens. If it fails an exception is caught and presented on the command console where WebLogic was started. Scrolling back on the console, the following message was found:

```
java.sql.SQLException: ORA-08177: can't serialize access for this transaction
```

The problem could be that the application was trying to access a record that was locked at that moment. There could be other reasons as well, but this problem immediately showed a weakness in the code written by the Wonder Troops. As the database failed, JTS produced an exception. The `storeOrder()` method caught the exception but did nothing with it!

This is a nice example of code that seems to be pretty good and will work well on simple tests. However, when a load test comes around these little subtleties show up. The troops are really happy that they went through the trouble of load testing the application.

Let us take time out to understand what it means to lose an order in this context. The fact that the order did not make it into the database when the deliver button was clicked did not mean that the order was lost, it just meant that the operator had to click on the deliver button again, as all the information was still contained in the session. This is unacceptable behavior, the test proving is that under a small size load the application misbehaves.

The solution is to retry the database when this exception occurs. But what if the exception happened again? How many times should the Troops repeat before giving up? Gut feeling decided that 5 retries was enough. If it failed, the current click of the deliver button would fail and the operator would have to click it again.

The following code was added to the `OrderMaintenanceS` servlet:

```
int attempts = 0;
while (attempts < MAXATTEMPTS) {
  try {
    currentOrder.storeOrder();
    if (attempts > 0) {
      attempts++;
      System.err.println("OrderMaintenanceServlet: "  +
                         "order stored in attempt #" + attempts);
    }
    break;
  } catch(Exception de) {
    attempts++;
    System.err.println("OrderMaintenanceServlet: " +
                       "failed attempt to OrderSF.storeOrder() #" +
                       attempts);
    if (attempts > MAXATTEMPTS) {
      session.putValue("message", "Order not stored due to: " +de);
      System.err.println(de);
      return;
    }
  }
}
```

The test was started again. To the surprise of the Troops things were still not working. When a transaction was rolled back and another attempt was tried, it still did not work. Other tests were conducted with all sorts of debug output. They finally figured it out. What was happening was that the `OrderBeanSF` bean uses a local variable, `isNew`, to find out if it is a new order or an existing order. When the transaction is rolled back, the value of this variable goes into limbo.

As the troops discussed what could be done, one of them found information on the `SessionSynchronization` interface. This interface allows the recovery of conversational state. It has three methods available:

- `afterBegin()`, called right after the start of a new transaction. If you want to store attributes that you may need reverted, do it here.

- `beforeCompletion()`, called immediately before the completion of a transaction. It is not known if it is committed or rolled back at this point.

- `afterCompletion(boolean committed)`, called after the completion of a transaction. The transaction was successful if `committed` is `true`, otherwise its value is `false`. It is in this method that you would recover the state.

The additions to the `OrderBeanSF` code are the following:

```
/**
 * Used to revert the EJB Conversational State in the case
 * of a rolled back transaction.
 */
public boolean previouslyNew;
```

```
/**
 * Used to revert the EJB Conversational State in the case
 * of a rolled back transaction.
 * It is part of the javax.ejb.SessionSynchronization interface
 */
public void afterBegin() {
  previouslyNew = isNew;
}
/**
 * Used to revert the EJB Conversational State in the case
 * of a rolled back transaction.
 * It is part of the javax.ejb.SessionSynchronization interface
 */
public void beforeCompletion() {
}

/**
 * Used to revert the EJB Conversational State in the case
 * of a rolled back transaction.
 * It is part of the javax.ejb.SessionSynchronization interface
 */
public void afterCompletion(boolean commited) {
  if (! commited) {
    isNew = previouslyNew;
  }
}
```

Now things seemed to be under control again, the troops are ready to run the test one more time. The message, which was placed in the command console, was presented at the time of the transaction being committed:

```
OrderMaintenanceServlet: order delivered in attempt #2
```

The results for this test are the following:

Test 11.5.1	ART	TPS
url0	87.67	11.41
url1	9.18	108.89
url2	68.08	14.69
url3	97.22	10.29
url4	58.01	17.24
url5	71.06	14.07
url6	83.87	11.92
url7	78.02	12.82
url8	508.34	1.97
url9	23.37	42.79
Total	**1084.82**	**0.92**

The response time is about 50% higher than the previous test with 60 users. This could be blamed on the overhead of the entity beans. Shown below is the graph with the CPU usage of Grace:

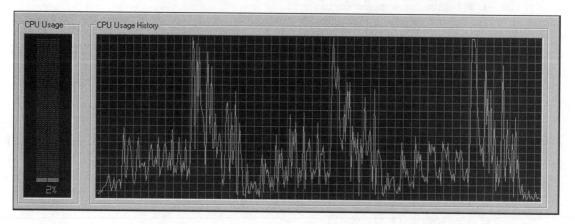

The CPU usage on Maria is pretty much the same as it was on the previous set of runs. Below is a screenshot of the WebLogic console. The interesting information for this run is that there were no passivations for either bean. The OrderMasterEB bean has 180 instances in the cache, which is correct as there are 60 users creating 3 orders each. The OrderDetailEB bean has 541 instances in the cache, which is also correct. Each order has 3 items, multiplied by 180 it gives 540 details. Since there was one item that was committed on the second try, it gives a total of 541.

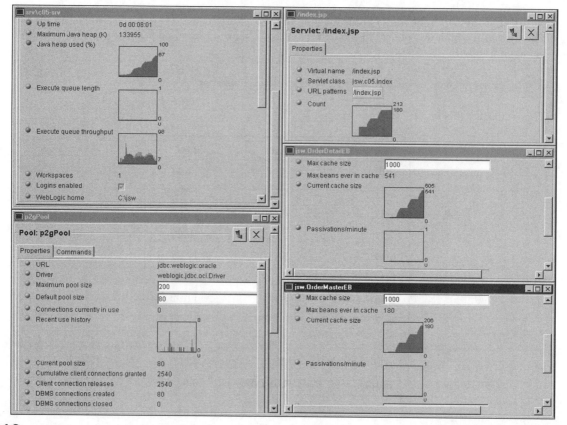

Test 11.5.2 – 120 Users

Continuing with the established pattern of incremental loads, the results for 120 simultaneous users are:

Test 11.5.2	ART	TPS
url0	27.72	36.08
url1	20.31	49.24
url2	69.95	14.30
url3	93.13	10.74
url4	68.63	14.57
url5	120.94	8.27
url6	162.43	6.16
url7	142.06	7.04
url8	1302.63	0.77
url9	35.79	27.94
Total	**2043.59**	**0.49**

Just about double the response time of the previous run. Looking at the console nothing seems out of order. There are no passivations and even though the total order detail beancount is 1080 (120 customers, 3 orders each, 3 items on each order) it reaches the 1000 limit and starts reusing beans from the cache.

The CPU usage of Grace (shown below) is quite high, whereas the CPU usage of Maria remains relatively unchanged.

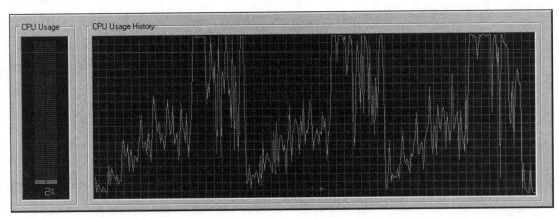

Test 11.5.3 – 160 Users

This test had one error caused by a socket closing, so 1 transaction was lost. The results for this test are the following:

Test 11.5.3	ART	TPS
url0	30.62	32.66
url1	16.10	62.10
url2	72.25	13.84
url3	83.06	12.04
url4	75.95	13.17
url5	144.06	6.94
url6	258.14	3.87
url7	229.02	4.37
url8	4451.13	0.22
url9	37.33	26.79
Total	**5397.66**	**0.19**

Again the response time doubles. The console reveals that at the very last moment of execution there was a burst of passivation activity for the order detail bean, at the rate of 417 per minute. Everything else looks pretty normal.

Here is the CPU usage of Grace:

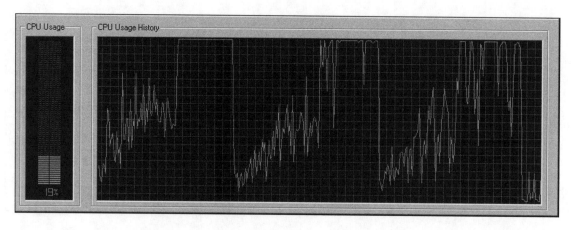

Test 11.5.4 – 200 Users

The results for this test are as follows:

Test 11.5.4	ART	TPS
url0	413.64	2.42
url1	139.94	7.15
url2	254.47	3.93
url3	222.75	4.49
url4	202.73	4.93
url5	320.38	3.12
url6	1159.91	0.86
url7	1903.91	0.53
url8	11080.09	0.09
url9	724.76	1.38
Total	**16422.57**	**0.06**

This time the degradation is nearly three times the response from the previous test and the TPS drop significantly. Looking at the screenshot of the console presented overleaf, you can see that the passivation activity reaches up to 379 per minute. Looking at the CPU usage of Grace (below the Weblogic console figure) we can see that it is spending a lot of time at 100%.

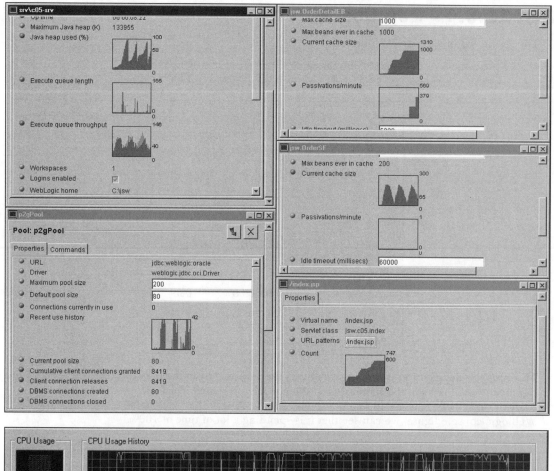

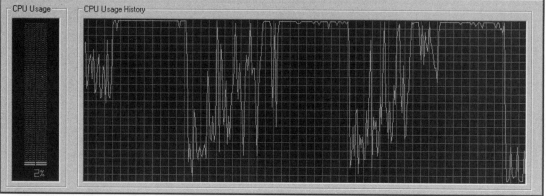

The Troops have the feeling that they are reaching a limit, which is again more related to the hardware than to WebLogic.

Test 11.5.5 – isModified()

Rather the trying to optimize the previous run by enlarging the cache size of the order detail bean, the Troops decide to give it a try with the isModified() method-name deployment parameter. By default WebLogic will call the ejbStore() method at the successful completion of every transaction even if no persistent fields of the EJB were updated. This can lead to unnecessary writes to the database.

The parameter is used by providing the name of a method written by the developer that will return true if the persistent data has been updated and false if not. Needless to say that you should use this very carefully.

```
/**
 * This field is for the "isModified" version.
 */
private transient boolean isDirty;


/**
 * Returns whether the EJBean has been modified or not.
 * This is for the "isModified" version.
 *
 * @return                  boolean isDirty
 */
public boolean isModified() {
  return isDirty;
}


/**
 * Sets the EJBean's modified flag.
 * This is for the "isModified" version.
 *
 * @param flag              Modified Flag
 */
public void setModified(boolean flag) {
  isDirty = flag;
}


/**
 * Sets the OrderDetail information of this E-EJB.
 * @exception P2GException
 *               If the given OrderDetail <tt>od_number</tt> field
 *               does not match the primary key that is in the E-EJB.
 */
public void setOrderDetail(OrderDetail orderDetail)
    throws P2GException{

  //the primary key is never modified!!
  if (od_number != orderDetail.getOd_number())
    throw new P2GException("Cannot modify a different order detail");

  od_or_number = orderDetail.getOd_or_number();
  od_pizza = orderDetail.getOd_pizza();
  od_quantity = orderDetail.getOd_quantity();
  od_dough = orderDetail.getOd_dough();
```

```
      setModified(true); //"isModified" version: to force writing
  }


  /**
   * This function transforms the data loaded from the database.
   * It creates a Pizza object initialized with the loaded
   * data, and stores it in the <tt>od_pizza</tt> field.
   */
  public void ejbLoad() {
    od_pizza = new Pizza();
    od_pizza.setP_name(od_p_name);
    od_pizza.setP_size(od_p_size);
    setModified(false); //"isModified" version: to avoid writing
  }


  /**
   * This function transforms the data to be stored in the database.
   * It updates the data in fields <tt>od_p_name</tt> and
   * <tt>od_p_size</tt> from the data in field <tt>od_pizza</tt>.
   */
  public void ejbStore() {
    od_p_name = od_pizza.getP_name();
    od_p_size = od_pizza.getP_size();
    setModified(false); //"isModified" version: to avoid writing
```

This test run is done again with 200 users. One transaction was lost due to the familiar socket closed error. The results are:

URL	ART	TPS
url0	236.07	4.24
url1	122.87	8.14
url2	186.97	5.35
url3	162.26	6.16
url4	175.84	5.69
url5	465.92	2.15
url6	995.54	1.00
url7	870.72	1.15
url8	8257.32	0.12
url9	292.20	3.42
Total	**11765.70**	**0.08**

The performance is better. On the console the passivations decreased rapidly to an average of about 140 per minute. The CPU usage graph of Grace, however remained the same.

Test 11.5.6 – dbIsShared()

The default behavior of WebLogic is to call the `ejbLoad()` method at the beginning of every transaction. This makes sense in an environment where many sources may update the database, because the bean will always get the freshest data. But if the environment is based on a single WebLogic server, this is unnecessary and it causes extra overhead.

By setting this deployment parameter to `false`, we achieve the behavior where it will not make unnecessary calls to `ejbLoad()`.

This test run is done with `dbIsShared()` set to `false` on both entity beans. Again with 200 users we obtain the following results:

Test 11.5.6	ART	TPS
url0	97.51	10.26
url1	26.45	37.80
url2	83.48	11.98
url3	119.35	8.38
url4	112.57	8.88
url5	199.95	5.00
url6	385.75	2.59
url7	469.44	2.13
url8	4377.62	0.23
url9	149.78	6.68
Total	**6021.89**	**0.17**

Here you can see the dramatic difference this parameter can have. In the console (shown overleaf) you can see that there are very few passivations of the order detail bean until the end of the test where it surges to 555 per minute. The CPU usage chart for Grace remains pretty much the same as for the two previous tests.

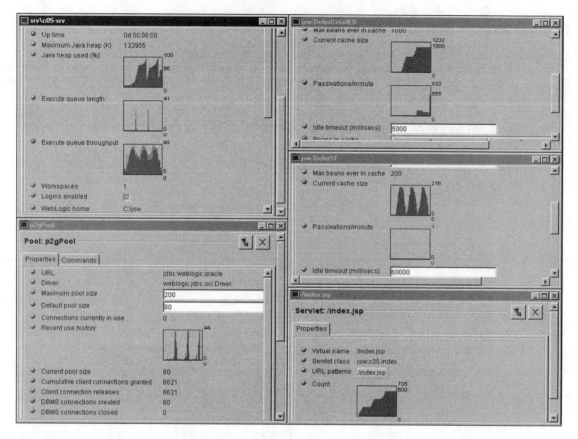

The CPU usage of Maria is a little lighter on this run than the two previous ones. A screenshot is presented below.

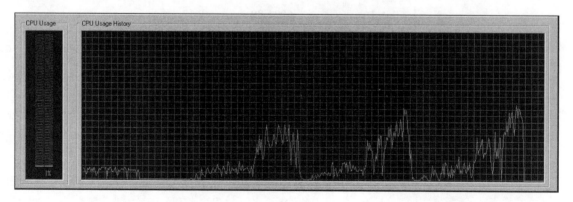

Conclusion

After such a long period of rigorous testing, the Wonder Troops picked out three important factors, which could help improve performance:

❑ The use of the `isModified()` deployment parameter improves performance here by as much as 30%. You have to be very careful when using it though, as now the control of when persistent data is committed to the database is in your code.

❑ The `dbIsShared()` parameter is also very powerful, but you have to be aware that it will not work in a clustered environment. If you are planning to grow your application to a cluster of WebLogic servers then do not use this parameter as the results will be disastrous.

❑ A careful selection of the size of the cache for the beans can make a difference.

A Comparative Analysis

The objective of this section is to compare the various test runs that have been done so far. This will be done with two cases, one where the applications have not been particularly loaded and another with a medium size load. In this case the troops will use the numbers generated by the test runs for 60 and 160 users.

The comparison will be done using the following results of the various tests:

❑ **Test series 2**: Servlets, Oracle stored procedures using JDBC access.

❑ **Test series 3**: Servlets, stateless session beans using the JTA driver. The representative test run for 60 users is Test 11.3.2, which does not add connections to the JDBC pool during execution.

❑ **Test series 4**: Servlets, stateless and stateful session beans using the JTA driver.

❑ **Test series 5**: Servlets, stateless and stateful session beans, and entity beans.

The analysis will be done using the average response time instead of transactions per second (TPS), as it will better represent the actual performance of each step. The following table presents the response times of the test runs with 60 users:

60 Users	Servlets	Stateless	Stateful	Entity
url0	13.91	83.79	64.42	87.67
url1	8.11	9.11	9.74	9.18
url2	48.32	62.51	68.93	68.08
url3	68.57	116.59	103.04	97.22
url4	63.49	166.22	58.14	58.01

Table continued on following page

60 Users	Servlets	Stateless	Stateful	Entity
url5	56.74	247.63	70.34	71.06
url6	57.29	225.28	62.49	83.87
url7	50.84	244.59	54.38	78.02
url8	53.31	213.91	207.01	508.34
url9		14.11	11.67	23.37
Total ART	**420.58**	**1383.74**	**710.16**	**1084.82**

With a small load of 60 users it is clear that the better combination of Enterprise JavaBeans is to use the stateful session bean. The price to be paid for the convenience of using entity beans is over 50%. The following table presents the results for the test runs with 160 users:

160 Users	Servlets	Stateless	Stateful	Entity
url0	20.53	99.33	25.77	30.62
url1	11.11	13.47	12.19	16.1
url2	50.61	145.66	98.93	72.25
url3	84.19	341.78	191.67	83.06
url4	89.81	887.59	258.32	75.95
url5	89.60	2752.3	387.43	144.06
url6	85.90	4874.67	534.14	258.14
url7	81.65	5205.24	537.17	229.02
url8	73.97	6119.59	1308.95	4451.13
url9		148.47	85.56	37.33
Total ART	**587.37**	**20588.10**	**3440.13**	**5397.66**

With a larger load of 160 users, the usage of the stateful session bean remains the choice when using EJBs. The ratio between using entity beans or not maintains itself at about 50%. In the chart presented opposite above, you can see how badly the stateless session beans option scales.

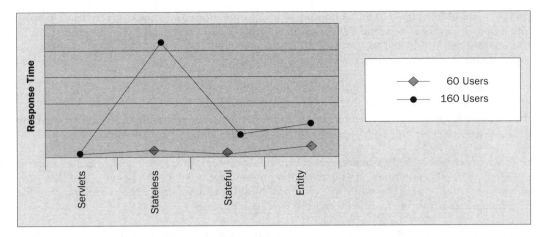

In order to be able to understand what is really happening, we need to eliminate the noise and concentrate in the URLs that are significant. The significant URLs occur when:

❏   An order is created – URL 3

❏   An item is added to the order – there are 3 choices, the troops select URL 5

❏   The order is updated, prices are calculated per item, etc – URL 7

❏   The order is committed to the database and the inventory is updated – URL 8

Using the results from the runs with 60 users the following chart is built:

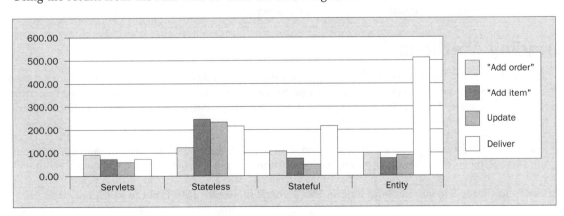

Starting with the servlets, we can see that the response time is very similar for the 4 operations chosen. These are performed by the Oracle stored procedures.

Using the stateless session beans these operations are significantly more expensive. Every one of these operations requires the instantiation of a bean plus access to the database using JTA. As discussed earlier, in this case the transaction isolation level is defined to be `serializable`, the most restricting of all. It was later brought to the attention of the Troops that the way in which Oracle implements this isolation level is not very solid. In this case using an isolation level of `read committed` should be enough. This should substantially improve the response times of this set of tests.

Using the stateful bean the add item and update order operations are comparatively faster because they happen in memory, but the actual delivery operation has to access the database to update both the order master and order detail tables. As it all happens in one single transaction this operation takes about the same time as the one in the stateless-only test.

The test using entity beans is more or less the same as when they are not used, until we get to the delivery operation. Here you can really appreciate the price you have to pay for using this infrastructure. Even if the entity beans are optimized by using the is-modified deployment parameter improving the response time by about 25%, this is still takes about double the time.

The controversy that arose in Chapter 5 seems to be resolved. Using entity beans implies a performance hit of about 50%. The question is if you are willing to pay that price for the benefits that they offer. Some people will not, accept it while others will. Yet others will use entity beans and improve the performance by using brute force with more powerful computers.

The final conclusion is that in this particular pizza case, using the stateful session bean model is very attractive. It scales pretty decently considering that it is running on a Pentium III machine with 256MB of memory and a heap of 128MB. Even though the response time is higher than the servlet model, the problems occurring when coordinating transactions and catching rollbacks would have been very tricky to program in the servlet model.

Testing JMS Point to Point

This set of tests will deal with the application developed on Chapter 7 to send a pizza order from the central location to the outlet. This is a good opportunity to learn how to use the Grinder with a Java method to create the load instead of the HTTP test scripts.

Grinding Methods

The basic idea is to write a method that replicates the functionality of what is going to be load tested. The easiest way to do this is just to copy and paste the actual method of the application and instrument it. This becomes a class that is called by the Grinder for execution, and this class can call the other classes that make up the original system.

For this set of tests two plugins will be created, one that will act as the producer of messages simulating the Pizza2Go central location, and another to consume the pizza orders, thus simulating the outlet.

The following is a fragment of the plug-in PTPSndBmk that sends JMS Point to Point messages:

```
/**
 * This class is a Grinder plug-in for sending Point-to-Point
 * JMS messages.
 * This plug-in is specific for testing application from
 * chapter 7 of the book.
 */
public class PTPSndBmk
  implements com.ejbgrinder.grinder.GrinderPlugin {

  public void init(GrinderContext gc) {
    System.out.println("calling init");
```

```
      _serverURL = gc.paramAsString("serverURL");
      _queueName = gc.paramAsString("queue");
      _outlets = gc.paramAsInt("outlets");
      _persistentDelivery = gc.paramAsBoolean("persistentDelivery");
      _details = gc.paramAsInt("details");

      try {
        _ctx = getInitialContext(_serverURL);
        _queueConnectionFactory = (QueueConnectionFactory)
                          _ctx.lookup(JMS_FACTORY);
        _queueConnection = _queueConnectionFactory.createQueueConnection();
        _queueSession = _queueConnection.createQueueSession(false,
                        Session.AUTO_ACKNOWLEDGE);
        try {
          _queue = (Queue) _ctx.lookup(_queueName);
        }
        catch(NamingException ne){
          _queue = _queueSession.createQueue(_queueName);
          _ctx.bind(_queueName, _queue);
        }
        _sender = _queueSession.createSender(_queue);
        if (_persistentDelivery)
          _sender.setDeliveryMode(DeliveryMode.PERSISTENT);
        else
          _sender.setDeliveryMode(DeliveryMode.NON_PERSISTENT);
        _queueConnection.start();
        System.out.println("PTPSndBmk: JMS connection opened");

        _outletNumber = 1;
      } catch(Exception e) {
        System.err.println("PTPSndBmk: an exception has occurred " +
                        "when trying to open a JMS connection:");
        System.err.println("PTPSndBmk: " + e);
      }
    }

  public void send() {
    //System.out.println("calling send");
    ObjectMessage msg = null;
    Hashtable ht = null;
    try {
      msg = _queueSession.createObjectMessage();
      ht = prepareOrder(_outletNumber);
      msg.setLongProperty("outletNumber",
                        ((Long)ht.get("outletNumber")).longValue());
      msg.setObject(ht);
      _sender.send(msg);
      //System.out.println("PTPSndBmk: JMS message (id=" + _messagesSent +
                        ") sent to outlet: " + _outletNumber);
      _messagesSent++;
      _outletNumber = 1 + (_messagesSent % _outlets);
    } catch(Exception e) {
      System.err.println("PTPSndBmk: an exception has occurred " +
                        "when trying to send a JMS message:");
      System.err.println("PTPSndBmk: " + e);
    }
  }
}
```

Next is a fragment of the plugin `PTPRcvBmk` that receives JMS Point to Point messages:

```java
/**
 * This class is a Grinder plug-in for receiving Point-to-Point JMS
 * messages.
 * This plug-in is specific for testing application from
 * chapter 7 of the book.
 */
public class PTPRcvBmk
    implements com.ejbgrinder.grinder.GrinderPlugin {

  public void init(GrinderContext gc) {
    System.out.println("calling init");
    _serverURL = gc.paramAsString("serverURL");
    _queueName = gc.paramAsString("queue");
    _outletNumber = gc.paramAsInt("outletNumber");

    try {
      _ctx = getInitialContext(_serverURL);
      _queueConnectionFactory = (QueueConnectionFactory)
                                _ctx.lookup(JMS_FACTORY);
      _queueConnection = _queueConnectionFactory.createQueueConnection();
      _queueSession = _queueConnection.createQueueSession(false,
                        Session.AUTO_ACKNOWLEDGE);
      try {
        _queue = (Queue) _ctx.lookup(_queueName);
      } catch(NamingException ne) {
        _queue = _queueSession.createQueue(_queueName);
        _ctx.bind(_queueName, _queue);
      }
      String selector = "outletNumber = " + _outletNumber;
      _receiver = _queueSession.createReceiver(_queue, selector);
      _queueConnection.start();
      System.out.println("PTPRcvBmk: JMS connection opened");
    } catch(Exception e) {
      System.err.println("PTPRcvBmk: an exception has occurred when " +
                        "trying to open a JMS connection:");
      System.err.println("PTPRcvBmk: " + e);
    }
  }

  public void receive() {
    //System.out.println("calling receive");
    Message msg = null;
    Hashtable ht = null;
    try {
      msg = _receiver.receive();
      _messagesReceived++;
      //System.out.println("PTPRcvBmk: JMS message received");
      //System.out.println("outletNumber=" +
      //                    msg.getLongProperty("outletNumber"));
      if (msg instanceof ObjectMessage) {
          ht = (Hashtable)((ObjectMessage)msg).getObject();
        Customer c = (Customer)ht.get("customer");
        OrderMaster or = (OrderMaster)ht.get("orderMaster");
```

```
        Vector vOd = (Vector)ht.get("orderDetail");
        saveOrder(c, or, vOd);
      }
      else {
      }
    } catch(Exception e) {
      System.err.println("PTPRcvBmk: an exception has occurred when " +
                          "trying to receive a JMS message:");
      System.err.println("PTPRcvBmk: " + e);
    }
  }
```

Once these classes have been completed, the next step is to prepare the `grinder.properties` file to execute them. Let us start with the producer. First the test class is defined:

```
grinder.cycleClass=jsw.c11.PTPSndBmk
```

Then the methods of the test class are defined:

```
grinder.cycleMethods=init,send,end
```

And finally, the parameters that are to be passed to the class for execution:

```
grinder.cycleParams=[serverURL]t3://grace:7001,\
                    [queue]jsw.orderQueue,\
                    [outlets]3,\
                    [persistentDelivery]true,\
                    [details]2
```

In this case we are specifying the server and queue to be used, as well as that it has to produce messages for three outlets, which are persistent and contain 2 items (pizzas). Finally, the number of cycles is set to 12,000:

```
grinder.times=12000
```

For the consumer, the test script is similar. The test class, its methods, and parameters are specified:

```
grinder.cycleClass=jsw.c11.PTPRcvBmk

grinder.cycleMethods=init,receive,end

grinder.cycleParams=[serverURL]t3://grace:7001,\
                    [queue]jsw.orderQueue,\
                    [outletNumber]1
```

The parameters are the server and queue it should listen to. In this example the Grinder will be simulating outlet number 1. Finally the number of cycles is set to 4,000.

The Test Environment

For this set of test runs, the computer architecture used is presented in the following diagram. All the machines are connected via a 100Mb network, although the ideal scenario would be to have the consumer machines connected to the network via a slow connection, like a 64K line. This would be closer to the reality of Pizza2Go.

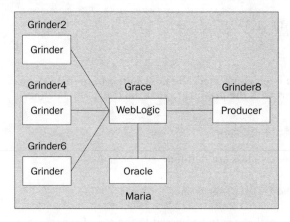

The troops decide that the tests will consist of only one producer (the application when sending the order) and three consumers (outlets). Admittedly, the system could be tested with more than one producer (the various instances of the bean producing the message) or with more outlets listening to the queue. But since the messages are defined as persistent, it was felt that these additions would have more of an impact on the database than on the JMS system.

They designed four tests:

❏ The producer runs alone, sending the messages to the persistent queue. The objective is to simulate that the outlets are not connected.

❏ The consumers run alone getting their messages from the queue. This is to measure the effort a consumer must go through to retrieve a large number of messages after a lengthy period of disconnection.

❏ The producer and the consumers run simultaneously, as would be the case in reality.

❏ The producer and consumers run simultaneously and the messages are not persistent. This is just to understand the price of persistence.

The tests are based on having the producer blast 4,000 messages to the 3 outlets for a total of 12,000 messages. Each of the outlets will then consume the 4,000 messages. The size of the message (the pizza order) is about 2K.

Test 11.6.1 – Producer Alone

The results are quite impressive. The producer generated messages at the rate of 54.79 per second, or to view from another angle, the response time per message was of 18.25 milliseconds. The CPU usage of Grace averaged about 30% during the test as can be seen below:

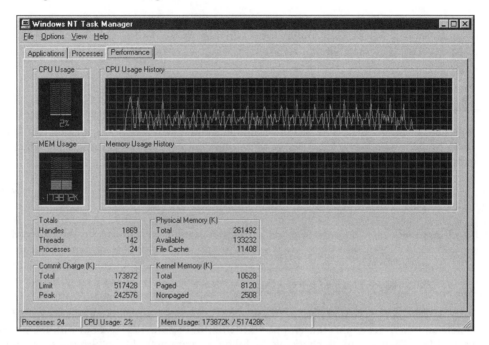

The CPU usage of Maria where the database is running shows a steady 40% as presented here:

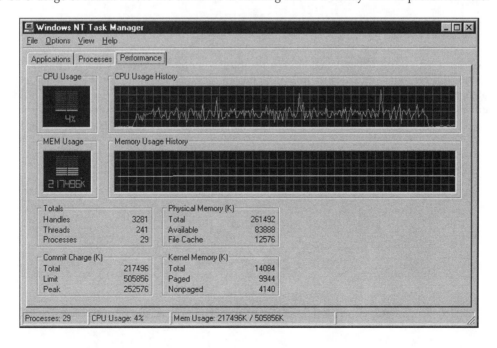

Test 11.6.2 – Consumers Alone

In this test the 3 consumers will go to the JMS server to read the 4,000 messages that are directed to each of them. The producer is not generating messages during this execution. The results are presented as an average of the response time of the 3 consumers, which is 81.27 milliseconds. This is about 12.30 transactions per second.

The CPU usage of Grace presents a similar pattern to that during the previous test, but the average has increased to 35%. The same applies for the CPU usage of Maria, where the average has now increased to 50%.

Test 11.6.3 – Producer and Consumers

This test gets closer to reality as both producer and consumers will be working together. It is a combination of the previous two tests. The producer now has a response time of 27.70, which is about 50% more than on the test where it ran alone.

The average response time of the 3 consumers was 83.17, which is pretty close to the result where the consumers worked alone.

The CPU usage of Grace is about the same as during the previous run; however, the pattern is different with the peaks and valleys closer together. The CPU usage by the database remains the same.

Test 11.6.4 – No Persistence

As discussed in Chapter 7, the pizza application cannot afford to work without persistency. However, just to understand the price of this the Troops decide to run the previous test but with the persistency of messages disabled. They do this by changing the following parameter in the Grinder properties file of the producer:

```
[persistentDelivery] false, \
```

The results are incredible. The producer has a response time of 3.52 milliseconds or 284.02 TPS. This is only 13% of the response time of the run with persistency. For the consumers the average response time is 10.61 milliseconds or 94.24 TPS. This also represents 13% of the previous test. Based on this data we can conclude that the cost of persistency in a JMS PTP message is about 8 times more expensive.

Conclusion

Based on this tests we can see that the code developed by the Wonder Troops is pretty solid, as it behaved well under what can be considered high load. The Troops also obtain a better understanding of the performance of JMS and can now do some capacity planning based on this data. It is also interesting to see that most of the overhead of the JMS PTP system comes from persistency.

Testing JMS Publish and Subscribe

The intent is to test the reservation system created with the JMS Publish and Subscribe system in the second half of Chapter 7.

The Test Methods

As in the previous set of tests, this one will be using publisher and subscriber plugins.

The publisher's init() and send() methods are defined as follows (taken from the plugin PubSubSndBmk):

```
/**
 * This class is a Grinder plug-in for sending
 * Publish and Subscribe JMS messages.
 * This plug-in is specific for testing application from
 * chapter 7 of the book.
 *
 *
 */
public class PubSubSndBmk
  implements com.ejbgrinder.grinder.GrinderPlugin {

  public void init(GrinderContext gc) {
    System.out.println("calling init");
    _serverURL   = gc.paramAsString("serverURL");
    _matchNumber = gc.paramAsInt("matchNumber");
    _begin       = gc.paramAsInt("begin");
    _step        = gc.paramAsInt("step");
    _last        = _begin;

    try {
      _ctx = getInitialContext(_serverURL);
      TicketServicesSLHome tH = (TicketServicesSLHome)
        _ctx.lookup("jsw.c07.TicketServicesSL");
      _ts = tH.create();
      System.out.println("PubSubSndBmk: EJB contacted");
    } catch(Exception e) {
      System.err.println("PubSubSndBmk: an exception has occurred when " +
                        " trying to contact the EJB:");
      System.err.println("PubSubSndBmk: " + e);
    }
  }
```

```
    public void send() {
      //System.out.println("calling send");
      try {
        Vector v = new Vector();
        Ticket ticket = null;

        int max = _last + _step;
        while (_last < max){
          ticket = new Ticket();
          ticket.setTi_id("" + _last);
          ticket.setTi_ma_number(_matchNumber);
          ticket.setTi_c_country_code(1);
          ticket.setTi_c_area_code(303);
          ticket.setTi_c_phone(5551212);
          v.addElement(ticket);
          _last++;
        }
        int n = _ts.buy(v, 1);
        _messagesSent++;
        //System.out.println("PubSubSndBmk: EJB/JMS message sent");
      } catch(Exception e) {
        System.err.println("PubSubSndBmk: an exception has occurred when " +
                           "trying to call an EJB method:");
        System.err.println("PubSubSndBmk: " + e);
      }
    }
```

The subscriber's init() and receive() methods are as follows (taken from the plugin PubSubRcvBmk):

```
/**
 * This class is a Grinder plug-in for receving
 * Publish and Subscribe JMS messages.
 * This plug-in is specific for testing application from
 * chapter 7 of the book.
 *
 */
public class PubSubRcvBmk
  implements com.ejbgrinder.grinder.GrinderPlugin {

  public void init(GrinderContext gc) {
    System.out.println("calling init");
    _serverURL = gc.paramAsString("serverURL");
    _topicName = gc.paramAsString("topic");
    _matchNumber = gc.paramAsInt("matchNumber");
    _sleepMillis = gc.paramAsInt("sleepMillis");
    _timeoutMillis = gc.paramAsInt("timeoutMillis");
    _maxAttempts = gc.paramAsInt("maxAttempts");

    try {
      _ctx = getInitialContext(_serverURL);
      _topicConnectionFactory = (TopicConnectionFactory)
                          _ctx.lookup(JMS_FACTORY);
      _topicConnection = _topicConnectionFactory.createTopicConnection();
```

```
        _topicSession = _topicConnection.createTopicSession(false,
                        Session.AUTO_ACKNOWLEDGE);
      try {
        _topic = (Topic) _ctx.lookup(_topicName);
      } catch(NamingException ne) {
        _topic = _topicSession.createTopic(_topicName);
        _ctx.bind(_topicName, _topic);
      }
      String selector = "matchNumber = " + _matchNumber;
      _subscriber = _topicSession.createSubscriber(_topic, selector,
                    false);
      _topicConnection.start();
      System.out.println("PubSubRcvBmk: JMS connection opened");
    } catch(Exception e) {
      System.err.println("PubSubRcvBmk: an exception has occurred when " +
                         "trying to open a JMS connection:");
      System.err.println("PubSubRcvBmk: " + e);
      e.printStackTrace(System.err);
    }
  }

  public void receive() {
    //System.out.println("calling receive");
    Message msg = null;
    Hashtable ht = null;
    try {
      int attempt = 0;
      while( (msg == null) && (attempt < _maxAttempts) ) {
        msg = _subscriber.receive(_timeoutMillis);
        if (msg != null) {
          _messagesReceived++;
          //System.out.println("PubSubRcvBmk: JMS message received");
          if (msg instanceof MapMessage) {
            int available  = ((MapMessage)msg).getInt("availableSeats");
            String tickets = ((MapMessage)msg).getString("tickets");
            String type    = ((MapMessage)msg).getString("type");
            showSeats(available, tickets, type);
          }
          else {
          }
        }
        else {
          attempt++;
        }
      }
      if (msg == null) {
        System.err.println("PubSubRcvBmk: no message received in " +
                           _maxAttempts +
                           " receive attempts with receive timeout of " +
                           _timeoutMillis + ".");
      }
    } catch(Exception e) {
      System.err.println("PubSubRcvBmk: an exception has occurred when " +
                         "trying to receive a JMS message:");
      System.err.println("PubSubRcvBmk: " + e);
    }
  }
}
```

The Test Environment

The network architecture remains the same as for the previous set of runs. This set of test runs is quite simple. The first test is based on 1 producer generating 1000 reservations each containing 2 seats for sports event number 1. On the other end there will be 3 consumers subscribed to sports event number 1. The consumers will sleep 100 milliseconds between receiving events to simulate that they are doing something with the message (such as displaying it).

The second test is the inverse of the first one. For this one there are 3 producers each generating 1000 reservations with 2 seats for sports event number 1. There is only one consumer subscribed to sports event number 1. It is set to receive 3,000 messages and will sleep 100 milliseconds between events.

The database is initialized with a venue large enough to accommodate the 6,000 seats that will be reserved. Also, the tests are done in such a way that the requested seats are always available, to make sure that the request does not fail.

The Grinder script for the producer is defined in a similar fashion to that for the previous run. The class and methods are defined. Then the parameters are set defining the JMS server, the event number, the first seat for the reservations, and the number of seats per reservation:

```
grinder.cycleClass=jsw.c11.PubSubSndBmk
grinder.cycleMethods=init,send,end
grinder.cycleParams=[serverURL]t3://grace:7001,\
                    [matchNumber]1,\
                    [begin]1,\
                    [step]2
```

The consumer test script is similar:

```
grinder.cycleClass=jsw.c11.PubSubRcvBmk
grinder.cycleMethods=init,receive,sleep,end
grinder.cycleParams=[serverURL]t3://grace:7001,\
                    [topic]jsw.ticketTopic,\
                    [matchNumber]1,\
                    [sleepMillis]100,\
                    [timeoutMillis]1000,\
                    [maxAttempts]5
```

Now that this is done, the Troops are ready to start.

Test 11.7.1 – One Against Many

For this run the producer had a response time of 58.95 milliseconds, or 16.96 TPS. The average response time of the consumers was 12.21 milliseconds or 81.87 TPS. The CPU usage of Grace was of the order of 80% while the usage of Maria averaged 20%.

Test 11.7.2 – Many Against One

As there will be various producers, the Grinder scripts of each one has to be modified so that the reservation starts on different seats and they do not fail. The arrangement is that Grinder 2 starts from seat 1, Grinder 4 from seat 2001 and Grinder 6 from seat 4001.

The average response time for the producers is 70.53 milliseconds or 14.18 TPS, whereas the response time for the consumer is 108.03 milliseconds or 9.26.

The CPU usage of Grace now increases to average 95% and Maria is now at 40%.

Conclusion

In this set of tests the Troops learned about the performance of JMS pub/sub. It is interesting to see that subscribers can receive events at such a high rate (82 TPS) and even under triple the load they can still handle 9 TPS. These timings exclude the sleep time of 100 milliseconds. In the real world the subscribers will do something with the event they receive so the capacity for processing an event is really restricted by the processing of the event itself.

Summary

In this chapter we learned how to use the Grinder and tested almost all the code developed in the book under various stress conditions. We saw how to improve the performance of the various elements that make up a J2EE application and discussed the advantages and disadvantages of the various ways of using the J2EE technology.

In the next chapter we will be doing the same, but in a clustered environment using two and three computers running the WebLogic server.

Grinding in a Cluster

In the previous chapter we conducted a number of tests sequentially increasing the user load on the different applications developed throughout the book. We saw that as we increased the load we started reaching various execution limits related to the hardware being used and to the WebLogic server. In this chapter we will be running similar tests to the previous chapter but using the clustering functionality of WebLogic to see how it can cope with an increased number of users. We will also be looking at the failover capabilities included with clustering.

Clustering

Every hardware and software vendor has a different definition of clustering, so it is important to define clustering in relation to the WebLogic server. It is the ability to have two or more WebLogic servers working together in such a way that the clients think they are dealing with one single monolithic WebLogic server. By 'working together' we mean that the members of a cluster coordinate their actions to provide scalability and highly available services. The main objective is to make this totally transparent to the users and, as much as possible, to the developers as well (meaning that you don't have to be a brain surgeon to develop code that makes use of this functionality).

The main features of clustering are:

❑   **Scalability** – achieved by allowing the addition of WebLogic servers in a dynamic fashion to increase capacity.

❑   **High availability** – the ability to send the load of a failed server to another member of the cluster. A server in the cluster could have "failed" because of an orderly shutdown to perform some maintenance or because of a crash.

Clustering is done at the WebLogic level based on careful state management and highly optimized protocols based on commodity technologies such as IP multicast, resulting in a software-only functionality. No specialized hardware is required to make clustering available on the multiple platforms for which WebLogic is certified.

To achieve full scalability, WebLogic uses load balancing. There are various algorithms available for this:

❑ **Round Robin** – the WebLogic instance to which the work will be sent is selected from a list of instances. The list is cycled through in a sequential fashion, and once the end of the list is reached, it starts again from the beginning. This works well when the hardware being used is homogeneous. This is the default.

❑ **Weighted Round Robin** – every member has a number from 0 to 100 representing the proportion of work it will take. If all but one instance has values of 100 with the other having a value of only 50, the latter will only take half as many requests as the others. This algorithm is an improvement over the simple Round Robin when handling non-homogeneous hardware in a cluster.

❑ **Random** – selects the next instance randomly.

❑ **Parameter-based routing** – when the developers create their own mechanism to select the next instance.

Because of the different underlying nature of the J2EE technologies, WebLogic handles clustering for servlets differently from for objects (EJBs, RMI objects). This will be detailed further in this chapter.

One of the powerful features of the WebLogic server is the flexibility it offers regarding the architectural design of a cluster. A cluster can run on the same computer (though usually only one server instance per processor) or distributed among various computers. It can also use a combination, where various instances of WebLogic can run on the same computer and this can be replicated over various computers.

You can also have functional divisions of clusters, for example one cluster for servlets and another one for objects. The cluster for servlets could be running on one or various machines, as could the object cluster.

In all cases you will need a web server acting as a proxy in front of the cluster. The proxy can run on one or more web servers in a separate cluster. The diagram below presents a functional architecture. One example of a hardware configuration is where the proxy is a cluster of iPlanet web servers, the servlet cluster is based on ten Pentium class machines each running one instance of WebLogic and the object cluster is based on two Sun machines each running two instances of WebLogic.

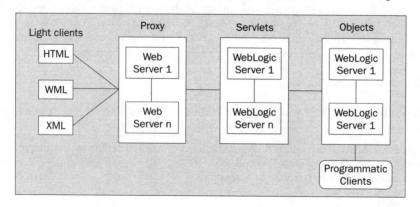

There are no specific rules on how to design a cluster architecture, but do not get too creative, for example do not have a cluster over a wide area network and do not run it on standard hardware. There are a couple of other points to consider:

❑ Using one or more instances of WebLogic on the same computer. Typically you will use only one instance per machine when the computer is not very powerful. Multiple instances on the same computer are used when the computer is powerful enough to handle them. In this case the operating system will do a better job handling several JVMs than only one single JVM, which uses up lots of memory. Here the main consideration is the garbage collection impact during execution. Obviously the execution of the GC will take longer when working with a 2 GB heap space than with 512 MB. So it makes more sense to have several instances of WebLogic running with smaller heap spaces.

❑ Functional separation. The considerations here are having separate clusters for servlets and objects. When servlets and objects are running in the same instance of WebLogic they benefit from being in the same memory space. Sometimes architects prefer to separate servlets from objects when the first are used substantially more than the latter. The options in this case are either to have the instances of WebLogic run on the same machine or on separate ones. If they run on different computers there is a price to be paid by having the requests travel over the network (a network jump), whereas if they run on the same computer there is no network jump. In some cases the price of the network jump is worthwhile because of the scalability gained from having the load distributed over various machines.

Servlet Clustering

As explained earlier, a cluster requires a web server in front that acts as a proxy. When a new session is started, the proxy selects a WebLogic instance to service it according to the selected load balancing algorithm. From that moment on the requests associated to that session would be forwarded to the same server.

Possible web servers are WebLogic, iPlanet web server (Netscape), Apache, or Microsoft IIS. In the case of WebLogic, the proxy functionality is enabled by changing the value of a property in the `weblogic.properties` file. For the iPlanet web server there is an NSAPI plugin that performs the proxy role. There are also plugins for Apache and IIS.

High availability is achieved by replicating the `HttpSession` object. When replication is enabled, the proxy works with the cluster by defining a primary and a secondary server. Every time there is a call to `session.setAttribute()` the session object of the primary server is replicated to the secondary server. If the primary server is no longer available, the proxy turns the secondary server into the new primary and selects a new secondary server based on the selected load balancing algorithm. Replication is only needed when failover is required, which is not always the case.

If the amount of session data is large, it is likely to be more efficient if multiple name/value pairs are stored in the session rather than a single object. For example, the following statements:

```
Customer cust = new Customer();
cust.setFirstName(fname);
cust.setLastName(lname);
cust.setAddress(addr);
session.setAttribute("Customer", cust);
```

Can be re-defined as:

```
session.setAttribute("FirstName", fname);
session.setAttribute("LastdName", lname);
session.setAttribute("Address", addr);
```

Changing one of the fields looks like this:

```
session.setAttribute("Address", newAddr);
```

whereas in the object construct it would be done as:

```
Customer cust = (Customer) session.getAtrribute("Customer");
cust.setAddress(newAddr);
session.setAttribute(cust);
```

The same data changes are made in both cases, but in the former case only a small amount is replicated, while in the latter a larger amount is replicated. Nevertheless, replication of a small amount of data has its cost for multiple changes, the execution of three `setAttribute()` statements versus only one in the single object approach.

Replication can be done in memory or to a database. Obviously in-memory replication will be substantially faster that replicating the information to a database.

Clustering the Pizza Servlets

The Wonder Troops are now ready to start testing the clustering capabilities of the WebLogic server. They will start by testing the application they developed in Chapter 3, which only uses servlets and the Oracle stored procedures.

For these tests they will be using the hardware configuration presented below.

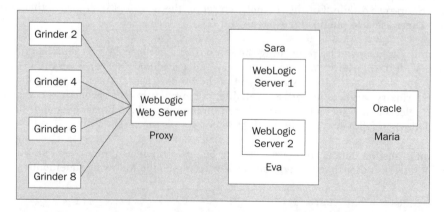

The new machines, Sara and Eva have the same configuration as Grace, and the Proxy has the same configuration as the Grinder machines.

The Wonder Troops follow the instructions for setting up the cluster from http://www.weblogic.com/docs51/cluster/index.html.

They decide to use the Round Robin load balancing algorithm, which is the default of WebLogic. They set up the proxy as follows:

```
weblogic.allow.execute.weblogic.servlet=everyone

weblogic.httpd.register.cluster=\
        weblogic.servlet.internal.HttpClusterServlet

weblogic.httpd.initArgs.cluster=\
        defaultServers=sara:7001:7002|eva:7001:7002

weblogic.httpd.defaultServlet=cluster
```

This is situated in the `weblogic.properties` file for the proxy server. The first line is the ACL, which grants servlet execution permission to everyone. Then the cluster servlet is registered, along with its `init` arguments – that is, the list of servers in the cluster, with their default and SSL listening ports. Finally, the cluster servlet is registered as the default servlet for the proxy, meaning all the requests are handled by the cluster.

The syntax of the `defaultServers` init argument is the following:

```
defaultServers=machine_1:port:ssl_port|machine_2:port:ssl_port
```

The machine value can be expressed using the host name or its IP address. Additional `init` arguments can be added such as the `DebugConfigInfo` option, used to test the configuration:

```
defaultServers=sara:7001:7002|eva:7001:7002, DebugConfigInfo=ON
```

Test Series 12.1.1 – Two Servers

This set of tests will be conducted using only two computers, Sara and Eva, each one running only one instance of the WebLogic server. The setup of the WebLogic server is as follows.

Each server in the cluster must start in cluster mode, therefore the following property has to be added to the `startWls.cmd` startup script:

```
-Dweblogic.cluster.enable=true
```

This option is added as a system property in the call to the JVM, as in the following lines from the `startWls.cmd` script:

```
%J_J% -ms32m -mx64m
        -classpath %J_C%
        -Dweblogic.cluster.enable=true
        -Dweblogic.class.path=%W_C%;%P_C%
        -Dweblogic.system.name=%P_S%
        -Dweblogic.system.home=%P_H%
        -Dweblogic.home=%W_H%
        -Djava.security.manager
        -Djava.security.policy==.\weblogic.policy
        weblogic.Server
```

445

There are other cluster-specific properties like the cluster name and multicast address. The cluster can be started with the default values of these other properties.

However, the following properties must also be added to the `weblogic.properties` file of each server in the cluster:

```
weblogic.httpd.clustering.enable=true
weblogic.httpd.session.persistence=false
```

The first property must be enabled when there are servlets deployed in a cluster, even if servlet session persistence is disabled, as declared by the second property.

After running the modified `startWls.cmd` script, the WebLogic server will start in cluster mode and you will see a message similar to:

```
Joined Cluster mycluster at address 237.0.0.1
```

Test 12.1.1.1 – No Replication

This first test is done with 200 simultaneous users and no replication. The results are:

Test 12.1.1.1	ART	TPS
url0	3.89	18.56
url1	14.39	69.52
url2	65.14	15.35
url3	99.77	10.02
url4	113.33	8.82
url5	134.97	7.41
url6	153.35	6.52
url7	131.70	7.59
url8	86.40	11.57
Total	**852.92**	**1.17**

As compared with the corresponding run in Chapter 11 (Test 11.2.4) there is an increase in the response time of about 8%. This is the overhead price of clustering. If you think about it, 8% is not a big overhead, but let us wait and see how it behaves as we increase the user load.

The CPU usage of the proxy is presented below.

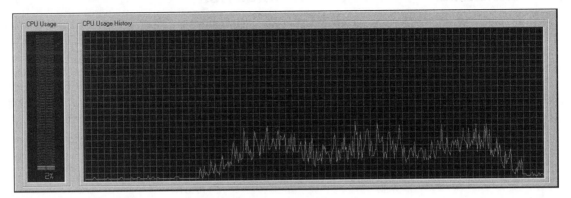

The behavior of both servers is almost the same as you can see in the screenshot beneath. The console contains a view of the basic statistics of both servers. Notice that the execution queue throughput graphs are not the same, but they are similar, presented in different scales. Looking at the usage of the JDBC connections we can see that they also behaved in a similar fashion.

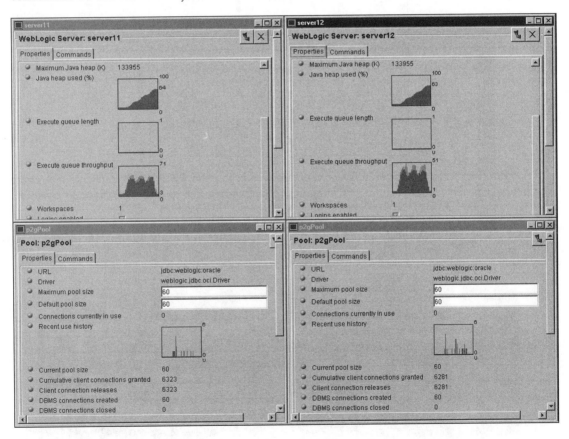

Test 12.1.1.2 – In-Memory Replication

For the next test run, the Troops decide to add **in-memory replication**. This will help in case of a failure of either member of the cluster. Everything remains the same for the run other than changing the `weblogic.properties` for each member of the cluster as follows:

```
weblogic.httpd.session.persistence=true
weblogic.httpd.session.persistentStoreType=replicated
```

The run is done again with 200 users and the results are:

Test 12.1.1.2	ART	TPS
url0	58.59	17.07
url1	20.21	49.48
url2	86.35	11.58
url3	110.45	9.05
url4	114.55	8.73
url5	133.00	7.52
url6	149.50	6.69
url7	138.15	7.24
url8	94.41	10.59
Total	**905.21**	**1.10**

In this case we can easily calculate the price of replication in memory to be about 6%, which is not very expensive considering that for this you get failover. Comparing this with the corresponding run in Chapter 11 (Test 11.2.4), the overhead of clustering remains at about 8%.

The CPU usages of Sara and Eva are very similar, which indicates that the Round Robin load balancing is doing its job. A snapshot of the CPU usage is shown below. Checking all the other information available from the run, it appears to be similar to the previous one.

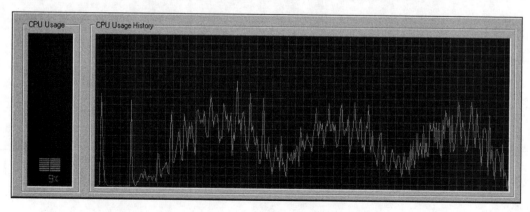

Test 12.1.1.3 – 280 Users

As failover is one of the features that the Troops require for their system, they will conduct the rest of the tests with in-memory replication enabled. The next test is going to increase the load to 280 users. The results are:

Test 12.1.1.3	ART	TPS
url0	71.53	13.98
url1	24.72	40.46
url2	91.28	10.95
url3	127.79	7.83
url4	159.58	6.27
url5	192.19	5.20
url6	209.69	4.77
url7	187.55	5.33
url8	132.51	7.55
Total	**1196.84**	**0.83**

The increase in user load is reflected by a response time increase of 32%. However, when compared with the same run on one server in Chapter 11 (Test 11.2.6), the response time decreased a dramatic 48%. This proves that the scaling of the cluster does work.

The CPU usage of Eva and Sara is quite efficient as can be seen in the graph below. The behavior presented in the WebLogic console overleaf is also good, but be sure to note the different scales on the charts.

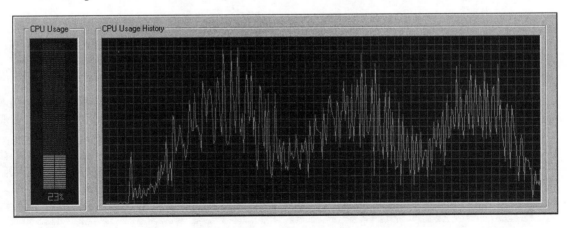

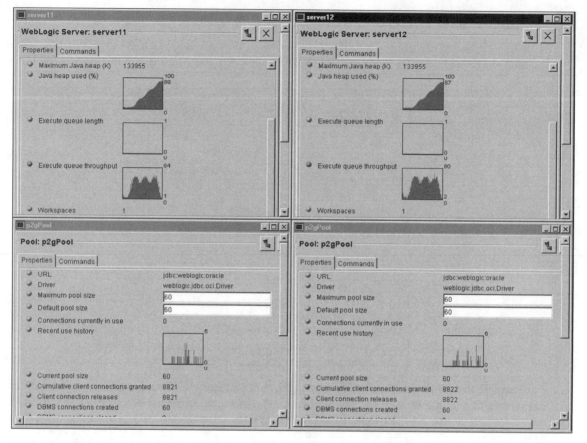

Below is the CPU usage of Maria, where the database is running. As you can see, the load is starting to increase noticeably.

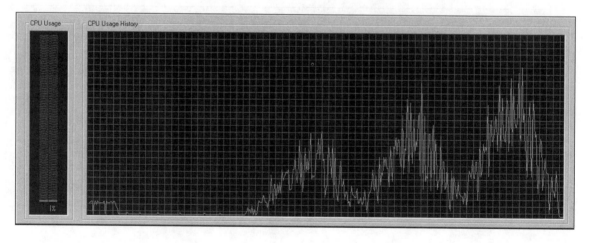

Test 12.1.1.4 – 320 Users

Increasing the load a little more, we get the following results:

Test 12.1.1.4	ART	TPS
url0	80.02	12.50
url1	25.95	38.54
url2	104.28	9.59
url3	139.70	7.16
url4	165.63	6.04
url5	197.34	5.07
url6	224.23	4.46
url7	198.43	5.04
url8	145.48	6.87
Total	**1281.05**	**0.78**

The difference is barely noticeable as we have effectively increased the load by 20 users per server. This represents about a 7% decrease in the response time.

Test 12.1.1.5 – 400 Users

As the previous test can be considered successful, the Troops retry it with 400 users to see how it scales. Surprisingly this run was plagued with errors. A total of 353 transactions were lost and all of them could be traced to the database not responding to the high number of requests from the two WebLogic servers.

In the Chapter 11 runs, where only one server was used, the server was saturated before it could generate enough requests to the database to create problems. Now that we have two servers hitting the database simultaneously, the database is outpaced much more easily.

Let us try to understand what an error means in this context. When the Pizza2Go operator clicks the button to add an item to the pizza, failure occurs because the database cannot cope with the request. The operator will have to go back one page and resubmit since the information is still active in the session. Something that looks really bad in the test (losing a transaction) in reality is nothing more than a resubmit of a form.

The results of this run are:

Test 12.1.1.5	ART	TPS
url0	101.17	9.88
url1	39.90	25.06
url2	176.00	5.68
url3	319.80	3.13
url4	487.39	2.05
url5	605.85	1.65
url6	677.34	1.48
url7	603.68	1.66
url8	439.49	2.28
Total	**3450.64**	**0.29**

In the following figure we can see that the CPU usages of Eva and Sara are starting to hit 100% at the beginning of the run. It seems that if the database ran on a more powerful machine then this run would nearly saturate WebLogic anyway.

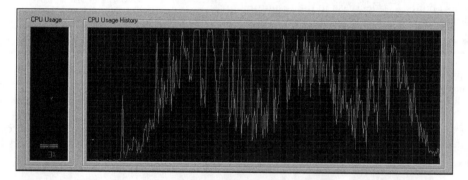

Here you can see how the CPU of Maria is very busy, almost reaching 100% at the peak of the third cycle of the test.

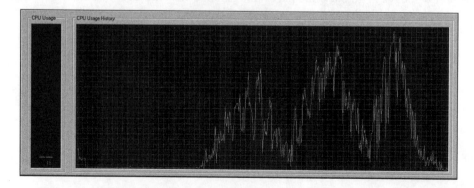

Test Series 12.1.2 – Three Servers

As the Troops had reached a hard limit on the tests, they decided to add one more server into the cluster and see how it behaved. Grace is added into the mix by changing the following line in the `weblogic.properties` file of the proxy:

```
defaultServers=sara:7001:7002|eva:7001:7002|grace:7001:7002
```

Test 12.1.2.1 – 280 Users

The first test with three servers is done with 280 users and the results are:

Test 12.1.2.1	ART	TPS
url0	165.83	6.03
url1	120.07	8.33
url2	136.36	7.33
url3	131.34	7.61
url4	132.76	7.53
url5	162.70	6.15
url6	222.70	4.49
url7	289.77	3.45
url8	276.83	3.61
Total	**1638.36**	**0.61**

Comparing this response time with the one obtained from Test 12.1.1.2 presents a decrease of about 37%, due to the overhead of running the extra server. However, it still is about 30% better than the corresponding run in Chapter 11 with only one server.

Below you can see a snapshot of the console, presenting all three servers in similar conditions and capable of handling more load.

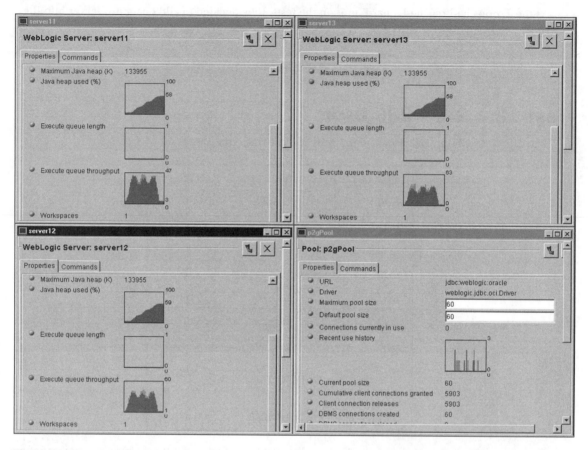

The following graph shows the CPU usage of Grace (similar to Eva and Sara), which is relatively busy, but with room for more.

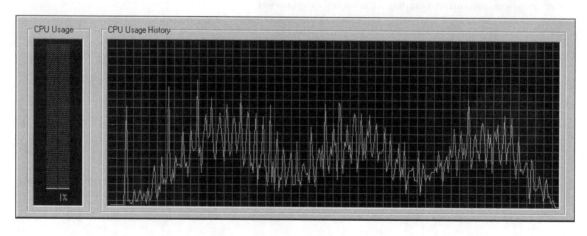

Test 12.1.2.2 – 320 Users

The next test increases the number of users by 40 to total 320 users. The results are the following:

Test 12.1.2.2	ART	TPS
url0	286.82	3.49
url1	200.52	4.99
url2	486.63	2.05
url3	536.47	1.86
url4	591.66	1.69
url5	640.26	1.56
url6	668.58	1.50
url7	668.55	1.50
url8	802.18	1.25
Total	**4881.66**	**0.2**

By just adding 40 users the response time has increased by 280%, from 1638 ms. There were no errors, but we are reaching a threshold. The database must be overwhelmed with requests, but not quite enough to start producing errors.

Whereas the WebLogic servers and the proxy exhibit a normal behavior, the database server shows a high usage of CPU as can be seen here:

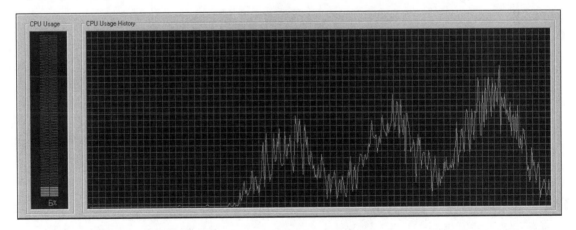

Test 12.1.2.3 – 400 users

As expected, this run with 400 users had a large number of errors, 288. Again all of them are directly traceable to the database. The CPU usage of Maria is quite heavy, as can be seen in the following screenshot:

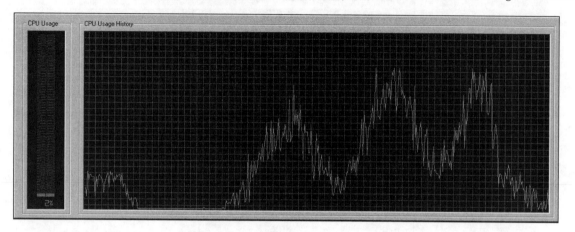

The rest of the data from the execution of the WebLogic servers and the proxy remains within acceptable ranges showing that more load could be handled easily. The results of this run are:

Test 12.1.2.3	ART	TPS
url0	264.25	3.78
url1	211.96	4.72
url2	538.80	1.86
url3	552.59	1.81
url4	661.28	1.51
url5	766.23	1.31
url6	814.70	1.23
url7	726.25	1.38
url8	744.68	1.34
Total	**5280.75**	**0.19**

Test 12.1.3 – Failure

The next test is focused on understanding how failover works. For this the Troops decide to test using 3 servers and 280 users. Just when the test is in the second half of the second cycle they pull the network connection from Grace effectively removing it from the cluster.

What happens next is that all the activity suddenly stops for the next 160 seconds, after which it ramps up again and continues up to the end of the test. The reason it takes this amount of time is related to the TCP/IP stack parameters, specifically the socket timeouts. The tests were made with the default values for these parameters on the NT operating system. Setting smaller values for the timeout parameters can make the proxy react sooner and the cluster recover more quickly. On the other hand, small values for timeouts allows the proxy to mark a server 'unavailable' when in reality it is just busy at that point in time. The latter approach could make the cluster more vulnerable under heavy load.

As the Troops have clearly identified when the failure occurs, they proceed to conduct an analysis of the response times for every cycle, which can be found in the following table:

Test 12.1.3	Cycle 0	Cycle 1	Cycle 2
url0	50.30	352.71	22316.76
url1	24.90	285.51	4247.11
url2	145.55	750.12	7205.68
url3	177.68	773.30	1527.19
url4	149.38	2613.99	420.29
url5	167.97	8939.25	331.05
url6	271.29	14395.13	285.98
url7	366.21	19438.03	222.21
url8	510.01	23279.99	225.20
Total	**1863.29**	**70828.03**	**36781.46**

The first cycle has a decent response time, considering that the optimizer of the JVM has not started producing results. Compared to the previous test, where the response time is averaged over the three cycles that make up the test, there is a difference of only 225 milliseconds. As expected, the response time for the second cycle increases dramatically, since this is where the failure occurs. On the third cycle the response time improves substantially, almost halving.

Conclusion

This set of tests demonstrates how the servlet clustering works, scales, and reacts to a failure. The first conclusion is that it is easy for a cluster of WebLogic servers to overrun a database server, so be prepared to have a more powerful machine running the database than the ones running WebLogic.

Finally, while the recovery from a failed WebLogic server is automatic and effortless, the cluster requires a period of time to recover. Therefore it is not as transparent as one would like it to be.

Object Clustering

A clustered object is one that is available on all the members of a cluster. This is called **symmetric clustering**. It is a requirement of WebLogic that the clustered object be deployed on all the members of the cluster.

The implementation of object clustering in WebLogic is based on a lightweight, message-passing kernel that supports both multi-tier architecture (required by EJB) and peer-to-peer architecture (required by RMI). At the core of it there is a very simple but powerful abstraction called a Remote Java Virtual Machine (RJVM). These RJVMs pass messages between themselves using a variety of protocols, including TCP/IP, SSL, HTTP, and IIOP. The RJVMs create and maintain all the sockets necessary to support these protocols and share them in a very efficient way between all the objects in the upper layers. They also support routing, which means that an RJVM can forward messages from one server to another.

The normal way of calling an RMI object or an EJB is to instantiate a stub. This stub will then reference a remote object. When using the WebLogic clustering a **smart stub** is initiated.

Smart Stubs

Smart stubs, also known as replica-aware stubs, are the first of two building blocks that make this kind of clustering possible in the WebLogic server. The reason these stubs are 'smart' is because they provide all the necessary information for failover and load balancing. More specifically, a smart stub has a replica handler that determines the specific algorithms that it must use for load balancing and failover. A developer has the choice of using predefined replica handlers or creating their own, the latter not being high on the list of suggestions.

When the invocation of a method fails, the replica handler determines if a retry should be attempted. Retries are not always warranted, but when it is possible, the replica handler will choose a new server offering that specific service to handle the request.

Load balancing occurs in a similar fashion. Immediately before invoking any method, the replica handler chooses a server to handle the request. The handler will not always select another server, as it prefers to use what is called the 'cheapest' invocation, it will try to use existing sockets or choose the server where all (or most) of the objects related to this invocation live.

Interestingly enough, all these algorithms can be 'sticky', which means that the replica handler will be used for load balancing only the first time a method is called on a stub.

Replicated Naming Service

Replicated naming service is the second building block for object clustering support in the WebLogic Server. WebLogic uses JNDI extensively within the server. It is also used as a key element of clustering. When a client requests the initial context from the JNDI tree in a clustered environment, it can request it from any member of the cluster. This is because the naming tree is replicated across all the members of a cluster.

When a member of the cluster wants to offer a service, it advertises this by placing a stub on the corresponding node of its naming tree. The stub is actually placed in a service pool at the node. This service pool contains all the stubs belonging to the members of the cluster offering the service. The result of a lookup in a JNDI tree will be the smart stub, which is aware of all the service providers in the cluster.

The JNDI naming tree is replicated on all the members of a cluster by means of the WebLogic Service Advertisement Protocol (WSAP). WSAP is based on IP multicasting and it transmits three different types of messages: heartbeats, announcements, and state dumps.

- ❑ **Heartbeats** are the actual messages sent between WebLogic servers. If there are no messages to be sent, then the server will issue a simple heartbeat. If a server does not receive a heartbeat from another server after a certain timeout period it will consider that server down and will cancel all the services offered by that server.

- ❑ An **announcement** contains an offer or retraction of a service. It will travel as a heartbeat and there is a sophisticated mechanism to deal with lost announcements.

- ❑ A **state dump** contains a complete list of services offered by a member of a cluster, and is what is multicasted when a new member joins an existing cluster.

Clustered EJBs

All EJBs can be clustered; however, this does not necessarily mean that all the instances of an EJB are clustered. Let us have a look at this in more detail.

Home Interfaces

All the home interfaces of the EJBs can be clustered. When a bean is deployed in a cluster, the home interface is bound into the replicated naming service. When a client looks up a home interface with JNDI, it gets a smart stub with reference to the actual home on each server that deployed the bean. When the `create()` or `find()` methods are called, the smart stub routes the call to the appropriate server based on the selected load balancing algorithm. That server will then create an instance of the bean.

Stateless Session Beans

Because, as their name suggests, these beans do not hold state on behalf of the client, the smart stub is free to send any call to any one of the servers that hosts the bean. The behavior for failover is dependent on the bean being **idempotent** or not. Idempotent is when a method returns the same result every time it is called with the same arguments.

If a bean is considered idempotent, this can be declared in the deployment descriptor and the failover will always happen.

In other words, stateless session beans are fully aware of the cluster without the developer making any effort other than defining that they are idempotent.

Stateful Session Beans

Because these kinds of beans do hold state in behalf of the client, all the calls must be sent to the specific instance of the bean. This is described as the bean being **pinned** to a server.

In this particular case the bean instance is not cluster-aware, even though the home interface is. This means that every new instance will be load balanced at the moment of creation, but if a failure occurs, it is the responsibility of the developer to catch the exception and deal with the recovery.

At the time of writing, BEA has a beta version of clustering available, which handles replication of stateful beans, thus making life easier for the developer in this case.

Entity Beans

The instances of these kinds of beans are pinned to the server that created them. As with the stateful session beans, the home interface is cluster-aware but the instance itself is not. The developer has to deal with the exception thrown by a server failure and handle the recovery.

If the bean is declared as read-only, the bean is fully cluster aware and a `find()` or `create()` will return a smart stub that will initiate the appropriate load balancing and failover.

RMI Objects

The implementation of RMI in a cluster in WebLogic is based on special extensions, which are used to create the smart stubs. The implementation of EJB in a WebLogic cluster is based on this clustered RMI.

Other Clustered Services

JDBC

With the JDBC/RMI driver it is possible to obtain load balancing and failover capabilities for JDBC connections. This is based on a `DataSource` object, which defines the connection to the database and can be registered in the replicated naming tree.

When a client looks up a data source object with JNDI, the load balancing and failover logic described earlier is used to select a server in the cluster that will handle the requested connection. Once a connection is obtained, it will be pinned to that server in order to maintain the database context.

JMS

At the time of writing, the engineering group of WebLogic are working on a version of clustering that can load balance JMS. A future version will also be able to handle failover.

Clustered Object Tests

At the time of writing the WebLogic clustering fully supports stateless session beans. The tests for this section will be limited to using the code developed in the first section of Chapter 4, which uses stateless beans.

Clustering the Pizza Stateless Beans

Using the same configuration of the test environment as for the previous tests in this chapter, the Troops are ready to test the code based on the stateless session beans.

Test Series 12.2.1 – Two Servers

Similar to the previous tests, the first set of tests will use only two machines, each running one instance of WebLogic. The setup is analogous to the test series 12.1.1, but deploying the code for Chapter 4a.

Test 12.2.1.1 – 200 Users

The Troops changed the test scripts in the Grinder to conform to the requirements of the stateless session bean version of the application. They then started testing with 200 simultaneous users. The results of this run are:

Test 12.2.1.1	ART	TPS
url0	79.88	12.52
url1	16.39	61.02
url2	84.04	11.90
url3	137.88	7.25
url4	202.73	4.93
url5	344.84	2.90
url6	544.25	1.84
url7	573.25	1.74
url8	520.66	1.92
url9	21.38	46.78
Total	**2525.29**	**0.4**

In comparison to the test in Chapter 11 (Test 11.3.5), the results are dramatically better, from a response time of almost 34 seconds to 2.5 seconds. This seems to make sense if you consider that each server is working with 100 simultaneous users. The response time for this test is in between the response times for the tests of 60 and 120 users with the single server.

In the screenshot of the console presented you can see that both servers behave similarly:

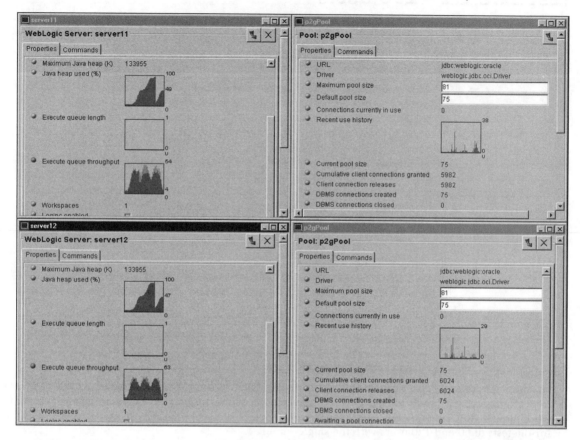

It is interesting to also note that the database is very busy, presenting a load level close to where there were failures in the previous set of runs. This can be seen below:

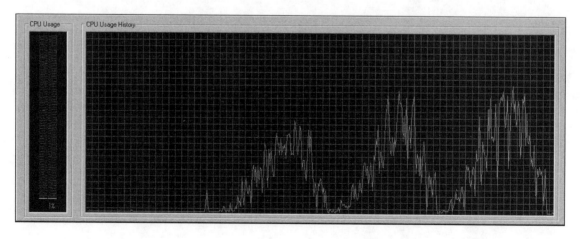

Test 12.2.1.2 – 280 Users

For this test the Troops increased the user load to 280. After seeing the load that Maria was having in the last run it comes as no surprise that there are errors on this test. In this case there were only two errors caused by the database not responding. The results are:

Test 12.2.1.2	ART	TPS
url0	60.47	16.54
url1	16.87	59.29
url2	87.52	11.43
url3	154.12	6.49
url4	331.15	3.02
url5	767.71	1.30
url6	1231.45	0.81
url7	1392.15	0.72
url8	1879.52	0.53
url9	43.71	22.88
Total	**5964.65**	**0.17**

This response time represents an increase of 136% over the previous run. We have already seen that this particular version of the application does not scale very well in the single machine tests. For those tests the maximum number of users it could handle was 200. Here it is doing a much better job with 280 users, but it is getting close to overrunning the database given the errors it has produced.

With a high CPU usage on the two servers running WebLogic, as presented below, the database almost reached 100% on the peak of the third cycle.

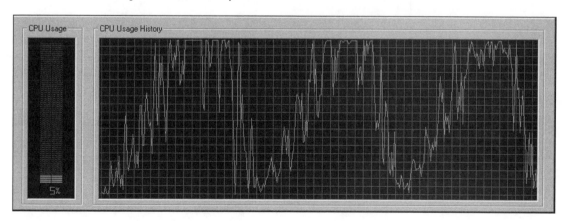

Test 12.2.1.3 – 320 Users

Interestingly enough this run only produced one error due to the database, which again showed a very high level of activity using the CPU. Both servers running WebLogic, Eva and Sara did show long peaks of cycle at 100% of CPU usage as can is shown in the figure below.

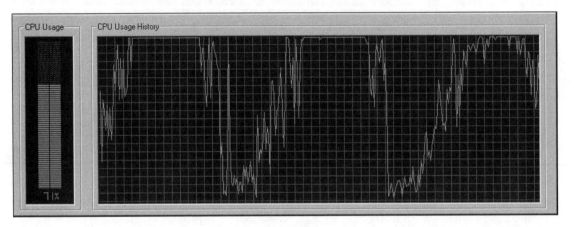

The response times for this test are:

Test 12.2.1.3	ART	TPS
url0	91.81	10.89
url1	26.22	38.14
url2	85.56	11.69
url3	200.47	4.99
url4	696.88	1.43
url5	2079.55	0.48
url6	4516.26	0.22
url7	4515.84	0.22
url8	7751.77	0.13
url9	97.89	10.22
Total	**20062.26**	**0.05**

Once again the WebLogic server is saturated producing response times that are over 3 times that of the previous run. It is the moment to add one more server to the cluster.

Test Series 12.2.2 – Three Servers

The procedure to add the third server is the same as the last time.

Test 12.2.2.1 – 280 Users

Starting from a higher base line, the results for 280 users are:

Test 12.2.2.1	ART	TPS
url0	282.45	3.54
url1	239.81	4.17
url2	444.16	2.25
url3	535.69	1.87
url4	678.00	1.47
url5	763.03	1.31
url6	866.62	1.15
url7	1021.24	0.98
url8	1071.03	0.93
url9	307.60	3.25
Total	**6209.63**	**0.16**

The response time is only 4% higher than the same run with two servers – showing that there is some overhead in the clustering when adding another server.

The database is using the CPU at a very high rate as seen below, but it is coping better with the requests as there are no errors.

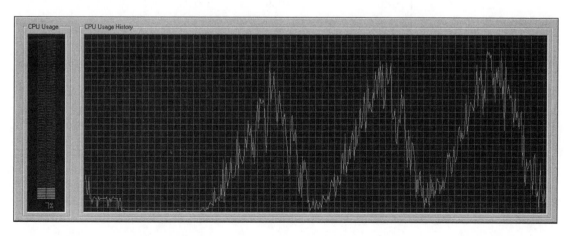

It is interesting to note the CPU usage chart of one of the WebLogic servers. The peaks for each cycle are decreasing as can be seen below. This can be attributed to the optimizer of the JVM.

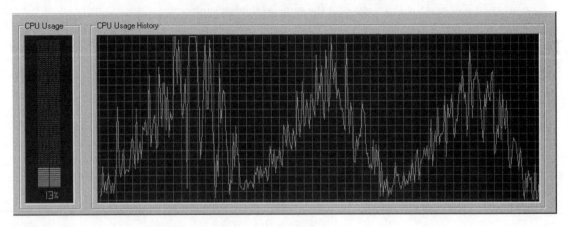

Test 12.2.2.2 – 320 Users

The execution of this test with 320 users did not produce any errors. The results are:

Test 12.2.2.2	ART	TPS
url0	295.04	3.39
url1	224.11	4.46
url2	477.62	2.09
url3	677.36	1.48
url4	715.34	1.40
url5	920.99	1.09
url6	1059.61	0.94
url7	1227.94	0.81
url8	1221.09	0.82
url9	330.82	3.02
Total	**7149.91**	**0.14**

This is a 15% increase in the response time as compared with the previous run; however, it is about three times less than the response time of the run with 2 servers for the same number of users. The figure below shows a screenshot of the console where you can observe the behavior of all three servers.

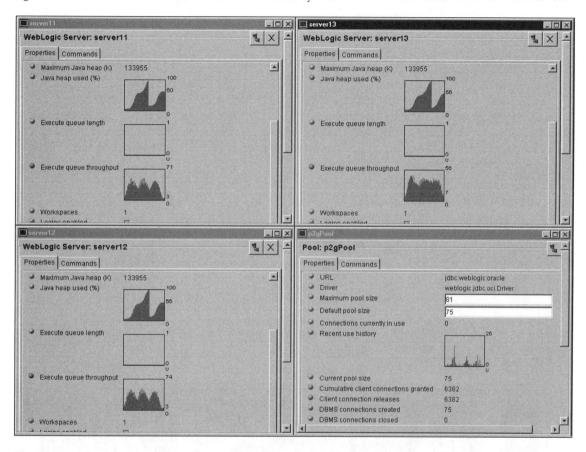

Now the database has reached a few peaks of 100% towards the middle of the third cycle. The WebLogic servers are experiencing a proportionally similar CPU usage.

Test 12.2.2.3 – 400 Users

This run had 39 errors due to the database and produced the following results:

URL	ART	TPS
url0	234.47	4.26
url1	203.85	4.91
url2	550.63	1.82
url3	632.41	1.58
url4	1203.62	0.83
url5	2422.12	0.41
url6	3673.13	0.27
url7	3172.06	0.32
url8	4811.48	0.21
url9	365.86	2.73
Total	**17269.62**	**0.06**

This is about 2.5 times the response time of the previous test. Here we have hit a limit with the number of machines in the cluster as well as the database as can be seen in the following figure that contains the CPU usage of Maria:

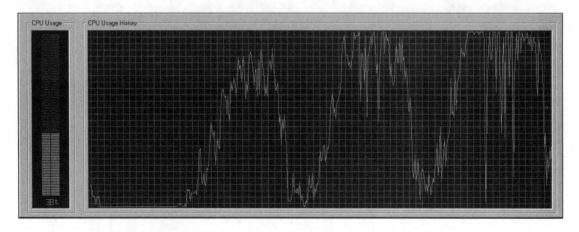

The CPUs of the three servers are having the peaks of the cycles at 100% and are very busy, as can be seen below:

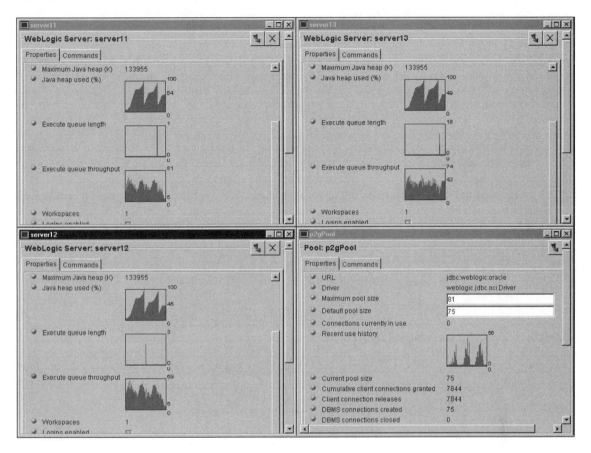

Conclusion

This set of tests used the stateless session bean version developed in Chapter 4. It can be said that the scalability is obvious, although not as good as for the tests using the servlets version.

In this particular case because the database is accessed in a different manner from for the servlet tests (it uses the JTA driver), it takes a larger user load to overrun the database.

Using the NSAPI Plugin

The NSAPI plugin is loaded by the iPlanet server by setting up two parameters in the `obj.conf` configuration file for the web server.

The first parameter is to instruct iPlanet to load the native library as an NSAPI module. The native library is provided with WebLogic and can be found under the `bin` directory of the WebLogic installation. There are several versions of the NSAPI library for distinct platforms and server versions. In this test scenario, an NT platform, the Troops included the following lines into the `obj.conf` file:

```
Init fn="load-modules" funcs="wl-proxy,wl-init" \
     shlib="C:/weblogic/bin/proxy36.dll"
Init fn="wl-init"
```

The second parameter is to let iPlanet know which request the WebLogic NSAPI plugin should handle. For this purpose, an object definition is declared. The following object definition tells iPlanet to redirect all requests to the servers in the cluster:

```
<Object name="weblogic" ppath="*">
   Service fn=wl-proxy WebLogicCluster="sara:7001,maria:7001" \
           PathTrim=""
</Object>
```

Test 12.3.1 – 280 Users

Just to test the usage of the NSAPI plugin, the Troops decide to give it a run with 280 users. The results are:

URL	ART	TPS
url0	123.54	8.09
url1	53.42	18.72
url2	157.60	6.35
url3	277.27	3.61
url4	596.01	1.68
url5	1283.40	0.78
url6	1634.66	0.61
url7	1599.98	0.63
url8	1891.89	0.53
url9	69.14	14.46
Total	**7686.91**	**0.13**

The response time is over 20% greater compared to the same run using the WebLogic server as a proxy (Test 12.2.1.2). The graphs of CPU usage are relatively similar, so it seems that it would be more efficient to use the WebLogic server as a proxy than the iPlanet web server with the NSAPI plugin.

Summary

In this chapter we learned how WebLogic clustering works for servlets and for objects. We saw the details of each one and used the versions of the application developed in Chapter 3 and 4 to test out the scalability and fault tolerance of the clustering capability of WebLogic. It is obvious that using the clustering functionality of the WebLogic server allows the application to scale, as well as providing failover.

It also proves that the database can soon become the bottleneck of the application. We are certain that by having the database fine-tuned and running on more powerful hardware, we could have increased the user loads and experienced little difficulty.

And Finally...

The Wonder Troops have illustrated why BEA WebLogic Server is the best choice for their application, and have shown the importance of the J2EE platform. The book has attempted to trace the Troops endeavors to help the reader in building their own e-commerce site.

For the Troops, their application has helped them keep a detailed record of stock, orders, and customers using the Oracle database, and use messaging techniques to communicate between different outlets and the Operation Center. On the customer side, they can now order pizzas in a secure web environment using the new interface, and confirmations of received orders are sent out.

Over the course of the chapters the Troops have meticulously constructed, developed, and tested their web site. The development of the site to use servlets, then stateless session beans and finally stateful session and entity beans was motivated by a desire to add functionality to support e-commerce (client log-in, order details and history, transactional ordering). The book has presented in detail the architecture behind these techniques. The testing balances that desire for functionality with some quantitative measures of the resultant resource requirements, strength, speed, and robustness.

The importance of simulating this real-life situation in which to test the code on the web site cannot be stressed enough. For a company like Pizza2Go, which relies on a fast and reliable relationship with its customers, the architecture behind the scenes has to be as robust as possible, and the Troops felt it necessary to perform these Grinder tests before allowing their new-fangled web site anywhere near the Internet.

> *In order that you can use and develop the Grinder for your own application, we've made it available under the GNU General Public License.*

The last word belongs to Mr Chairman Of The Board, who is very happy with the progress. His gamble regarding the employment and deployment of such luminaries such as Mr Wonderboy, Mr Senior Developer, and Mrs Chief Architect has certainly paid off, and he is pleased with Mr Yesman for bringing such talented staff to the fore in the Pizza2Go e-commerce revolution. After all, an ability to master the Internet is a major incentive to invest in a modern business. He is also impressed with the progress of the WAP interface the Troops developed in Chapter 9, as he anticipates public desire for mobile technology will only grow. Hopefully, this may finally allow the company to expand beyond North America into Europe.

Finally, and perhaps most importantly, we hope that reading this book has inspired you to experiment with your e-commerce site and to try to find the best solution for your situation.

HTTP

The Hypertext Transfer Protocol (HTTP) is an application-level protocol for distributed hypermedia information systems. It is a generic, stateless protocol, which can be used for many tasks beyond its use for hypertext. A feature of HTTP is the typing and negotiation of data representation, allowing systems to be built independently of the data being transferred.

The first version of HTTP, referred to as HTTP/0.9, was a simple protocol for raw data transfer across the Internet. HTTP/1.0, as defined by RFC 1945 improved the protocol by allowing messages to be in a MIME-like format, containing meta-information about the data transferred and modifiers on the request/response semantics. The current version HTTP/1.1, first defined in RFC 2068 and more recently in RFC 2616, made performance improvements by making all connections persistent and supporting absolute URLs in requests.

URL Request Protocols

A URL is a pointer to a particular resource on the Internet at a particular location and has a standard format as follows:

```
Protocol Servername Filepath
```

In order, the three elements are the protocol used to access the server, the name of the server and the location of the resource on the server. For example:

```
http://www.mydomain.com/
https://www.mydomain.com:8080/
ftp://ftp.mydomain.com/example.txt
mailto:me@world.com
file:///c:\Windows/win.exe
```

The `servername` and `filepath` pieces of the URL are totally dependent on where files are stored on your server and what you have called it, but there is a standard collection of protocols, most of which you should be familiar with:

- ❑ `http`: Normal HTTP requests for documents.
- ❑ `https`: Secure HTTP requests. The specific behavior of these depends on the security certificates and encryption keys you have set up.
- ❑ `JavaScript`: Executes JavaScript code within the current document.
- ❑ `ftp`: Retrieves documents from an FTP (File Transfer Protocol) server.
- ❑ `file`: Loads a file stored on the local (Client) machine. It can refer to remote servers but specifies no particular access protocol to remote file systems.
- ❑ `news`: Used to access Usenet newsgroups for articles.
- ❑ `nntp`: More sophisticated access to news servers.
- ❑ `mailto`: Allows mail to be sent from the browser. It may call in assistance from a helper app.
- ❑ `telnet`: Opens an interactive session with the server.
- ❑ `gopher`: A precursor to the World Wide Web.

This book exclusively deals with the first five of these.

HTTP Basics

Each HTTP client (web browser) request and server response has three parts: the request or response line, a header section, and the entity body.

Client Request

The client initiates a web page transaction – client page request and server page response – as follows.

The client connects to an HTTP-based server at a designated port (by default, 80) and sends a request by specifying an HTTP command called a method, followed by a document address, and an HTTP version number. The format of the request line is:

```
Method      Request-URI      Protocol
```

For example:

```
GET    /index.html    HTTP/1.0
```

uses the `GET` method to request the document `/index.html` using version 1.0 of the protocol. We'll come to a full list of HTTP Request Methods later.

Next, the client sends optional header information to the server about its configuration and the document formats it will accept. All header information is sent line by line, each with a header name and value in the form:

```
Keyword: Value
```

For example:

```
User-Agent:     Lynx/2.4 libwww/5.1k
Accept:         image/gif, image/x-xbitmap, image/jpeg, */*
```

The request line and the subsequent header lines are each terminated by a carriage return/linefeed (\r\n) sequence. The client sends a blank line to end the headers. We'll return with a full description of each HTTP Header value later on in the Appendix.

Finally, after sending the request and headers the client may send additional data. This data is mostly used by CGI programs using the POST method. This additional information is called a request entity. Finally a blank line (\r\n\r\n) terminates the request. A complete request might look like the following:

```
GET /index.html HTTP/1.0
Accept: */*
Connection: Keep-Alive
Host: www.w3.org
User-Agent: Generic
```

HTTP Request Methods

HTTP request methods should not be confused with URL protocols. The former are used to instruct a web server how to handle the incoming request while the latter define how client and server talk to each other. In version 1.1 of the HTTP protocol, there are seven basic HTTP request methods:

Method	Description
OPTIONS	Used to query a server about the capabilities it provides. Queries can be general or specific to a particular resource.
GET	Asks that the server return the body of the document identified in the Request-URI.
HEAD	Responds similarly to a GET, except that no content body is ever returned. It is a way of checking whether a document has been updated since the last request.
POST	This is used to transfer a block of data to the server in the content body of the request.
PUT	This is the complement of a GET request and stores the content body at the location specified by the Request-URI. It is similar to uploading a file with FTP.
DELETE	Provides a way to delete a document from the server. The document to be deleted is indicated in the Request-URI.
TRACE	This is used to track the path of a request through firewalls and multiple proxy servers. It is useful for debugging complex network problems and is similar to the traceroute tool.

Server Response

The HTTP response also contains three parts.

Firstly, the server replies with the status line containing three fields: the HTTP version, status code, and description of status code, in the following format.

```
Protocol    Status-code    Description
```

For example, the status line:

```
HTTP/1.0    200    OK
```

indicates that the server uses version 1.0 of the HTTP in its response. A status code of 200 means that the client request was successful.

After the response line, the server sends header information to the client about itself and the requested document. All header information is sent line by line, each with a header name and value in the form:

```
Keyword: Value
```

For example:

```
HTTP/1.1 200 OK
Date: Wed, 19 May 1999 18:20:56 GMT
Server: Apache/1.3.6 (Unix) PHP/3.0.7
Last-Modified: Mon, 17 May 1999 15:46:21 GMT
ETag: "2da0dc-2870-374039cd"
Accept-Ranges: bytes
Content-Length: 10352
Connection: close
Content-Type: text/html; charset=iso-8859-1
```

The response line and the subsequent header lines are each terminated by a carriage return/linefeed (\r\n) sequence. The server sends a blank line to end the headers. Again, we'll return to the exact meaning of these HTTP headers in a minute.

If the client's request if successful, the requested data is sent. This data may be a copy of a file, or the response from a CGI program. This result is called a **response entity**. If the client's request could not be fulfilled, additional data sent might be a human-readable explanation of why the server could not fulfill the request. The properties (type and length) of this data are sent in the headers. Finally a blank line (\r\n\r\n) terminates the response. A complete response might look like the following:

```
HTTP/1.1 200 OK
Date: Wed, 19 May 1999 18:20:56 GMT
Server: Apache/1.3.6 (Unix) PHP/3.0.7
Last-Modified: Mon, 17 May 1999 15:46:21 GMT
ETag: "2da0dc-2870-374039cd"
Accept-Ranges: bytes
Content-Length: 10352
Connection: close
Content-Type: text/html; charset=iso-8859-1
```

```
<!DOCTYPE HTML PUBLIC "-//W3C//DTD HTML 4.0 Transitional//EN"
"http://www.w3.org/TR/REC-html40/loose.dtd">
<html>

    ...

</html>
```

In HTTP/1.0, after the server has finished sending the response, it disconnects from the client and the transaction is over unless the client sends a `Connection: KeepAlive` header. In HTTP/1.1, however, the connection is maintained so that the client can make additional requests, unless the client sends an explicit `Connection: Close header`. Since many HTML documents embed other documents as inline images, applets, and frames, for example, this persistent connection feature of HTTP/1.1 protocol will save the overhead of the client having to repeatedly connect to the same server just to retrieve a single page.

HTTP Headers

These headers can appear in requests or responses. Some control how the web server behaves, others are meant for proxy servers and some will affect what your browser does with a response when it is received. You should refer to the HTTP 1.1 specification for a full description. You can download it from:

ftp://ftp.isi.edu/in-notes/rfc2616.txt

The authentication is covered in a little more detail in:

ftp://ftp.isi.edu/in-notes/rfc2617.txt

Other RFC documents from the same source may be useful and provide additional insights.

This table summarizes the headers you'll find most helpful. There are others in the specification but they control how the web server manages the requests and won't arrive in the CGI environment for you to access:

Header	Request	Response	Description
Accept:	✓		Lists the types that the client can cope with.
Accept-Charset:	✓		Lists the character sets that the browser can cope with.
Accept-Encoding:	✓		List of acceptable encodings or none. Omitting this header signifies that all current encodings are acceptable.
Accept-Language:	✓		List of acceptable languages.

Table Continued on Following Page

Header	Request	Response	Description
Age:		✓	A cache control header used to indicate the age of a response body.
Allow:		✓	Determines the available methods that the resource identified by the URI can respond to.
Authorization:	✓		Authorization credentials. Refer to RFC 2617 for more information on Digest authentication.
Cache-Control:	✓	✓	A sophisticated proxy-controlling header. Can be used to describe how proxies should handle requests and responses.
Code:	✓		Defines an encoding for the body data. This would normally be Base64.
Content-Base:		✓	Used to resolve relative URLs within the body of the document being returned. It overrides the value in the Content-Location header.
Content-Encoding:		✓	Specifies encodings that have been applied to the body prior to transmission.
Content-Language:		✓	This specifies the natural language of the response content.
Content-Length:		✓	The length of the body measured in bytes should be put here. CGI responses may defer to the web server and allow it to put this header in.
Content-Location:		✓	The actual location of the entity being returned in the response. This may be useful when deploying resources that can be resolved in several ways. The specifically selected version can be identified and requested directly.
Content-MD5:		✓	This is a way of computing a checksum for the entity body. The receiving browser can compare its computed value to be sure that the body has not been modified during transmission.

Header	Request	Response	Description
Content-Type:		✓	The type of data being returned in the response is specified with this header. These types are listed later in this appendix.
Expires:		✓	The date after which the response should be considered to be stale.
From:	✓		The client e-mail address is sent in this header.
Host:	✓		The target virtual host is defined in this header. The value is taken from the originating URL when the request is made.
Last-Modified:		✓	This indicates when the content being returned was last modified. For static files, the web server would use the file's timestamp. For a dynamically generated page, you might prefer to insert a value based on when a database entry was last changed. Other more sophisticated cache control headers are provided in the HTTP specification. Refer to RFC 2616 for details.
Location:		✓	Used to redirect to a new location. This could be used as part of a smart error handling CGI.
Referrer:	✓		The source of the current request is indicated here. This would be the page that the request was linked from. You can determine whether the link was from outside your site and also pick up search engine parameters from this too, if your URI was requested via Yahoo, for example.
User-Agent:	✓		This is the signature field of the browser. You can code round limitations in browsers if you know this. Be aware of some of the weird values that can show up in this header now that developers are building their own web browsers and spiders.
Warning:		✓	This is used to carry additional information about the response and whether there are risks associated with it.

Server Environment Variables

By and large, the headers in the request correspond with environment variables that are present when a CGI handler executes. Not all headers make it as far as the CGI environment. Some may be 'eaten up' by a proxy server, others by the target web server. Some environment variables are created as needed by the web server itself, without there having been a header value to convert.

Here is a summary of the environment variables you are likely to find available. There may be others if the web server administrator has configured them into the server or if the CGI adapter has been modified to pass them in. You can access them with the `Clib.getenv()` function. These are considered to be standard values and they should be present:

(Editor's Note: This list is written with respect to ScriptEase CGI scriptwriters. In JSP, the HTTP headers and server variables are accessible via the `ServletRequest, HTTPServletRequest, HTTPServletResponse,` *and* `ServletConfig, ServletContext` *classes)*

AUTH_TYPE

The value in this environment variable depends on the kind of authentication used in the server and whether the script is even security protected by the server. This involves server configuration and is server-specific and also protocol-specific. The value may not be defined if the page is insecure. If it is secure, the value indicating the type of authentication may only be set after the user is authenticated. An example value for AUTH_TYPE is BASIC.

CONTENT_LENGTH

If the request used the POST method, then it may have supplied additional information in the body. This is passed to the CGI handler on its standard input. However, ScriptEase will assimilate this for you, extract any query strings in the body and decode them into variables that you can access more conveniently.

CONTENT_TYPE

The data type of any content delivered in the body of the request. With this, you could process the standard input for content bodies that are some type other than form data. This is relatively unexplored territory and likely to be very much server- and platform-dependent. If it works at all, you might choose a reading mechanism based on content type and then use other headers to process the binary data in the body. If you are using this just to upload files, then the HTTP/1.1 protocol now supports a PUT method which is a better technique and is handled inside the server.

DOCUMENT_ROOT

This is the full path to the document root for the web server. If virtual hosts are being used and if they share the same CGI scripts, this document root may be different for each virtual host. It is a good idea to have separately owned cgi-bin directories unless the sites are closely related. For example, a movie site and a games site might have separate cgi-bin directories. Three differently branded versions of the movie site might have different document roots but could share the same cgi-bin functionality. In some servers, this may be a way to identify which one of several virtual hosts is being used.

FROM

If the user has configured their browser appropriately, this environment variable will contain their e-mail address. If it is present, then this is a good way to identify the user, given the assumption that they are the owner of the computer they are using.

GATEWAY_INTERFACE

You can determine the version number of the CGI interface being used. This would be useful if you depend on features available in a later version of the CGI interface but you only want to maintain a single script to be used on several machines.

HTTP_ACCEPT

This is a list of acceptable MIME types that the browser will accept. The values are dependent on the browser being used and how it is configured and are simply passed on by the web server. If you want to be particularly smart and do the right thing, check this value when you try to return any oddball data other than plain text or HTML. If the browser doesn't say it can cope, it might just crash on the user when you try and give them some unexpected data.

HTTP_ACCEPT_LANGUAGE

There may not be a value specified in this environment variable. If there is, the list will be as defined by the browser.

HTTP_CONNECTION

This will indicate the disposition of the HTTP connection. It might contain the value "Keep-Alive" or "Close" but you don't really have many options from the ScriptEase:WSE-driven CGI point of view. You might need to know whether the connection to the browser will remain open but since SE:WSE won't currently support streaming tricks it won't matter much either way.

HTTP_COOKIE

The cookie values sent back by the browser are collected together and made available in this environment variable. You will need to make a cookie cutter to separate them out and extract their values. Which particular cookies you receive depend on whereabouts in the site's document root you are and the scope of the cookie when it was created.

HTTP_HOST

On a multiple virtual host web server, this will tell you the host name that was used for the request. You can then adjust the output according to different variations of the site. For example, you can present different logos and backgrounds for www.mydomain.com and test.mydomain.com. This can help solve a lot of issues when you set up a co-operative branding deal to present your content via several portal sites. They do like to have their logo and corporate image on the page sometimes.

HTTP_PRAGMA

This is somewhat deprecated these days but will likely contain the value "no-cache". Cache control is handled more flexibly with the new response headers available in HTTP/1.1. Caching and proxy server activity can get extremely complex and you may want to study the HTTP specification for more info: ftp://ftp.isi.edu/in-notes/rfc2616.txt.

HTTP_REFERER

This is the complete URL for the page that was being displayed in the browser and which contained the link being requested. If the page was a search engine, this may also contain some interesting query information that you could extract to see how people found your web site. There are some situations where there will be no referrer listed. When a user types a URL into a location box, there is no referrer. This may also be true when the link was on a page held in a file on the user's machine. There are some browser-dependent issues as well. Some versions of Microsoft Internet Explorer do not report a referrer for HTML documents in framesets. If you have the referrer information it can be useful, but there are enough times when the referrer may be blank that you should have a fall back mechanism in place as well.

HTTP_USER_AGENT

The User Agent is a cute name for the browser. It is necessary because the page may not always be requested by a browser. It could be requested by a robot or so-called web spider. It may be requested by offline readers or monitoring services and it's not uncommon for static page generators to be used on a site that was originally designed to be dynamic. Rather than try to cope with all variants of the browsers, you should focus on determining whether you have a browser or robot requesting your documents. That way, you can serve up a page that is more appropriate to a robot when necessary. There is no point in delivering a page that contains an advert, for example. You can make your site attractive to the sight-impaired user community by detecting the use of a text-only browser such as Lynx. You could then serve a graphically sparse but text rich page instead. When examining this value, be aware that there is much weirdness in the values being returned by some browsers. This may be intentional or accidental, but since the Netscape sources were released, developers have been busy writing customized browsers. Some of these will send User-Agent headers containing control characters and binary data. Whether this is an attempt to exploit bugs in web servers, CGI handlers, or log analysis software is arguable. You will encounter e-mail addresses, URLs, command line instructions and even entire web pages in this header.

PATH

This is the list of directories that will be searched for commands that you may try to execute from within your CGI handler. It is inherited from the parent environment that spawned the handler. It is platform-dependent and certainly applies to UNIX systems. It may not be present on all of the others.

PATH_INFO

This is a way of extracting additional path information from the request. Here is a URL as an example: http://www.domain.com/cgi-bin/path.jsh/folder1/file. This will run the SE:WSE script called `path.jsh` and store the value `/folder1/file` in the PATH_INFO environment variable. This can be an additional way of passing parameters from the HTML page into the server-side script.

PATH_TRANSLATED

This is only implemented on some servers and may be implemented under another environment variable name on others. It returns the full physical path to the script being executed. This might be useful if you have shared code that you include into several scripts.

QUERY_STRING

The query string is that text in the URL following a question mark. This environment variable will contain that text. SE:WSE will unwrap it and present the individual items as variables you can access directly.

REMOTE_ADDR

This is the remote IP address of the client machine that initiated the request. You might use this to control what is displayed or to deny access to users outside your domain.

REMOTE_HOST

It is very likely this value will be empty. It requires the web server to resolve the IP address to a name via the DNS. Whether that would even work depends on the remote user's machine even being listed in a DNS database. It is most often disabled because it imposes significant performance degradation if the web server needs to perform a DNS lookup on every request. You could engineer a local DNS and run that separately, only looking up IP addresses when you need to. Even so, that would still impose a turnaround delay on handling the request and time is definitely of the essence here.

REMOTE_IDENT

This is a deprecated feature. It relies on both the client and server supporting RFC 931 but, since the end user can define the value to be anything they like, the chances of it being useful are quite small. This is probably best avoided altogether and you will be very fortunate if you ever see a meaningful value in it. Of course, in a captive intranet situation where you have more control, you might make use of it.

REMOTE_USER

If the user has been authenticated and has passed the test, the authenticated username will be placed in this variable. Other than that, this variable and AUTH_TYPE are likely to be empty. Even after authentication, this value may be empty when the request is made for a document in a non-secured area.

REQUEST_METHOD

This is the HTTP request method. It is likely you will only ever see GET or POST in here. You usually don't need to deliver different versions of a document based on this value but it might be important to verify that the access was made correctly from your page via the correct method. Apart from the size of the data being larger with a POST, there is another more subtle difference between GET and POST. Using a GET more than once should always result in the same data being returned. Using POST more than once may result in multiple transactions to the back-end. For example, placing an order more than once due to reposting a form. This is one area where the back button on the browser works against you and you may want to interlock this somehow within your session-handling code to prevent duplicate financial transactions happening. You should be aware that this is happening when the browser displays an alert asking whether you want to repost the same form data.

SCRIPT_FILENAME

This is effectively the same as the PATH_TRANSLATED environment variable. It is the full path to the script being executed. Once you have established which of these your server provides (if either), you should be able to stick with it.

SCRIPT_NAME

This is the logical name of the script. It is basically the Request-URI portion of the URL that was originally sent. It is the full path of the script without the document root or script alias mapping. This would be portable across several virtual hosts where the SCRIPT_FILENAME/PATH_TRANSLATED values might not be. This is also useful for making scripts relocatable. You can use this value to rebuild a form so that it will call the same script again. The result is that the script does not then contain a hard-coded path that will need to be edited if it is renamed or moved.

SERVER_ADMIN

If it is configured, the e-mail address of the server administrator is held in this environment variable. You could build this into the security mechanisms to alert the administrator when a potential break-in is detected. Be careful not to mailbomb the server administrator with thousands of messages though.

SERVER_NAME

This is the name of the server and may, on some systems, be equivalent to the HTTP_HOST value. This can be useful for manufacturing links elsewhere in a site or detecting the site name so you can build site-specific versions of a page.

SERVER_PORT

The port number that the request arrived on is stored here. Most web sites operate on port 80. Those that don't may be test sites or might operate inside a firewall. It is possible that ancillary servers for adverts and media may use other port numbers if they run on the same machine as the main web server. Most web servers allow you to configure any port number. In the case of the Apache web server you can set up individual virtual hosts on different ports. This means that you could develop a test site and use this value to activate additional debugging help knowing that it would be turned off if the script were run on the production site.

SERVER_PROTOCOL

This is the protocol level of the request being processed. This area is quite ambiguous in the specifications and previously published books. The browser can indicate a preferred protocol level that it can accommodate. This is the value it puts in the request line. However, the server may choose to override that and serve the request with a sub-set of that functionality that conforms to an earlier protocol level. The server configuration may determine a browser match and override it internally or the request may be simple enough that it can be served by HTTP/1.0 protocol even though the browser indicates that it could cope with HTTP/1.1 protocol. From a CGI scripting point of view, it is unlikely you would need to build alternative versions of a page according to this value. It might determine whether you could provide streaming media but that technique is not currently supported by SE:WSE anyway.

SERVER_SOFTWARE

For example, Apache/1.3.6, but dependent on your server.

UNIQUE_ID

This is available in CGI environments running under an Apache web server that has been built with the unique_id module included. You could select the first one of these that arrives in a session, and use it as the session key thereafter, as another alternative way of generating unique session keys. It also might provide some useful user-tracking possibilities.

Pizza2Go

JSP Syntax Reference

This appendix reviews the syntax for JavaServer Pages 1.1. It is intended to provide more information than the syntax card on particular options, while being more compact than the specification.

> The JSP specifications 1.0 and 1.1 plus PDF syntax cards are available from
> http://java.sun.com/products/jsp, while the older specifications are archived at
> http://www.kirkdorffer.com/jspspecs/jsp092.html and jsp091.html.

A word on the syntax of the syntax:

- ❑ Italics show what you'll have to specify.

- ❑ Bold shows the default value of an attribute. Attributes with default values are optional attributes, if you're using the default.

- ❑ When an attribute has a set of possible values, those are shown, delimited by |.

The page Directive

The page directive specifies attributes for the page – all the attributes are optional, as the essential ones have default values, shown in bold.

```
<%@ page language="java"
        extends="package.class"
        import="package.class, package.*, ..."
        session="true|false"
```

```
          buffer="none|8kb|sizekb"
          autoFlush="true|false"
          isThreadSafe="true|false"
          info="Sample JSP to show tags"
          errorPage="ErrorPage.jsp"
          contentType="text/html; charset=ISO-8859-1"
          isErrorPage="true|false"
%>
```

❑ The errorPage attribute contains the relative URL for the error page to which this page should go if there's an unhandled error on this page.

❑ The specified error page file must declare isErrorPage="true" to have access to the exception object.

❑ The contentType attribute sets the mime type and the character set for the page.

```
<%@ page language="java"
          isErrorPage="true" %>
```

```
<html>
<body>
<!-- The fully-qualified class that is the exception -->
<%= exception.toString() %>
<br>
<!-- The exception's message to the world -->
<%= exception.getMessage() %>
</body>
</html>
```

taglib Directive

The taglib directive defines a tag library namespace for the page, mapping the URI of the tag library descriptor to a prefix that can be used to reference tags from the library on this page.

```
<%@ taglib uri="/META-INF/taglib.tld" prefix="tagPrefix" %>

...

<tagPrefix:tagName attributeName="attributeValue" >
  JSP content
</tagPrefix:tagName>
<tagPrefix:tagName attributeName="attributeValue" />
```

The tag library descriptor (.tld file) looks like this:

```
<?xml version="1.0" encoding="ISO-8859-1" ?>
<!DOCTYPE taglib
        PUBLIC "-//Sun Microsystems, Inc.//DTD JSP Tag Library 1.1//EN"
        "http://java.sun.com/j2ee/dtds/web-jsptaglibrary_1_1.dtd">
<taglib>
  <tlibversion>1.0</tlibversion>
```

```
    <jspversion>1.1</jspversion>
    <shortname>projsp</shortname>
    <uri>http://www.wrox.com</uri>
    <info>
      Info on the tag library
    </info>

    <tag>
      <name>tagName</name>
      <tagclass>package.class</tagclass>
      <teiclass> package.TagExtraInfoClass</teiclass>
      <bodycontent>empty|JSP|tagdependent</bodycontent>
      <info>
        Information on the tag
      </info>

      <attribute>
        <name>attributeName</name>
        <required>true|false</required>
        <rtexprvalue>true|false</rtexprvalue>
      </attribute>
    </tag>

</taglib>
```

The `teiclass`, `bodycontent`, `info`, and `attribute` tags are optional. Within the `attribute` tag, the `required` and `rtexprvalue` tags are also optional. The value of `rtexprvalue` determines whether expressions are allowed to determine the value of the `attribute`.

Include Tags

There are two include tags – the `include` directive and the `jsp:include` tag.

The `include` directive includes a static file, specified by a relative URL, at translation time, adding any JSP in that file to this page for run-time processing:

```
<%@ include file="Header.html" %>
```

The `jsp:include` tag includes a static or dynamically-referenced file, so it's handled at run time:

```
<jsp:include page="relativeURL"
             flush="true" >
  <jsp:param name="parameterName" value="parameterValue"/>
</jsp:include>
```

❏   The `page` attribute can be the result of some run-time expression.

❏   Future releases of the Servlet API will provide some options for the `flush` attribute.

❏   The `jsp:param` tag provides a mapping between a name and a value. The value can be a run-time expression. Here the parameters are appended to the original request, in a comma-delimited list and if the parameter `name` already exists, the new parameter `value` takes precedence.

Bean-handling Tags

There are three tags to instantiate and handle JavaBeans from the page:

jsp:useBean Tag

The jsp:useBean tag checks for an instance of a bean of the given class and scope. If one exists it references it with the id, otherwise it instantiates it. The bean is available within its scope with its id attribute.

You can include code between the jsp:useBean tags, as shown in the second example – this code will only be run if the jsp:useBean tag successfully returns a reference to a bean instance.

```
<jsp:useBean id="aBeanName"
             scope="page|request|session|application"
             class="package.class"
/>
```

```
<jsp:useBean id="anotherBeanName"
             scope="page|request|session|application"
             class="package.class"
>
  <jsp.setProperty name="anotherBeanName"
                   property="*|propertyName" />
</jsp:useBean>
```

Note that the class package must be imported in the page directive

There is a lot of flexibility in specifying the bean. You can use:

❑   class="package.class"

❑   type="typeName"

❑   class="package.class" type="typeName" (and with terms reversed)

❑   beanName="beanName" type="typeName" (and with terms reversed)

where:

❑   typeName is the class of the scripting variable defined by the id attribute, that is the class that the Bean instance is cast to (whether the class, a parent class or an interface the class implements).

❑   beanName is the name of the Bean, as used in the instantiate() method of the java.beans.Beans class.

jsp:setProperty Tag

The `jsp:setProperty` tag we used above sets the property of the bean referenced by `name` using the `value`:

```
<jsp.setProperty name="anotherBeanName"
                 property="*|propertyName"
                 value="newValue" />
```

The property attribute can be any of the following:

- ❑   property="*propertyName*" value="*propertyValue*"
- ❑   property="*"
- ❑   property="*propertyName*" param="*parameterName*"
- ❑   property="*propertyName*"

where:

- ❑   The * setting tells the tag to iterate through the `request` parameters for the page, setting any values for properties in the Bean whose names match parameter names.
- ❑   The `param` attribute specifies the parameter name to use in setting this property.
- ❑   Omitting `value` and `param` attributes for a property assumes that the Bean property and `request` parameter name match.
- ❑   The `value` attribute can be any run-time expression as long as it evaluates to a `String`.
- ❑   The `value` attribute `String` can be automatically cast to `boolean`, `byte`, `char`, `double`, `int`, `float`, `long`, and their class equivalents. Other casts will have to be handled explicitly in the Bean's set*PropertyName*() method.

jsp:getProperty Tag

The final bean-handling tag is `jsp:getProperty`, which gets the named property and outputs its value for inclusion in the page as a String:

```
<jsp:getProperty name="anotherBeanName" property="propertyName" />
```

Comments

Two sorts of comments are allowed in addition to comments in Java code – JSP and HTML:

```
<!-- HTML comments remain in the final client page.
     Can include JSP expressions
-->
<%-- JSP comment which is hidden from the final client page --%>
```

Declarations

The following syntax allows you to declare variables and functions for the page:

```
<%!
  int i = 0;
  char ch = 'a';
  boolean isTrue(boolean b) {
    // Is this true?
  }
%>
```

Scriptlets

Scriptlets enclose Java code (on however many lines) that is translated and evaluated to generate dynamic content:

```
<%
  // Java code
%>
```

Expressions

Expressions return a value from the scripting code as a String to the page:

```
<br>My word, is it <%= userName %>? It's been a while...<br>
```

Supporting Applets and Beans

The jsp:plugin tag enables the JSP to include a bean or an applet in the client page. It has the following syntax:

```
<jsp:plugin type="bean|applet"
            code="class"
            codebase="classDirectory"
            name="instanceName"
            archive="archiveURI"
            align="bottom|top|middle|left|right"
            height="inPixels"
            width="inPixels"
            hspace="leftRightPixels"
            vspace="topBottomPixels"
            jreversion="1.1|number"
            nspluginurl="pluginURL"
            iepluginurl="pluginURL" >
  <jsp:params>
    <jsp:param name="parameterName" value="parameterValue">
  </jsp:params>
  <jsp:fallback>Problem with plugin</jsp:fallback>
</jsp:plugin>
```

Most of these attributes are direct from the HTML spec – the exceptions are type, jreversion, nspluginurl, and iepluginurl.

❑ The name, archive, align, height, width, hspace, vspace, jreversion, nspluginurl, and iepluginurl attributes are optional

❑ The jsp:param tag's value attribute can take a run-time expression

Forwarding the Request

To forward the client request to another URL, whether it be an HTML file, JSP or servlet, use the following syntax:

```
<jsp:forward page="relativeURL" />

<jsp:forward page="relativeURL" >
  <jsp:param name="parameterName" value="parameterValue" />
</jsp:forward>
```

❑ The page attribute for jsp:forward can be a run-time expression

❑ The value attribute for jsp:param can be a run-time expression

Implicit Objects

Implicit objects	Type	Scope
application	javax.servlet.ServletContext	Application
session	javax.servlet.HttpSession	Session
request	javax.servlet.ServletRequest	Request
pageContext	javax.servlet.jsp.PageContext	Page
out	javax.servlet.jsp.JspWriter	Page
config	javax.servlet.ServletConfig	Page
exception	java.lang.Throwable	Page
page	java.lang.Object	Page
response	javax.servlet.ServletResponse	Page

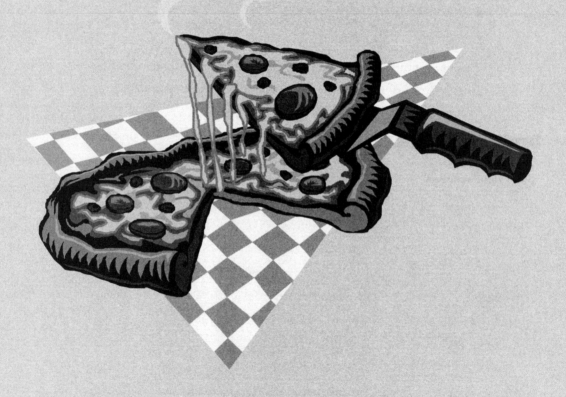

Pizza2Go

C

Support, Errata, and p2p.wrox.com

One of the most irritating things about any programming book is when you find that bit of code you've just spent an hour typing simply doesn't work. You check it a hundred times to see if you've set it up correctly and then you notice the spelling mistake in the variable name on the book page. Of course, you can blame the authors for not taking enough care and testing the code, the editors for not doing their job properly, or the proofreaders for not being eagle-eyed enough, but this doesn't get around the fact that mistakes do happen.

We try hard to ensure no mistakes sneak out into the real world, but we can't promise that this book is 100% error free. What we can do is offer the next best thing by providing you with immediate support and feedback from experts who have worked on the book and try to ensure that future editions eliminate these gremlins. We also now commit to supporting you not just while you read the book, but once you start developing applications as well through our online forums where you can put your questions to the authors, reviewers, and fellow industry professionals.

In this appendix we'll look at how to:

❑   Enroll in the peer to peer forums at http://p2p.wrox.com

❑   Post and check for errata on our main site, http://www.wrox.com

❑   e-Mail technical support a query or feedback on our books in general

Between all three support procedures, you should get an answer to your problem in no time flat.

The Online Forums at P2P.Wrox.Com

Join the Pro JSP mailing list for author and peer support. Our system provides **programmer to programmer™ support** on mailing lists, forums, and newsgroups all in addition to our one-to-one e-mail system, which we'll look at in a minute. Be confident that your query is not just being examined by a support professional, but by the many Wrox authors and other industry experts present on our mailing lists.

How To Enroll for Support

Just follow this four-step system:

1. Go to p2p.wrox.com in your favorite browser. Here you'll find any current announcements concerning P2P – new lists created, any removed and so on.

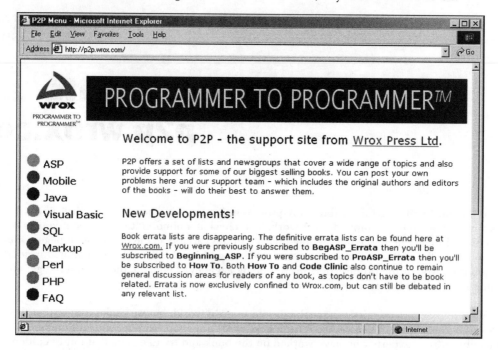

2. Click on the Java button in the left hand column.

3. Choose to access the pro_ jsp list.

4. If you are not a member of the list, you can choose to either view the list without joining it or create an account in the list, by hitting the respective buttons.

5. If you wish to join, you'll be presented with a form in which you'll need to fill in your e-mail address, name and a password (of at least four alphanumeric characters). Choose how you would like to receive the messages from the list and then hit Save.

6. Congratulations. You're now a member of the pro_ jsp mailing list.

Why This System Offers the Best Support

You can choose to join the mailing lists or you can receive them as a weekly digest. If you don't have the time or facilities to receive the mailing list, then you can search our online archives. You'll find the ability to search on specific subject areas or keywords. As these lists are moderated, you can be confident of finding good, accurate information quickly. Mails can be edited or moved by the moderator into the correct place, making this a most efficient resource. Junk and spam mail are deleted, and your own e-mail address is protected by the unique Lyris system from web-bots that can automatically hoover up newsgroup mailing list addresses. Any queries about joining, or leaving, lists or any query about the list should be sent to: moderatorprojsp@wrox.com.

Checking the Errata Online at www.wrox.com

The following section will take you step-by-step through the process of posting errata to our web site to get that help. The sections that follow, therefore, are:

- ❑ Wrox Developer's Membership
- ❑ Finding a list of existing errata on the web site
- ❑ Adding your own errata to the existing list
- ❑ What happens to your erratum once you've posted it (why doesn't it appear immediately)?

There is also a section covering how to e-mail a question for technical support. This comprises:

- ❑ What your e-mail should include
- ❑ What happens to your e-mail once it has been received by us

So that you only need view information relevant to yourself, we ask that you register as a Wrox Developer Member. This is a quick and easy process, which will save you time in the long-run. If you are already a member, just update membership to include this book.

Wrox Developer's Membership

To get your FREE Wrox Developer's Membership click on Membership in the top navigation bar of our home site – http://www.wrox.com. This is shown in the screenshot overleaf:

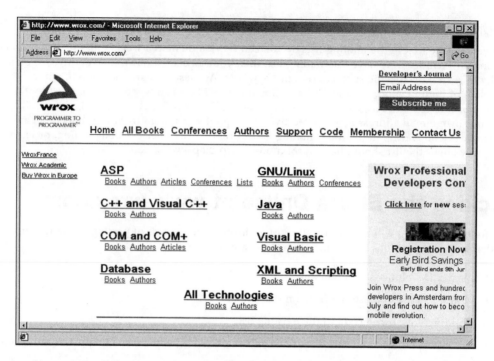

Then, on the next screen (not shown), click on **New User**. This will display a form. Fill in the details on the form and submit the details using the **Register** button at the bottom. Before you can say 'The best read books come in Wrox Red' you will get the following screen:

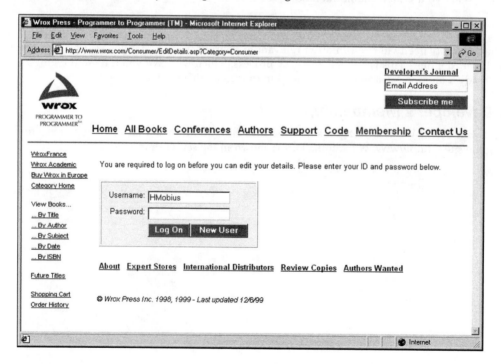

Type in your password once again and click Log On. The following page allows you to change your details if you need to, but now you're logged on, you have access to all the source code downloads and errata for the entire Wrox range of books.

Finding an Erratum on the Web Site

Before you send in a query, you might be able to save time by finding the answer to your problem on our web site – http://www.wrox.com.

Each book we publish has its own page and its own errata sheet. You can get to any book's page by clicking on Support from the top navigation bar.

Halfway down the main support page is a drop down box called Title Support. Simply scroll down the list until you see Professional J2EE with BEA Weblogic Server. Select it and then hit Errata.

This will take you to the errata page for the book. Select the criteria by which you want to view the errata, and click the Apply criteria button. This will provide you with links to specific errata. For an initial search, you are advised to view the errata by page numbers. If you have looked for an error previously, then you may wish to limit your search using dates. We update these pages daily to ensure that you have the latest information on bugs and errors.

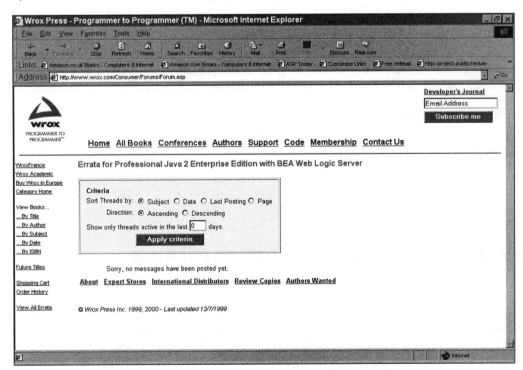

Add an Erratum : e-Mail Support

If you wish to point out an erratum to put up on the web site or directly query a problem in the book page with an expert who knows the book in detail then e-mail support@wrox.com, with the title of the book and the last four numbers of the ISBN in the subject field of the e-mail. A typical e-mail should include the following things:

> The **name**, **last four digits of the ISBN** and **page number** of the book in the Subject field
>
> Your **name**, **contact info** and the **problem** in the body of the message

We won't send you junk mail. We need the details to save your time and ours. If we need to replace a disk or CD we'll be able to get it to you straight away. When you send an e-mail it will go through the following chain of support:

Customer Support

Your message is delivered to one of our customer support staff who are the first people to read it. They have files on most frequently asked questions and will answer anything general immediately. They answer general questions about the book and the web site.

Editorial

Deeper queries are forwarded to the technical editor responsible for that book. They have experience with the programming language or particular product and are able to answer detailed technical questions on the subject. Once an issue has been resolved, the editor can post the erratum to the web site.

The Authors

Finally, in the unlikely event that the editor can't answer your problem, they will forward the request to the author. We try to protect the author from any distractions from writing. However, we are quite happy to forward specific requests to them. All Wrox authors help with the support on their books. They'll mail the customer and the editor with their response, and again all readers should benefit.

What We Can't Answer

Obviously with an ever-growing range of books and an ever-changing technology base, there is an increasing volume of data requiring support. While we endeavor to answer all questions about the book, we can't answer bugs in your own programs that you've adapted from our code. So, while you might have loved the chapters on file handling, don't expect too much sympathy if you cripple your company with a routine which deletes the contents of your hard drive. But do tell us if you're especially pleased with the routine you developed with our help.

How to Tell Us Exactly What You Think

We understand that errors can destroy the enjoyment of a book and can cause many wasted and frustrated hours, so we seek to minimize the distress that they can cause.

You might just wish to tell us how much you liked or loathed the book in question. Or you might have ideas about how this whole process could be improved. In which, case you should e-mail feedback@wrox.com. You'll always find a sympathetic ear, no matter what the problem is. Above all you should remember that we do care about what you have to say and we will do our utmost to act upon it.

Index

A Guide to the Index

The index is arranged hierarchically, in alphabetical order, with symbols preceding the letter A. Most second-level entries and many third-level entries also occur as first-level entries. This is to ensure that users will find the information they require however they choose to search for it.

F

fat clients, 20
  JMS, **264-71**
File API, 23
fileStats property, Grinder, 357
filtering, 314
  connections, 24
finder methods, 165
  bean managed persistence, **192-97**
firewalls, 19, 283, 284
First In First Out (FIFO) algorithm, 240
first tiers, 24
form based authentication, 286
forward action, JSP, 47
forward method, RequestDispatcher interface, 52, 98
FROM environment variable, HTTP, 481
From header, HTTP, 479
functional architecture, 24-27

G

GATEWAY_INTERFACE environment variable, HTTP, 481
GET command, HTTP, 97-98, 475
GET command, WAP, 324
getParameter method, request object, 97, 99
getProperty tag, JSP, 50, 73, 491
global.asa file, ASP, 216, 227, 228
GMD (guaranteed message delivery), 239
go element, WML, 324
Grinder, 346-65, 371-439
  architecture, **358-60**
  console, **364-65**
  dat files, 351, 352, 377, 378
  err files, 351, 353, 377
  load testing, **362-64**
  out files, 351, 377
  properties file, **353-58**
  test environment, **372-78**, **438-39**
guaranteed message delivery (GMD), 239

H

HEAD request method, HTTP, 475
headers, HTTP, 477-79
headers, JMS, 243-44
heartbeats, 459
home interface, EJBs, 105, 106
  clustering, **459**
  entity beans, **165**, 168-71
Host header, HTTP, 479
hostId property, Grinder, 356
hot deployment, 139
htmlKona API, 89-93

HTTP (Hypertext Transfer Protocol), 473-84
  authentication, **285-86**
  environment variables, 480-84
  headers, 477-79
  request methods, 475
  requests, 474-75
  responses, 476-77
  URLs, 473-74
HTTP_ACCEPT environment variable, 481
HTTP_ACCEPT_LANGUAGE environment variable, 481
HTTP_CONNECTION environment variable, 481
HTTP_COOKIE environment variable, 481
HTTP_HOST environment variable, 481
HTTP_PRAGMA environment variable, 481
HTTP_REFERER environment variable, 482
HTTP_USER_AGENT environment variable, 482
HttpServlet class, 44

I

idempotent beans, 459
IDLs (interface definition languages), 17
IIOP (Internet Inter-ORB Protocol), 18
IIS (Internet Information Server), 235
implicit objects, JSP, 48
include action, JSP, 47, 72
include directive, JSP, 47, 58, 489
include tag, JSP, 489
initialSleepTimes property, Grinder, 355, 358
initialWait property, Grinder, 357
interface definition languages (IDLs), 17
Internationalization and Localization Tool Kit, 63
Internet Information Server (IIS), 235
Internet Inter-ORB Protocol (IIOP), 18
is-modified-method-name element, 167, 179
isolation, transactions, 107
  translation isolation, **163-64**

J

Java, 24, 228
Java Database Connectivity
  See "JDBC".
Java IDL, 17
Java Message Service
  See "JMS".
Java Native Interface (JNI), 279
Java Transaction API (JTA), 16-17
Java Transaction Service (JTS), 16
Java virtual machines
  See "JVMs".
JavaBeans, 49-50
  action tags, **50**
  See also "EJBs".
JavaMail, 17
JavaServer Pages
  See "JSP".
JDBC (Java Database Connectivity), 15-16
  clusters, **460**
  connection pools, **60-62**

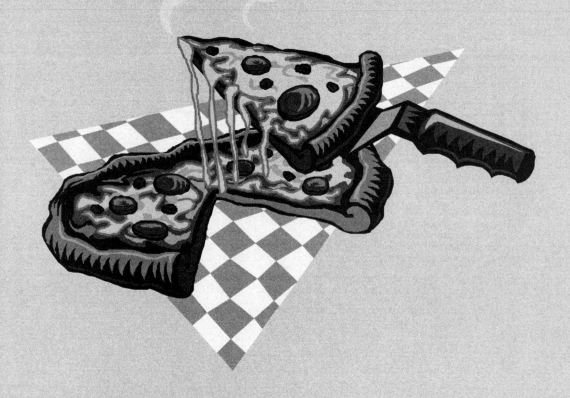